DISCOVERING *the* WESTERN PAST

A Look at the Evidence Volume I: To 1715

MERRY E. WIESNER
University of Wisconsin—Milwaukee

JULIUS R. RUFF
Marquette University

WILLIAM BRUCE WHEELER
University of Tennessee, Knoxville

Houghton Mifflin Company Boston

Dallas Geneva, Illinois Palo Alto Princeton, New Jersey

Acknowledgments

Pages 11–13: Extracts from Naphtali Lewis and Meyer Reinhold, eds. and trans., *Roman Civilization*. Copyright © 1955 Columbia University Press. Used by permission. Page 14: Extract from B. K. Workman, ed. and trans., *They Saw It Happen in Classical Times*. Permission granted by Barnes & Noble Books, Totowa, New Jersey. © Basil Blackwell, Publishers. Pages 25–30: Extracts from Thucydides, *History of the Peloponnesian War*, trans. Rex Warner. Copyright © Rex Warner, 1954. Reproduced by permission of Penguin Books Ltd. Pages 30–32: Extract from Aristotle, *The Politics*, trans. T. A. Sinclair. Copyright © the Estate of T. A. Sinclair, 1962, revised material copyright © Trevor J. Saunders, 1981. Reproduced by permission of Penguin Books Ltd. Pages 32–33: Extract from B. K. Workman, ed. and trans., *They Saw It Happen in Classical Times*. Permission granted by Barnes & Noble Books, Totowa, New Jersey. © Basil Blackwell, Publishers. Used by permission. Pages 50–58; Extracts from Naphtali Lewis and Meyer Reinhold, eds. and trans., *Roman Civilization*, vol. 2, *The Empire*. Copyright © 1955 Columbia University Press. Used by permission. Pages 74–75: Extract from THE MEDIEVAL CHURCH by Roland H. Bainton © 1962 by Roland H. Bainton. Reprinted by permission of Wadsworth, Inc. Pages 75–77: Extract from BEDE: A HISTORY OF THE ENGLISH CHURCH AND PEOPLE, trans. by Leo Sherley-Price (London: Penguin, 1955, 1968), pp. 66, 68–71. Copyright © Leo Sherley-Price, 1955, 1968. Reproduced by permission of Penguin Books Ltd. Pages 77–78: Extract from *Documents of the Christian Church*, 2 ed., edited by Henry Bettenson (Oxford: Oxford University Press, 1963). Reprinted by permission of Oxford University Press. Pages 78–80: Extract from James Harvey Robinson, ed. and trans., *Readings in European History*, vol. 1. Published by Silver, Burdett & Ginn, Inc. Pages 80–81: Extract from *Documents of the Christian Church*, 2 ed., edited by Henry Bettenson (Oxford: Oxford University Press, 1963). Reprinted by permission of Oxford University Press. Page 81: Extract from THE MEDIEVAL CHURCH by Roland H. Bainton © 1962 by Roland H. Bainton. Reprinted by permission of Wadsworth, Inc. Pages 82–83: Extracts from James Harvey Robinson, ed. and trans., *Readings in European History*, vol. 1. Published by Silver, Burdett & Ginn, Inc. Pages 83–85: Extract from Carolly Erickson, THE RECORDS OF MEDIEVAL EUROPE (Garden City, N.Y.: Doubleday, 1971). Used by permission. Pages 85–87: Extracts from James Harvey Robinson, ed. and trans., *Readings in European History*, vol. 1. Published by Silver, Burdett & Ginn, Inc. Pages 99–102; Extracts from Margaret L. Faull and Marie Stinson, eds., *Domesday Book*, vol. 30, *Yorkshire*. Reproduced by kind permission from the Phillimore edition of DOMESDAY BOOK (General Editor John Morris), volume 30 Yorkshire (County Editors Margaret L. Faull and Marie Stinson) published in 1986 by Phillimore & Co., Shopwyke Hall, Chichester, West Sussex, England. Pages 103–104: Extracts from DOMESDAY ENGLAND by H. C. Darby (New York: Cambridge University Press, 1977). Pages 123–124: Extract from THE PORTABLE MEDIEVAL READER, ed. James Bruce Ross and Mary Martin McLaughlin. Copyright 1949 by The Viking Press, Inc. Copyright renewed © 1976 by James Bruce Ross and Mary Martin McLaughlin. All rights reserved. Reprinted by permission of Viking Penguin Inc. Pages

Acknowledgments continue following page 309.

Cover: G. Braun and F. Hogenberg, *Londinum Feracissimi Angliae Regni Metropolis*, 1574. Photograph courtesy of the Museum of London.

Printed in the U.S.A.

Library of Congress Catalog Card Number: 88-81367

ISBN: 0-395-47585-6

DEFGHIJ-VH-9543210

CONTENTS

PREFACE

The title of this book begins with a verb, a choice that reflects our basic philosophy about history. History is not simply something one learns about; it is something one does. One discovers the past, and what makes this pursuit exciting is not only the past that is discovered but the process of discovery itself. This process can be simultaneously exhilarating and frustrating, enlightening and confusing, but it is always challenging enough to convince those of us who are professional historians to spend our lives at it.

The recognition that history involves discovery as much as physics or astronomy does is often unshared by students, whose classroom experience of history frequently does not extend beyond listening to lectures and reading textbooks. The primary goal of *Discovering the Western Past: A Look at the Evidence* is to allow students enrolled in the Western Civilization course to *do* history in the same way we as historians do—to examine a group of original sources in order to answer a question about the past. We feel that contact with original sources is an excellent means of communicating the excitement of doing history, but incorporating complete works or a collection of documents into a Western Civilization course can be problematic for many instructors.

The evidence in this book thus differs from that in most source collections in its variety. We have included such visual evidence as coins, paintings, aerial photographs, cartoons, buildings, architectural plans, maps, and political posters. In choosing written evidence we again have tried to offer a broad sample—songs, plays, poems, court records, notarial contracts, statistical data, and work regulations all supplement letters, newspapers, speeches, autobiographies, and other more traditional sources.

In order for students to learn history the way we as historians do, they must not only be confronted with the evidence; they must also learn how to use that evidence to arrive at a conclusion. In other words, they must learn historical methodology. Too often methodology (or even the notion that historians *have* a methodology) is reserved for upper-level majors or graduate students; beginning students are simply presented with historical facts and interpretations without being shown how these were unearthed or formulated. They may learn that historians hold different interpretations of the significance of an event or individual or different ideas about causation, but they are not informed of how historians come to such conclusions.

Thus, along with evidence, we have provided explicit suggestions about how one might analyze that evidence, guiding students as they reach their own conclusions. As they work through the various chapters, students will discover not only that the sources of historical information are wide-ranging, but that the methodologies appropriate to understanding and using them are equally diverse. By doing it themselves, students will learn how intellectual historians handle philosophical treatises, economic historians quantitative data, social historians court records, and political and diplomatic historians theoretical treatises and memoirs. They will also be asked to consider the limitations of their evidence, to explore what historical questions it cannot answer as well as those it can. Instead of passive observers, students become active participants.

Following an approach that we have found successful in many different classroom situations, we have divided each chapter into five parts: The Problem, Sources and Method, The Evidence, Questions to Consider, and Epilogue. The section called "The Problem" presents the general historical background and context for the evidence offered and concludes with the central question or questions explored in the chapter. The section titled "Sources and Method" provides specific information about the sources and suggests ways in which students might best study and analyze this primary evidence. It also discusses how previous historians have evaluated such sources and mentions any major disputes about methodology or interpretation. "The Evidence" forms the core of each chapter, presenting a variety of original sources for students to use in completing the central task. In "Questions to Consider," suggestions are offered about connections among the sources, and students are guided to draw deductions from the evidence. The final section, "Epilogue," traces both the immediate effects of the issue under discussion and its impact on later developments.

Within this framework, we have tried to present a series of historical issues and events of significance to the instructor as well as of interest to the student. We have also aimed to provide a balance among political, social, diplomatic, intellectual, and cultural history. In other words, we have attempted to create a kind of historical sampler that we believe will help students learn the methods and skills used by historians. Not only will these skills—analyzing arguments, developing hypotheses, comparing evidence, testing conclusions, and reevaluting material—enable students to master historical content; they will also provide the necessary foundation for a productive, meaningful life beyond college.

Discovering the Western Past is designed to accommodate any format of the Western Civilization course, from the small lecture/discussion class of a liberal arts or community college to the large lecture with discussions led by teaching assistants of a sizable university. The chapters may be used for individual assignments, team projects, class discussions, papers, and exams. Each is self-contained, so that any combination may be assigned. The book is not intended to replace a standard textbook, and it was written to accompany any Western Civilization text the instructor chooses. The Instructor's Manual provided with the book offers further suggestions for class discussion as well as a variety of ways in which students' learning may be evaluated and annotated lists of suggestions for further reading.

In the completion of this book, the authors received assistance from a number of persons. All three authors would like to acknowledge the initial work on this project by Professors Carol L. Lansing and Michael J. McDonald of the University of Tennessee, Knoxville. The organization and concepts that they proposed for these volumes provided a foundation for the work of the present authors. Our colleagues and students at the University of Wisconsin—Milwaukee, Marquette University, and the University of Tennessee, Knoxville have been generous with their ideas and time. Merry E. Wiesner (-Hanks) wishes especially to thank Ann Healy and Carolyn Ashbaugh for their critiques and suggestions and Neil Wiesner-Hanks and Kai Wiesner-Hanks for their help in maintaining the author's perspective. Julius R. Ruff wishes to acknowledge the assistance of the Reverend John Patrick Donnelly, S.J., Joseph Mikolajczak, Michael Sibalis, Laura B. Ruff, and Julia B. Ruff. Edwin Trainer of the University of Tennessee, Knoxville has been especially supportive, as has Palmira Brummett, who offered invaluable assistance on the non-Western perspective.

We wish particularly to acknowledge the following historians, who read and commented on the manuscript through its stages of development:

Susan Amussen, *Connecticut College*
James G. Baughman, *Jefferson Community College*
Rebecca Boehling, *University of Dayton*
John Bohnstedt, *California State University, Fresno*
Ronald Brown, *Charles County Community College*
Craig Buettinger, *Jacksonville University*
Helen Callahan, *Augusta College*
Gerald Herman, *Northeastern University*
Jean Knoll, *De Paul University*
Sharon Strocchia, *Emory University*

Finally, we wish to thank the staff of Houghton Mifflin Company for their enthusiastic support.

M.E.W. J.R.R. W.B.W.

CHAPTER ONE

THE NEED FOR WATER IN ANCIENT SOCIETIES

THE PROBLEM

The title of the course for which you are using this book is likely a variant of "Western Civilization." Why do we use the term "civilization"? What distinguishes human cultures that are labeled "civilizations" from those that are not? Though great differences separate them, all civilizations share some basic characteristics. The most important of these similarities is the presence of cities; indeed, the word "civilization" comes from the Latin word *civilis* (meaning "civic"), which is also the root of "citizen" and "civil." Historians and archeologists generally define a city as a place inhabited by more than 5,000 people, and they have discovered the remains of the earliest communities of this size in ancient Mesopotamia, present-day Iraq.

Why should the presence of cities be the distinguishing mark of cultural development? It is not the cities themselves but what they imply about a culture that makes them so important. Any society in which thousands of people live in close proximity to one another must have some sort of laws or rules governing human behavior. These may be either part of an oral tradition or, as in ancient Mesopotamia, written down. A city must provide its residents with a constant supply of food, which means developing ways to transport food into the city from the surrounding farmland, to store food throughout the year, and to save it for years marked by poor harvests. Not only does the presence of cities indicate that people could transport and store food effectively, it also reveals that they were producing enough surplus food to allow for specialization of labor. If all work time had been devoted to farming, it would not have been possible to build roads, produce storage bins, or enforce laws on which the city depended. This specialization of labor, then, allowed some members of society the opportunity and time to create and produce goods and artifacts not directly essential to daily survival. Urban residents in Mesopotamia began to construct large buildings and decorate them with sculptures, paintings, and mosaics, write poetry and history, and develop religious and philosophical ideas, all of which are pursuits we consider essential to a civilization. As the cities themselves grew, greater and greater amounts of food were required to feed their inhabitants, which led to further technological development.

Mesopotamia was in many ways an odd location for the beginning of a civilization. True, the soil is so rich that the region is called the "Fertile Crescent," but it does not receive enough natural rainfall to grow crops steadily year after year. In fact, this region is not where agriculture began in the West; that happened closer to the Mediterranean, where the rainfall was more regular. Apparently, as techniques of planting and harvesting crops spread into Mesopotamia, the inhabitants realized they would be able to use these techniques effectively only through irrigation. They needed to tap the waters flowing in the Tigris and Euphrates rivers, a project requiring the cooperation of a great many people. Thus, rather than proving a block to further development, the need for irrigation in ancient Mesopotamia may have been the real spur that led to the growth of cities. We may never be able to know this with certainty, because irrigation systems were already in place when written records began and because cities and irrigation expanded at the same time. We do know that in Mesopotamia, neither could have existed without the other; cities could survive only where irrigation had created a food surplus, and irrigation only where enough people were available to create and maintain ditches and others parts of the system.

Building irrigation systems presented both technical and organizational problems. The Tigris and Euphrates were fast-flowing rivers that carried soil as well as water down from the highlands. This rich soil created new farmland where the rivers emptied into the Persian Gulf. (The ancient Persian Gulf ended more than 100 miles north of its present boundary; all that land was created as the rivers filled in the delta.) The soil also rapidly clogged up the irrigation ditches, which consequently required constant cleaning. Every year this deposit was excavated and piled on the banks until the sides of the ditches grew so tall that cleaning could no longer be easily accomplished. At this point the old ditch was abandoned and a new ditch cut, tasks that required a great deal of work and the cooperation of everyone whose land was watered by that ditch.

Mesopotamian farmers used several types of irrigation. One technique, known as *basin irrigation*, was to level large plots of land fronting the rivers and main canals and build up dikes around them. In the spring and other times during the year when the water was high, farmers knocked holes in the dikes to admit water and fresh soil. Once the sediment had settled, they let the water flow back into the channel. They also built small waterways between their fields to provide water throughout the year, thereby developing a system of *perennial irrigation*. In the hillier country of northern Mesopotamia, farmers built *terraces* with water channels running alongside. The hillside terraces provided narrow strips of flat land to farm, and the waterways were dug to connect with brooks and streams.

Farmers could depend on gravity to bring water to their fields during spring and flood seasons, but at other times they needed water-raising machines. Numerous types of machines were devised, some of which are still in use in many parts of the world today. These solved some problems but created others, as farmers with machines could drain an irrigation ditch during times of low water, leaving their neighbors with nothing. How were rights to water to be decided? Solving this problem would be crucial to human social organization, and the first recorded laws regarding property rights are in fact not rights to land but rights to water. In Mesopotamia, land was useless unless it was irrigated.

Many of the irrigation techniques developed in Mesopotamia either spread to Egypt or were developed independently there. Because it received even less rainfall than Mesopotamia, Egypt was totally dependent on the Nile for watering crops. Fortunately, the Nile was a much better source of water than the Tigris and Euphrates because it flooded regularly, allowing easy basin irrigation. The rise and fall of the Nile was so regular, in fact, that the Egyptians based their 365-day calendar on its annual flooding. The Egyptians also constructed waterways and water-lifting machines to allow for perennial irrigation. Here, too, irrigation both caused and resulted from the growth of cities; it contributed as well to the power of the kings, whom the Egyptian people regarded as responsible for the flood of the Nile.

Irrigation was more difficult in places that did not have flood-prone rivers, including many parts of North Africa and the Near East. Here people adapted techniques to conserve water from sporadic heavy rainfalls. They dammed the temporary lakes (termed *wadis*) created by these rainfalls and built ditches to convey the water to fields, rather than allowing it simply to flow off onto the desert. Sometimes this wadi irrigation involved a whole series of small dams down the course of rivers that ran only after storms. Besides providing water, wadi irrigation also built up terraces because the rivers carried soil with them.

The earliest water systems were for crop irrigation, but people also began to demand good drinking water. In many parts of the ancient world the demand for drinking water led to the setting up of a second system, because river water that is suitable for irrigation may be brackish, unpleasant, or even unhealthful to drink. In southern Europe, where lakes were often not far from growing cities, the problem was solved by building channels made of timber, stone, or clay earthenware that carried water from the lakes to the city. These channels might be open or closed, depending on the terrain and level of technical development of the culture that built them. Generally they relied on gravity flow and fed into underground tanks or reservoirs in the city; the oldest known water channels are in Jerusalem and date from about 1000 B.C. The construction of such systems, which demanded even more technical expertise than irrigation ditches, provoked additional legal problems about ownership of the right to this clean, cool water.

When lakes were not located close enough to make above-ground channels feasible, people had to rely on water from *aquifers*, underground water-bearing layers of gravel or porous rock. The water could be obtained from wells drilled in the ground, but wells could only supply a small amount of water at a time. Once an aquifer had been discovered, however, a horizontal channel could be dug to lead the water to an outside channel or reservoir. A horizontal channel only worked in hilly areas where the aquifer stood higher than a nearby valley, but such channels, called *qanats*, have been found in Iran, Syria, Egypt, and Turkey that are over 2,000 years old. If the amount of water was large enough, the qanat could be used for irrigation as well as drinking water.

When the Romans conquered the Middle East and North Africa in the second century B.C., they inherited irrigation systems that had already been in existence in some cases for more than 2,000 years. The Romans carried many ideas to other parts of their empire and made innovations as the terrain or distance required. Most of the European territory in the Roman Empire received adequate rainfall for farming without irrigation, but many Roman cities, especially Rome itself, experienced a chronic shortage of drinking water. The Romans solved this problem by building *aqueducts*, covered or uncovered channels that brought water into the cities from lakes and springs. The first of these in Rome was built in 312 B.C., and the system expanded continuously up to about A.D. 150. Over 300 miles of aqueducts served the city of Rome alone, with extensive systems in the outlying provinces as well. Although Roman engineers went to great lengths to avoid valleys, they were occasionally forced to construct enormous bridges to carry the aqueduct over a valley. Some of these bridges were over 150 feet high, and a few, such as the bridge-aqueduct in Segovia, Spain, still bring water to city residents. The Romans' sophisticated architectural and construction techniques—the arch and water-resistant cement, for example—enabled them to build water systems undreamed of in Mesopotamia and Egypt. Legal problems were not as easily solved, however, and disputes about water rights recur frequently throughout the long history of Rome.

Supplying cities with water was not simply a technological problem but one with economic, legal, and political implications. Through their solutions to these complex problems, ancient societies created what we call civilization. Your task in this chapter will be to use both visual and written evidence of ancient water systems to answer the question: How did the need for a steady supply of water shape civilization?

SOURCES AND METHOD

Historians use a wide variety of sources when examining ancient irrigation and water supply systems. Many of these systems were created before the development of writing, so archeological evidence is extremely important, especially in examining technological development. This evidence may be the actual remains of ancient ditches, machines, or aqueducts, but in many areas these have completely disappeared. This does not mean they have left no trace, however, for the ancient uses of modern landscapes are often revealed through patterns of depressions and discoloration.

The easiest way to see these patterns is through aerial photography. Analyzing aerial photographs can be a difficult task, however, and it takes a great deal of training to learn how to read ancient land use patterns through the overlay of modern development. Occasionally the older patterns can be quite clear, however, and only a small amount of additional information is necessary for you to begin to decode them. The first piece of evidence, Source 1, is an aerial photograph of the site of a pre-Roman city in Italy. Examine the picture carefully. Can you see the old grid pattern of irrigation ditches, which shows up as light and dark marsh grass? The dark lines are the outlines of ancient irrigation ditches, the lighter squares are ancient fields, and the white parallel lines superimposed on the top are part of a modern drainage system. To examine the ancient system, you will mentally need to strip away the modern system. What do you think the broader black strip at the top left is? Does this system look like basin or perennial irrigation? Look at the flatness of the landscape. Would silting be a problem?

A more sophisticated type of aerial photography involves the use of satellites rather than airplanes. Satellites can take extremely detailed pictures of the earth's surface that reveal natural and artificially constructed features, both ancient and contemporary. The sharpest images are produced by high-resolution military satellites whose pictures are not available to the public. Low-power images produced by LANDSAT, the only U.S. commercial imaging satellite system, are adequate for most archeological and historical purposes, however. Source 2 is a map of the major ancient irrigation ditches between the Tigris and Euphrates rivers that were identifiable in a recent LANDSAT image. What does the size of the system reveal about Mesopotamian technology? What does it imply about the political systems in this area—would you expect, for example, the cities in Mesopotamia to be hostile to each other? New technologies such as LANDSAT imagery not only provide answers to questions but also guide future research. How could you use this map to plan further investigations of irrigation systems?

Aerial photography provides visual evidence of entire irrigation systems but not of the specific tools and machines used to lift water to the fields. For these we must look to the remains of the tools themselves or to depictions of them in tomb paintings, mosaics, and pottery. Comparing these pictures with machines still in use today shows that many techniques for lifting water have remained virtually unchanged for thousands of years.

Sources 3 through 6 show four different machines for raising water that we know were in use in ancient times: the shaduf, saqiya, Archimedes' screw, and noria. To assess their role and importance, you must consider a number of different factors while carefully examining the four diagrams. Some of these factors are technical: How complicated is the machine to build? Does it have many moving parts that must all be in good repair? How much water can it lift? How high can it lift the water? Can it work with both flowing and stationary water? Some factors are economic: Does the machine require a person to operate it, thus taking that person away from other types of labor? Does it require a strong adult, or can it be operated by a child? Does it require an animal, which must be fed and cared for? Some factors are both economic and political: Does the machine require a variety of raw materials to build, more than one family might possess? Does it require any raw materials, like metal, that would have to be imported? (Such questions are political because someone has to decide which families get the raw materials necessary for their fields.) Some factors are legal: Does the machine raise so much water that laws about distribution would become necessary? At this point, you may want to make a chart summarizing your assessment of the advantages and disadvantages of each machine, which will help you in making your final conclusions.

We will now turn from visual to written sources. Because water is such a vital commodity, mention of water systems appears very early in recorded human history. The next five sources are written accounts of the construction or operation of water systems. Source 7 contains sections from the Code of Hammurabi, a Babylonian legal code dating from 1750 B.C., that refer to irrigation. Source 8 is a description of the Roman aqueduct system written by Vitruvius during the first century B.C., and Source 9 a description of the water system projects undertaken by Emperor Claudius during his reign (A.D. 41–54), written by the Roman historian Suetonius. The next selection is a discussion of some of the problems associated with Rome's water system, written about A.D. 100

by Frontinus, who was commissioner of the water supply. The last is a proclamation issued by Emperor Theodosius in 438 as part of his code of laws, an edict that had probably been in effect for many decades earlier as well.

As you read these sources, notice first of all the technical issues the authors are addressing. What problems in tapping, transportation, and storage of water do they discuss? What solutions do they suggest? Then look at legal problems, which you can find most clearly stated in the selection by Frontinus and the law codes of Hammurabi and Theodosius. Keep in mind when you are reading the law codes that laws are generally written to address those problems already taking place, not those the lawmakers are simply anticipating. The presence of a law, especially one that is frequently repeated, is often a good indication that the prohibited activity was probably happening, and happening often. How did people misuse or harm the water systems? What penalties were provided for those who did? Who controlled the legal use of water, and who decided how water was to be distributed?

The written sources also include information about political and economic factors in ancient water supply systems that is nearly impossible to gain from archeological evidence. Careful reading can reveal who paid for the construction of such systems and who stood to gain financially from them once they were built. What reasons, other than the simple need for water, might rulers have had for building water systems? What political and economic factors entered into decisions about the ways in which water was to be distributed?

THE EVIDENCE

Source 1 from Leo Deuel, Flights Into Yesterday: The Story of Aerial Archeology *(New York: St. Martin's Press, 1969), p. 236. Photo by Fotoaerea Valvassori, Ravenna.*

1. Aerial Photograph of Pre-Roman City in Italy

Source 2 from Robert MaC. Adams, Heartland of Cities; Surveys of Ancient Settlements and Land Use on the Central Floodplains of the Euphrates *(Chicago: University of Chicago Press, 1981), p. 34.*

2. Major Ancient Levees Identifiable in LANDSAT Imagery

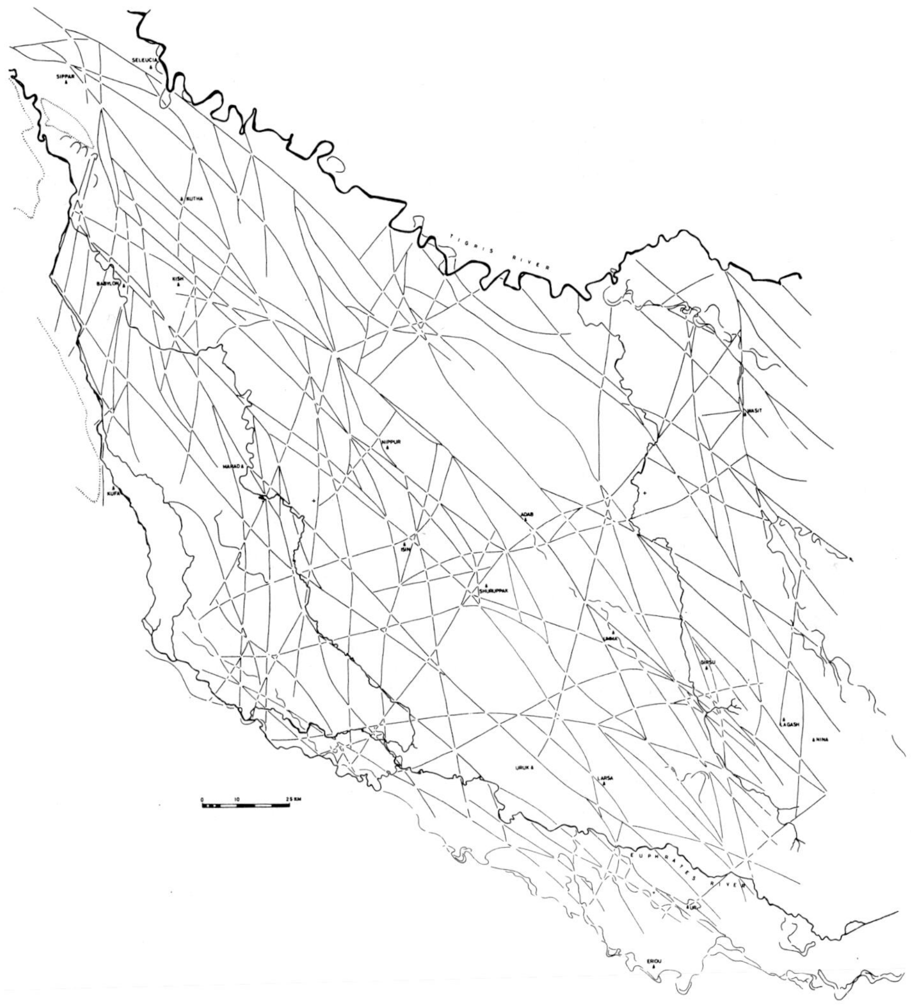

Sources 3 through 6 adapted from sketches by Merry E. Wiesner.

3. Shaduf

4. Saqiya

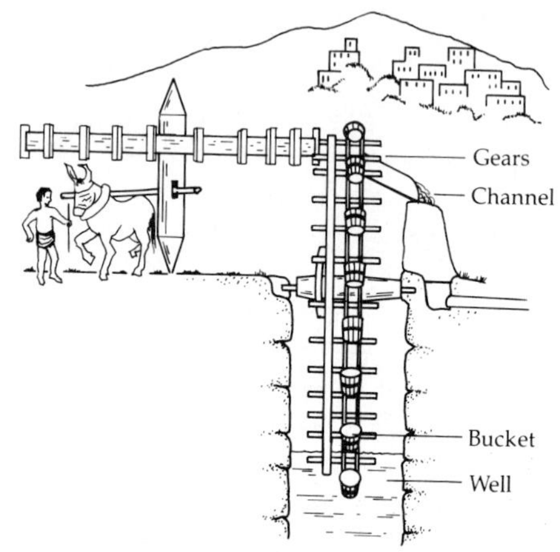

5. Archimedes' Screw

6. Noria

Source 7 from Robert F. Harper, The Code of Hammurabi *(Chicago: University of Chicago Press, 1904).*

7. Sections from the Code of Hammurabi Referring to Irrigation, 1750 B.C.

53. If a man neglects to maintain his dike and does not strengthen it, and a break is made in his dike and the water carries away the farmland, the man in whose dike the break has been made shall replace the grain which has been damaged.

54. If he is not able to replace the grain, they shall sell him and his goods and the farmers whose grain the water has carried away shall divide (the results of the sale).

55. If a man opens his canal for irrigation and neglects it and the water carries away an adjacent field, he shall pay out grain on the basis of the adjacent field.

56. If a man opens up the water and the water carries away the improvements of an adjacent field, he shall pay out ten *gur* of grain per *bur* [of damaged land]. . . .

66. If a man has stolen a watering-machine from the meadow, he shall pay five shekels of silver to the owner of the watering-machine.

Sources 8 and 9 from Naphtali Lewis and Meyer Reinhold, editors and translators, Roman Civilization *(New York: Columbia University Press, 1955), pp. 304–306; pp. 151–152.*

8. Vetruvius's Description of the Roman Aqueduct System, first century B.C.

The supply of water is made by three methods: by channels through walled conduits, or by lead pipes, or by earthenware pipes. And they are arranged as follows. In the case of conduits, the structure must be very solid; the bed of the channel must be leveled with a fall of not less than half a foot in 100 feet. The walled conduits are to be arched over so that the minimum amount of sun may strike the water. When it comes to the city walls, a reservoir is to be made. To this reservoir a triple distribution tank is to be joined to receive the water; and three pipes of equal size are to be placed in the reservoir, leading to the adjoining tanks, so that when there is an overflow from the two outer tanks, it may deliver into the middle tank. From the middle tank pipes will be laid to all basins and fountains; from the second tank to the baths, in order to furnish an annual revenue to the treasury; to avoid a deficiency in the public supply, private houses are to be supplied from the third, for private persons will not be able to divert the water, since they have their own limited supply from the distribution sources. Another reason why I have made these divisions is that those who take private supplies into their houses may by their taxes paid through tax farmers contribute to the maintenance of the water supply.

If, however, there are hills between the city and the source, we must proceed as follows: underground channels are to be dug and leveled to the fall mentioned above. If the bed is of tufa or stone, the channel may be cut in it; but if it is of soil or sand, the bed of the channel and the walls with the vaulting must be constructed, and the water should be thus conducted. Air shafts are to be so constructed that they are 120 feet apart.

But if the supply is to be by lead pipes, first of all a reservoir is to be built at the source. Then the opening of the pipe is to be determined in accordance with the amount of water, and these pipes are to be laid from the source reservoir to a reservoir which is inside the city.

When an aqueduct is to be made with lead pipes it is to have the following arrangement. If there is a fall from the source to the city and the intervening hills are not high enough to interrupt the supply, then if there are valleys, we must build substructures to bring it up to a level, as in the case of channels and conduits. If the way round the valley is not long, a circuit should be used; but if the valleys are expansive, the course will be directed down the hill, and when it reaches the bottom it is carried on a low substructure so that the level there may continue as far as possible. This will form a "belly," which the Greeks call *koilia*. When the "belly" comes to the hill opposite, and the long distance of the "belly" makes the water slow in welling up, the water is to be forced to the height of the top of the hill. . . .

Again, it is not without advantage to put reservoirs at intervals of 24,000 feet, so that if a break occurs anywhere neither the whole load of water nor the whole structure need be disturbed, and the place where it has occurred may be more easily found. But these reservoirs are to be neither in the descent nor on the level portion of the "belly," nor at risings, nor anywhere in a valley, but on unbroken level ground.

But if we wish to employ a less expensive method, we must proceed as follows. Earthenware pipes are to be made not less than two inches thick, but these pipes should be so tongued at one end that they can fit into and join one another. The joints are to be coated with quicklime mixed with oil. . . . Everything also is to be fixed as for lead pipes. Further, when the water is first let in from the source, ashes are to be put in beforehand, so that if any joints are not sufficiently coated they may be lined with the ashes.

Water supply by earthenware pipes has these advantages. First, in the construction: if a break occurs, anybody can repair it. Again, water is much more wholesome from earthenware pipes than from lead pipes. For it seems to be made injurious by lead, because white lead is produced by it; and this is said to be harmful to the human body. So if what is produced by anything is injurious, there is no doubt that the thing itself is not wholesome. We can take an example from the workers in lead who have complexions affected by pallor. For when lead is smelted in casting, the fumes from it settle on the members of the body and, burning them, rob the limbs of the virtues of the blood. Therefore it seems that water should by no means be brought in lead pipes if we desire to have it wholesome. Everyday life can be used to show that the flavor from earthenware pipes is better, because everybody (even those who load their table with silver vessels) uses earthenware to preserve the purity of water.

But if we are to create springs from which the water supplies come, we must dig wells.

But if the soil is hard, or if the veins of water lie too deep, then supplies of water are to be collected from the roofs or higher ground in concrete cisterns. . . . If the cisterns are made double or triple, so that they can be changed by percolation, they will make the supply of water much more wholesome. For when the sediment has a place to settle in, the water will be more limpid and will keep its taste without any smell. If not, salt must be added to purify it.

9. Suetonius's Description of the Water Projects Undertaken by Emperor Claudius (r. A.D. 41–54)

The public works which Claudius completed were great and essential rather than numerous; they were in particular the following: an aqueduct begun by Caligula; also the drainage channel of Lake Fucine and the harbor at Ostia, although in the case of the last two he knew that Augustus had refused the former to the Marsians in spite of their frequent requests, and that the latter had often been considered by the deified Julius but given up because of its difficulty. He brought to the city on stone arches the cool and abundant springs of the Claudian aqueduct . . . and at the same time the channel of the New Anio, distributing them into many beautifully ornamented fountains. He made the attempt on the Fucine Lake as much in the hope of gain as of glory, inasmuch as there were some who offered to drain it at their own cost provided the land that was drained be given them. He finished the drainage canal, which was three miles in length, partly by leveling and partly by tunneling a mountain, a work of great difficulty requiring eleven years, although he had 30,000 men at work all the time without interruption.

Source 10 from B. K. Workman, editor and translator, They Saw It Happen in Classical Times *(New York: Barnes & Noble, 1964), pp. 179–181.*

10. Frontinus's Discussion of Rome's Water System, ca A.D. 100

The New Anio[1] is drawn from the river in the district of Sinbrinum, at about the forty-second milestone along the Via Sublacensis. On either side of the river at this point are fields of rich soil which make the banks less firm, so that the water in the aqueduct is discoloured and muddy even without the damage done by storms. So a little way along from the inlet a cleansing basin was built where the water could settle and be purified between the river and the conduit. Even so, in the event of rain, the water reaches the city in a muddy state. The length of the New Anio is about 47 miles, of which over 39 are underground and more than 7 carried on structures above the ground. In the upper reaches a distance of about two miles in various sections is carried on low structures or arches. Nearer the city, from the seventh Roman mile-stone, is half a mile on substructures and five miles on arches. These arches are very high, rising in certain places to a height of 109 feet.

. . . All the aqueducts reach the city at different levels. So some serve the higher districts and some cannot reach loftier ground. For the hills of Rome have gradually increased in height because of the rubble from frequent fires. There are five aqueducts high enough at entrance to reach all the city, but they supply water at different pressures. . . .

Anyone who wants to tap water for private consumption must send in an application and take it, duly signed by the Emperor, to the Commissioner. The latter must take immediate action on Caesar's grant, and enrol one of the Imperial freedmen to help him in the business. . . . The right to water once granted cannot be inherited or bought, and does not go with the property, though long ago a privilege was extended to the public baths that their right should last in perpetuity. . . . When grants lapse, notice is given and record made in the ledgers, which are consulted so that future applicants can be given vacant supplies. The previous custom was to cut off these lapsed supplies at once, to make some profit by a temporary sale to the landowners or even to outsiders. Our Emperor felt that property should not suddenly be left without water, and that it would be fairer to give thirty days' notice for other arrangements to be made by the interested party. . . .

Now that I have explained the situation with regard to private supply, it will be pertinent to give some examples of the ways in which men have broken these very sound arrangements and have been caught red-handed. In some reservoirs I have found larger valves in position than had been

1. An aqueduct completed under the emperor Claudius in A.D. 52.

granted, and some have not even had the official stamp on them. When a stamped valve exceeds the legal dimensions, then the private advantage of the controller who stamped it is uncovered. When a valve is not even stamped, then both parties are clearly liable, chiefly the purchaser, but also the controller. Sometimes stamped valves of the correct dimensions open into pipes of a larger cross-section. The result is that the water is not kept in for the legal distance, but forced through a short, narrow pipe and easily fills the larger one which is joined to it. So care must be taken that, when a valve is stamped, the pipes connected to it should be stamped as of the correct length ordered by Senatorial decree. For then and only then will the controller be fully liable when he knows that only stamped pipes must be positioned.

When valves are sited, good care must be taken to see that they are placed in a horizontal line, not one above the other. A lower inlet gets a greater pressure of water, the upper one less, because the supply of water is taken by the lower. In some pipes no valves are positioned at all. These are called "free" pipes, and are opened and closed to suit the watermen.

Another of the watermen's intolerable practices is to make a new outlet from the cistern when a water-grant is transferred to a new owner, leaving the old one for themselves to get water from for sale. I would say that it was one of the Commissioner's chief duties to put a stop to this. For it affects not only the proper protection of the supply, but also the upkeep of the reservoir which would be ruined if needlessly filled with outlets.

Another financial scheme of the watermen, which they call "puncturing," must also be abolished. There are long separate stretches all over the city through which the pipes pass hidden under the pavement. I found out that these pipes were being tapped everywhere by the "puncturers," from which water was supplied by private pipe to all the business premises in the area, with the result that only a meagre amount reached the public utilities. I can estimate the volume of water stolen in this way from the amount of lead piping which was removed when these branch pipes were dug up.

Source 11 from Naphtali Lewis and Meyer Reinhold, editors and translators, Roman Civilization *(New York: Columbia University Press, 1955), pp. 479–480.*

11. Proclamation of Emperor Theodosius, A.D. 438

It is our will that the landholders over whose lands the courses of aqueducts pass shall be exempt from extraordinary burdens, so that by their work the aqueducts may be cleansed when they are choked with dirt. The said landholders shall not be subject to any other burden of a superindiction,[2] lest

2. That is, any special taxes.

they be occupied in other matters and not be present to clean the aqueducts. If they neglect this duty, they shall be punished by the forfeiture of their landholdings; for the fisc[3] will take possession of the landed estate of any man whose negligence contributes to the damage of the aqueducts. Furthermore, persons through whose landed estates the aqueducts pass should know that they may have trees to the right and left at a distance of fifteen feet from the aqueducts, and your[4] office shall see to it that these trees are cut out if they grow too luxuriantly at any time, so that their roots may not injure the structure of the aqueduct.

QUESTIONS TO CONSIDER

Now that you have looked at both visual and written evidence, you will need to put together the information you have gathered from each type of source to achieve a more complete picture. Because sources for the earliest period of human development are so scanty, we need to use every shred available and use them somewhat creatively, making speculations where no specific evidence exists.

Take all the evidence about technical problems first. Keeping in mind that the ancient world had no power equipment and no tools more elaborate than axes, hammers, saws, and drills (the Romans also had planes and chisels), what would you judge to be the most difficult purely technical problem involved in constructing water systems? In keeping them operating? The four diagrams of the water-raising machines are arranged in chronological order of their development: the shaduf as old as 2500 B.C. and the other three not until a thousand years later. Looking at your chart on the advantages and disadvantages of each machine, in what ways did the later machines improve on the shaduf? What additional problems might these improvements have produced? What types of technological experimentation did the need for water encourage?

Technological advance is not always an unmitigated blessing. For example, water standing in irrigation ditches can become brackish, providing a good breeding ground for mosquitoes and other carriers of disease. Cities that depend on irrigation suffer food shortages and famine when ditches cannot be kept clear or when river levels are low. The diversion of large quantities of water for irrigation makes rivers much smaller when they finally reach their deltas, which means the deltas become increasingly salty from seawater and unable to support the types of plant and animal life they originally fostered. Judging by the aerial photograph and

3. **fisc:** the imperial treasury.

4. This proclamation was addressed to the administrator of the water supply, the same office that Frontinus held earlier.

the LANDSAT map, would you expect any of these problems in ancient Italy or Mesopotamia? Do you find evidence in the written sources for problems in the later Roman water systems that were caused by technical advances? Do the written sources offer suggestions for solving these problems?

Now consider what you have learned about the economic issues associated with water systems. You have doubtless noticed that tremendous numbers of people were needed to construct irrigation ditches and aqueducts. Some of the written sources, such as the extract from Suetonius, provide exact figures. The size and complexity of the systems in all of the sources also imply substantial workforce, given the lack of elaborate equipment. The rulers of Mesopotamia and Rome saw the necessity of a large labor force as no problem; it was rather a solution to the greater problem of unemployment. A story is told about the Roman emperor Vespasian, who, when offered a labor-saving machine, refused to allow its use because that would put people out of work and lead to social problems in Rome. We might regard this concern for full employment as positive social attitude, but it should also tell you something about the value of labor in ancient societies. What would you expect wages to be for construction workers? What class of people would you expect to find working on these water systems?

Large numbers of workers were not only needed to build but also to maintain irrigation systems and to operate water-lifting machines. What does this fact tell you about the value of labor? What would happen with a sudden drop in the population, such as that caused by a famine or epidemic? How would a loss of workers affect the available food supply?

The sources also reveal information about political factors associated with water-systems. What does the construction of these systems indicate about the power of rulers to coerce or hire labor? How do rulers control the building and maintenance of machines and ditches? How might their control affect the power and independence of local communities or of individual families? What does this tell you about the role of water in expanding centralized political power?

Finally, the sources provide evidence of alterations in the law made necessary by the search for water. Previously unrestricted and unregulated actions now came under the control of public authorities, which meant that the number of enforcement agents and courts had to increase. What would this do to taxation levels? In what ways would political concerns shape the regulations?

Political issues affect not only the types of laws to be passed, but also the stringency or selectivity with which those laws are enforced. We have very little information about how rigidly law codes were implemented in ancient societies, for court records (if there were any) have not survived; law codes were frequently recopied and reissued, but the outcome of individual cases was not. It is therefore dangerous to assume that the prescribed penalties were actually levied or that the law was regularly obeyed. (Think for a minute the mistake a person 2,000 years from now would make in describing traffic patterns in twentieth-century America by assuming that the posted speed limit described the actual speed at which traffic moved!) Looking again at the law codes of Hammurabi and Theodosius, would you expect the penalties to be carried out, or do they appear to serve more as a strong warning? How would the penalties differ in their effects on poor and rich people?

You are now ready to answer the question posed at the beginning of the chapter: How did the need for a steady supply of water affect the development of civilization in the West?

EPILOGUE

The irrigation and water supply systems of the ancient world not only required huge amounts of labor, they also made necessary a strong central authority to coerce or hire that labor and to enforce laws to keep the channels flowing. At first, each Mesopotamian city managed its own irrigation system, but the wealthy and advanced cities were attractive targets for foreign conquerors. The political history of ancient Mesopotamia was one of wave after wave of conquerors coming down from the north—the Akkadians, Babylonians, Assyrians, Persians, Greeks, and finally Romans. Most of these conquerors realized the importance of irrigation and ordered the conquered residents to maintain or expand their systems. When the Muslims invaded the region in the seventh century, they also learned Mesopotamian techniques and spread these westward into North Africa and Spain, where Roman irrigation systems had in many places fallen apart.

In the intervals between these powerful conquerors, however, and after the thirteenth century, when the area was conquered by the Mongols, the irrigation ditches were often not maintained and they silted irreparably. The fertile farmland that had been so laboriously built up in the delta became salinized from the salty waters of the Persian Gulf, making it useless for farming. Once the irrigation ditches were no longer functional, the cities could not survive. Centuries of irrigation combined with too little fertilization made even land that was still being irrigated less and less productive.

The benefits and problems brought by irrigation are not limited to the ancient world, however; they can be seen in many modern societies. One of the best modern examples comes from the same part of the world we have been studying in this chapter. Throughout the twentieth century, Egypt has expanded its irrigation system watered by the Nile with a series of dams, culminating in the Aswan High Dam begun in 1960 to provide hydroelectric power and limit the free flow of water at the height of the flood season. The enormous reservoir formed by the dam can also be tapped at low-water times to allow for perennial irrigation. The Aswan Dam serves all its intended purposes very well, but it has also created some unexpected problems. The river's regular flooding had brought new fertile soil to the Nile Valley and carried away the salts that resulted from evaporation. Once the dam stopped the flooding, Egyptian fields needed artificial fertilizer to remain productive, a commodity many farmers could not afford. The soil of the Nile Valley has a high clay content, rendering drainage difficult, and a steady supply of water makes many fields waterlogged and unusable. The large reservoir created by the dam sits in the middle of the Sahara, allowing a tremendous amount of evaporation and significantly decreasing the total flow of water in the Nile; it has also put many acres of farmland under water and forced the relocation of tens of thousands of people. The current drought in North Africa has further lowered the Nile's level, decreasing the amount of hydroelectric power the river can produce. Ending the flooding also allowed snails carrying bilharzia or schistosomiasis—an intestinal parasite that makes people very weak—to proliferate in the fields and irrigation ditches. Thus, like the lead pipes that brought water to the Romans, the Aswan High Dam has proved a mixed blessing in modern Egypt.

As you reflect on what you have discovered in this chapter, you may want to think about problems associated with the distribution of water in your own region. How does the need for water affect the political and economic structures of your city or state? What technological solutions has your region devised, and how have these worked?

CHAPTER TWO

THE IDEAL AND THE REALITY OF CLASSICAL ATHENS

THE PROBLEM

Athens during the fifth century B.C. is often identified as one of the main sources of Western values and standards. Later Europeans and Americans regarded the Athenians as the originators of democracy, drama, representational or realistic art, history, philosophy, and science. At different times over the past 2,500 years they also attempted to imitate this "Golden Age" of classical Athens in everything from buildings to literature. Many U.S. state capitols and government buildings are modeled on the Parthenon or other temples, complete with statuary of former governors in the manner of Greek gods. We still divide drama into tragedies and comedies in the same way the Athenians did, though now we sometimes use a prerecorded laugh track instead of grinning masks to indicate that a given work is a comedy. During some historical periods, such as the Renaissance, thinkers and writers made conscious attempts to return to classical ideals in all areas of life, combing the works of Athenian authors for previously overlooked material in their quest to draw guidance and learn everything possible from this unique flowering of culture.

Even more than a model for literature and art, classical Athens has continued to serve as a relevant source for answers to basic questions about human existence. Though all cultures have sought to identify the ultimate aim and meaning of human life, the ancient Greeks, especially the Athenians, were the first in the West to provide answers that were not expressed in religious or mythological terms. Their thoughts on these matters grew out of speculations on the nature of the universe made by earlier Greeks, particularly Thales and his followers Anaximander and Heraclitus. These thinkers, living in the seventh and sixth centuries B.C., theorized about how the universe had been formed and what it was made of by means of rational explanations drawn from observation rather than from myth or religious tradition. Because they believed the natural universe could be explained in other than supernatural terms, they are often termed the first true scientists or first philosophers.

During the fifth century B.C., several Athenian thinkers turned their attention from the world around them to the human beings living in that world. They used this new method of philosophical inquiry to question the workings of the human mind and the societies humans create. They asked such questions as: How do we learn things? What should we try to learn? How do we know what is right or wrong, good or bad? If we can know what is good, how can we create things that are good? What kind of government is best? This type of questioning is perhaps most often associated with Socrates (469–399 B.C.) and his pupil Plato (427?–347 B.C.), who are generally called the founders of Western philosophy. Thales and his followers are thus known as the "pre-Socratics"; and a twentieth-century philosopher, Alfred North Whitehead, noted—only half jokingly—that "the European philosophical tradition . . . consists of a series of footnotes to Plato."

Both Socrates and Plato believed that goodness is related to knowledge and that excellence could be learned. For Plato especially, true knowledge was gained not by observation of the world but by contemplation of what an ideal world would be like. To understand goodness, justice, or beauty, it is necessary to think about what pure and ultimate goodness, justice, or beauty means. Plato thus introduced into Western thought a strong strain of *idealism* and was the first to write works on what an ideal society or set of laws would look like. He also described the education required to train citizens for governing this ideal state as well as the social and economic structure necessary to keep them at their posts. Though he probably recognized these standards could never be achieved, he believed that the creation of ideals was an important component of the discipline of philosophy, a sentiment shared by many Western thinkers after him.

Plato's most brilliant pupil, Aristotle (384–322 B.C.), originally agreed with his teacher but then began to depart somewhat from idealism. Like the pre-Socratics, Aristotle was fascinated by the world around him, and many of his writings on scientific subjects reveal keen powers of observation. Even his treatises on standards of human behavior, such as those concerning ethics and politics, are based on close observation of Athenian society and not simply on speculation. Aristotle further intended that these works should not only describe ideal human behavior or political systems but also provide suggestions about how to alter current practice to conform more closely to the ideal. Thus though Aristotle was still to some degree an idealist, both the source and the recipient of his ideals was the real world.

In classical Athens, human nature was a subject contemplated not only by scientists and philosophers but also by historians, such as Herodotus and Thucydides. They, too, searched for explanations about the natural order that did not involve the gods; for Herodotus and Thucydides, the Persian and Peloponnesian wars were caused by human failings, not by actions of vengeful gods such as those Homer, following tradition, depicted in the *Iliad* as causing the Trojan War. Like Aristotle, they were interested in describing real events and finding explanations for them; like Plato, they were also interested in the possible as well as the actual. History, in their opinion, was the best arena for observing the true worth of various ideals to human society.

To the Athenians, war was the ultimate test of human ideals, morals, and values, but these could also be tested and observed on a much smaller scale in the way people conducted their everyday lives. Although for Plato the basis of an ideal government was the perfectly trained ruler or group of rulers, for Aristotle and other writers it was the perfectly managed household, which they regarded as a microcosm of society. Observing that the household was the smallest economic and political unit in Athenian society, Aristotle began his consideration of the ideal governmental system with thoughts on how households should be run. Other writers on politics and economics followed suit, giving advice after observing households they regarded as particularly well managed.

Whereas Plato clearly indicated that he was describing an ideal, in the case of Aristotle and other Athenians it is sometimes difficult to determine whether they were attempting to describe reality, what they wished were reality, or a pure ideal. Your task in this chapter will be to examine the relationship between ideal and reality in the writings of several Athenian philosophers, historians, and commentators as well as in architectural diagrams of Athenian buildings and houses. What ideals do the writers set forth for the individual, the household, and the government? How are these ideals reflected in more realistic descriptions of life in Athens and in the way Athenians built their houses and city?

SOURCES AND METHOD

All the written sources we will use come from Athenians who lived during the classical period and are thus what we term original or primary sources. They differ greatly from modern primary sources, however, in that their textual accuracy cannot be checked. Before the development of the printing press, the only way to obtain a copy of a work was to write it out by hand yourself or hire someone to do it. Therefore each manuscript copy might be slightly different. Because the originals of the works of Aristotle or Thucydides have long since disappeared, what we have to work with are translations of composites based on as many of the oldest copies still in existence after 2,500 years that the translators could find.

The problem of accuracy is further complicated with some of the authors we will read because they did not actually write the works attributed to them. Many of Aristotle's works, for instance, are probably copies of his students' notes combined with (perhaps) some of his own. If you think of the way in which you record your own instructors' remarks, you can see why we must be cautious about assuming that these secondhand works contain everything Aristotle taught exactly as he intended it. Socrates, in fact, wrote nothing at all; all his ideas and words come to us through his pupil Plato. Scholars have long debated how much of the written record represents Socrates and how much Plato, especially when we consider that Socrates generally spoke at social gatherings or informally while walking around Athens, when Plato was not taking notes. These problems do not mean we should discount these sources but simply realize they differ from the printed documents and tape-recorded speeches of later eras.

We will begin our investigation with what is probably the most famous description of classical Athens: a funeral speech delivered by Pericles. Pericles, one of the leaders of Athens when the Peloponnesian War opened, gave this speech in 430 B.C. in honor of those who had died during that first year of the war. It was recorded by Thucydides and, though there is some disagreement over who actually wrote it, reflects Pericles' opinions. Read the speech carefully. Is Pericles describing an ideal he hopes Athens will achieve or reality as he sees it? How does he depict Athenian democracy and the Athenian attitude toward wealth? How does Athens treat its neighbors? What role does Pericles see for Athenian women? Before going on to the next readings, jot down some words that you feel best describe Athens and the Athenians. Would you want to live in the Athens Pericles describes?

Source 2 comes from a later section of Thucydides' *Peloponnesian War*, and it describes Athenian actions in the sixteenth year of the war. As you read it, think about the virtues that Pericles ascribed to the Athenians. Are these virtues reflected in the debate with the Melians, or in the actions against them? How do the Athenians justify their actions? After reading this selection, jot down a few more words you think describe the Athenians. Would you now erase some entries from your first list?

Source 3 is taken from the first book of Aristotle's *Politics*. In this selection he describes the proper functioning of a household and the role of each person in it. As you read it, you will notice that Aristotle is concerned equally with the economic role of household members and their moral status. What qualities does he see as important in the ideal head of household? the ideal wife or child? the ideal slave? How does he justify the differences between household members? How do these qualities compare with those described by Pericles or exhibited by the Athenians in their contact with the Melians? Add a few more words to your list describing the Athenians.

The fourth selection, by an unknown author, presents his views of Athenian democracy and the Athenian empire. This passage was written about five years after the speech made by Pericles and about ten years before the Melian debate. How does this author view democracy and Athens' relations with its neighbors? What words might he add to your list to describe his fellow Athenians? How do you think he would have responded had he been in the audience listening to Pericles' funeral speech?

The fifth selection is a discussion of household management cast in the form of a dialogue, from a treatise by Xenophon called *The Economist*. What does the main speaker, whose name is Ischomachus, see as the main roles of husband and wife? Would he have agreed with Aristotle's conclusions about the qualities necessary in an ideal husband and wife? What suggestions does he make for encouraging ideal behavior in wives and slaves? Does he appear to be describing an actual or an ideal marital relationship? What words would you now add or subtract from your list?

The sixth selection is a very small part of *The Republic*, in which Plato sets out his views on the ideal government. Plato did not favor democracy; he advocated training of a group of leaders, whom he called *guardians*, to work for the best interests of all. What qualities does Plato feel are most important in the guardians? What economic and family structures does he feel will help them maintain these qualities? How does his description of the ideal female guardian compare with Pericles' and Xenophon's description of the ideal Athenian wife? Do the qualities he finds important in guardians match up with any of those on your list?

Once you have read all the selections carefully, go back to Pericles' speech and read it again. Do you still have the same opinion about whether he is describing ideal or reality? Which of the original words are left on your list describing Athens?

Now look at the two diagrams, which are based on archeological discoveries. They are thus clear representations of physical reality in classical Greece but tell us something about ideals as well, for people construct the space they live in according to their ideas about how society should operate. The first diagram is the floor plan of a house from fifth-century B.C. Olynthos. Does the actual house correspond to the one described by Xenophon? How does the layout of the house reinforce the roles prescribed for the ideal husband and wife? The second diagram is a plan of the Athenian *agora*, the open square in the center of Athens that served as both the political and commercial center of the city. The west side of the agora was a line of government buildings, including the *bouleuter*, where the council met. The agora was bordered by several *stoa*, roofed-over open colonnades in front of lines of shops and offices. Because the climate of Greece is mild a good part of the year, much business could take place outside or in one of the stoa. What qualities from your list does the openness of the agora encourage? As you can see from the diagram, the agora was bordered by buildings with religious, governmental, and commercial functions. What does the placement of these buildings indicate about how Athenians valued the different areas of their lives?

THE EVIDENCE

Sources 1 and 2 from Thucydides, History of the Peloponnesian War, *translated by Rex Warner (Baltimore: Penguin, 1954), pp. 117–123; pp. 358–363.*

1. Pericles' Funeral Speech, 430 B.C.

I have no wish to make a long speech on subjects familiar to you all: so I shall say nothing about the warlike deeds by which we acquired our power or the battles in which we or our fathers gallantly resisted our enemies, Greek or foreign. What I want to do is, in the first place, to discuss the spirit in which we faced our trials and also our constitution and the way of life which has made us great. After that I shall speak in praise of the dead, believing that this kind of speech is not inappropriate to the present occasion, and that this whole assembly, of citizens and foreigners, may listen to it with advantage.

Let me say that our system of government does not copy the institutions of our neighbours. It is more the case of our being a model to others, than of our imitating anyone else. Our constitution is called a democracy because power is in the hands not of a minority but of the whole people. When it is a question of settling private disputes, everyone is equal before the law; when it is a question of putting one person before another in positions of public responsibility, what counts is not membership of a particular class, but the actual ability which the man possesses. No one, so long as he has it in him to be of service to the state, is kept in political obscurity because of poverty. And, just as our political life is free and open, so is our day-to-day life in our relations with each other. We do not get into a state with our next-door neighbour if he enjoys himself in his own way, nor do we give him the kind of black looks which, though they do no real harm, still do hurt people's feelings. We are free and tolerant in our private lives; but in public affairs we keep to the law. This is because it commands our deep respect.

We give our obedience to those whom we put in positions of authority, and we obey the laws themselves, especially those which are for the protection of the oppressed, and those unwritten laws which it is an acknowledged shame to break.

And here is another point. When our work is over, we are in a position to enjoy all kinds of recreation for our spirits. There are various kinds of contests and sacrifices regularly throughout the year; in our own homes we find a beauty and a good taste which delight us every day and which drive away our cares. Then the greatness of our city brings it about that all the good things from all over the world flow in to us, so that to us it seems just as natural to enjoy foreign goods as our own local products. . . .

Our love of what is beautiful does not lead to extravagance; our love of the things of the mind does not make us soft. We regard wealth as something to be properly used, rather than as something to boast about. As for poverty, no one need be ashamed to admit it: the real shame is in not taking practical measures to escape from it. Here each individual is interested not only in his own affairs but in the affairs of the state as well: even those who are mostly occupied with their own business are extremely well informed on general politics—this is a peculiarity of ours: we do not say that a man who takes no interest in politics is a man who minds his own business; we say that he has no business here at all. We Athenians, in our own persons, take our decisions on policy or submit them to proper discussions: for we do not think that there is an incompatibility between words and deeds; the worst thing is to rush into action before the consequences have been properly debated. And this is another point where we differ from other people. We are capable at the same time of taking risks and of estimating them beforehand. Others are brave out of ignorance; and, when they stop to think, they begin to fear. But the man who can most truly be accounted brave is he who best knows the meaning of what is sweet in life and of what is terrible, and then goes out undeterred to meet what is to come.

Again, in questions of general good feeling there is a great contrast between us and most other people. We make friends by doing good to others, not by receiving good from them. This makes our friendship all the more reliable, since we want to keep alive the gratitude of those who are in our debt by showing continued goodwill to them: whereas the feelings of one who owes us something lack the same enthusiasm, since he knows that, when he repays our kindness, it will be more like paying back a debt than giving something spontaneously. We are unique in this. When we do kindnesses to others, we do not do them out of any calculations of profit or loss: we do them without afterthought, relying on our free liberality. Taking everything together, then, I declare that our city is an education to Greece, and I declare that in my opinion each single one of our citizens, in all the manifold aspects of life, is able to show himself the rightful lord and owner of his own person, and do this, moreover, with exceptional grace and exceptional versatility. And to show that this is no empty boasting for the present occasion, but real tangible fact, you have only to consider the power which our city possesses and which has been won by those very qualities which I have mentioned. Athens, alone of the states we know, comes to her testing time in a greatness that surpasses what was imagined of her. In her case, and in her case alone, no invading enemy is ashamed at being defeated, and no subject can complain of being governed by people unfit for their responsibilities. Mighty indeed are the marks and monuments of our empire which we have left. Future ages will wonder at us, as the present age wonders at us now. We do not need the praises of a Homer, or of anyone else whose words may delight us for the moment, but whose estimation of facts will fall short of what is really true. For our adventurous spirit has forced an entry into every sea and into every land; and everywhere we have left behind us everlasting memorials of good done to our friends or suffering inflicted on our enemies.

This, then, is the kind of city for which these men, who could not bear the thought of losing her, nobly fought and nobly died. . . .

Perhaps I should say a word or two on the duties of women to those among you who are now widowed. I can say all I have to say in a short word of advice. Your great glory is not to be inferior to what God has made you, and the greatest glory of a woman is to be least talked about by men, whether they are praising you or criticizing you. I have now, as the law demanded, said what I had to say. For the time being our offerings to the dead have been made, and for the future their children will be supported at the public expense by the city, until they come of age. This is the crown and prize which she offers, both to the dead and to their children, for the ordeals which they have faced. Where the rewards of valour are the greatest, there you will find also the best and bravest spirits among the people. And now, when you have mourned for your dear ones, you must depart.

2. The Melian Debate, 445 B.C.

The Athenians also made an expedition against the island of Melos. They had thirty of their own ships, six from Chios, and two from Lesbos; 1,200 hoplites,[1] 300 archers, and twenty mounted archers, all from Athens; and about 1,500 hoplites from the allies and the islanders.

The Melians are a colony from Sparta. They had refused to join the Athenian empire like the other islanders, and at first had remained neutral without helping either side; but afterwards, when the Athenians had brought force to bear on them by laying waste their land, they had become open enemies of Athens.

Now the generals Cleomedes, the son of Lycomedes, and Tisias, the son of Tisimachus, encamped with the above force in Melian territory and, before doing any harm to the land, first of all sent representatives to negotiate. The Melians did not invite these representatives to speak before the people, but asked them to make the statement for which they had come in front of the governing body and the few. The Athenian representatives then spoke as follows: . . . . What we shall do now is to show you that it is for the good

1. **hoplite:** a footsoldier armed with a shield and spear; hoplites were trained to attack in a close formation called a **phalanx.**

of our own empire that we are here and that it is for the preservation of your city that we shall say what we are going to say. We do not want any trouble in bringing you into our empire, and we want you to be spared for the good both of yourselves and of ourselves.

MELIANS: And how could it be just as good for us to be the slaves as for you to be the masters?

ATHENIANS: You, by giving in, would save yourselves from disaster; we, by not destroying you, would be able to profit from you.

MELIANS: So you would not agree to our being neutral, friends instead of enemies, but allies of neither side?

ATHENIANS: No, because it is not so much your hostility that injures us; it is rather the case that, if we were on friendly terms with you, our subjects would regard that as a sign of weakness in us, whereas your hatred is evidence of our power.

MELIANS: Is that your subjects' idea of fair play—that no distinction should be made between people who are quite unconnected with you and people who are mostly your own colonists or else rebels whom you have conquered?

ATHENIANS: So far as right and wrong are concerned they think that there is no difference between the two, that those who still preserve their independence do so because they are strong, and that if we fail to attack them it is because we are afraid. So that by conquering you we shall increase not only the size but the security of our empire. We rule the sea and you are islanders, and weaker islanders too than the others; it is therefore particularly important that you should not escape.

MELIANS: But do you think there is no security for you in what we suggest? For here again, since you will not let us mention justice, but tell us to give in to your interests, we, too, must tell you what our interests are and, if yours and ours happen to coincide, we must try to persuade you of the fact. Is it not certain that you will make enemies of all states who are at present neutral, when they see what is happening here and naturally conclude that in course of time you will attack them too? Does not this mean that you are strengthening the enemies you have already and are forcing others to become your enemies even against their intentions and their inclinations?

ATHENIANS: As a matter of fact we are not so much frightened of states on the continent. They have their liberty, and this means that it will be a long time before they begin to take precautions against us. We are more concerned about islanders like yourselves, who are still unsubdued, or subjects who have already become embittered by the constraint which our empire imposes on them. These are the people who are most likely to act in a reckless manner and to bring themselves and us, too, into the most obvious danger.

MELIANS: Then surely, if such hazards are taken by you to keep your empire and by your subjects to escape from it, we who are still free would show ourselves great cowards and weaklings if we failed to face everything that comes rather than submit to slavery.

ATHENIANS: No, not if you are sensible. This is no fair fight, with honour on one side and shame on the other. It is rather a question of saving your lives and not resisting those who are far too strong for you. . . . Our opinion of the gods and our knowledge of men lead us to conclude that it is a general and necessary law of nature to rule wherever one can. This is not a law that we made ourselves, nor were we the first to act upon it when it was made. We found it already in existence, and we shall leave it to exist for ever among those who come after us. . . . For in many cases men have still been able to see the dangers ahead of them, but this thing called dishonour, this word, by its own force of seduction, has drawn them into a state where they have surrendered to an idea, while in fact they have fallen voluntarily into irrevocable disaster, in dishonour that is all the more dishonourable because it has come to them from their own folly rather than their misfortune. You, if you take the right view, will be careful to avoid this. You will see that there is nothing disgraceful in giving way to the greatest city in Hellas when she is offering you such reasonable terms—alliance on a tribute-paying basis and liberty to enjoy your own property. And, when you are allowed to choose between war and safety, you will not be so insensitively arrogant as to make the wrong choice. This is the safe rule—to stand up to one's equals, to behave with deference towards one's superiors, and to treat one's inferiors with moderation. Think it over again, then, when we have withdrawn from the meeting, and let this be a point that constantly recurs to your minds—that you are discussing the fate of your country, that you have only one country, and that its future for good or ill depends on this one single decision which you are going to make.

The Athenians then withdrew from the discussion. The Melians, left to themselves, reached a conclusion which was much the same as they had indicated in their previous replies. Their answer was as follows:

MELIANS: Our decision, Athenians, is just the same as it was at first. We are not prepared to give up in a short moment the liberty which our city has enjoyed from its foundation for 700 years. We put our trust in the fortune that the gods will send and which has saved us up to now, and in the help of men—that is, of the Spartans; and so we shall try to save ourselves. But we invite you to allow us to be friends of yours and enemies to neither side, to make a treaty which shall be agreeable to both you and us, and so to leave our country. . . .

The Athenian representatives then went back to the army, and the Athenian generals, finding that the Melians would not submit, immediately commenced hostilities and built a wall completely round the city of Melos, dividing the work out among the various states. . . .

Meanwhile the Melians made a night attack and captured the part of the Athenian lines opposite the marketplace. They killed some of the troops, and then, after bringing in corn and everything else useful that they could lay their hands on, retired again and made no further move, while the Athenians took measures to make their blockade more efficient in future. So the summer came to an end.

In the following winter the Melians again captured another part of the Athenian lines where there were only a few of the garrison on guard. As a result of this, another force came out afterwards from Athens under the command of Philocrates, the son of Demeas. Siege operations were now carried on vigorously and, as there was also some treachery from inside, the Melians surrendered unconditionally to the Athenians, who put to death all the men of military age whom they took, and sold the women and children as slaves. Melos itself they took over for themselves, sending out later a colony of 500 men.

Source 3 from Aristotle, The Politics, *translated by T. A. Sinclair (Baltimore: Penguin, 1962), pp. 26–27, 31, 34, 50–53.*

3. From Aristotle, *The Politics*

We shall, I think, in this as in other subjects, get the best view of the matter if we look at the natural growth of things from the beginning. . . .

It was out of the association formed by men with these two, women and slaves, that the first household was formed; and the poet Hesiod was right when he wrote, "Get first a house and a wife and an ox to draw the plough." (The ox is the poor man's slave.) This association of persons, established according to the law of nature and continuing day after day, is the household. . . .

Now property is part of a household and the acquisition of property part of the economics of a household; for neither life itself nor the good life is possible without a certain minimum standard of wealth. Again, for any given craft the existence of the proper tools will be essential for the performance of its task. Tools may be animate as well as inanimate; a ship's captain uses a lifeless rudder, but a living man for watch; for the worker in a craft is, from the point of view of the craft, one of its tools. So any piece of property can be regarded as a tool enabling a man to live; and his property is an assemblage of such tools, including his slaves; and a slave, being a living creature like any other servant, is a tool worth many tools. . . .

The "slave by nature" then is he that can and therefore does belong to another, and he that participates in the reasoning faculty so far as to understand but not so as to possess it. For the other animals serve their owner not by exercise of reason but passively. The use, too, of slaves hardly differs at all from that of domestic animals; from both we derive that which is essential for our bodily needs. . . . It is clear then that in household management the people are of greater importance than the material property, and their quality of more account than that of the goods that make up their wealth, and also that free men are of more account than slaves. About slaves the first question to be asked is whether in addition to their value as tools and servants there is some other quality or virtue, superior to these, that belongs to slaves. Can they possess self-respect, courage, justice, and virtues of that kind, or have they in fact nothing but the serviceable quality of their persons?

The question may be answered in either of two ways, but both present a difficulty. If we say that slaves have these virtues, how then will they differ from free men? If we say that they have not, the position is anomalous, since they are human beings and capable of reason. Roughly the same question can be put in relation to wife and child: Have not these also virtues? Ought not a woman to be self-respecting, brave, and just? Is not a child sometimes naughty, sometimes good? . . .

This mention of virtue leads us straightaway to a consideration of the soul; for it is here that the natural ruler and the natural subject, whose virtue we regard as different, are to be found. In the soul the difference between ruler and ruled is that between the rational and the nonrational. It is therefore clear that in other connexions also there will be natural differences. And so generally in cases of ruler and ruled; the differences will be natural but they need not be the same. For rule of free over slave, male over female, man over boy, are all natural, but they are also different, because, while parts of the soul are present in each case, the distribution is different. Thus the deliberative faculty in the soul is not present at all in a slave; in a female it is inoperative, in a child undeveloped. We must therefore take it that the same conditions prevail also in regard to the ethical virtues, namely that all must participate in them but not all to the same extent, but only as may be required by each for his proper function. The ruler then must have ethical virtue in its entirety; for his task is simply that of chief maker and reason is chief maker. And the other members must have what amount is appropriate to each. So it is evident that each of the classes spoken of must have ethical virtue. It is also clear that there is some variation in the ethical virtues; self-respect is not the same in a man as in a woman, nor justice, nor courage either, as Socrates thought; the one is courage of a ruler, the other courage of a servant, and likewise with the other virtues.

If we look at the matter in greater detail it will become clearer. For those who talk in generalities and say that virtue is "a good condition of the soul," or that it is "right conduct" or the like, delude themselves. Better than those who look for general definitions are those who, like Gorgias, enumerate the different virtues. So the poet Sophocles singles out "silence" as "bringing credit to a woman," but that is not so for a man. This method of assessing virtue according to function is one that we should always follow. Take the child: he is not yet fully developed and his function is to grow up, so we cannot speak of his virtue as belonging absolutely to him, but only in relation to the progress of his development and to whoever is in charge of him. So too with slave and master; we laid it down that a slave's function is to perform menial tasks; so the amount of virtue required will not be very great, only enough to ensure that he does not neglect his work through loose living or mere fecklessness.

Source 4 from B. K. Workman, editor and translator, They Saw It Happen in Classical Times *(New York: Barnes & Noble, 1964), pp. 32–34.*

4. An Unknown Author's View of Athenian Democracy

Insolent conduct of slaves and resident aliens is everywhere rife in Athens. You cannot strike a slave there, and he will not get out of your way in the street. There is a good reason for this being the local custom. If the law allowed a free-born citizen to strike a slave, an alien, or a freedman, then you would often strike an Athenian citizen in the mistaken impression that he was a slave. For the common people dress as poorly as slaves or aliens and their general appearance is no better. . . .

The common people take no supervisory interest in athletic or aesthetic shows, feeling that it is not right for them, since they know that they have not the ability to become expert at them. When it is necessary to provide men to put on stageshows or games or to finance and build triremes,[2] they know that impresarios come from the rich, the actors and chorus from the people. In the same way, organizers and ship-masters are the rich, while the common people take a subordinate part in the games and act as oarsmen for the triremes. But they do at least think it right to receive pay for singing or running or dancing or rowing in the fleet, to level up the incomes of rich and poor. The same holds good for the law courts as well; they are more interested in what profit they can make than in the true ends of justice. . . .

Of the mainland cities in the Athenian Empire, the large ones are governed by fear, the small ones by want. For all states must import and export, and this they cannot do unless they remain subject to the mistress of the seas. Secondly, sea powers can do what land powers cannot—ravage a superior enemy's country. For they can sail where few or no enemy troops are stationed, and, if some enemies do arrive, they can embark and sail somewhere else. This causes fewer difficulties than military assistance by land. A third advantage is that naval powers can sail from their own lands in any direction they choose, but journeys of several days cannot be made by land powers, for the travelling is slow and marching men cannot get provisions for any length of time. Furthermore a land force must either march through friendly

2. **trireme:** standard Greek warship, about 120 feet long and rowed by 150 to 175 men; a ram on the bow was the trireme's main weapon.

country or be prepared to overcome opponents in battle. But a sea power can land where it has superiority, and lie off where it has not, or rather sail on until it comes to a friendly coast or to a people weaker than itself. A last point is that natural diseases to crops are a sore burden to land powers but not to sea powers. Since the whole world does not suffer from such diseases at the same time, crops from healthy districts can be brought to the cities of those who command the sea.

Source 5 from Julia O'Faolain and Lauro Martines, editors, Not in God's Image: Women in History from the Greeks to the Victorians *(New York: Harper & Row, 1973), pp. 20–22. Adapted from several translations.*

5. From Xenophon, *The Economist*

"Here's another thing I'd like to ask you," said I. "Did you train your wife yourself or did she already know how to run a house when you got her from her father and mother?"

"What could she have known, Socrates," said he, "when I took her from her family? She wasn't yet fifteen. Until then she had been under careful supervision and meant to see, hear, and ask as little as possible. Don't you think it was already a lot that she should have known how to make a cloak of the wool she was given and how to dole out spinning to the servants? She had been taught to moderate her appetites, which, to my mind, is basic for both men's and women's education."

"So, apart from that," I asked, "it was you, Ischomachus, who had to train and teach her her household duties?"

"Yes," said Ischomachus, "but not before sacrificing to the gods. . . . And she solemnly swore before heaven that she would behave as I wanted, and it was clear that she would neglect none of my lessons."

"Tell me what you taught her first. . . ."

"Well, Socrates, as soon as I had tamed her and she was relaxed enough to talk, I asked her the following question: 'Tell me, my dear,' said I, 'do you understand why I married you and why your parents gave you to me? You know as well as I do that neither of us would have had trouble finding someone else to share our beds. But, after thinking about it carefully, it was you I chose and me your parents chose as the best partners we could find for our home and our children. Now, if God sends us children, we shall think about how best to raise them, for we share an interest in securing the best allies and support for our old age. For the moment we only share our home. . . .'"

"My wife answered, 'But how can I help? What am I capable of doing? It is on you that everything depends. My duty, my mother said, is to be well behaved.'"

"'Oh, by Zeus,' said I, 'my father said the same to me. But the best behavior in a man and woman is that which will keep up their property and increase it as far as may be done by honest and legal means.'"

"'And do you see some way,' asked my wife, 'in which I can help in this?'"

"'. . . It seems to me that God adapted women's nature to indoor and man's to outdoor work. . . . As Nature has entrusted woman with guarding the household supplies, and a timid nature is no disadvantage in such a job, it has endowed woman with more fear than man. . . . It is more proper for a woman to stay in the house than out of doors and less so for a man to be indoors instead of out. If anyone goes against the nature given him by God and leaves his appointed post . . . he will be punished. . . . You must stay indoors and send out the servants whose work is outside and supervise those who work indoors, receive what is brought in, give out what is to be spent, plan ahead what should be stored and ensure that provisions for a year are not used up in a month. When the wool is brought in, you must see to it that clothes are made from it for whoever needs them and see to it that the corn is still edible. . . . Many of your duties will give you pleasure: for instance, if you teach spinning and weaving to a slave who did not know how to do this when you got her, you double her usefulness to yourself, or if you make a good housekeeper of one who didn't know how to do anything. . . .' Then I took her around the family living rooms, which are pleasantly decorated, cool in summer and warm in winter. I pointed out how the whole house faces south so as to enjoy the winter sun. . . . I showed her the women's quarters which are separated from the men's by a bolted door to prevent anything being improperly removed and also to ensure that the slaves should not have children without our permission. For good slaves are usually even more devoted once they have a family; but good-for-nothings, once they begin to cohabit, have extra chances to get up to mischief."

Source 6 from B. Jowett, translator, The Dialogues of Plato, *revised edition, vol. 3 (Oxford: Oxford University Press, 1895, revised 1924), pp. 58, 100–101, 103, 106, 140–142, 147–148, 151, 159.*

6. From Plato, *The Republic*

Is not the love of learning the love of wisdom, which is philosophy?

They are the same, he replied.

And may we not say confidently of man also, that he who is likely to be gentle to his friends and acquaintances, must by nature be a lover of wisdom and knowledge?

That we may safely affirm.

Then he who is to be a really good and noble guardian of the State will require to unite in himself philosophy and spirit and swiftness and strength?

Undoubtedly.

Then we have found the desired natures; and now that we have found them, how are they to be reared and educated? Is not this an enquiry which may be expected to throw light on the greater enquiry which is our final end—How do justice and injustice grow up in States?

Adeimantus thought that the enquiry would be of great service to us. . . .

Come then, and let us pass a leisure hour in storytelling, and our story shall be the education of our heroes.

By all means.

And what shall be their education? Can we find a better than the traditional sort?—and this has two divisions, gymnastic for the body, and music[3] for the soul.

True. . . .

Very good, I said; then what is the next question? Must we not ask who are to be rulers and who subjects?

Certainly.

There can be no doubt that the elder must rule the younger.

Clearly.

And that the best of these must rule.

That is also clear.

Now, are not the best husbandmen those who are most devoted to husbandry?

Yes.

And as we are to have the best of guardians for our city, must they not be those who have most the character of guardians?

Yes. . . .

Then there must be a selection. Let us note among the guardians those who in their whole life show the greatest eagerness to do what is for the good of their country, and the greatest repugnance to do what is against her interests.

Those are the right men.

And they will have to be watched at every age, in order that we may see whether they preserve their resolution, and never, under the influence either of force or enchantment, forget or cast off their sense of duty to the State. . . . And he who at every age, as boy and youth and in mature life, has come out of the trial victorious and pure, shall be appointed a ruler and guardian of the State; he shall be honoured in life and death, and shall receive sepulture[4] and other memorials of honour, the greatest that we have to give. But him who fails, we must reject. I am inclined to think that this is the sort of way in which our rulers and guardians should be chosen and appointed. I speak generally, and not with any pretension to exactness.

And, speaking generally, I agree with you, he said. . . .

3. By "music," the Athenians meant all that was sacred to the **muses**, the patron goddesses of the arts and sciences.

4. **sepulture:** a special burial ceremony.

Then let us consider what will be their way of life, if they are to realize our idea of them. In the first place, none of them should have any property of his own beyond what is absolutely necessary; neither should they have a private house or store closed against any one who has a mind to enter; their provisions should be only such as are required by trained warriors, who are men of temperance and courage; they should agree to receive from the citizens a fixed rate of pay, enough to meet the expenses of the year and no more; and they will go to mess and live together like soldiers in a camp. Gold and silver we will tell them that they have from God; the diviner metal is within them, and they have therefore no need of the dross which is current among men, and ought not to pollute the divine by any such earthly admixture; for that commoner metal has been the source of many unholy deeds, but their own is undefiled. And they alone of all the citizens may not touch or handle silver or gold, or be under the same roof with them, or wear them, or drink from them. And this will be their salvation, and they will be the saviours of the State. But should they ever acquire homes or lands or moneys of their own, they will become housekeepers and husbandmen instead of guardians, enemies and tyrants instead of allies of the other citizens; hating and being hated, plotting and being plotted against, they will pass their whole life in much greater terror of internal than of external enemies, and the hour of ruin, both to themselves and to the rest of the State, will be at hand. For all which reasons may we not say that thus shall our State be ordered, and that these shall be the regulations appointed by us for our guardians concerning their houses and all other matters?

Yes, said Glaucon. . . .

The part of the men has been played out, and now properly enough comes the turn of the women. Of them I will proceed to speak, and the more readily since I am invited by you.

For men born and educated like our citizens, the only way, in my opinion, of arriving at a right conclusion about the possession and use of women and children is to follow the path on which we originally started, when we said that the men were to be the guardians and watchdogs of the herd.

True.

Let us further suppose the birth and education of our women to be subject to similar or nearly similar regulations; then we shall see whether the result accords with our design.

What do you mean?

What I mean may be put into the form of a question, I said: Are dogs divided into hes and shes, or do they both share equally in hunting and in keeping watch and in the other duties of dogs? or do we entrust to the males the entire and exclusive care of the flocks, while we leave the females at home, under the idea that the bearing and suckling their puppies is labour enough for them?

No, he said, they share alike; the only difference between them is that the males are stronger and the females weaker.

But can you use different animals for the same purpose, unless they are bred and fed in the same way?

You cannot.

Then, if women are to have the same duties as men, they must have the same nurture and education?

Yes. . . .

My friend, I said, there is no special faculty of administration in a state which a woman has because she is a woman, or which a man has by virtue of his sex, but the gifts of nature are alike diffused in both; all the pursuits of men are the pursuits of women also, but in all of them a woman is inferior to a man.

Very true.

Then are we to impose all our enactments on men and none of them on women?

That will never do.

One woman has a gift of healing, another not; one is a musician, and another has no music in her nature?

Very true.

And one woman has a turn for gymnastic and military exercises, and another is unwarlike and hates gymnastics?

Certainly.

And one woman is a philosopher, and another is an enemy of philosophy; one has spirit, and another is without spirit?

That is also true.

Then one woman will have the temper of a guardian, and another not. Was not the selection of the male guardians determined by differences of this sort?

Yes.

Men and women alike possess the qualities which make a guardian; they differ only in their comparative strength or weakness.

Obviously.

And those women who have such qualities are to be selected as the companions and colleagues of men who have similar qualities and whom they resemble in capacity and in character?

Very true. . . .

The law, I said, which is the sequel of this and of all that has preceded, is to the following effect—"that the wives of our guardians are to be common, and their children are to be common, and no parent is to know his own child, nor any child his parent."

Yes, he said, that is a much greater wave than the other; and the possibility as well as the utility of such a law are far more questionable. . . .

Both the community of property and the community of families, as I am saying, tend to make them more truly guardians; they will not tear the city in pieces by differing about "mine" and "not mine"; each man dragging any acquisition which he has made into a separate house of his own, where he has a separate wife and children and private pleasures and pains; but all will be affected as far as may be by the same pleasures and pains because they are all of one opinion about what is near and dear to them, and therefore they all tend towards a common end.

Certainly, he replied.

Source 7 adapted from Orestis B. Doumanis and Paul Oliver, editors, Shelter in Greece *(Athens: Architecture in Greece Press, 1974), p. 25.*

7. Floor Plan of a House from Olynthos, 5th century B.C.

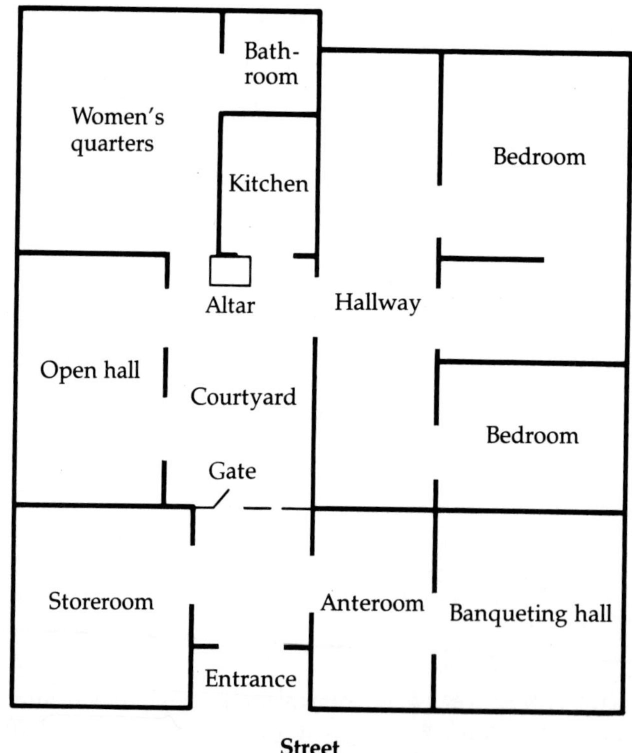

Source 8 from A. W. Lawrence, Greek Architecture *(Baltimore: Penguin Books, 1957), p. 257.*

8. The Athenian Agora, 4th century B.C.

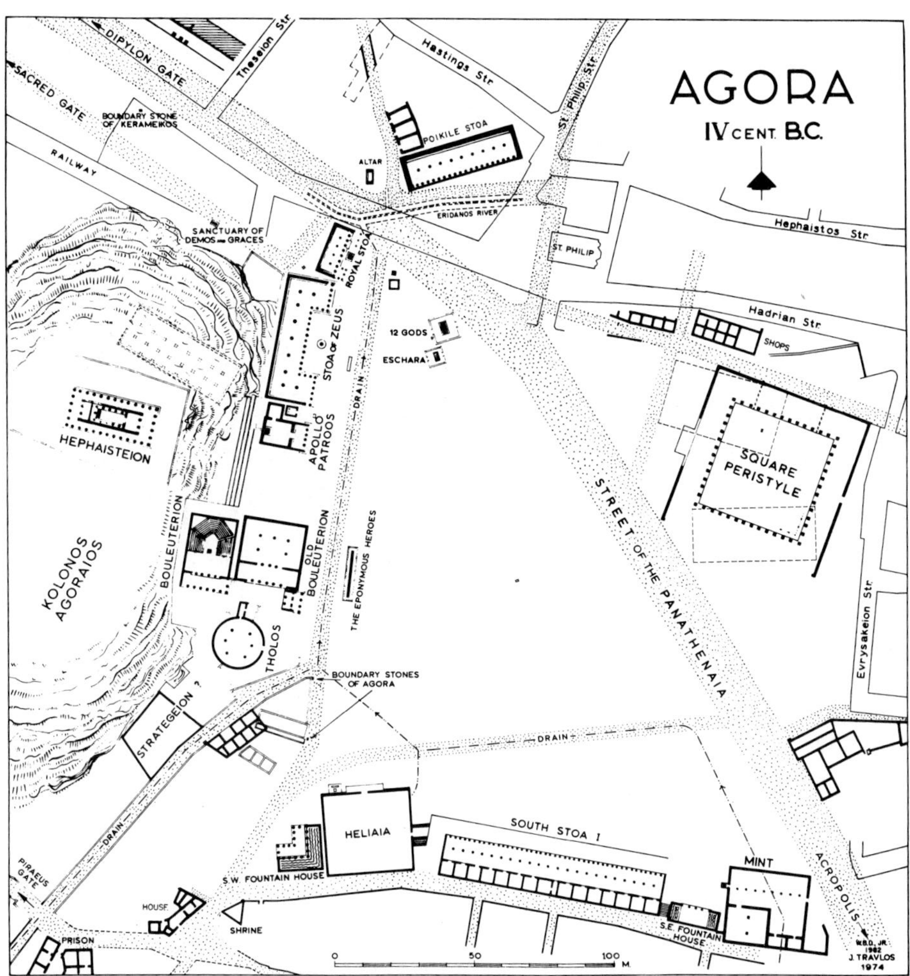

QUESTIONS TO CONSIDER

Before you start to think about the questions in this section, you may want to turn to your text to read (or reread) the section on Athens during the classical period. This can give you more background on the authors and on the political events that might have affected what they wrote.

Though some of the written selections in this chapter clearly describe ideals and others reality, still others blend realism and idealism, creating an idealized view of actual persons or situations. Which selections would you put in this last category? Why would these authors describe reality in an idealized manner? (To answer this question, you need to think about both the purpose of each selection and whether the author truly thought that what he was describing actually existed—in other words, whether this was a conscious or unconscious alteration of reality.)

Once you have labeled the written sources as ideals, reality, and idealizations of reality, go back to your list of the personal qualities of Athenians. Which qualities would you put in each of these three categories? Now that you know you are describing only an ideal or real characteristic, would you add any further qualities? The next step is to divide your list into categories of persons, for it is clear most of the authors make great distinctions between male and female, adult and child, slave and free. Do all the authors agree on the qualities important in an ideal man, woman, or slave? Which authors have opposing ideas? Why might this be so? Sometimes distinctions between categories are not clearly set out by the author; when Pericles, for instance, uses the words "person" and "people" in his funeral oration, one might think he was talking about all Athenians. Looking at your list divided into categories, of whom is Pericles speaking when he says "person" and "people"? Do any of the authors make distinctions between individuals of the same category based on such factors as wealth or education; for example, do they describe wealthy men differently from poormen, or set out different ideals for women interested in learning than for those who are not? If Athenians lived up to the ideals prescribed for them, what types of people would you expect to meet in the agora? What types of people would you not expect to meet?

Turning from the individual to social units, what qualities should the ideal Athenian household possess? How might real households work to emulate these ideals? Judging from information in the selections and in your text about Athenian marriage patterns, family life, and social life in general, did real Athenian households approach the ideal at all? How did their beliefs about the way households should be run affect the way Athenians designed their houses? How did the layout of a house work to make reality correspond with those ideals?

The qualities of governments as presented in the selections may also be classified as real, ideal, or idealized. Were any of the words you used to describe the Athenian government after first reading Pericles included in your final list? Does his idealized view of Athens come closer to the realistic view provided in the Melian debate or to the purely ideal view of Plato? After reading all the selections, would you put the quality "democracy" into the real or ideal column for Athens? How would Athenians define democracy? How does the layout of the agora reflect this definition? Do all the authors agree that democracy is a desirable form of government? Judging from information in your text about politics in Athens in the fifth century, why would authors disagree on this matter? If you put democracy in the ideal column, what changes in existing conditions would have been necessary for it to become a reality?

The selections you have read offer varying opinions on a great many subjects, including the benefits of wealth and private property, the relationship between dominant and dependent states and between dominant and dependent individuals, the reasons for the differences between men and women, the role of naval power in foreign policy, and the causes of imperialism. All these issues have both ideal and real components, and you may want to think about them before you draw your final conclusions about classical Athens. How well did Athens live up to the ideals it set for itself? How did the different ideals held up for different categories of persons affect their participation in Athenian life?

EPILOGUE

We can find the ideals of the Athenians expressed not only in their philosophy, history, and architecture, as you have discovered here, but also in their drama, poetry, and sculpture. Indeed, most of the original sources we have from Athens are not realistic descriptions but either thoughts about ideals or idealizations of actual persons and episodes. That they are idealizations may be very clear to us as modern skeptical readers, but for a long time the statements in these sources were taken as literal truth. To give you an example, here is a quotation from Edith Hamilton, one of the foremost historians of Greece, published in 1930:

> For a hundred years Athens was a city where the great spiritual forces that war in men's minds flowed together along in peace; law and freedom, truth and religion, beauty and goodness, the objective and the subjective—there was a truce to their eternal warfare, and the result was the balance and clarity, the harmony and completeness, that the word Greek has come to stand for.[5]

Given what you have just read, would you agree with her? Do you think everyone living in classical Athens would have agreed with her?

No matter how you have judged the relationship between ideal and reality in classical Athens, the ideals for the individual and state created there have significantly shaped the development of Western philosophy and social institutions. Roman philosophers closely studied Plato's *Republic,* and medieval philosophers were strongly influenced by Aristotle's *Politics*. Writers from the Renaissance until the present have invented ideal societies, "utopias" guided by wise leaders like Plato's guardians. Occasionally small groups of people have actually tried to set up working

5. Edith Hamilton, *The Greek Way* (New York: Norton, 1930), p. 206.

replicas of these ideal societies, frequently forbidding private property and the nuclear family as Plato did. Educational theorists have devised "perfect" school systems that, if not entirely successful when put into practice, have had their effect on real-life pedagogy. The Athenian ideal of government by the people is reflected in the constitutions of modern democratic states, with the category "people" now including groups unthinkable to Pericles.

In terms of Athenian history, democracy was an extremely short-lived phenomenon. Widespread revolt broke out in the Athenian empire, and Sparta ultimately defeated Athens, bringing the Peloponnesian War to a close after twenty-seven years. This did not end warfare in Greece, however, as the city-states continued to battle among themselves. Finally, in 338 B.C., Greece was conquered by Philip of Macedonia and Athens became simply one small part of a much larger empire. From that point on, Athenian ideals of individual behavior would be emulated in Western culture, but democratic government would not again be attempted as an experiment in the real world for another 2,000 years.

CHAPTER THREE
THE ACHIEVEMENTS OF AUGUSTUS

THE PROBLEM

For many centuries, the seat of power in Rome was the Senate, a body of men drawn from the most powerful and prominent Roman families that made all major political and military decisions. Under the leadership of the Senate, Rome had gradually taken control of the entire Italian peninsula. It then conquered southern France and much of Spain, and, after defeating Carthage in the Punic Wars, occupied northern Africa. These territorial conquests altered the nature of power in Rome, however, because the armies that conquered and held the new territories pledged loyalty to their military leaders and not to the Senate. During the first century before Christ, several of these semi-independent armies challenged the Senate's power and civil war erupted in many parts of the Roman territory. The city itself was plundered several times by rival legions, and trade and communications were frequently disrupted. In 60 B.C., three army generals—Pompey, Crassus, and Julius Caesar—decided to form a political alliance, the Triumvirate, leaving the Senate intact but without much actual power.

All three of these generals were ambitious men who were unwilling to share power with anyone for very long. The Senate was especially worried about Julius Caesar, who was gathering an increasingly larger army in Gaul (present-day France), and decided to put its trust in Pompey, whose base of power lay in Greece. (Crassus had meanwhile died in battle.) It ordered Caesar to disband his army and not to return to Rome, setting the Rubicon River near Ravenna in northern Italy as the line he must not cross. In 49 B.C., Caesar crossed the Rubicon, an expression we still use for an irrevocable decision, directly challenging the power of the Senate and of Pompey. His armies quickly defeated those of the Senate in Italy, and within a few months he held the entire Italian peninsula. From there Caesar turned his attention to Pompey's army, which his forces also defeated by 45 B.C., leaving him in control of all the Roman territory. Though he did not disband the Senate, he did begin to shape the government to his liking, appointing officials and army officers and directly overseeing the administration of the provinces. He increased the size of the Senate from 600 to 900 members by padding it with his followers, many of whom came from the provinces.

Caesar's meteoric and extralegal rise to power created great resentment among many Roman senators. Intensely proud of Roman traditions and of their own families' long-standing political power, they felt that Caesar was degrading the Senate by adding unsophisticated rural representatives. A group of senators, led by Brutus and Cassius, decided to assassinate Caesar, which they did on the steps of the Roman Senate on March 15, 44 B.C. The conspirators had not thought much beyond this act, however, and Caesar's death led not to peace but to a renewal of civil war. Some of the army was loyal to the assassins; some to Mark Antony, an associate of Caesar's; and some to Caesar's nephew and adopted son, Octavian. At first Mark Antony and Octavian cooperated to defeat the assassins, but then they turned against each other. The war dragged on for over a decade, with Octavian's forces gradually gaining more territory. Octavian won the support of many Romans by convincing them that Antony was plotting with Cleopatra, queen of Egypt, and in 31 B.C. his forces decisively defeated those of Antony at the naval battle of Actium. Antony and his ally Cleopatra committed suicide, leaving Octavian sole ruler of the Mediterranean world.

The problem now facing Octavian was the same one Julius Caesar had confronted twelve years earlier: how to transform a state won by military force into a stable political system. Caesar's answer—personal, autocratic rule—had led to his assassination at the hands of disgruntled senators. This lesson was not lost on Octavian, who realized that directly opposing the strong republican tradition in Rome could be very dangerous.

This tradition had arisen from both political reality—the Senate had held actual power for many generations—and Roman political theory. The Romans held that their form of government had been given to them by the gods, who had conferred authority on Romulus, the mythical founder of Rome. That authority was later passed on to the Senate, whose original function was to consult the gods about actions Rome should take. The Senate in turn passed on authority to the rest of the government bureaucracy and to male heads of household, for in Rome households were considered, as in Athens, the smallest unit of government. Only male heads of household could sit in the Senate, for only such individuals were regarded as worthy enough to consult the gods on matters of great importance to the state. This meant that Roman society was extremely patriarchal, with fathers having (at least in theory) absolute control over their wives, children, and servants.

This divinely ordained authority could always be distributed downward as the political bureaucracy grew, but to do away with existing institutions was extremely dangerous. Any radical transformation of the structure of government, especially any change in the authority of the Senate, would have been regarded as impious.

Octavian had himself grown up in this tradition and at least to some degree shared these ideas about authority and the divine roots of the Roman political system. He realized that he could be more effective—and probably would live longer—if he worked through, rather than against, existing political institutions. Moreover, serious problems existed that had to be faced immediately; after years of civil war, the government bureaucracy was no longer firmly in place to deal with them. He needed to appoint officials and governors and reestablish law and order throughout Roman territory without offending the Senate by acting like an autocrat or dictator.

In the eyes of many of his contemporaries, Octavian accomplished this admittedly difficult task very well. The Senate conferred on him the name he is usually known by, Augustus, meaning "blessed" or "magnificent." Later historians regarded Augustus, rather than Julius Caesar, as the creator of the Roman Empire. Your task in this chapter will be to evaluate these judgments. How did Augustus transform the Roman republic into an empire? Why was he successful where Julius Caesar had not been?

SOURCES AND METHOD

As you think about these questions, you can see that they involve two somewhat different components: the process by which Augustus made changes and the results of these changes, or what we might term the *means* and the *ends*. Both are important to consider in assessing the achievements of any political leader, and both have been used by the contemporaries of Augustus, later Roman writers, and modern historians in evaluating the first Roman emperor's reign.

One of the best sources for observing the process of political change are laws, especially basic laws such as constitutions that set out governmental structure. Rome was a society in which law was extremely important and was explicitly written down, unlike many early societies in which laws were handed down orally from generation to generation. As the Romans conquered Europe and the Mediterranean, they brought their legal system with them; consequently, Roman law forms the basis of most modern Western legal systems, with England and thus the United States the most notable exceptions.

We encounter some serious difficulties in using laws as our source material for the reign of Augustus, however. Given Roman ideas about authority and the strength of Roman tradition, would you expect him to have made major legal changes? Augustus, after all, described his aims and his actions as restoring republican government; if we use only the constitution of Rome as a source, we might be tempted to believe him. No new office was created for the emperor; what he did instead was to preserve carefully all traditional offices while gradually taking over many of them himself. Augustus was both a consul and a tribune, though the former office was usually reserved for a patrician and the latter for a plebeian. Later the Senate appointed him *imperator,* or commander-in-chief of the army, and gave him direct control of many of the outlying provinces. These provinces furnished grain supplies essential to the people of Rome as well as soldiers loyal to Augustus rather than to the Senate. The Senate also gave him the honorary title of *princeps* (or "first citizen"), the title he preferred, which gradually lost its republican origins and gained the overtones of "monarch" evident in its modern English derivative, "prince." Augustus recognized the importance of religion to most Romans, and in 12 B.C. had himself named *pontifex maximus* or supreme priest. He encouraged the building of temples dedicated to "Rome and Augustus," laying the foundations for the growth of a ruler cult closely linked with patriotic loyalty to Rome.

None of these innovations required any alteration in the basic constitution of Rome. What did change, however, was the tone of many laws, particularly those from the outlying provinces, where Augustus could be more open about the transformation he was working without bringing on the wrath of the senate. Our first two selections, then, are decrees and laws from Roman territories, where we can perhaps see some hint of the gradual development of the republic into an empire.

Source 1 is a decree by Augustus himself, an inscription dated 4 B.C. from the Greek city of Cyrene. As with all laws, it is passed in response to a perceived problem. What problem does the decree confront? What procedure does it provide to solve this problem? What complications does it anticipate, and how does it try to solve them? You will notice that the decree itself is set within a long framework giving the reasons it was issued. This is true for many laws, including the American Constitution, which begins, "We the people of the United States, in order to form a more perfect union, establish justice, insure domestic tranquillity." Why does Augustus say he is passing this law? This framework can also give you clues to the relationship between Augustus and the Senate. How is this relationship described, and what does Augustus's attitude appear to be?

The second law is an inscription dated A.D. 11 from an altar in the city of Narbonne in southern France, passed by the local government, not the central Roman authorities. What does it order the population to do? Although the law itself does not state why it was passed, what might some reasons have been? What does the law indicate about attitudes toward Augustus and toward Roman authorities?

Another valuable source for examining the achievements of Augustus consists of the comments of his contemporaries and later Roman historians. Because Romans had such a strong sense of their own traditions, they were fascinated by history and were ever eager to point out how the hand of the gods operated in a way that allowed Rome to conquer most of the Western world. In the century before Augustus took over, it looked to many Romans as if the gods had forgotten Rome, leaving its citizens to kill each other in revolutions and civil wars. Augustus's military successes and political acumen seemed to show that he had the gods on his side, so writers delighted in extolling his accomplishments. Augustus's astuteness also extended to the world of literature and the arts, and he hired writers, sculptors, architects, and painters to glorify Rome, causing his own reputation no harm in the process. Many of the poems and histories are blatant hero worship; others communicate a more balanced view and, because Augustus was not totally successful at winning everyone over to his side, some authors are openly critical.

Sources 3 through 6 are assessments by various Romans of Augustus's rule. As you read them, first try to gauge each author's basic attitude toward Augustus. What does he find to praise or blame? Does his judgment appear overly positive or negative? Does he sound objective? In answering these questions, you will need to pay attention not only to the content of the selection but also to the specific words each author chooses. What kinds of adjectives does he use to describe Augustus's person and political actions? Once you have assessed the basic attitude of each author, identify what he regards as important in Augustus's reign. To what factors does he attribute Augustus's success? How does he describe the process by which the Roman republic was turned into an empire? What reasons does he give for Augustus's success and Julius Caesar's failure?

A bit of background on each of these selections will help you put them in better perspective. Source 3 was written by Horace, a poet living at the court of Augustus. This is an excerpt from his *Odes*, a literary rather than primarily historical work. Source 4, an excerpt from Suetonius's biography of Augustus, was composed during the first half of the second century; Suetonius, private secretary to the emperor Hadrian, was keenly interested in the private as well as public lives of the Roman emperors. Source 5 is taken from the long history of Rome by the politician and historian Dio Cassius (c. 150–235). Source 6 is drawn from the *Annals* of Tacitus, an orator and historian from a well-to-do Roman family. Sources 4 through 6 were written between one and two centuries after the events they present and are thus "history" as we know it, describing events after they happened.

Source 7 is a third type of evidence, namely, Augustus's own description of his rule. Usually called the *Res Gestae Divi Augusti*, it is an inscription he composed shortly before the end of his life. In this piece, following a long Roman tradition of inscriptions commemorating distinguished citizens, he describes the honors conferred on him as well as his accomplishments. Like all autobiographical statements, it is not simply intended as an objective description of a ruler's deeds but specifically as a vehicle for all that Augustus most wanted people to remember about this reign. Even though it is subjective, the *Res Gestae* is unique and invaluable as a primary source because it gives us Augustus's own version of the transformations he wrought in Roman society. As you read it, compare Augustus's descriptions of his deeds with those of the historians you have just read. What does Augustus regard as his most important accomplishments?

Many of the best sources for Augustus, of course, as for all of ancient history, are not written but archeological. As the Romans conquered land after land, they introduced not only their legal code but their monetary system as well. Roman coins have been found throughout all of Europe and the Near East, far beyond the borders of the Roman Empire. *Numismatics*, the study of coins, can thus provide us with clues available from no other source, for coins have the great advantage of being both durable and valuable. Though their value sometimes works to render them less durable—people melt them down to make other coins or to use the metal in other ways—it also makes them one of the few material goods that people hide in great quantities. Their owners intend to dig them up later, of course, but die or forget where they have buried them, leaving great caches of coins for later archeologists and historians.

Roman coins differ markedly from modern coins in some respects. Though the primary function of both is to serve as a means of exchange, Roman coins were also transmitters of political propaganda. One side usually displayed a portrait of the emperor, chosen very carefully by the emperor himself to emphasize certain qualities. The reverse side often depicted a recent victory, anniversary, or other important event, or the personification of an abstract quality or virtue such as health or liberty. Modern coins also feature portraits, pictures, and slogans, but they tend to stay the same for decades and so we pay very little attention to what is on them. Roman emperors, on the other hand, issued new coins frequently, expecting people to look at them. Most of the people who lived in the Roman Empire were illiterate, with no chance to read about the illustrious deeds of the emperor, but they did come into contact with coins nearly every day. From these coins they learned what the emperor looked like, what he had recently done, or what qualities to associate with him, for even illiterate people could identify the symbols for such abstract virtues as liberty or victory. Over 100 different portraits of Augustus have been found on coins that provide us with additional clues about the achievements he most wanted to emphasize.

Once you have read the written documents, look at the two illustrations of coins. On the first, issued in 2 B.C., the lettering reads CAESAR AUGUSTUS DIVI F PATER PATRIAE, or "Augustus Caesar, son of a God, Father of the Fatherland." (Julius Caesar had been deified by the Senate after his assassination, which is why Augustus named himself "son of a God.") Augustus is crowned with what appears to be a wreath of corn ears; this crown was the exclusive right of the priests of one of Rome's oldest religious groups that honored agricultural gods. The second coin, issued between 20 and 16 B.C., shows Augustus alongside the winged figure of the goddess Victory in a chariot atop a triumphal arch that stands itself on top of a viaduct; the inscription reads QUOD VIAE MUN SUNT, "because the roads have been reinforced." Think about the message Augustus was trying to convey with each of these coins. Even if you could not read the words, what impression would you have of the emperor from coins like these?

Issuing coins was one way for an emperor to celebrate and communicate his achievements; building was another. As you have read in Augustus's autobiography, he had many structures—stadiums, marketplaces, and temples—built for various purposes. He, and later Roman emperors, also built structures that were purely symbolic, the most impressive of which were celebratory arches, built to commemorate an achievement or military victory. The second coin shows Augustus standing on top of such an arch; Source 12 is a photograph of the arch of Augustus that still stands at Rimini. This arch was built at one end of the Flaminian Way that Augustus reconstructed, as you have read in his autobiography; a similar arch was built at the other end in Rome. As you did when looking at the coins, think about the message such an arch conveys. It was put up with the agreement of the Senate; does it give you a sense of republicanism or empire?

Roads are another prime archeological source, closely related to the aqueducts we examined in Chapter 1. The Romans initially built roads to help their army move more quickly; once built, however, the road system facilitated trade and commerce as well. Roads are thus symbols of power as well as a means to maintain and extend it. Archeologists have long studied the expansion of the Roman road system, and their findings can most easily be seen diagrammed on maps. Though maps do not have the immediacy of actual archeological remains, they are based on such remains and enable us to detect patterns and make comparisons over time.

Selections 10 and 11 are maps of the major Roman roads existing before the reign of Augustus, those built or reconstructed during his reign, and the Roman road system at its farthest extent. Compare the first map with the information you have obtained from Augustus himself about his expansion of the frontiers of Rome (Source 7, paragraph 26). Notice that he mentions only the western part of the Roman Empire; do the roads built during his reign reflect this western orientation? What do the later road-building patterns shown in Source 11 tell us about the goals and successes of later Roman emperors?

THE EVIDENCE

Sources 1 through 3 from Naphtali Lewis and Meyer Reinhold, editors and translators, Roman Civilization, *vol. 2,* The Empire *(New York: Columbia University Press, 1955), pp. 39–42; p. 62; p. 20.*

1. Decree Issued by Emperor Augustus, 4 B.C.

The Emperor Caesar Augustus, *pontifex maximus,* holding the tribunician power for the nineteenth year, declares:

A decree of the senate was passed in the consulship of Gaius Calvisius and Lucius Passienus, with me as one of those present at the writing. Since it affects the welfare of the allies of the Roman people, I have decided to send it into the provinces, appended to this my prefatory edict, so that it may be known to all who are under our care. From this it will be evident to all the inhabitants of the provinces how much both I and the senate are concerned that none of our subjects should suffer any improper treatment or any extortion.

DECREE OF THE SENATE

Whereas the consuls Gaius Calvisius Sabinus and Lucius Passienus Rufus spoke "Concerning matters affecting the security of the allies of the Roman people which the Emperor Caesar Augustus, our *princeps,* following the recommendation of the council which he had drawn by lot from among the senate, desired to be brought before the senate by us," the senate passed the following decree:

Whereas our ancestors established legal process for extortion so that the allies might more easily be able to take action for any wrongs done them and recover moneys extorted from them, and whereas this type of process is sometimes very expensive and troublesome for those in whose interest the law was enacted, because poor people or persons weak with illness or age are dragged from far-distant provinces as witnesses, the senate decrees as follows:

If after the passage of this decree of the senate any of the allies, desiring to recover extorted moneys, public or private, appear and so depose before one of the magistrates who is authorized to convene the senate, the magistrate—except where the extorter faces a capital charge—shall bring them before the senate as soon as possible and shall assign them any advocate they themselves request to speak in their behalf before the senate; but no one who has in accordance with the laws been excused from this duty shall be required to serve as advocate against his will. . . .

The judges chosen shall hear and inquire into only those cases in which a man is accused of having appropriated money from a community or from private parties; and, rendering their decision within thirty days, they shall order him to restore such sum of money, public or private, as the accusers prove was taken from them. Those whose duty it is to inquire into and pronounce judgment in these cases shall, until they complete the inquiry and pronounce their judgment, be exempted from all public duties except public worship. . . .

The senate likewise decrees that the judges who are selected in accordance with this decree of the senate shall pronounce in open court each his several finding, and what the majority pronounces shall be the verdict.

2. Inscription from the City of Narbonne, A.D. 11

In the consulship of Titus Statilius Taurus and Lucius Cassius Longinus, September 22. Vow taken to the divine spirit of Augustus by the populace of the Narbonensians in perpetuity: "May it be good, favorable, and auspicious to the Emperor Caesar Augustus, son of a god, father of his country, *pontifex maximus,* holding the tribunician power for the thirty-fourth year; to his wife, children, and house; to the Roman senate and people; and to the colonists[1] and residents of the Colonia Julia Paterna of Narbo Martius,[2] who have bound themselves to worship his divine spirit in perpetuity!"

The populace of the Narbonensians has erected in the forum at Narbo an altar at which every year on September 23—the day on which the good fortune of the age bore him to be ruler of the world—three Roman *equites* from the populace and three freedmen shall sacrifice one animal each and shall at their own expense on that day provide the colonists and residents with incense and wine for supplication to his divine spirit. And on September 24 they shall likewise provide incense and wine for the colonists and residents. Also on January 1 they shall provide incense and wine for the colonists and residents. Also on January 7, the day on which he first entered upon the command of the world, they shall make supplication with incense and wine, and shall sacrifice one animal each, and shall provide incense and wine for the colonists and residents on that day. And on May 31, because on that day in the consulship of Titus Statilius Taurus and Manius Aemilius

1. The word "colonist" has a very specific meaning in Roman history. **Colonists** were Romans, often retired soldiers, who were granted land in the outlying provinces in order to build up Roman strength there. They were legally somewhat distinct from native residents, which is why this law uses the phrase "colonists and residents" to make it clear that both groups were required to follow its provisions.

2. The long phrase "Colonia Julia Pasterna of Narbo Martius" is the official and complete Roman name for the town of Narbo, which we now call Narbonne.

Lepidus he reconciled the populace to the decurions,[3] they shall sacrifice one animal each and shall provide the colonists and residents with incense and wine for supplication to his divine spirit. And of these three Roman *equites* and three freedmen one. . . . [The rest of this inscription is lost.]

3. From Horace, *Odes*

Thine age, O Caesar, has brought back fertile crops to the fields and has restored to our own Jupiter the military standards stripped from the proud columns of the Parthians[4]; has closed Janus' temple[5] freed of wars; has put reins on license overstepping righteous bounds; has wiped away our sins and revived the ancient virtues through which the Latin name and the might of Italy waxed great, and the fame and majesty of our empire were spread from the sun's bed in the west to the east. As long as Caesar is the guardian of the state, neither civil dissension nor violence shall banish peace, nor wrath that forges swords and brings discord and misery to cities. Not those who drink the deep Danube shall violate the orders of Caesar, nor the Getae, nor the Seres,[6] nor the perfidious Parthians, nor those born by the Don River. And we, both on profane and sacred days, amidst the gifts of merry Bacchus, together with our wives and children, will first duly pray to the gods; then, after the tradition of our ancestors, in songs to the accompaniment of Lydian flutes we will hymn leaders whose duty is done.

Source 4 from Suetonius, The Lives of the Twelve Caesars, *edited and translated by Joseph Gavorse (New York: Modern Library, 1931), p. 89.*

4. From Suetonius, *Life of Augustus*

The whole body of citizens with a sudden unanimous impulse proffered him the title of "father of his country"—first the plebs, by a deputation sent to Antium, and then, because he declined it, again at Rome as he entered the theater, which they attended in throngs, all wearing laurel wreaths; the

3. **decurion:** member of a town council.

4. The Parthians were an empire located in the region occupied by present-day Iraq. They had defeated Roman armies led by Mark Antony and had taken the Roman military standards, that is, the flags and banners of the army they defeated. Augustus recovered these standards, an important symbolic act, even though he did not conquer the Parthians.

5. This was a small temple in Rome that was ordered closed whenever peace reigned throughout the whole Roman Empire. During the reign of Augustus it was closed three times.

6. The Getae and the Sedes were people who lived in the regions occupied by present-day Rumania and the Ukraine.

senate afterwards in the senate house, not by a decree or by acclamation, but through Valerius Messala. He, speaking for the whole body, said: "Good fortune and divine favor attend thee and thy house, Caesar Augustus; for thus we feel that we are praying for lasting prosperity for our country and happiness for our city. The senate in accord with the Roman people hails thee 'Father of thy Country.'" Then Augustus with tears in his eyes replied as follows (and I have given his exact words, as I did those of Messala): "Having attained my highest hopes, members of the senate, what more have I to ask of the immortal gods than that I may retain this same unanimous approval of yours to the very end of my life?"

Sources 5 through 7 from Naphtali Lewis and Meyer Reinhold, editors and translators, Roman Civilization, *vol. 2,* The Empire *(New York: Columbia University Press, 1955), pp. 4–8; p. 4; pp. 9–10, 12, 14–16, 17, 19.*

5. From Dio Cassius, *Roman History*

In this way the power of both people and senate passed entirely into the hands of Augustus, and from this time there was, strictly speaking, a monarchy; for monarchy would be the truest name for it, even if two or three men later held the power jointly. Now, the Romans so detested the title "monarch" that they called their emperors neither dictators nor kings nor anything of this sort. Yet, since the final authority for the government devolves upon them, they needs must be kings. The offices established by the laws, it is true, are maintained even now, except that of censor; but the entire direction and administration is absolutely in accordance with the wishes of the one in power at the time. And yet, in order to preserve the appearance of having this authority not through their power but by virtue of the laws, the emperors have taken to themselves all the offices (including the titles) which under the Republic possessed great power with the consent of the people—with the exception of the dictatorship. Thus, they very often become consuls, and they are always styled proconsuls whenever they are outside the *pomerium.*[7] The title *imperator* is held by them for life, not only by those who have won victories in battle but also by all the rest, to indicate their absolute power, instead of the title "king" or "dictator." These latter titles they have never assumed since they fell out of use in the constitution, but the actuality of those offices is secured to them by the appellation *imperator.* By virtue of the titles named, they secure the right to make levies, collect funds, declare war, make peace, and rule foreigners and citizens alike everywhere and always—even to the extent of being able to put to death both

7. **pomerium:** the city limits of Rome.

equites and senators inside the *pomerium*—and all the other powers once granted to the consuls and other officials possessing independent authority; and by virtue of holding the censorship they investigate our lives and morals as well as take the census, enrolling some in the equestrian and senatorial orders and removing others from these orders according to their will. By virtue of being consecrated in all the priesthoods and, in addition, from their right to bestow most of them upon others, as well as from the fact that, even if two or three persons rule jointly, one of them is *pontifex maximus*, they hold in their own hands supreme authority over all matters both profane and sacred. The tribunician power, as it is called, which once the most influential men used to hold, gives them the right to nullify the effects of the measures taken by any other official, in case they do not approve, and makes their persons inviolable; and if they appear to be wronged in even the slightest degree, not merely by deed but even by word, they may destroy the guilty party as one accursed, without a trial.

Thus by virtue of these Republican titles they have clothed themselves with all the powers of the government, so that they actually possess all the prerogatives of kings without the usual title. For the appellation "Caesar" or "Augustus" confers upon them no actual power but merely shows in the one case that they are the successors of their family line, and in the other the splendor of their rank. The name "Father" perhaps gives them a certain authority over us all—the authority which fathers once had over their children; yet it did not signify this at first, but betokened honor and served as an admonition both to them to love their subjects as they would their children, and to their subjects to revere them as they would their fathers. . . .

The senate as a body, it is true, continued to sit in judgment as before, and in certain cases transacted business with embassies and envoys from both peoples and kings; and the people and the plebs, moreover, continued to come together for the elections; but nothing was actually done that did not please Caesar. At any rate, in the case of those who were to hold office, he himself selected and nominated some; and though he left the election of others in the hands of the people and the plebs, in accordance with the ancient practice, yet he took care that no persons should hold office who were unfit or elected as the result of factious combinations or bribery.

Such were the arrangements made, generally speaking, at that time; for in reality Caesar himself was destined to have absolute power in all matters for life, because he was not only in control of money matters (nominally, to be sure, he had separated the public funds from his own, but as a matter of fact he spent the former also as he saw fit) but also in control of the army. At all events, when his ten-year period came to an end, there was voted him another five years, then five more, after that ten, and again another ten, and then ten for the fifth time, so that by the succession of ten-year periods he continued to be sole ruler for life. And it is for this reason that the subsequent monarchs, though no longer appointed for a specified period but for their whole life once for all, nevertheless always held a celebration every ten years, as if then renewing their sovereignty once more; and this is done even at the present day.

Now, Caesar had received many privileges previously, when the question of declining the sovereignty and that of apportioning the provinces were under discussion. For the right to fasten laurels to the front of the imperial residence and to hang the civic crown above the doors was then voted him to symbolize the fact that he was always victorious over enemies and savior of the citizens. The imperial palace is called Palatium, not because it was ever decreed that this should be its name but because Caesar dwelt on the Palatine and had his military headquarters there. . . . Hence, even if the emperior resides somewhere else, his dwelling retains the name of Palatium.

And when he had actually completed the reorganization, the name Augustus was at length bestowed upon him by the senate and by the people. . . . He took the title of Augustus, signifying that he was more than human; for all most precious and sacred objects are termed *augusta.* For which reason they called him also in Greek *sebastos* . . . meaning an august person.

6. From Tacitus, *Annals*

After the death of Brutus and Cassius, there was no longer any army loyal to the Republic. . . . Then, laying aside the title of triumvir and parading as a consul, and professing himself satisfied with the tribunician power for the protection of the plebs, Augustus enticed the soldiers with gifts, the people with grain, and all men with the allurement of peace, and gradually grew in power, concentrating in his own hands the functions of the senate, the magistrates, and the laws. No one opposed him, for the most courageous had fallen in battle or in the proscription. As for the remaining nobles, the readier they were for slavery, the higher were they raised in wealth and offices, so that, aggrandized by the revolution, they preferred the safety of the present to the perils of the past. Nor did the provinces view with disfavor this state of affairs, for they distrusted the government of the senate and the people on account of the struggles of the powerful and the rapacity of the officials, while the protection afforded them by the laws was inoperative, as the provinces were repeatedly thrown into confusion by violence, intrigue, and finally bribery. . . .

At home all was peaceful; the officials bore the same titles as before. The younger generation was born after the victory of Actium, and even many of the older generation had been born during the civil wars. How few were left who had seen the Republic!

Thus the constitution had been transformed, and there was nothing at all left of the good old way of life. Stripped of equality, all looked to the directives of a *princeps* with no apprehension for the present, while Augustus in the vigorous years of his life maintained his power, that of his family, and peace.

7. From Augustus, *Res Gestae Divi Augustus*

1. At the age of nineteen, on my own initiative and at my own expense, I raised an army by means of which I liberated the Republic, which was oppressed by the tyranny of a faction. For which reason the senate, with honorific decrees, made me a member of its order in the consulship of Gaius Pansa and Aulus Hirtius, giving me at the same time consular rank in voting, and granted me the *imperium*. It ordered me as propraetor, together with the consuls, to see to it that the state suffered no harm. Moreover, in the same year, when both consuls had fallen in the war, the people elected me consul and a triumvir for the settlement of the commonwealth.

2. Those who assassinated my father I drove into exile, avenging their crime by due process of law; and afterwards when they waged war against the state, I conquered them twice on the battlefield.

3. I waged many wars throughout the whole world by land and by sea, both civil and foreign, and when victorious I spared all citizens who sought pardon. Foreign peoples who could safely be pardoned I preferred to spare rather than to extirpate. . . . Though the Roman senate and people unitedly agreed that I should be elected sole guardian of the laws and morals with supreme authority, I refused to accept any office offered me which was contrary to the traditions of our ancestors. . . .

9. The senate decreed that vows for my health should be offered up every fifth year by the consuls and priests. In fulfillment of these vows, games were often celebrated during my lifetime, sometimes by the four most distinguished colleges of priests, sometimes by the consuls. Moreover, the whole citizen body, with one accord, both individually and as members of municipalities, prayed continuously for my health at all the shrines.

10. My name was inserted, by decree of the senate, in the hymn of the Salian priests. And it was enacted by law that I should be sacrosanct in perpetuity and that I should possess the tribunician power as long as I live. I declined to become *pontifex maximus* in place of a colleague while he was still alive, when the people offered me that priesthood, which my father had held. A few years later, in the consulship of Publius Sulpicius and Gaius Valgius, I accepted this priesthood, when death removed the man who had taken possession of it at a time of civil disturbance; and from all Italy a multitude flocked to my election such as had never previously been recorded at Rome. . . .

17. Four times I came to the assistance of the treasury with my own money, transferring to those in charge of the treasury 150,000,000 sesterces. And in the consulship of Marcus Lepidus and Lucius Arruntius I transferred out of my own patrimony 170,000,000 sesterces to the soldiers' bonus fund, which

was established on my advice for the purpose of providing bonuses for soldiers who had completed twenty or more years of service.

18. From the year in which Gnaeus Lentulus and Publius Lentulus were consuls, whenever the provincial taxes fell short, in the case sometimes of 100,000 persons and sometimes of many more, I made up their tribute in grain and in money from my own grain stores and my own patrimony. . . .

20. I repaired the Capitol and the theater of Pompey with enormous expenditures on both works, without having my name inscribed on them. I repaired the conduits of the aqueducts which were falling into ruin in many places because of age, and I doubled the capacity of the aqueduct called Marcia by admitting a new spring into its conduit. I completed the Julian Forum and the basilica which was between the temple of Castor and the temple of Saturn, works begun and far advanced by my father, and when the same basilica was destroyed by fire, I enlarged its site and began rebuilding the structure, which is to be inscribed with the names of my sons; and in case it should not be completed while I am still alive, I left instructions that the work be completed by my heirs. In my sixth consulship I repaired eighty-two temples of the gods in the city, in accordance with a resolution of the senate, neglecting none which at that time required repair. In my seventh consulship I reconstructed the Flaminian Way from the city as far as Ariminum,[8] and also all the bridges except the Mulvian and the Minucian. . . .

22. I gave a gladiatorial show three times in my own name, and five times in the names of my sons or grandsons; at these shows about 10,000 fought. Twice I presented to the people in my own name an exhibition of athletes invited from all parts of the world, and a third time in the name of my grandson. I presented games in my own name four times, and in addition twenty-three times in the place of other magistrates. On behalf of the college of fifteen, as master of that college, with Marcus Agrippa as my colleague, I celebrated the Secular Games[9] in the consulship of Gaius Furnius and Gaius Silanus. In my thirteenth consulship I was the first to celebrate the Games of Mars, which subsequently the consuls, in accordance with a decree of the senate and a law, have regularly celebrated in the succeeding years. Twenty-six times I provided for the people, in my own name or in the names of my sons or grandsons, hunting spectacles of African wild beasts in the circus or in the Forum or in the amphitheaters; in these exhibitions about 3,500 animals were killed.

8. Present-day Rimini, Italy.

9. The Secular Games were an enormous series of athletic games, festivals, and banquets that Augustus ordered held in 17 B.C. Though called "secular," they were held in honor of the gods and were directed by the College of Fifteen, a board that oversaw sacrifices to the gods. All adult Roman citizens were expected to view the games out of religious duty.

23. I presented to the people an exhibition of a naval battle across the Tiber where the grove of the Caesars now is, having had the site excavated 1,800 feet in length and 1,200 feet in width. In this exhibition thirty beaked ships, triremes or biremes, and in addition a great number of smaller vessels engaged in combat. On board these fleets, exclusive of rowers, there were about 3,000 combatants. . . .

26. I extended the frontiers of all the provinces of the Roman people on whose boundaries were peoples subject to our empire. I restored peace to the Gallic and Spanish provinces and likewise to Germany, that is, to the entire region bounded by the Ocean from Gades to the mouth of the Elbe River. I caused peace to be restored in the Alps, from the region nearest to the Adriatic Sea as far as the Tuscan Sea, without undeservedly making war against any people. My fleet sailed the Ocean from the mouth of the Rhine eastward as far as the territory of the Cimbrians,[10] to which no Roman previously had penetrated either by land or by sea. . . .

34. In my sixth and seventh consulships, after I had put an end to the civil wars, having attained supreme power by universal consent, I transferred the state from my own power to the control of the Roman senate and people. For this service of mine I received the title of Augustus by decree of the senate, and the doorposts of my house were publicly decked with laurels, the civic crown was affixed over my doorway, and a golden shield was set up in the Julian senate house, which, as the inscription on this shield testifies, the Roman senate and people gave me in recognition of my valor, clemency, justice, and devotion. After that time I excelled all in authority, but I possessed no more power than the others who were my colleagues in each magistracy.

35. When I held my thirteenth consulship, the senate, the equestrian order, and the entire Roman people gave me the title of "father of the country" and decreed that this title should be inscribed in the vestibule of my house, in the Julian senate house, and in the Augustun Forum on the pedestal of the chariot which was set up in my honor by decree of the senate. At the time I wrote this document I was in my seventy-sixth year.

10. Near present-day Hamburg, West Germany.

Sources 8 and 9 from The American Numismatic Society, New York.

8. Roman Coin Issued 2 B.C.

9. Roman Coin Issued 20–16 B.C.

Source 10 adapted from sketches by Merry E. Wiesner.

10. Main Roads, 31 B.C.–A.D. 14

—— Roads built before reign of Augustus

- - - - Roads built or renovated under Augustus

Source 11 from Victor W. Von Hagen, The Roads That Led to Rome *(Cleveland and New York: World Publishing Co., © 1967 by George Weidenfeld and Nicolson, London), pp. 18–19.*

11. Main Roman Roads at Their Greatest Extent, A.D. 180

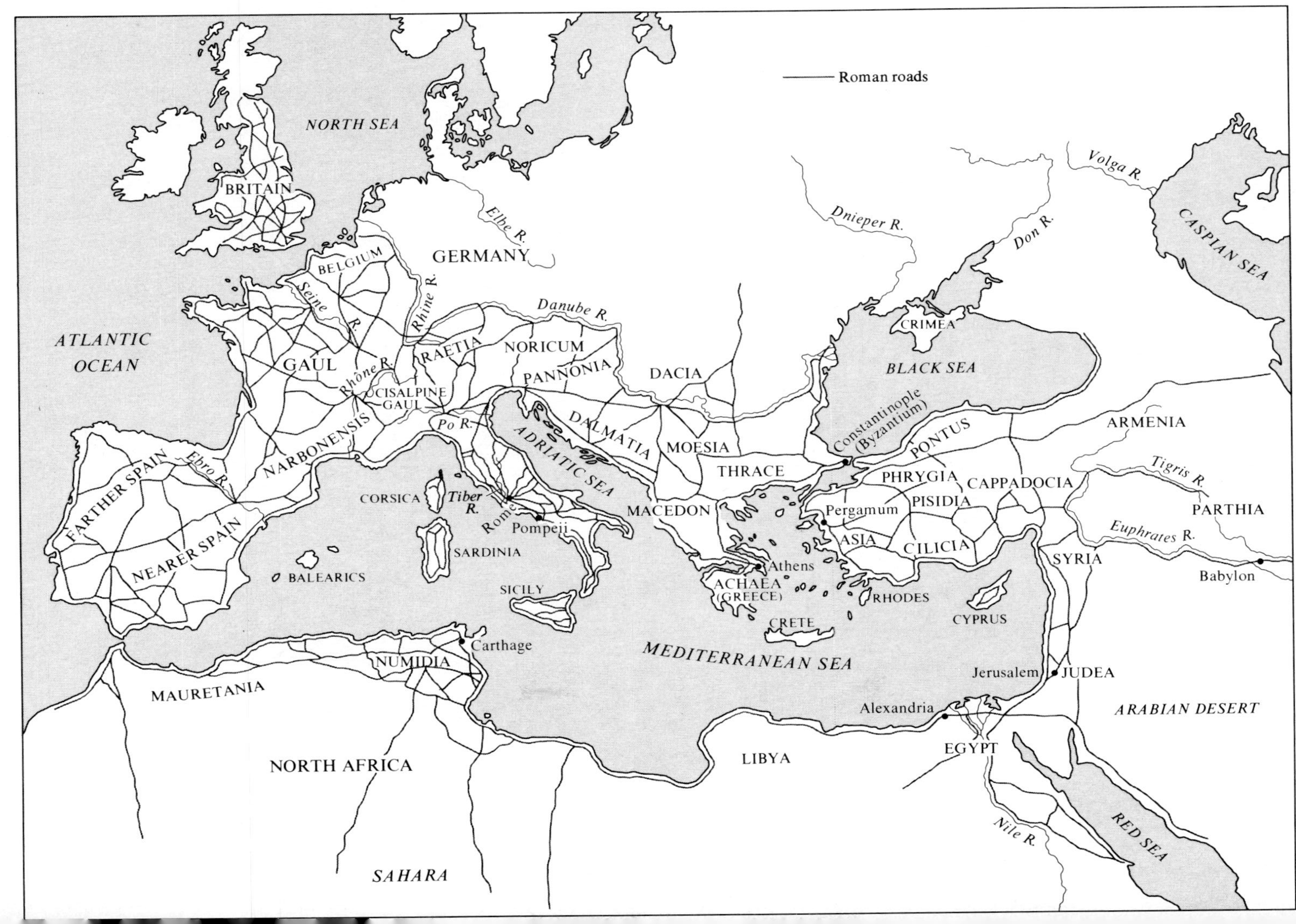

Source 12 from Alinari/Art Resource. Photo by Stab D. Anderson, 1931.

12. Arch of Augustus at Rimini

QUESTIONS TO CONSIDER

Now that you have examined various pieces of evidence, you need to put them together to arrive at a conclusion you can support. Do not worry about not having all the evidence you need; no historian can ever discover "all" the facts about an event or person. He or she makes conclusions on the basis of the evidence available, alters those conclusions when new material is discovered, and uses those conclusions as a framework for further research. In this respect, historians operate just like physicists learning how the universe works. Do not worry if some of your sources disagree; ten people who witness an auto accident often come up with ten quite contradictory accounts of the event. Why might accounts of Augustus's rule be even more contradictory?

The sources have made you aware of the operation of Roman government on two levels: that of the formal constitution, which remained a republic, and that of the actual locus of power, which was increasingly the emperor. The changes that Augustus instituted thus took place at the second level, and in many areas we can ignore the formal constitution of Rome in describing the process of change. Comparing all the sources, how would you describe the means by which Augustus transformed the republic into a different type of government? Which steps were most important? Which observers seemed to have the clearest view of this process, Augustus himself and those living during his lifetime or later historians? In considering this last question, you need to think about the advantages and disadvantages of eyewitness reports versus later, secondary accounts.

The second question concerns results, not process: Why was Augustus successful? To answer this, we must consider not only the changes themselves, but people's perceptions of them. A ruler's place in history depends not only on real accomplishments but also on how these accomplishments are perceived and judged by later generations. Rulers perceived as good or successful are often given credit for everything good that happened during their reigns, even if they had nothing to do with it. Conversely, rulers regarded as unsuccessful, weak, or bad get blamed for many things that were not their fault. A reputation is generally based on actual achievements, but occasionally it is also determined by a ruler's successful manipulation of public opinion, and sometimes on that manipulation alone.

Augustus clearly recognized the importance of public opinion, which in Rome was tied to upholding tradition. How does he make use of Roman traditions in the laws and coins he issues? How do other observers judge his connection with tradition? Many of Rome's traditions were incorporated into public rituals and ceremonies. What sorts of ceremonies did Romans participate in or view? How did Augustus use these ceremonies to demonstrate his power or his personal connections with Roman tradition? Along with rituals, titles are also important demonstrations of power. What does Augustus call himself and what do others call him, both in the written documents and on the coins? Why is there so much discussion of his accepting or not accepting various titles?

Now that you have considered the opinions of a range of commentators, assessed some actual legal changes and road-building patterns, examined some coins, and heard from Augustus himself, you are ready to answer the questions: How did Augustus transform the Roman republic into an empire? Why was he successful? Once you have made your assessment, think about how you would use it to structure future research. What other evidence would be useful in supporting your conclusions? Where might you go to find that evidence?

EPILOGUE

Though Augustus said that his own aim was a restoration of the republic, in reality he transformed Roman government into an empire ruled by one individual. His reign is generally termed the *Principate*, a word taken from Augustus's favorite title *princeps*, but the rulers of Rome after him would not hesitate to use the title *emperor*. Like him, they would also retain the titles *pontifex maximus*, supreme priest, and *imperator*, commander-in-chief. It is interesting to see how many of our words denoting aspects of royal rule come from Augustus: not only *prince, emperor,* and *czar* (the Russian variant of "Caesar") but also *palace*, from Palatine, the hill where Augustus had his house.

The emperors who came after Augustus would build on his achievements, both literally and figuratively. They extended the borders of the Roman Empire even farther, so that at its largest it would stretch from Scotland to the Sudan and from Spain to Syria. The Roman road system was expanded to over 50,000 miles, longer than the current interstate highway system in the United States; some of those roads are still usable today. Roman coins continued to be stamped with the emperor's picture and have been found as far away as southern India. Later emperors continued Augustus's building projects in Rome and throughout the empire. Vespasian built the Colosseum, which could seat 50,000 people; Trajan, the Forum with a number of different buildings and an enormous 125-foot column with his statue on top; Hadrian, the Pantheon and a wall dividing England and Scotland. The emperor Nero may have even ordered part of Rome burned to make room for his urban renewal projects.

Augustus's successors also continued his centralization of power. His stepson Tiberius stripped the assemblies of their right to elect magistrates, and later emperors would take this power away from the Senate as well. Bureaucrats appointed by the emperor oversaw the grain trade, the army, and the collection of taxes, with the Senate gradually dwindling into a rubber stamp for the emperor's decisions. New territories were ruled directly by the emperor through governors and generals; in these jurisdictions the Senate did not have even the pretense of power.

The cult of ruler worship initiated somewhat tentatively in the provinces under Augustus grew enormously after his death, when, like Julius Caesar, he was declared a god. Later emperors were not willing to wait so long. Caligula declared himself a god at the age of twenty-five, spent much of his time in the temple of Castor and Pollux, and talked to the statue of Jupiter as an equal. Though Caligula was probably insane and later was stabbed to death, ruler worship in general was serious business for most Romans, closely linked as it was to tradition and patriotism. Groups like the Christians, who did not offer sacrifices to the emperor or at least to the emperor's "genius" were felt to be unpatriotic, disloyal, and probably traitorous.

Thus in many ways Augustus laid the foundation for the success and durability of his empire. Historians have always been fascinated with the demise of the Roman Empire, but considering the fact that it lasted more than 400 years after Augustus in western Europe—and, in a significantly altered form, almost 1,500 years in eastern Europe—a more appropriate question might be why it lasted so long. Though the weaknesses that led to the empire's eventual collapse were also outgrowths of the reign of Augustus, the latter still represents a remarkable success story.

We must be careful of attributing too much to one man, however. As we have seen, Augustus had an extremely effective network of supporters and advisors, including Rome's most important men of letters. Their rendering of the glories of Roman civilization and the brilliance of Augustus has shaped much of what has been written about Rome since; you may only need to check the adjectives used to describe Augustus in your text to confirm this. Myths or exaggerations told about a ruler die hard, especially those that have been repeated for nearly 2,000 years.

CHAPTER FOUR

THE TRANSFORMATION OF CHRISTIANITY

THE PROBLEM

The Christian religion began as a minority sect within Judaism in an outlying region of the vast Roman Empire. Usually the Romans tolerated the religions of the people they conquered as long as these religions did not appear to be politically or socially revolutionary and as long as the people would also participate in ceremonies honoring and appeasing the Roman gods. In fact, Romans often adopted the gods of conquered peoples, believing that by honoring these new gods they would gain still further protection for the Roman state. The Romans' respect for their own traditions led them to make an exception, in the case of the Jews, to the requirement that all people under their rule honor Roman gods, for they recognized that Jewish monotheism had an equally long tradition. Because the Jews in addition did not actively seek converts, the Romans did not have to worry that Judaism would spread.

A source of genuine concern for the Romans, however, was the growing popularity of other religions, called *mystery religions,* during the time Christianity began. These religions practiced rites that were not open to the general public—hence the name *mystery*—and promised their followers special benefits not available to the uninitiated, such as life after death. Because of their exclusivity and secret nature, the mystery religions contrasted sharply with traditional Roman religion, which was characterized by public ceremonies to honor and appease the gods and to which everyone belonged automatically simply by virtue of being born a Roman citizen. Mystery religions were gaining increasing numbers of adherents during the last two centuries B.C. as many Romans became dissatisfied with their formal traditional religion and began to seek more personal forms of religious expression. These religious groups appeared subversive and dangerous to Roman authorities not only because they had secret rituals, but also because they were not tied to the traditions of any one people or ethnic group and were actively seeking new converts.

In the eyes of Roman officialdom, Christianity was yet another mystery religion. Like the religion of the Egyptian goddess Isis, it featured an initiation ritual involving purification by water and honored the figure of a mother holding an infant son. Like the followers of the god Mithras, Christians shared a ceremonial meal of bread and wine; like those of the goddess Cybele, they celebrated an annual feast of resurrection every spring. Christians were thus included in the authorities' general distrust of all mystery religions, and certain of their beliefs and ceremonies made them appear even more dangerous than their rival sects. Christians talked about their king, who sounded like a rival to the emperor, and held ceremonies in which they claimed to eat and drink the body and blood of this king, which to Romans appeared to be nothing more than cannibalism. Christian husbands and wives called each other brother and sister, suggesting incest. They spoke of the imminent end of the world, which would of course mean the end of the Roman Empire, and thus appeared to preach political revolution. Their ideas were not part of traditional Judaism, and were in fact causing disputes in the Jewish community, so the Romans did not feel this group of dissidents warranted the same respect that Jews did.

During the reign of the emperor Nero, Roman officials initiated their campaigns of persecution against Christians, especially when unrest broke out in the empire. Christians were blamed for not honoring the traditional gods, thus provoking the gods' displeasure and leading to turmoil and crisis. Persecution of this group did not have the desired effect, however. The courage of Christians facing death convinced many people throughout the Roman Empire that Christianity offered something unique. Already weary of traditional religion, they embraced Christianity rather than other mystery religions. The first three centuries after the death of Christ saw a gradual but steady growth in the number of Christians, particularly in urban areas. Christians began to organize support networks for new converts, providing them not only with spiritual guidance but also with food and shelter if they needed it, which further increased the attractiveness of the new religion.

Some new and highly educated Christians began to expand the original teachings into a more complex philosophical and theological system, which made Christianity more appealing and acceptable to those educated in Greek philosophy. Christianity found adherents at all social levels, especially among upper-class women; gradually even Roman government officials converted. Though it is very difficult to determine exact numbers, scholars estimate that by A.D. 300 perhaps as many as 20 percent of the inhabitants of the Roman Empire were Christian, even though the religion was still officially prohibited.

If we skip ahead another three hundred years, however, we find not simply further growth but a complete transformation. By 600 Christianity was the only legal religion in the Roman Empire (which by this time consisted only of the eastern half of the original Roman Empire), and it was the official religion in all the kingdoms that had replaced the Roman Empire in the West. Missionary efforts had also reached far beyond the borders of the old Roman Empire, so that Ireland and parts of Germany were also Christian. The next few centuries would extend the religion even further as eastern Europe, Scandinavia, and Russia gradually became Christianized.

Not only did the Christian religion expand in numbers of converts during this period of the early Middle Ages, it also grew in economic strength and political power. In many parts of Europe, the Church came to own about a quarter of all land, gradually acquiring property through gifts and bequests from individuals and rulers alike. *Bishops*, the regional Church officials, became advisors to rulers and also rulers of territory themselves. The increased power of the Church was most dramatically evident in western Europe, where, after the collapse of the Roman Empire, Church leaders often took over many of the functions of the secular government. As it grew in power, the western Church also became more centralized as the Bishop of Rome began to claim authority over all other bishops and, eventually, authority over all secular rulers as well. By 600, and even moreso by several centuries later, Christianity was western Europe's most powerful political, cultural, and economic institution—an institution centralized under the authority of one man, the Bishop of Rome, who had taken the title *pope*, a word derived from the Latin word *papa*, which means "father."

The Church's preeminent position during the Middle Ages was not an outcome that could have been predicted during the first decades of Christianity, and probably not even in the year 300. How was Christianity transformed from an outlawed minority sect to the most powerful religious and secular institution in all of Europe?

SOURCES AND METHOD

Studying the history of religious movements poses special problems for historians because the available primary sources are rarely objective. Such records were written by either hostile observers or, more likely, followers of the religion whose intentions were not simply to describe real events but to bolster the faith of other followers or to win new converts. You can see this lack of objectivity most clearly in studying the earliest decades of Christianity. The only contemporary written sources describing the events in the life of Jesus and in the lives of his first followers are the books of the New Testament. These were written primarily not to record historical facts but to spread the good news (which is what *gospel* means) and to give advice to new

Christians. We can extract historical information from the New Testament, but we have no way of checking it against other sources.

The problem is somewhat different for the later period we are investigating here. Many more primary sources are available, but almost all were written by Christians, most of whom were members of the clergy. This is particularly true in western Europe, where all schools, the only places one could learn to read and write, were run by the Church. Secular rulers and Church officials often hired writers to compose chronicles and biographies, but because of their training these writers always felt it important to stress events of religious significance. The subject of the biography as well often wanted emphasis laid on his or her piety and Christian devotion.

Many of the sources from the early Middle Ages have an even stronger religious purpose, for they are biographies of those individuals whom the Church judged to be saints and were written to provide other Christians with models of behavior. Though they are not fiction, these works often mold the events of the real person's life to fit the model expected of a saint and always include *miracles*—acts of God unexplainable by the laws of nature—for these happenings were a requirement for sainthood. Once we understand their limitations, however, these saints' lives, called *hagiography*, can provide a great deal of information about missionaries and Church leaders and about how the Church developed. Because stories about saints were repeated orally by missionaries and preachers, they also explain how people who could not read were introduced to Christianity.

This chapter's sources were thus written by people who were not simply recording human actions but trying to show the hand of God at work in the establishment of the Christian religion. Just those human actions, however, are what interest us as historians, so we must make distinctions between the real and the miraculous when we use these sources. To answer the questions posed in this chapter, your first task will be to extract specific information about human actions from the documents. You may want to make a list of the factors you see as important in explaining the rapid and widespread growth of Christianity. What types of people played a significant role in building this religion? What tactics did they use? What institutions did the Church create to help build up its power? What ideas were developed to help justify the changes?

The first three sources are all from biographies of rulers or histories written by members of the clergy. The first is from the life of the Roman emperor Constantine, written shortly after his death in 337 by his friend and advisor Bishop Eusebius. Constantine, searching for ways to build up the power of Rome, thought that new gods might provide one answer. How does Eusebius describe Constantine's conversion to Christianity? What role did the existing Christian clergy play? (Eusebius does not call them priests but simply "those who were acquainted with the mysteries of His doctrines.") Source 2, describing the conversion of King Clovis of the Franks in 496, is taken from the *History of the Franks* by Bishop Gregory of Tours, who lived in the sixth century. What inspired Clovis to convert? What role did the Bishop play in his conversion? Source 3, from the *History of the English Church and People* written in the eighth century by the English scholar and monk Bede, also describes a royal conversion. What role did the pope (*pontiff*) play in the events described? What reservations did King Ethelbert have about accepting Christianity? What ultimately persuaded him to convert?

Before you continue, compare the three conversion accounts. What role did the miraculous play in each? What kinds of clergy were important? What influence did the ruler's wife exert? What aspects of Christianity attracted the rulers? What actions did the rulers take after converting to Christianity?

Sources 4 and 5 provide additional information about imperial or royal actions. Selection 4 presents two extracts from the law code of the Roman emperor Theodosius II, who ruled from 408 to 450. Constantine had legalized Christianity after his conversion; how did Theodosius further transform the status of Christianity? How did he propose to enforce his proclamation? Source 5, a selection from the thirteenth-century sagas of the Norse kings written by an unknown author, describes events that occurred much later than those presented in the preceding documents, because Christianity was slow in reaching the remote parts of northern Europe. King Olaf's actions were quite similar to those of Theodosius, however, and followed a pattern set by earlier rulers. How did Olaf convince his subjects to convert? How did he and Theodosius justify violent actions or the use of force in the name of religion? How would you compare their actions with those of King Ethelbert from Source 3?

From the five sources you have read so far, what types of people have you included in your list of important players in the development of Christianity? What types of tactics? How would you describe the relationship between the rulers and the Church? How would you compare the roles of the ruler and his subjects in these sources; that is, was conversion always imposed from the top down? What sorts of activities did the clergy participate in? How were these activities important in the growth of the Church?

Several of the sources you have read so far have referred to the pope; the next five documents discuss the papacy directly. Source 6 comes from a sermon by Pope Leo in 446 that states his reasons for believing that the pope should have supreme control over the church. On what foundation does Leo base papal authority? Source 7 provides another perspective on this issue, namely, that of the emperor. This is an edict from the emperor Valentinian III in 445. What bases does Valentinian see for papal power? Why does he think it important for the Church that only one individual hold power? Why does he feel this is important for the empire as well? What role does he envision for the emperor in enforcing papal authority? Source 8, an excerpt from a letter by Pope Gelasius to the emperor during the late fifth century, provides an example of how the popes' conception of their own authority had developed by the fifth century. How does Gelasius describe the relationship between the pope's power and that of the secular ruler? What would you expect the emperor's reaction to have been? How would you compare the relationship between pope and emperor described here with that described by Valentinian in the previous document?

Papal authority may have been based on theoretical statements, but it grew out of direct papal actions. Sources 9 and 10 give two versions of the same historical event, the meeting between Pope Leo I and Attila the Hun in 452. The ninth selection was written by Prosper, a Christian chronicler, about three years after the meeting took place; the tenth, by a later unknown author. How would this meeting have helped build up papal authority? Why might the later author have expanded the account in the way that he did? Reading these documents about the papacy has doubtless prompted you to add entries to your list of individuals and institutions. What ideas did the popes choose to emphasize as they gained power?

The sources you have read so far have primarily viewed the expansion of Christianity from the perspective of emperors, kings, and popes. They have, however, described the actions of individual missionaries and Church officials, and the last three sources describe several of these men in detail. All are taken from saints' lives that were written shortly after the death of each saint by one of his followers. Source 11 comes from the life of St. Bonitus, a seventh-century bishop of Auvergne in France; Source 12 from the life of St. Boniface, an eighth-century English missionary to the Germans; and Source 13 from the life of St. Sturmi, one of Boniface's converts and disciples. Because miracles were an essential prerequisite for sainthood, all three selections describe miraculous events, but they also provide other clues about why these men were successful missionaries and Church leaders. As you read Source 11, note those aspects of Bonitus's background that might help explain his high Church position. What was his family like? What kind of education did he receive? What sorts of relationships did he develop with political rulers? How would these factors have helped in building up the power of a bishop? As you read Source 12, note those people whom Boniface selected to work with him as he prepared to cut down the oak of Thor. Why would he choose not to perform this act alone?

At first glance, the last source might appear to contradict some of what you have read so far. Unlike Bonitus, Sturmi did not become a Church official but went deeper and deeper into the forests of Germany. In this retreat he was following a pattern begun many centuries earlier by Christians who already were questioning the growing worldliness of their religion. During the reign of Constantine, some Christian thinkers wondered whether the Church could be powerful and holy at the same time and whether it should have close relations with secular powers. Many of these believers rejected the official Church and moved out into the deserts of Egypt to live what they regarded was the true Christian life of prayer, meditation, and devotion, sharply criticizing the wealthy bishops who built elaborate churches and wore luxurious robes of office. These "desert fathers" (and mothers) often tried to live as hermits, but as their reputations for holiness grew they attracted disciples. Soon whole communities sprang up in the desert, communities that came to be called *monasteries*, supporting themselves by their own labor and generally forbidding marriage and private property to their members.

Initially a reaction against the organized and institutional church, the monasteries became increasingly popular and, as the monastic movement spread to Europe, they too became institutionalized. Elaborate codes of rules were laid down regulating the running of monasteries and the lives of their occupants. Though their original founders were opposed to the Church's extreme wealth, many monasteries prospered themselves as people gave them land or money in return for those spiritual services, such as prayers for the soul, offered by monks and nuns. The bishops and the pope alike realized that the monks, who were often very devoted and consequently held in high regard for their piety and moral life, made effective missionaries for the Christian religion. Monks, as you have read in the third selection on Augustine, were sent out by the pope to gain converts and were able to bring large areas under his religious jurisdiction.

The life of St. Sturmi provides some evidence about how this process happened. What were Sturmi's original aims? What sort of life did the monks lead at first? How did Boniface change things? What kind of relationship developed between the monastery and the secular rulers?

Careful reading of the sources has given you a great deal of information about the development of Christianity as a religion and a secular power during this period. Reviewing your list of people, tactics, and institutions, which of these factors appear most important to the sheer growth in numbers of Christians? Which to the growth of church power? How did Christian ideology and teachings change as the Church developed into a powerful institution?

THE EVIDENCE

Source 1 from R. Schaff and H. Wace, editors, The Library of the Nicene and Post-Nicene Fathers, *vol. 1 (New York: The Christian Literature Society, 1890), pp. 489–491.*

1. The Conversion of Constantine, early 4th century

Being convinced, however, that he [Constantine] needed some more powerful aid than his military forces could afford him,[1] on account of the wicked and magical enchantments which were so diligently practiced by the tyrant [Maxentius], he sought Divine assistance, deeming the possession of arms and a numerous soldiery of secondary importance, but believing the cooperating power of Deity invincible and not to be shaken. He considered, therefore, on what God he might rely for protection and assistance. . . .

Accordingly he called on Him with earnest prayer and supplications that he would reveal to him who He was, and stretch forth His right hand to help him in his present difficulties. And while he was thus praying with fervent entreaty, a most marvelous sign appeared to him from heaven, the account of which it might have been hard to believe had it been related to any other person. But since the victorious emperor himself long afterwards declared it to the writer of this history, when he was honored with his acquaintance and society, and confirmed his statement by an oath, who could hesitate to accredit the relation, especially since the testimony of after-time has established its truth? He said that about noon, when the day was already beginning to decline, he saw with his own eyes the trophy of a cross of light in the heavens, above the sun, and bearing the inscription, CONQUER BY THIS. At this sight he himself was struck with amazement, and his whole army also, which followed him on this expedition, and witnessed the miracle.

He said, moreover, that he doubted within himself what the import of this apparition could be. And while he continued to ponder and reason on its meaning, night suddenly came on; then in his sleep the Christ of God appeared to him with the same sign which he had seen in the heavens, and commanded him to make a likeness of that sign which he had seen in the heavens, and to use it as a safeguard in all engagements with his enemies.

At the dawn of day he arose, and communicated the marvel to his friends: and then, calling together the workers in gold and precious stones, he sat in the midst of them, and described to them the figure of the sign he had seen, bidding them represent it in gold and precious stones. And this representation I myself have had an opportunity of seeing. . . .

1. In A.D. 312, Constantine, who ruled Gaul and Britain, was about to invade Italy and try to gain the throne of the western Roman Empire by defeating Maxentius, who ruled Rome.

The emperor constantly made use of this sign of salvation as a safeguard against every adverse and hostile power, and commanded that others similar to it should be carried at the head of all his armies.

These things were done shortly afterwards. But at the time above specified, being struck with amazement at the extraordinary vision, and resolving to worship no other God save Him who had appeared to him, he sent for those who were acquainted with the mysteries of His doctrines, and enquired who that God was, and what was intended by the sign of the vision he had seen.

They affirmed that He was God, the only begotten Son of the one and only God: that the sign which had appeared was the symbol of immortality, and the trophy of that victory over death which He had gained in time past when sojourning on earth. They taught him also the causes of His advent, and explained to him the true account of His incarnation. Thus he was instructed in these matters, and was impressed with wonder at the divine manifestation which had been presented to his sight. Comparing, therefore, the heavenly vision with the interpretation given, he found his judgment confirmed; and, in the persuasion that the knowledge of these things had been imparted to him by Divine teaching, he determined thenceforth to devote himself to the reading of the inspired writings.

Source 2 from Roland H. Bainton, The Medieval Church *(Princeton: D. VanNostrand, 1962), pp. 99–101.*

2. The Conversion of Clovis, 496

The queen [Clotilde] never ceased to entreat the king [Clovis] to recognize the true God and give up idols, but nothing could move him to believe these things until he was engaged in a war with the Alemanni[2] in which he was compelled by constraint to confess what he had refused to do voluntarily. It came to pass that his army was in danger of being wiped out. Thereupon, lifting his eyes to heaven, with compunction of heart and moved to tears, he cried, "Jesus Christ, who art according to Clotilde the Son of the living God, who art said to give aid to those in trouble and victory to those who hope in Thee. . . . I beseech Thee . . . if Thou wilt give me victory over mine enemies I will believe in Thee and be baptized in Thy name. I have called upon my gods and they are far removed from helping me. Hence I believe they are powerless, since they do not succour their followers. I now call upon Thee. Only save me from mine enemies." When he had thus spoken the Alemanni turned their backs and took to flight. . . . Clovis returning related to the queen how he had won the victory by calling upon the name

2. **Alemanni:** one of the German tribes.

of Christ. Then the queen with haste secretly summoned Remigius, the bishop of Rheims, that he should instruct the king in the word of salvation. He then began privately to tell his majesty that he should believe in the true God, the maker of heaven and earth and should give up idols. The king said, "Willingly, holy father, but there is one difficulty. My people will not give up their gods. But I will go and speak to them according to your word." But before he had opened his mouth all the people cried, "Pious king, we reject the mortal gods and are ready to follow the immortal God, whom Remigius preaches." Then the bishop with great joy gave orders to prepare the fount. The church was resplendent with banners, flickering candles and the scent of wax and incense, so that those present believed that they partook of the savor of heaven. The king asked that he be baptized by the pontiff. Like a new Constantine Clovis ascended to the laver,[3] putting off his former leprosy. As he went down into the water the bishop said, "Bow thy neck. Adore what you have burned. Burn what you have adored." Now the holy bishop Remigius, a man of consummate learning and of great sanctity, may fitly be compared to the holy Sylvester [*who baptized Constantine*].

Source 3 from Bede, A History of the English Church and People, *translated by Leo Sherley-Price (Baltimore: Penguin, 1955), pp. 66, 68–71.*

3. The Conversion of King Ethelbert, 597

In the year of our Lord 582, Maurice, fifty-fourth in succession from Augustus, became Emperor, and ruled for twenty-one years. In the tenth year of his reign, Gregory, an eminent scholar and administrator, was elected Pontiff of the apostolic Roman see,[4] and ruled it for thirteen years, six months, and ten days. In the fourteenth year of this Emperor, and about the one hundred and fiftieth year after the coming of the English to Britain, Gregory was inspired by God to send his servant Augustine with several other God-fearing monks to preach the word of God to the English nation. . . .

At this time the most powerful king there was Ethelbert, who reigned in Kent and whose domains extended northwards to the river Humber, which forms the boundary between the north and south Angles. To the east of Kent lies the large island of Thanet, which by English reckoning is six hundred hides[5] in extent; it is separated from the mainland by a waterway about three furlongs[6] broad called the Wantsum, which joins the sea at either end and

3. **laver:** baptismal font.
4. **see:** official seat of authority of a bishop or the pope.
5. **hide:** approximately 125 square miles.
6. **furlong:** one-eighth of a mile.

is fordable only in two places. It was here that God's servant Augustine landed with companions, who are said to have been forty in number. At the direction of blessed Pope Gregory, they had brought interpreters from among the Franks, and they sent these to Ethelbert, saying that they came from Rome bearing very glad news, which infallibly assured all who would receive it of eternal joy in heaven and an everlasting kingdom with the living and true God. On receiving this message, the king ordered them to remain in the island where they had landed, and gave directions that they were to be provided with all necessaries until he should decide what action to take. For he had already heard of the Christian religion, having a Christian wife of the Frankish royal house named Bertha, whom he had received from her parents on condition that she should have freedom to hold and practice her faith unhindered with Bishop Liudhard, whom they had sent as her helper in the faith.

After some days, the king came to the island and, sitting down in the open air, summoned Augustine and his companions to an audience. But he took precautions that they should not approach him in a house; for he held an ancient superstition that, if they were practisers of magical arts, they might have opportunity to deceive and master him. But the monks were endowed with power from God, not from the Devil, and approached the king carrying a silver cross as their standard and the likeness of our Lord and Saviour painted on a board. First of all they offered prayer to God, singing a litany for the eternal salvation both of themselves and of those to whom and for whose sake they had come. And when, at the king's command, they had sat down and preached the word of life to the king and his court, the king said: "Your words and promises are fair indeed; but they are new and uncertain, and I cannot accept them and abandon the age-old beliefs that I have held together with the whole English nation. But since you have travelled far, and I can see that you are sincere in your desire to impart to us what you believe to be true and excellent, we will not harm you. We will receive you hospitably and take care to supply you with all that you need; nor will we forbid you to preach and win any people you can to your religion." The king then granted them a dwelling in the city of Canterbury, which was the chief city of all his realm, and in accordance with his promise he allowed them provisions and did not withdraw their freedom to preach. Tradition says that as they approached the city, bearing the holy cross and the likeness of our great King and Lord Jesus Christ as was their custom, they sang in unison this litany: "We pray Thee, O Lord, in all Thy mercy, that Thy wrath and anger may be turned away from this city and from Thy holy house, for we are sinners. Alleluia."

As soon as they had occupied the house given to them they began to emulate the life of the apostles and the primitive Church. They were constantly at prayer; they fasted and kept vigils; they preached the word of life to whomsoever they could. They regarded worldly things as of little importance, and accepted only the necessities of life from those they taught. They practised what they preached, and were willing to endure any hardship, and even to die for the truth which they proclaimed. Before long a number of heathen, admiring the simplicity of their holy lives and the comfort of their heavenly message, believed and were baptized. On the east side of the city stood an old church, built in honour of Saint Martin during the Roman occupation of Britain, where the Christian queen of whom I have spoken went to pray. Here they first assembled to sing the psalms, to pray, to say Mass, to preach, and to baptize, until the king's own conversion to the Faith gave them greater freedom to preach and to build and restore churches everywhere.

At length the king himself, among others, edified by the pure lives of these holy men and their gladdening promises, the truth of which they confirmed by many miracles, believed and was baptized. Thenceforward great numbers gathered each day to hear the word of God, forsaking their heathen rites and entering the unity of Christ's holy Church as believers. While the king was pleased at their faith and conversion, it is said that he would not compel anyone to accept Christianity; for he had learned from his instructors and guides to salvation that the service of Christ must be accepted freely and not under compulsion. Nevertheless, he showed greater favour to believers, because they were fellow-citizens of the kingdom of heaven. And it was not long before he granted his teachers in his capital of Canterbury a place of residence appropriate to their station, and gave them possessions of various kinds to supply their wants.

Source 4 from Henry Bettenson, editor and translator, Documents of the Christian Church *(London: Oxford, 1963), p. 22 (first part); James Harvey Robinson, editor and translator,* Readings in European History, *vol. 1 (Boston: Ginn, 1904), p. 26 (second part).*

4. From the Theodosian Code, 438

It is our [Theodosius's] desire that all the various nations which are subject to our Clemency and Moderation, should continue in the profession of that religion which was delivered to the Romans by the divine Apostle Peter, as it hath been preserved by faithful tradition; and which is now professed by the Pontiff Damasus and by Peter, Bishop of Alexandria, a man of apostolic holiness. According to the apostolic teaching and the docrine of the Gospel, let us believe the one deity of the Father, the Son and the Holy Spirit, in equal majesty and in a holy Trinity. We authorize the followers of this law to assume the title of Catholic Christians; but as for the others, since, in our judgement, they are foolish madmen, we decree that they shall be branded with the ignominious name of heretics, and shall not presume to give to their conventicles the name of churches. They will suffer in the first place the chastisement of the divine condemnation, and in the second the punishment which our authority, in accordance with the will of Heaven, shall decide to inflict.

We command that their [the heretics'] books, which contain the substance of their criminal teachings, be sought out with the utmost care and burnt with fire under the eyes of the magistrates. Should any one perchance be convicted of concealing, through deceit or othrwise, and of failing to produce, any work of this kind, let him know that as the possessor of harmful books written with criminal intent he shall suffer capital punishment.

Source 5 from Samuel Laing, translator, Heimskringla or the Sagas of the Norse Kings *(London: J. C. Nimmo, 1889), pp. 150–151.*

5. Conversion of Scandinavia, 996–997

When Harald Gormson, king of Denmark, had adopted Christianity, he sent a message over all his kingdom that all people should be baptized. . . . In Viken many were baptized [*but subsequently lapsed*]. But now (996) that Olaf Trygveson was king of Norway, he remained long during the summer in Viken [*and summoning his relatives he declared that he would*] either bring it to this that all Norway should be Christian or die. . . . King Olaf immediately made it known to the public that he recommended Christianity to all the people in his kingdom, which message was well received and approved of by those who had before given him their promise; and these being the most powerful among the people assembled, the others followed their example, and all the inhabitants of the east part of Viken allowed themselves to be baptized. The king then went to the north part of Viken, and invited every man to accept Christianity; and those who opposed him he punished severely, killing some, mutilating others, and driving some into banishment. . . . During that summer (996) and the following winter (997) all Viken was made Christian.

Source 6 from James Harvey Robinson, editor and translator, Readings in European History, *vol. 1 (Boston: Ginn, 1904), pp. 69–71.*

6. Sermon by Pope Leo, 446

A single person, Peter, is appointed from the whole world as a leader in the calling of all peoples, and is placed above all the other apostles and the fathers of the Church. Although there are many priests among the people of God, and many pastors, Peter should of right rule all of those whom Christ himself rules in the first instance. Great and marvelous, my dear brethren, is the participation in its own power which it has pleased the Divine Excellency to grant to this man. And such powers as it granted to other leaders in common with Peter were granted only through Peter. Our Lord, indeed, asked all the apostles what men said of him, but so long as it was left to all to reply, so long was the hesitation of human ignorance clearly displayed. But when the opinion of the apostles was asked, he who was first in apostolic dignity was the first to reply; who when he had answered, "Thou art the Christ, the Son of the living God," Jesus said to him, "Blessed art thou, Simon Bar-jonah: for flesh and blood hath not revealed it unto thee, but my Father which is in heaven";[7]—that is to say, thou art blessed for this reason, for my father has taught thee, neither has mere earthly opinion misled thee, but thou art instructed by a heavenly inspiration. . . . I am the foundation than which none other can be established; yet thou too art a rock [*petra*] because thou art made firm by my strength, so that those things which I have in virtue of my power thou shalt have in common with me by participation. "And upon this rock I will build my church; and the gates of hell shall not prevail against it." . . .

And he said to the blessed Peter, "I will give unto thee the keys of the kingdom of heaven: and whatsoever thou shalt bind on earth shall be bound in heaven: and whatsoever thou shalt loose on earth shall be loosed in heaven." The right to this power passed also to the other apostles, and the provisions of this ordinance went forth to all the leaders of the Church. Still it was not in vain that what was made known to all was especially recommended to one. For this power was entrusted expressly to Peter, since Peter was placed as a model before all the rulers of the Church. Peter's prerogative remains and everywhere his judgment goes forth in equity. For never is severity too great nor forgiveness too lax where nothing is bound nor loosed except the blessed Peter bind or loose it.

Just before his passion,[8] which was about to shake the apostles' constancy, the Lord said to Simon, "Simon, Simon, behold, Satan asked to have you, that he might sift you as wheat: but I made supplication for thee, that thy faith fail not: and do thou, when once thou hast turned again, stablish thy brethren,"[9] that you should not enter into temptation. The danger of the temptation to yield to fear was common to all the apostles and all alike needed the aid of divine protection, since the devil desired to confound and ruin them all. Yet the Lord took special care of Peter and prayed especially that Peter might have faith, as if the state of the others would be more secure

7. Matthew xvi. 16–17.

8. **passion:** crucifixion and death.

9. Luke xxii. 31–32.

if the mind of their chief was not overcome. In Peter, therefore, the strength of all was confirmed and the aid of divine grace so ordered that the strength which was granted to Peter by Christ was in turn transmitted through Peter to the apostles.

Since, therefore, beloved brethren, we[10] behold this protection divinely appointed to us, we may properly and justly rejoice in the merits and dignity of our leader, sending up thanks to our eternal King and Redeemer, our Lord Jesus Christ, for giving such power to him whom he made the head of the whole Church: so that if anything, even in our own days, is rightly done by us and rightly ordained, it should be properly attributed to the influence and guidance of him to whom it was said: "When once thou hast turned again, stablish thy brethren." To whom, moreover, his Lord, after his resurrection, when Peter had three times professed his eternal love, said mystically three times, "Feed my sheep."[11] Like a faithful shepherd, he has beyond a doubt fulfilled his Lord's command, confirming us by his exhortations, and never ceasing to pray for us that we be not overcome by any temptation.

Source 7 from Henry Bettenson, editor and translator, Documents of the Christian Church *(London: Oxford, 1963), pp. 22–23.*

7. Edict of Emperor Valentinian III, 445

We are convinced that the only defence for us and for our Empire is in the favour of the God of heaven: and in order to deserve this favour it is our first care to support the Christian faith and its venerable religion. Therefore, inasmuch as the pre-eminence of the Apostolic See is assured by the merit of S. Peter, the first of the bishops, by the leading position of the city of Rome and also by the authority of the holy Synod,[12] let not presumption strive to attempt anything contrary to the authority of that See. For the peace of the churches will only then be everywhere preserved when the whole body acknowledge its ruler. Hitherto this has been observed without violation; but Hilary, Bishop of Arles,[13] as we have learnt from the report of that venerable man Leo, the pope of Rome, has with contumacious presumption

10. Popes, like emperors, refer to themselves as "we."

11. John xxi. 15 *sqq.*

12. **synod:** meetings of the Church bishops.

13. Hilary had presided at a synod which deposed Chelidonius, Bishop of Besançon. Chelidonius refused to resign, was excommunicated, went to Rome and appealed to Leo, who admitted him to communion. Hilary went to Rome to protest. But Leo acquitted Chelidonius, ordered his reinstatement, and deprived Hilary of the primacy he had exercised in the Gallican church.

ventured upon certain unlawful proceedings; and thus an abominable confusion has invaded the church beyond the Alps. . . . By such presumptuous acts confidence in the Empire, and respect for our rule is destroyed. Therefore in the first place we put down so great a crime: and, beyond that, in order that no disturbance, however slight, may arise among the churches, and the discipline of religion may not appear to be impaired in any case whatever, we decree, by a perpetual edict, that nothing shall be attempted by the Gallican[14] bishops, or by those of any other province, contrary to the ancient custom, without the authority of the venerable pope of the Eternal City. But whatsoever the authority of the Apostolic See has enacted, or shall enact, let that be held as law for all. So that if any bishop summoned before the pope of Rome shall neglect to attend, let him be compelled to appear by the governor of the province.

Source 8 from Roland H. Bainton, The Medieval Church *(Princeton: D. VanNostrand, 1962), p. 108.*

8. Letter of Pope Gelasius to the Emperor, late 5th century

There are indeed two [*powers*], most august Emperor, by which chiefly this world is ruled, the sacred authority of the pontiffs and the royal power. Of the two the priesthood has the greater weight to the degree that it must render an account for kings themselves in matters divine. Know then, most clement son, that although you preside with dignity in human affairs, as to the divine you are to submit your neck to those from whom you look for salvation and from whom you receive the celestial sacraments. You are to be subject rather than to rule in the religious sphere and bow to the judgment of the priests rather than seek to bend them to your will. For, if in the area of public discipline the priests recognize your authority as derived from above and obey your laws, lest in purely secular matters they should appear to resist, how much more willingly should you obey them who are charged with the administration of the venerable mysteries? . . . And if it is proper that the hearts of the faithful should be submitted to priests in general, by how much more should obedience be rendered to him who presides over that see which the Highest Divinity desired to be preeminent above all priests [*i.e., the see of Rome*]?

14. **Gallican:** French.

Sources 9 and 10 from James Harvey Robinson, editor and translator, Readings in European History, *vol. 1 (Boston: Ginn, 1904), pp. 49–50; pp. 50–51.*

9. Prosper's Account of the Meeting Between Pope Leo and Attila the Hun, 455

Now Attila, having once more collected his forces which had been scattered in Gaul [at the battle of Chalons], took his way through Pannonia into Italy. . . . To the emperor and the senate and Roman people none of all the proposed plans to oppose the enemy seemed so practicable as to send legates[15] to the most savage king and beg for peace. Our most blessed Pope Leo—trusting in the help of God, who never fails the righteous in their trials—undertook the task, accompanied by Avienus, a man of consular rank, and the prefect Trygetius. And the outcome was what his faith had foreseen; for when the king had received the embassy, he was so impressed by the presence of the high priest that he ordered his army to give up warfare and, after he had promised peace, he departed beyond the Danube.

10. Anonymous Account of the Meeting Between Pope Leo and Attila the Hun, 6th century

Attila, the leader of the Huns, who was called the scourge of God, came into Italy, inflamed with fury, after he had laid waste with most savage frenzy Thrace and Illyricum, Macedonia and Moesia, Achaia and Greece, Pannonia and Germany. He was utterly cruel in inflicting torture, greedy in plundering, insolent in abuse. . . . He destroyed Aquileia from the foundations and razed to the ground those regal cities, Pavia and Milan; he laid waste many other towns,[16] and was rushing down upon Rome.

Then Leo had compassion on the calamity of Italy and Rome, and with one of the consuls and a large part of the Roman senate he went to meet Attila. The old man of harmless simplicity, venerable in his gray hair and his majestic garb, ready of his own will to give himself entirely for the defense of his flock, went forth to meet the tyrant who was destroying all things. He met Attila, it is said, in the neighborhood of the river Mincio, and he spoke to the grim monarch, sayng: "The senate and the people of Rome, once conquerors of the world, now indeed vanquished, come before thee as sup-

15. **legate:** representative.

16. This is an exaggeration. Attila does not seem to have destroyed the buildings, even in Milan and Pavia.

pliants. We pray for mercy and deliverance. O Attila, thou king of kings, thou couldst have no greater glory than to see suppliant at thy feet this people before whom once all peoples and kings lay suppliant. Thou hast subdued, O Attila, the whole circle of the lands which it was granted to the Romans, victors over all peoples, to conquer. Now we pray that thou, who hast conquered others, shouldst conquer thyself. The people have felt thy scourge; now as suppliants they would feel thy mercy."

As Leo said these things Attila stood looking upon his venerable garb and aspect, silent, as if thinking deeply. And lo, suddenly there were seen the apostles Peter and Paul, clad like bishops, standing by Leo, the one on the right hand, the other on the left. They held swords stretched out over his head, and threatened Attila with death if he did not obey the pope's command. Wherefore Attila was appeased by Leo's intercession—he who had raged as one mad. He straightway promised a lasting peace and withdrew beyond the Danube.

Source 11 from Carrolly Erickson, The Records of Medieval Europe *(Garden City, New York: Anchor, 1971), pp. 98–100.*

11. Life of St. Bonitus, 7th century

Here Begins the Life of Saint Bonitus, Bishop and Confessor

The illustrous Bonitus was descended from Arvernian lineage. His father was called Theodatus, his mother Syagria; they were at least of senatorial rank, and from noble stock. Bonitus, then, before he was born, was held to have received a significant presage of devotion [*salutatio*] from a certain holy priest named Frigio. When this priest came to the paternal household he was received by Bonitus's mother-to-be with great joy, and when she, as was customary, asked for his blessing, she is said to have heard this reply given as a devotion: "Thou holy to God and venerable lord", he said, "give me your blessing." When the mother had grasped the meaning of what he had said, and silently weighing it, was pondering it in her heart, nonetheless inquiring of the servant of God, she spoke saying: "What is this you say, father?" . . . And he said: "I did not ask a blessing, as you think, from you, but from him who is in your womb, since I perceive him to be a most high priest, chosen by God." And she, praying, said: "I ask, O father, that that which you have spoken shall, through your prayers, come to pass."

Afterwards, when the child had become a boy and was settled with his parents in the forenamed city, he was trained in the rudiments of grammar, instructed in the Theodosian decrees, and excelling in related studies also, he was examined by his instructors, and advanced. When he was of the age of puberty, his father being dead, with God as his guide he went to the royal palace and put himself in the hands of Sigebert, a minister of the king. Because Sigebert had grown very fond of him, he was chosen to be the royal cup-bearer. Not long after this, he gained the office of master of requests, accepting the ring from the king's own hand; he fulfilled it so nobly that he gained the affections of the prince and all the nobles, all the duties having been handed over to him by the ministers of the palace. For he had, to be sure, bodily beauty, but was more beautiful in the mind and in the strength of his chastity.

Soon after this, he gratefully accepted a great honor from the prince. Then the prince died, and, his son being dead, his great-grandson succeeded him. So pleasing was Bonitus in his sight that he chose him to be prefect of Marseille, the first province, but he insisted to the suitors brought before him that he would rather be considered a priest than a judge. . . .

[Bonitus is raised to the episcopacy by the king.]

Having thus accepted the bishopric, he considered himself to have accepted not an honor, but a burden, and he augmented the labor of his daily obligations by his fasts and vigils, which he kept throughout the night, and by silent reading in private, most especially during the Lenten season; in all, he was so zealous that you would think him not only most worthy of the priesthood, but worthy to live the monastic life as well. He bore two- and three-day fasts; indeed, we know him to have fasted for as many as four days. . . .

Now I shall relate how the Lord worked miracles by his virtue. When the day of the Lord's resurrection dawned, the brothers begged him to perform the solemnities of the mass for them. But, when, as was his custom, he washed his hands at the altar . . . a certain incapacitated brother named Auderamnus came and asked for the *levita*,[17] so that he might drink water from the priestly hands.

Having done so, he was restored to his former health, and immediately overjoyed, sat down to table with the brothers.

And another brother in the same monastery named Natholenum, when he took some of the water, was, according to many, relieved of a fever by its virtue [alone]. These things which are related above were told us by the venerable father Adelfius. . . .

When the man of God, returning from Rome, came into the city of Chiusi in Tuscany, a certain blind woman begged his servants to give her the water in which he had washed his hands as a remedy to bathe her eyes. Although they were anxious to fulfil her request, the man of God, having washed his hands, ordered that the water be poured on the ground, as was his custom,

17. **levita:** a small vessel used in priestly ablutions.

so that they were able to steal hardly a drop of it; and giving it to the woman, they said: "Go and keep vigil tonight with this water in the basilica of the blessed Peter, which is in this city, and in the morning touch it to your eyes, as you have asked, according to your faith; we believe it will bring deliverance to you." The woman did as they said, and having fulfilled all, her eyesight restored, she beheld the light which she had sought with all her heart's desire. . . .

Now at that time nothing remained to him that he could give away as alms, and so as the gospel says he was naked, and did not even have two tunics to put on, and following the example of the blessed apostle Peter he had no gold or silver; but, restored by his divine virtues, he expended the treasure of health, which is more precious. Behold what the word of truth has said in the gospel: "He who hath forsaken all for my name's sake, shall receive a hundredfold, and shall inherit everlasting life. He receives a hundredfold who is established in the holiness and grace of God."[18] As blessed Paul said: "Our conversation is in heaven."[19] . . . Just so the blessed priest, who left much behind in this world, neither sought nor deserved anything earthly afterwards; but he received a hundredfold, since he shone with the grace of perfection, and now possesses eternal life with the saints in glory.

Then returning after this to Loudun, he remained there for four years, and continuing until the end, with God's aid, to do the good he had always done, he closed his days.

Here Ends the Life of Saint Bonitus, Bishop and Confessor.

Sources 12 and 13 from James Harvey Robinson, editor and translator, Readings in European History, *vol. 1 (Boston: Ginn, 1904), pp. 106–107; pp. 107–111.*

12. From the Life of St. Boniface, 8th century

Many of the people of Hesse were converted [by Boniface] to the Catholic faith and confirmed by the grace of the spirit: and they received the laying on of hands. But some there were, not yet strong of soul, who refused to accept wholly the teachings of the true faith. Some men sacrificed secretly, some even openly, to trees and springs. Some secretly practiced divining, soothsaying, and incantations, and some openly. But others, who were of sounder mind, cast aside all heathen profanation and did none of these things; and it was with the advice and consent of these men that Boniface

18. Mark 10, 29–30.
19. Phil. 3, 20.

sought to fell a certain tree of great size, at Geismar, and called, in the ancient speech of the region, the oak of Jove [i.e. Thor].

The man of God was surrounded by the servants of God. When he would cut down the tree, behold a great throng of pagans who were there cursed him bitterly among themselves because he was the enemy of their gods. And when he had cut into the trunk a little way, a breeze sent by God stirred overhead, and suddenly the branching top of the tree was broken off, and the oak in all its huge bulk fell to the ground. And it was broken into four parts, as if by the divine will, so that the trunk was divided into four huge sections without any effort of the brethren who stood by. When the pagans who had cursed did see this, they left off cursing and, believing, blessed God. Then the most holy priest took counsel with the brethen: and he built from the wood of the tree an oratory,[20] and dedicated it to the holy apostle Peter.

13. From the Life of St. Sturmi, 8th century

For almost three years he [Sturmi] fulfilled the duties of the priesthood, preaching and baptizing among the people. Then by the inspiration of God the purpose came into his soul to chasten himself by the straiter life and the hardships of the wilderness. He sought counsel thereupon from Boniface—his master in the spirit—who, when he understood Sturmi, knew that this purpose was inspired of God and rejoiced that God had designed to lead him by his grace. He gave Sturmi two companions, and when he had prayed and blessed them all he said: "Go forth into that solitude which is called Bochonia[21] and seek a place meet[22] for the servants of God to dwell in. For God is able to prepare for his servants a place in the wilderness."

And so those three went forth into the wilderness and entered into places solitary and rough, and saw almost nothing but heaven and earth and great trees; and they prayed Christ fervently that he would direct their feet in the path of peace. On the third day they came to the place which even to this day is called Hersfeld,[23] and when they had seen and explored the region round about, they asked Christ that the place might be blest to the dwellers therein. On the very spot where the monastery now stands they built poor huts of the bark of trees. There they tarried many days, serving God with holy fasts and watching and prayer. . . .

20. **oratory:** a small chapel.
21. **Bochonia:** central Germany.
22. **meet:** suitable.
23. **Hersfeld:** in central Germany.

[Boniface advised Sturmi to go farther and search for a more secluded place. He did and found a place that appeared right.]

When he had come thither straightway the holy man Sturmi was filled with exceeding great joy, for he knew that through the merits and prayers of the holy bishop Boniface the place had been revealed to him by God.

Then on the second day the man of God came again to Hersfeld and found his brethren there calling upon God with fervent prayers. He told them of the place he had found and bade them make ready to go thither with him. But Sturmi went straightway to the holy bishop Boniface to tell him how he had found a place for the brethren to dwell in. Together they rejoiced and gave God thanks and held sweet converse about the life and conversation of monks. Then did the bishop let Sturmi go back to his wilderness, while he went to the palace of Carloman, the king, to gain from him a grant of the place Sturmi had chosen.

When Boniface came before the king, he said to him: "We have found in the wilderness called Bochonia, beside the river named Fulda, a place meet for the servants of God to dwell in, where before us no man has dwelt. It is under your sway, and we do beg of your beneficence to give us this place, so that we may be enabled to serve God under your protection." . . . Then did the king before all the lords of his palace give over to the bishop the place he had asked for, saying, "This place which thou seekest on the bank of the river Fulda I give over whole and entire from my law to the law of God—from that place in all directions in a circle four thousand paces toward east and west and north and south, yet shall hold the region."

Then the king gave command that a charter be written to this end, and he sealed it with his own hand.

In the year of the incarnation of Christ 744, in the first month, the twelfth day of the month, while the brothers Carloman and Pippin were reigning over the Frankish people, did Sturmi arise, in the name of God, and with seven brethren he did go to the place where now the monastery stands. They prayed to the Lord Christ that he would ever protect and defend them by his power; and, serving God in sacred psalms and in fasts, vigils, and prayers by day and by night, they did busy themselves cutting down the forests and clearing the ground by their own labor so far as strength was given them.

When two months had passed by, and a multitude of men were gathered together, the reverend archbishop Boniface came unto them; and when he looked and saw the convenience and great resources of the place, he exulted in the Holy Spirit, giving thanks and praising Christ because he had deigned to bestow upon his servants such a lodge in the wilderness.

QUESTIONS TO CONSIDER

By now you have a good idea of some of the reasons for the growth and success of Christianity during the early Middle Ages, in particular the political and institutional factors involved. Reviewing your lists, how would you rank the factors you have identified in order of importance?

Your assessment of the development of Christianity is based on your extraction of the human element from documents that also pay great attention to the miraculous. This emphasis on human action is important in our understanding of historical change, but to understand how early medieval people viewed historical change we have to look at the miracles as well.

To gain some flavor of the medieval world view, return to the documents and this time read them only for the "acts of God." What role did the miraculous play in the royal conversions? Why might some of the accounts, such as Constantine's, put more emphasis on miracles than others? Why would the author of the second account of Pope Leo's meeting with Attila add the miraculous details he does? What sorts of miracles are included in the saints' lives? Do these seem to stress the power of God or the special holiness of the individual saint? Why do the miracles link the saints with other saints or with Biblical characters?

The accounts often flow very easily from historical to supernatural events. What does this tell you about ideas of the boundaries between the natural and the supernatural in the early Middle Ages? How might this world view have been shaped by the level of general understanding of disease, astronomical occurrences, or other natural phenomena at the time?

Your description of the development of Christianity is probably quite different from the account that one of these early medieval authors would have written. What might their list of shaping factors look like? How would they fit the factors you view as important into their story? How might their ranking of factors differ from yours? For example, you have read several different justifications for papal primacy—Biblical, political, and miraculous. Which do you feel is most important? Which do you feel contemporary observers regarded as the most important?

We currently term "miraculous" only those events that defy logical explanation, such as a military victory over a powerful opponent by a smaller or poorly equipped force. Do you think these early medieval writers would have agreed? Or might they have viewed military advantage as simply further evidence of God's favor? Using these documents as evidence, how would you compare early medieval and modern views of history?

EPILOGUE

The transformation of Christianity from a minority religious sect emphasizing the life and teachings of Jesus to the official religion of Europe was not universally regarded as positive by all Christians. We have already seen how the desert fathers and mothers attempted to separate themselves from the official Church, but the monastic movement they started itself became institutionalized and powerful in secular affairs.

Though this close relationship with the centralized Church was acceptable to many monks, others wanted to return to the original ideals of the movement, believing that worldly goods only corrupted the Church and that close relations between Church and state were not desirable. The entire Middle Ages witnessed calls for reform, for restoring what was perceived as the original message of Christianity. The institutional Church tolerated these protests as long as only a few people were involved; when such movements became large, however, the Church reacted by declaring them heresy and thus unacceptable. In some cases, the Church itself led military campaigns or crusades against these groups in the same way that earlier kings persecuted non-Christians once they became Christians themselves—and in the same way the Roman authorities once persecuted the Christian minority.

No single reform was effective in changing the basic structure of the Church that grew up in the early Middle Ages. From 330 on, Christianity would be closely connected with secular governments and would become a wealthy and powerful secular institution in its own right. The form adopted by the Roman church would even survive the theological change of the Protestant Reformation. Though Protestant areas broke with the papacy in Rome, they continued to set up state churches, magnificent buildings, and a hierarchy of officials with great power over many areas of life. Even today the close relationship between church and state begun by Constantine, Clovis, Ethelbert, and Olaf has not ended in Europe; Western European countries still support official Christian churches by taxation, even though actual church attendance is low in comparison with the United States.

CHAPTER FIVE

THE DOMESDAY BOOK AND MEDIEVAL STATISTICS

THE PROBLEM

In 1066 the Anglo-Saxon king of England, Edward the Confessor, died childless, leaving several claimants to the throne. Later that year the armies of William, Duke of Normandy and one of the contenders, defeated the armies of his Anglo-Saxon rival Harold at the Battle of Hastings. William then moved to subdue the rest of the country, quashing all attempts at resistance and replacing Anglo-Saxon officials with Normans. He built many castles at strategic points and stripped the leading Anglo-Saxon nobles of their lands. To keep any of his own nobles from becoming too powerful, he granted them fiefs scattered throughout the country so they would not be able to unite their forces to oppose the king. William declared himself sole owner of all land and required every feudal lord to swear an oath of allegiance to him.

These were all expensive tactics, and William imposed and collected a variety of taxes throughout his reign to finance them. Increasingly, though, he came to believe the country could yield still more revenue. He also wanted to sell off royal land, and at the highest possible price. At the meeting of his nobles held at Christmas in 1085, William called for a survey of the entire country that would assess each estate for tax purposes and let him know the extent and value of royal lands. The survey was also intended to count the population and determine the status of every person who lived in England—free, serf, or slave—as a further aid in making tax assessments. The nobles' estates were to be accurately described and valued, which would end disputes among them about land ownership and enable William to judge how many knights each of his nobles should supply for the royal army.

The king's officials set out immediately to take this survey and acted with a thoroughness that frightened rural residents, who were not used to such extensive royal involvement in their lives. In the words of an

Anglo-Saxon chronicler of William's reign:

> Then he sent his men all over England into every shire [county] to ascertain how many hundreds of hides[1] of land there were in each shire, and how much land and live-stock the king himself owned in the country, and what annual dues were lawfully his from each shire. He also had it recorded how much . . . each man who was a landholder here in England had in land or in livestock, and how much money it was worth. So very thoroughly did he have the inquiry carried out that there was not a single hide, not one virgate[2] of land, not even—it is shameful to record it, but did not seem shameful to him to do—not even one ox, nor one cow, nor one pig which escaped notice in his survey. And all the surveys were subsequently brought to him.[3]

Earlier medieval kings had also taken surveys, but never in such detail. Reminded of the survey of sinners and saved God would make at the Last Judgment, a scene depicted in many parish churches, people began to call William's survey the "Domesday [i.e., doomsday] Book." To many observers, including the chronicler quoted here, William was seeking details about their lives that only God should know, which is why William's thoroughness is dubbed "shameful."

The detail that so alarmed the English population makes the Domesday Book a unique source of information about everyday life in the Middle Ages. The vast majority of the medieval European population were peasants who lived in villages, and we have very few sources that describe their lives. Most literate people were clerics, who have left us many sources about theology and the church; lay authors of written accounts tended to live in cities and thus also wrote little about rural areas. Chroniclers were interested in the lives of kings and nobles, not in the peasants who farmed the land. The Domesday Book is one of the few primary documents to throw light on the lives of this invisible majority.

The Domesday Book is unique in another way. It not only gives us qualitative evidence in its descriptions of villages and people, but also quantitative evidence in its measurement of land and enumeration of human and animal populations. Because it is open to statistical interpretation in a way very few medieval sources are, we can use the Domesday Book to identify typical and specific features of medieval rural life. It provides reliable data for one time only, the year 1086, so the Domesday Book does not allow much analysis of change over time; it does, however, permit comparisons between one part of England and another.

Your task in this chapter will be twofold. First, we will evaluate the Domesday survey itself to answer the following question: What patterns of medieval rural life do the Domesday data reveal? We will then use figures drawn from the survey to answer a second question: What factors were

1. **hide:** a variable measure of land, 80–120 acres.
2. **virgate:** one-quarter of one hide.
3. *The Anglo-Saxon Chronicle,* translated by G. N. Garmonsway (London: J. M. Dent, 1953), p. 216.

important in determining the economic health of a village or area? The first question asks us to make some generalizations; the second asks for comparisons.

SOURCES AND METHOD

The way that surveys are constructed can reveal a great deal about a society. To begin with, survey takers generally divide whatever they are counting into those categories they rate as important. For example, modern census takers divide people by sex, race, occupation, age, income level, and place of residence because these categories are judged interesting or important in understanding economic, social, and geographic patterns. They also count certain material possessions, like televisions, telephones, and bathtubs, because these are held to be good indicators of economic status.

William's survey takers similarly counted specific objects as measures of economic status and divided people into categories they believed were meaningful. Though not every category appears on each page of the Domesday Book, certain categories appear over and over, enabling us to make generalizations. (It is important to keep in mind throughout this chapter that the categories in the Domesday Book were determined by William's officials, not by rural residents themselves. Domesday provides us with a perspective of rural society as seen from the top, which may not always correspond with the way rural people viewed themselves.)

The best place to begin your assessment of the Domesday Book is with the actual text. Source 1 consists of three parallel versions of the same text, part of the survey of the king's land in the county of Yorkshire. The first version is the original Domesday Book manuscript; the second is a printed transcription of the first two paragraphs. As you can see, the first challenge for anyone using the Domesday survey is to read and understand the actual document. The third version, an English translation of the entire page shown in Version 1, is the sample we will use to analyze the survey itself.

Even though this sample is in English, you will need to know a few more facts before you can make any generalizations. Like the entire Domesday Book, this extract is organized by *manor,* which generally meant a village and its surrounding lands. Easingwold is one manor, North Atherton a second, and so on. Most manors also controlled some land that was not directly adjacent and was either designated by a name (e.g., HUBY) or as an "outlier" (e.g., BIRKBY).

As you read the sample entries, make a list of what is being described and counted. As you would expect, the amount of taxable land appears first in each entry; the next figure is a note: "which *x* ploughs can plough." This figure is not a count of actual plows but an estimate of how many plows could possibly be used on the land if all the arable land were farmed. William wanted this figure, usually called the "ploughlands," to determine how well each manor was fulfilling its potential. The survey then notes who held the land before the Norman conquest and who currently held it. Following this are the actual counts of people, plows, and plowteams as well as other information the surveyors felt important to note, and in some cases an assessment of the worth of the land before 1066 along with its worth at the time of the survey. After this comes a description and measure of the various uses to which the manor's land could be put and a count of people and plowteams in the outliers.

As you read the entries, note that the people are divided into categories: This sample includes *freemen* (free peasants), *villagers* (serfs with some land), *smallholders* (serfs with little or no land), and *priests*. (Other categories, such as slaves, swineherds, and fishermen, appear elsewhere in the Domesday Book, but not for Yorkshire.) What do these categories indicate about the rural social structure of eleventh-century England? These numbers do not count every individual, only adult males. Though in actuality a free woman could be married to a serf, and vice versa, the officials chose to regard the status of a wife as identical to that of her husband. Note that the land is also divided into categories: arable, meadow, woodland and pasture, waste. Why did William's surveyors feel it important to measure meadows and pastures along with arable land? What does this indicate about medieval agriculture?

From just this small sample of seven manors, you can already make some generalizations about rural life, or at least about rural life on the king's land in Yorkshire. What types of people resided on the manors? What types of land did most manors contain? What had happened to the value of most manors after 1066? Judging by the change in value, what was the economic impact of the conquest? Besides houses, what other types of buildings could be found in villages?

The Domesday Book contains similar entries for a total of 13,418 manors. Historians, economists, and geographers have compiled these figures to arrive at generalizations of the sort you have just made that apply to all of England. In so doing, they came to realize that such generalizations may be highly misleading, that a typical manor could vary enormously from one part of England to another. Because the Domesday Book is arranged according to manors, however, and these manors are listed by county, comparisons between one part of England and another are possible; such comparisons are ultimately more meaningful than generalized statistics. We will now turn to the second question, which involves statistical comparisons of several English counties.

Analysis by county is appropriate historically because each county had its own administration and its own identity in the same way that each state in the United States does. Thirty-three counties were surveyed in the Domesday Book, a relatively large number, so the statistics you will be working with come from five different counties. This reduction in the number of cases, called *sampling*, is frequently done by anyone taking a survey; political polls, the Nielsen ratings for television, and the full U.S. census are all done today by sampling. Because we are comparing counties, it is not important which ones are included in the sample, so the five—Cornwall, Norfolk, Shropshire, Wiltshire, and Yorkshire—were chosen somewhat at random to represent a wide range of geographic areas. (If we were using our conclusions to make generalizations about all of England, we would need a more representative sample, like those modern political pollsters attempt to gather.) Before you turn to the statistics, look at the map below showing the counties' locations; keep referring to this map as you come up with explanations for the differences you find.

The Five Sample Counties

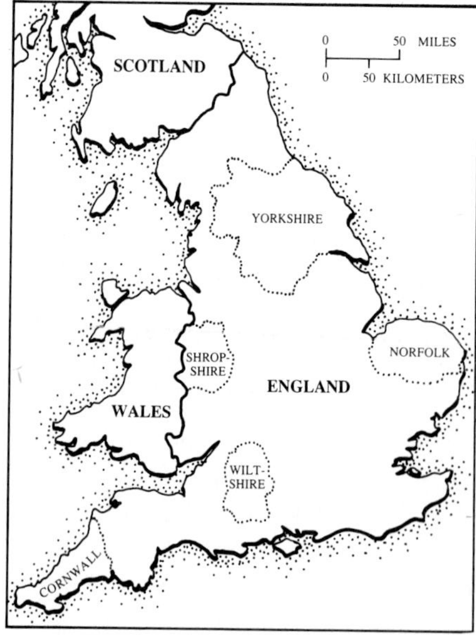

Modern governments and private industry both generate huge amounts of statistics measuring every conceivable aspect of life; economists and other social scientists have developed sophisticated quantitative techniques to make comparisons and evaluate how various factors and changes are related. They often use these measurements to predict the future, advising political leaders about the probable results of this or that policy. Quantitative techniques can also be used to understand the past, however, and historians are employing them increasingly to describe societies accurately and assess the relationships among various types of change. For instance, census data are now used to chart the ways in which immigrants become acculturated into American society; import and export statistics, to assess changes in trade patterns. The amount of statistical evidence available decreases the further back in time we go, however, and the problems of interpretation increase. For a period as early as the eleventh century, sophisticated techniques are not appropriate, and their results can be very misleading. Thus, to evaluate the evidence in this chapter, you will not need extensive knowledge of statistics, simply some basic understanding of math and a calculator.

The first stage in quantitative analysis—gathering and compiling the raw data—has already been done for you. The next stage is to transform the data into figures that will allow useful and significant comparisons. To do this, you will need to expand on the tables given here. To help you in this task, the worksheet that follows the sources allows you to gather all your calculations in one place. You should complete these calculations before you begin to draw up your explanation for the numbers you have generated, but you also need to keep in mind why certain measurements are important. Why, for instance, might population density be more significant than total population?

The statistical tables probably look familiar enough, but you need some additional information to understand the numbers and make your own calculations. Table 1 gives you the area of each county and the number of inhabitants as recorded in the Domesday Book. The first column needs no explanation, but remember that the second is not a count of all individuals, only adult males. To arrive at a total population, historians have to speculate about the size of the average household, taking into account what can be known about average age at marriage, fertility rates, likelihood of live-in servants, life expectancy, and so on. As you can imagine, little is known about many of these factors for the eleventh century, so household size remains an educated guess. Though there is disagreement, many historians use 4.5 persons as a rough estimate of average household size. For your first calculation—the total rural population in each county—you will thus need to multiply the number of inhabitants listed by 4.5.

This population figure is only preliminary, for several historians have pointed out that in some counties one factor may render population figures arrived at by simply multiplying by household size especially inaccurate—namely, the presence of slaves. Adult male slaves are included in the Domesday count, but they would not have had their own households; they should be counted simply as one person and not multiplied. Table 2 gives you the number of slaves in each county. To arrive at a more accurate total population than your first figure, you need to subtract this number from the original count, multiply that number by 4.5, and then add the number of slaves. Your second calculation will thus be a more accurate reflection of total population. (In this and in all calculations, be sure you understand exactly how you are arriving at the numbers you are, and why. Calculators and computers do the work for you, but they do not think.) Now you can make a third calculation—population density expressed in persons per square mile.

Table 3 gives you the number of manors in each county, so you can make a fourth calculation—the average size of the settlement expressed in persons per settlement. Table 4 provides the number of plowteams, which in Norman England consisted of eight oxen. With these figures you can make two more calculations—the population per plowteam and the number of plowteams per square mile.

So far we have been using only what was physically counted by William's officials—people, oxen, settlements. This count may be somewhat inaccurate because officials missed things or counted them twice, or because the records themselves are unclear. It did not, however, require a value judgment from the officials, which was the case with the next two tables. William not only wanted to know how much of everything he had, but also what everything was worth and what it might possibly be worth if worked to its fullest capacity. He therefore ordered his officials to assess the value of all land; in other words, to give an estimate of how much the grain, sheep, or other products of the land were worth in a year. Table 5 gives you these figures and also breaks them down in terms of value per square mile, adult male, and plowteam.

Table 6 offers an even more subjective figure, the number of "ploughlands." As we saw in the sample from Yorkshire, this figure is more or less an estimate of the total amount of arable land in each county, usually expressed in a phrase like "there are *x* carucates, which *y* teams can plow." By dividing the number of plowteams by the number of plowlands, you arrive at a measure of how well each county was working up to its theoretical capacity. Such a figure is best expressed as a percentage, so you should multiply this fraction by 100. No plowlands are mentioned for Norfolk in the Domesday Book, so you will have to leave this county out of these calculations.

As you can see, William's officials judged some counties to be producing much less than they could, others to be nearer optimum production levels. You can arrive at a further estimate—the highest annual value theoretically possible in each county—by dividing the annual value by the percentage of theoretical capacity each county is currently producing. (As an example, here are the calculations for Cornwall: 1,221 plowteams/2,557 plowlands = 0.48 or 48% capacity. If £670—the annual value for Cornwall given in Table 5—= 48%, 100% of Cornwall's possible annual value = 670/0.48, or 1,396. You can then perform these calculations per square mile and per adult male. Again, using Cornwall as an example: 10 shillings/sq mi/0.48 = 21 shillings/sq mi possible annual value; 3 shillings/man/0.48 = 6.3 shillings/man possible annual value.)

On your worksheet you now have ten columns of figures: (1) total rural population unadjusted for slaves, (2) total rural population adjusted for slaves, (3) population density, (4) average manor size, (5) population per plowteam, (6) plowteams per square mile, (7) percent of its theoretical capacity each county was currently producing, (8) highest annual value theoretically possible, (9) highest annual value possible per square mile, and (10) highest annual value possible per adult male.

You have completed the second stage of quantitative analysis—arriving at a series of figures that will make comparison possible—and are now ready to begin evaluating your numbers. Many different comparisons are possible, but here are a few suggestions: Look first at your figures for population density and size of manor. Which counties are heavily populated, and which have the largest settlements? Based on these figures alone, which counties have larger villages close together? Smaller villages close together? Larger villages far apart? Smaller villages far apart?

Now look at the columns for population per plowteam and plowteams per square mile of area. What do these figures indicate about the fertility of the land in each county? Yorkshire and Wiltshire have roughly equal populations per team yet vastly different numbers of plowteams per square mile. What does this circumstance indicate about agriculture and the condition of the land in these two counties? (It is important to keep in mind that a plowteam could only plow about 100 acres, or $\frac{1}{6}$ of a square mile, per year; therefore a county with fewer plowteams per square mile would have more untilled land, not plowteams that worked much larger areas.) Does this help explain why the villages in Yorkshire are smaller and farther apart from one another than those elsewhere?

Look at Table 5, showing annual values, and your own calculations for possible annual values. Which county is the most productive? The least? How are annual value and population density related? Does the presence of slaves affect the annual value? Cornwall and Yorkshire are about even in annual value per man yet very different in annual value per square mile. Why might this be? In which counties did William's officials see the greatest possibility for improvement in annual value? What suggestions might they have made to effect this (e.g., an increase in the number of plowteams working, an increase in the population)?

Population density, number of plows, and average manor size all help to explain some of the differences in agricultural production levels and economic well-being in these counties, but other factors also recorded in the Domesday Book might also help to explain the patterns you have discovered. As you remember from the sample, mills were always noted; Table 7 gives you the number of grain mills in each county, both total and broken down per 1,000 teams and 1,000 men. How do these figures relate to the figures for annual value? Might building mills have helped some counties increase their productivity? As you also remember, the Domesday Book classifies the rural population according to social status (free, villager, smallholder, slave) and, in some cases, occupation. Table 8 gives you these figures for the five counties. We have already considered the relationship between the presence of slaves and the annual value for each county. Do you see any relationship between the percentage of free peasants and the annual value? Between the presence of smallholders, who were not much better off than slaves? Does either the presence of mills or a rough understanding of the social structure help explain any anomalies in your earlier comparisons?

You are now ready to answer both questions: What does the Domesday survey reveal about medieval rural life? What factors were important in determining the economic health of a village or county?

THE EVIDENCE

Source 1 from the Public Records Office E 31/2, f. 299, London (version 1); Margaret L. Faull and Marie Stinson, editors, Domesday Book, *vol. 30,* Yorkshire, *part 1 (Chichester, England: Phillimore, 1986), 299a (versions 2 and 3).*

1. From the Domesday Book

VERSION 1

VERSION 2

TERRA REGIS *IN EVRVIC SCIRE*.

IN EISICEWALT sunt ad geldū . xii . carucatæ
terræ . q̄s . vii . carucæ possunt arare . H̄ tenuit Morcar
p̱ uno manerio . T.R.E . Modo . ē in manu regis . 7 sunt
ibi . x . uitti habentes . iiii . carucas . Æccła cū pb̄ro.
Silua pastilis . ii . lev̄ long̃ . 7 ii . lat̃ . Int̃ totū . iii . leug
long̃ . 7 ii . lat̃ . Tc̄ uał . xxxii . lib̃ . m̄ . xx . solidos.

Ad hoc Man̄ ptinet soca harū terrarū . In hobi.
iiii . car̃ . In Molzbi . iii . car̃ . In Mortune . ii . car̃ 7 di
mid̄ . In Torp Sudtune Chelesterd . 7 Carebi . xvii . car̃.
In Tormozbi . i . car̃ 7 dim̄ . In Hottune . vi . car̃ . In So
rebi . iii . car̃ . 7 duæ aliæ ad hallā ptinentes . cū Molen
dino . qd̄ redd̄ . xx . sol̃ . Int̃ totū sunt ad gld̄ . xxxix.
carucatæ . q̄s . xx . carucæ possunt arare . Non sunt
ibi nisi . ii . uitti 7 iiii . bord̄ . hn̄tes . i . car̃ 7 dimidiā,
Reliq̄ t̃ra wasta . ē . Silua tām pastilis . ē in aliq̄bz,
jn long̃ . i . leug̃ & dim̄ . 7 in lat̃ similit̃.

In Aluertune sunt ad gld̄ . xliiii . carucatæ t̃ræ.
q̄s xxx . car̃ poss̄ arare . H̄ tenuit Eduin̄ com̄ p̱ uno
manerio . T.R.E . 7 habeb̄ . lxvi . uittos cū xxx.v . car̃,
Huic M̄ appendeñ . xi . bereuuitæ . Bretebi . Smide
tune . Sourebi . Smitune . Kirkebi . Corketune . Lan
demot . Bergebi . Gristorentun . Romundebi . Jaforbe,
Modo . ē in manu regis . 7 wast̃ . ē . Tc̄ uał quat̃ . xx.
lib̃ . Ibi . ē p̄tū . xl . ac̄ . Silua 7 plan̄ . v . leug̃ lḡ
7 latū similit̃.

VERSION 3

LAND OF THE KING

In YORKSHIRE

[NORTH RIDING]

1 In EASINGWOLD there are 12 carucates[4] of land taxable, which 7 ploughs can plough. Morcar held this as one manor before 1066. Now it is in the King's hands; and

there are there 10 villagers who have 4 ploughs.

A church with a priest.

Woodland and pasture, 2 leagues long and 2 wide.

In all, 3 leagues long and 2 wide.

Value then £32;[5] now 20s.

To this manor belongs the jurisdiction of these lands: in HUBY, 4 carucates; in MOXBY (Hall), 3 carucates; in MURTON (Farm), 2½ carucates; in THORPE (Hill), SUTTON (on the Forest), KELSIT (Grange) and (Cold) KIRBY, 17 carucates; in THORMANBY, 1½ carucates; in (Sand) HUTTON, 6 carucates; In SOWERBY, 3 carucates and 2 others belonging to the hall, with a mill which pays 20s.

In all there are 39 carucates taxable, which 20 ploughs can plough.

There are there only 2 villagers and 4 smallholders who have 1½ ploughs.

The rest of the land is waste.

There is, however, woodland, pasturable in some parts, 1½ leagues in length and the same in width.

2 In (North) ALLERTON there are 44 carucates of land taxable, which 30 ploughs can plough. Earl Edwin held this as one manor before 1066, and he had

66 villagers with 35 ploughs.

To this manor are attached 11 outliers: BIRKBY; (Great) SMEATON; SOWERBY (under Cotcliffe); (Little) SMEATON; KIRBY (Wiske); (East) COWTON; LANDMOTH; BORROWBY; THORNTON (le Beans); ROMANBY; YAFFORTH. Now it is in the King's hands. Waste. Value then £80.

There is there, meadow, 40 acres; wood and open land, 5 leagues long and as wide.

To this manor belongs the jurisdiction of these lands: NEWSHAM (Grange); 'WESTHOUSE'; MAUNBY; WARLABY; AINDERBY (Steeple); YAFFORTH; LAZENBY (Hall); (Over) DINSDALE (Grange); (West) ROUNTON; IRBY (Manor); (West) HARLSEY; (Kirby) SIGSTON; COWESBY; THIMBLEBY; LEAKE; KNAYTON; RAVENSTHORPE (Manor); THORNTON (le Street); CROSBY (Grange); (North) OT-

4. **carucate:** approximately 140 acres.

5. 1 pound (£) = 20 shillings (s) = 240 pence (d).

TERINGTON; ROMANBY; BROMPTON; (North) KILVINGTON; KNAYTON. In all there are 85 carucates taxable which 45 ploughs can plough.

There is there, meadow, 60 acres.

There were there 116 Freemen.

Now waste.

3 In FALSGRAVE and NORTHFIELD (Farm), its outlier, there are 15 carucates of land taxable, which 8 ploughs can plough. Tosti held this as one manor. Now it is the King's.

There are there 5 villagers who have 2 ploughs.

Woodland pasture, 3 leagues long and 2 leagues wide.

In all, 6 leagues long and 4 wide.

Value before 1066 £56; now 30s.

To this manor belongs the jurisdiction of these lands: OSGODBY, 4 c.; LEBBERSTON; GRISTHORPE; 'SCAWTHORPE'; *ETERSTORP*; *RODEBESTORP*; FILEY; 'BURTON (Dale)'; (High, Middle and Low) DEEPDALE; (West) AYTON; 'NEWTON'; PRESTON (Hill); HUTTON (Buscel); MARTIN (Garth); WYKEHAM; RUSTON; THIRLEY (Cotes); STAINTON (dale); 299 b BURNISTON; SCALBY; CLOUGHTON. In all, there are 84 carucates taxable, which 42 ploughs can plough.

In these there were 108 Freemen with 46 ploughs; now there are 7 Freemen, 15 villagers and 14 smallholders who have 7½ ploughs. The rest waste.

4 In PICKERING there are 37 carucates of land taxable, which 20 ploughs can plough. Morcar held this as one manor with its outliers: BARTON (le Street), NEWTON, (High) BLANDSBY and EASTHORPE (House). Now the King has it. There is there 1 plough; and

20 villagers with 6 ploughs.

Meadow, ½ league long and as wide; nevertheless all the wood which belongs to the manor is 16 leagues long and 4 wide.

Value of this manor before 1066 £88; now 20s 4d.

To this manor belongs the jurisdiction of these lands: BROMPTON, 3 carucates; *ODULFESMARE*; EBBERSTON; ALLERSTON; WILTON; *FARMANBY*; ROXBY (Hill); KINGTHORPE (House); *CHILUESMARES*; *ASCHILESMARES*; *MAXUDESMARES*; SNAINTON; *CHIGOGEMERS*; ELLERBURN; THORNTON (Dale); LEVISHAM; MIDDLETON; BARTON (le Street). In all there are 50 carucates taxable which 27 ploughs can plough. Now there are there only 10 villagers who have 2 ploughs. The rest waste.

However, there are 20 acres of meadow.

In all, 16 leagues long and 4 wide.

[EAST RIDING]

5 In HEMINGBROUGH there are 3 carucates taxable which 2 ploughs can plough. Tosti held this as one manor. Now the King has there
5 villagers and 3 smallholders with 2 ploughs.
A priest is there and a church.
Meadow, 7 acres; woodland pasture, ½ league long and as wide.
In all, 1 league long and ½ wide.
Value before 1066, 40s; now 16s.

6 In (Market) WEIGHTON with SHIPTON (thorpe), its outlier, there are 30 carucates taxable, on which 30 ploughs possible. Morcar held this as one manor. Now the King has there 1 plough; and
8 villagers with 4 ploughs; and 5 smallholders.
Meadow, 1 league long and ½ wide.
The whole, 4 leagues long and 3 wide.
Value before 1066 £30; now 60s.
To this manor belongs jurisdiction in (North) CLIFFE of 1 carucate, which 1 plough can plough; in GOODMANHAM, 1½ carucates taxable, jurisdiction; in HOUGHTON, 4½ carucates taxable, jurisdiction.

7 In WARTER with its 3 outliers, HARSWELL, *TORP* and (Nun)-BURNHOLME, there are 29 carucates taxable, which 15 ploughs can plough. Morcar held this as one manor. Now the King has there
10 villagers with 2 ploughs.
A priest is there and a church.
A mill paying 2s; meadow, 20 acres;
The whole, 2 leagues long and as wide.
Value before 1066 £40; now 30s.
To this manor belongs the jurisdiction of 8 carucates in DUGGLEBY and *TURODEBI*, where 4 ploughs possible. In HOTHAM, 1 carucate of land; in SEATON (Ross), 4 carucates of land.
They are waste.

Source 2 from H. C. Darby, Domesday England *(New York: Cambridge University Press, 1977), appendices 1, 3, 13, 14.*

2. Statistical Tables

TABLE 1

County	Area (sq mi)	Population (adult males)
Cornwall	1,348	5,368
Norfolk	2,037	26,309
Shropshire	1,353	4,757
Wiltshire	1,379	9,944
Yorkshire	7,024	7,566

TABLE 2

County	Slaves
Cornwall	1,149
Norfolk	973
Shropshire	928
Wiltshire	1,588
Yorkshire	0

TABLE 3

County	Settlements
Cornwall	332
Norfolk	730
Shropshire	459
Wiltshire	344
Yorkshire	1,993

TABLE 4

County	Plowteams[a]
Cornwall	1,221
Norfolk	5,006
Shropshire	1,999
Wiltshire	3,003
Yorkshire	2,927

a. 1 plowteam = 8 oxen.

TABLE 5

County	Annual Value			
	Total (£)[a]	*Per sq mi* (s.)	*Per man* (s.)	*Per plowteam* (s.)
Cornwall	670	10	3	11
Norfolk	2,037	40	3	16
Shropshire	852	13	4	10
Wiltshire	4,470	69	11	32
Yorkshire	1,084	3	3	7

a. £1 = 20s.

TABLE 6

County	Plowlands
Cornwall	2,557
Norfolk	?
Shropshire	3,130
Wiltshire	3,475
Yorkshire	5,710

TABLE 7

	Mills		
County	*Total*	*Per 1,000 teams*	*Per 1,000 men*
Cornwall	6	50	1
Norfolk	538	107	21
Shropshire	94	53	34
Wiltshire	433	144	50
Yorkshire	120	41	16

TABLE 8

	Population by Social Category					
County	*Freemen*	*Villagers*	*Smallholders*	*Slaves*	*Others*	*Total*
Cornwall	0	1,704 (31%)	2,426 (45%)	1,149 (21%)	89	5,368
Norfolk	10,637 (40%)	4,607 (18%)	9,886 (38%)	973 (9%)	217	26,309
Shropshire	20 (0.4%)	1,833 (39%)	1,179 (25%)	928 (20%)	767	4,757
Wiltshire	0	3,497 (35%)	4,479 (45%)	1,588 (16%)	380	9,944
Yorkshire	450 (6%)	5,030 (66%)	1,822 (24%)	0	264	7,566

WORKSHEET

County	Unadjusted Total Rural Population	Total Rural Population Adjusted for Slaves	Population Density	Average Manor Size	Population per Plow-team	Plowteams per Sq Mi	Percent of Theoretical Capacity Currently Producing	Highest Theoretical Annual Value	Highest Theoretical Annual Value per Sq Mi	Highest Theoretical Annual Value per Adult Male
Cornwall										
Norfolk										
Shropshire										
Wiltshire										
Yorkshire										

1042

QUESTIONS TO CONSIDER

Information that can be quantified is extremely persuasive in assessing historical trends or making comparisons, but researchers using statistics must always be careful to ask several questions in weighing any conclusions drawn from the numbers. The first is the most basic: Do the conclusions make sense? It is easy to be led astray by numbers that seem to correlate without stepping back and trying to figure out why they do. As statisticians are fond of pointing out, all kinds of correlations can be discovered between entities that could in no way be causally related to each other, such as the price of wheat and the number of blue-eyed babies born in a certain year. Put the conclusions you have drawn about medieval rural life to this test. Do your findings pass the test of common sense?

Once you have satisfied yourself that your explanations are logical, you then need to examine the limitations of your data and think about what sorts of hidden assumptions are contained in the statistics that might influence the results. Is the survey large enough to be meaningful? Are the categories clearly defined, so that no room for ambiguity exists? Do the figures involve value judgments, so that two people gathering information might arrive at different figures? (A good example here is such categories as lower class, middle class, and upper class, which observers might define very differently.) What biases might have influenced those gathering information? What was the original intent of the survey, and how might this have affected the results? What does a government survey like Domesday leave out? What aspects of rural life does it reveal nothing about? How might a similar survey designed by villagers themselves differ from the Domesday Book? These are all questions you can ask of the Domesday Book.

A third line of questioning in any statistical study involves nonquantifiable factors that may have influenced the results. All statistical studies, even the most sophisticated computer-assisted ones that take dozens of different factors into account, possess some variance that cannot be explained by quantifiable factors. What sorts of nonquantifiable factors might have influenced the economic health of a village? How might productivity have been affected by people's attitudes about work? What about traditions of land use? How might the fact that the survey was taken by officials of a conquering ruler have affected the outcome? You can doubtless come up with many other factors that might have affected productivity.

Now that you have thought about the limitations of your statistics, you can also consider how your conclusions can be expanded. The way that surveys are constructed can reveal a great deal about a society in addition to the information the survey gathers. Think about the Domesday survey. What does the fact that only adult males were counted for Domesday tell you about the status of women in medieval society? What does the presence of slaves as late as the eleventh century indicate about the power of the Christian church, whose leaders encouraged the freeing of slaves? What does the fact that this survey counted only rural residents indicate about the importance of towns in eleventh-century England? From the Domesday Book, what can we learn about the personality of William the Conqueror? The monarchs of France and Germany never instituted similar surveys or even attempted to do so. What does this circumstance indicate about the power of the English kings as compared to those on the continent? As you can see, quantitative studies can also reveal many qualitative aspects of life.

EPILOGUE

The Domesday survey was immediately put to use by William, who began to sell his "royal land" at the highest possible price. He died the following year, but the survey remained one of the most important acts of his reign. Throughout the rest of the Middle Ages, individual landholders turned to the Domesday Book to answer all sorts of questions about land ownership and boundaries and the extent of royal forests. The Church used it in disagreements with the Crown over who held the rights to certain pieces of land. The most important of these questions was whether certain land was "ancient demesne," that is, former royal land; peasants on this land, such as the manors we examined in Yorkshire, were free of many labor services and were entitled to special legal privileges well into the nineteenth century. Copies of parts of the survey were often made, and the parchment on which it was written became yellowed and glossy from the oil of many human hands. The original document, kept with the records of the royal treasury, was one of the most carefully guarded treasures in all of England.

The Domesday Book gradually achieved a mythic status in the minds of many, who felt it contained the answers to all conceivable questions about land ownership. Later writers assumed its name came not from the thoroughness of the survey but from the fact that its word was regarded as final, just as God's word would be final at the Last Judgment. The document's reputation was greater than the information it contained, however, and by the eighteenth century a growing disappointment in its limitations combined with the increasing problems of interpretation to limit its use as a legal source.

Domesday remained extremely important as a historical source, however, and efforts were begun to make the document easier to use. It was first printed in 1783; the original was copied directly by photozincography, an early photographic process, in 1861. These procedures made the work accessible to a much wider audience, but using it still demanded knowledge of Latin as well as medieval handwriting and terminology.

Scattered translations and indexes were made for individual counties, but not until the 1980s did a full translation with new indexes appear; the sample from Yorkshire reprinted here was only published in 1986. At present, historians at the University of California, Santa Barbara and Hull University in England are computerizing the entire text so that statistics for every manor in every county will soon be available for scholars all over the world. By this means not just the numbers but the words themselves will finally be open to quantitative analysis, allowing conclusions about the medieval English economy drawn from the information in Domesday, like those you have made in this chapter, to be tested much more rigorously.

CHAPTER SIX

SYMBOLS AND CEREMONIES OF FEUDAL POWER

THE PROBLEM

Medieval Europe is commonly said to have had a *feudal* system of government, a description that perhaps confuses more than it clarifies. *Feudalism*, a word unknown in the Middle Ages, was invented later to describe medieval customs of landholding and delegation of authority. Used correctly, the term denotes a system of reciprocal rights and obligations in which individual warriors (knights) pledge their loyalty, aid, and assistance to a king or other powerful noble, thus becoming that lord's *vassals*. In turn, the lord promised his vassals protection and material support, which in the early Middle Ages often meant board and room in the lord's own household. As their vassals became more numerous or lived farther away, lords increasingly granted them land in recompense for their allegiance. Such a parcel of land, called a *fief* (*feudum* in Latin), in theory still belonged to the lord; the vassal only retained the use of it. Feudalism was thus a loose arrangement consisting of a mixture of personal and property ties. Unlike the Roman Empire or most modern governments, it did not involve allegiance to an abstract state or governmental system but simply amounted to an agreement between individuals.

This promise of allegiance and support could only be made by free persons; serfs, who were tied to the land, were not actually part of the feudal system. In the last chapter we looked at the economic system of medieval Europe, known as *manorialism*, and its estates or *manors* of various sizes worked by slaves, serfs, and free peasants. Fiefs were generally made up of manors and included the peasants who lived on them, but manorialism and feudalism are not synonymous. Manorialism describes an economic system, and feudalism a political one.

Though serfs were not included in the feudal system, Church officials were. Rulers rewarded Church officials with fiefs for their spiritual services or pledges of allegiance. In addition, the Church was a landholder in its own right and granted fiefs in return for oaths of loyalty from knightly vassals. In many feudal arrangements abbots and abbesses of monasteries, bishops, and archbishops were either lords[1] or vassals. Additionally, both secular and clerical vassals divided their fiefs still further, granting land to people who became their vassals in a process known as *subinfeudation*. By this means the same person could be lord in one relationship and vassal in another.

As you can see, such a system of rights and responsibilities could easily become chaotic, especially because it was easy to forget, once a family had held a piece of land for several generations, that this land actually belonged to the lord. This is more or less what happened in the centuries between 700 and 1050, as political power became completely decentralized and vassals began ruling their fiefs independently. Around the year 1050, however, this process of decentralization began to change and rulers increasingly manipulated feudal institutions to build up rather than diminish their power. Sometimes this accumulation of power and authority involved a show of force toward an unruly vassal, but it was more often accomplished through legal changes.

The rulers of England after the Norman conquest in 1066 were particularly successful in reorganizing feudal institutions to consolidate and extend their own power. William the Conqueror, who reigned from 1066 to 1087, called nobles and Church officials to serve as his advisors to the Great Council; in the Salisbury oath of 1086, he required every vassal to swear obedience directly to him. Henry II (1154–1189) sent royal judges throughout his realm to hear cases and punish crimes, a strategy that brought everyone under the same legal system and ensured that the king's will was carried out at the local level. Henry also increased the central bureaucracy, especially the Exchequer, or treasury. Later rulers of France, especially Philip II Augustus (1180–1223), and of Germany, especially Frederick Barbarossa (1152–1190), emulated the rulers of England as far as they were able. Gradually the purely feudal personal agreement was transformed into a system that might best be described as *feudal monarchy* or *feudal principality*, in which the monarchs held a great deal more power than they had in the early Middle Ages. Some historians emphasize the distinction between these two types of feudalism by calling the years 700 through 1050 the *first feudal age* and the years 1050 through 1300 the *second feudal age*.

Along with legal changes, medieval rulers also made use of public ceremony to demonstrate their power. Recognizing that their subjects regarded oaths as highly serious expressions of their duties as Christians, rulers began to require that their vassals swear allegiance regularly and in person during ceremonies of *homage* (allegiance) and *fealty*

1. Because abbesses and, in some parts of Europe, noblewomen who inherited land could grant fiefs and have vassals, the word *lord* in the context of feudalism did not always mean a man; it connotes rather "the person who holds the rights of lordship."

(loyalty). They enlarged the ceremonies of knighthood, impressing on young knights their duties of obedience and loyalty. Kings and other territorial rulers expanded their coronation ceremonies, turning these occasions into long, spectacular displays of royal wealth and power with compulsory attendance by all vassals. When rulers appeared in public, it was always together with the symbols of their authority, providing constant visual demonstration of royal power. Further recognizing that authority could be symbolized by buildings as well as ceremonies, they erected royal castles in rebellious areas and destroyed the castles of disobedient subjects.

It is not difficult for a modern reader of the media age to understand the manipulation of symbols as a means of promoting loyalty and allegiance. Because medieval people did not live in a world as full of visual stimulation as ours, however, by their standards the ceremonies surrounding a monarch were truly extraordinary spectacles. Not only did medieval rulers rely on secular badges of power such as flags and swords, they also began to incorporate religious emblems as well. This use of religious symbols by heads of state was accompanied by changes in the theory underlying kingship. In the first feudal age, the king was regarded simply as the greatest of the nobles, whose power derived from the personal agreements he had made with his vassals. This concept of authority continued into the second feudal age, but alongside it the notion developed that the king received his power from God as well. Rulers were increasingly seen not only as the pinnacle of a pyramid of vassals, but as their entire kingdom's representative to God as well. They were not regarded as divine in the way that ancient heads of state such as the Egyptian pharaohs and Roman emperors had been—Christianity would not allow this kind of deification—but in some ways they were considered sacred. Monarchs demonstrated the holy nature of their rule with purely religious articles such as crosses and chalices as well as with symbolic objects that were both religious and secular, such as the crown (which represented royal authority and also the crown of thorns worn by Jesus before the crucifixion), the orb (the ball surmounted by a cross that stood for the ruler's domination of the land and protection of the Church), and the scepter (a rod ornamented with both religious and secular designs). These insignia showed that the monarch united the power of church and state in one person. Seeing a monarch in full regalia would impress on anyone that this was not just the greatest of the nobles, but also a holy personage whose authority was supported by the full weight of Christian scripture.

Monarchs were not the only ones to use religious emblems to demonstrate their authority, however. As the European rulers were consolidating their own power, they attempted to wrest independent power not only from their vassals but also from the Church. Here they met a formidable opponent. Even kings as powerful as Henry II were forced to back down in their attempts to control the Church, and constant disputes with the pope were one of the reasons that the German emperors were not successful at establishing a unified country. Learning by example, Church officials patterned themselves after secular rulers; in the twelfth century they began to demand regular oaths of homage and loyalty, ensuring that the separate authority of the Church was clearly symbolized in any royal ceremony and in all ceremonies of knighthood. While secular rulers built castles, churchmen built cathedrals, permanent monuments in stone to the glory of God and the authority of the Church. The consecrations of churches and cathedrals came to rival the coronations of monarchs in splendor and pomp. In this regard the Church was fortunate, for opportunities for special ceremonies and celebrations were much more frequent in the religious sphere than they were for secular rulers. Even the regular mass could be used to convey the Church's might to all who observed it. The king may have claimed sacred authority, but Church officials wanted everyone to know that they did as well.

In this chapter we will analyze several medieval ceremonies to see the ways in which they were used as vehicles for expressing authority. We will also study several objects that served the same purpose. How did these ceremonies and objects both embody and influence the relationships between lord and vassal and between Church and state?

SOURCES AND METHOD

Traditionally, political history was thought to be the history of *politics*—the art and management of government—and its sources consisted of laws, decrees, parliamentary debates, and other written documents that provided information about the political framework of a given historical period. Recently, however, political history has been more broadly defined as the history not only of politics but of power, and a much greater range of sources is now being drawn on to understand the power relationships of past societies. Borrowing techniques from the discipline of anthropology, political historians now use artifacts of material culture as well as written documents to explore the ways in which power is publically displayed and dramatized as well as the ways it is used and manipulated. The study of symbols or insignia is a particularly effective way to approach questions of authority in the central Middle Ages, for the trappings of power predominated over theories and written laws as living expressions of political systems during this period.

A *symbol* is basically something that stands for something else, that possesses a meaning beyond its own identity. Symbols may be used deliberately or unintentionally, and they may be interpreted differently by individual observers. Anthropologists have pointed out that symbols can often be read at many different levels, so that understanding all their meanings can be a complicated task. The symbols we will be examining here are more accessible than many from other historical periods, however, because they were consciously employed by rulers and officials who wanted to be absolutely sure their correct meaning was understood. Because most of those viewing these spectacles were not highly educated or even literate, rulers chose objects that had clear associations for everyone in the European medieval world and used these tokens again and again as a further reinforcement of their authority. Many have much the same meaning to us today, so you will find them easier to analyze than symbols from unfamiliar cultures that anthropologists study.

Because the most permanent material signs of power in the Middle Ages were the buildings that rulers and Church officials constructed and the works of art that adorned them, we will look first at the visual evidence. Sources 1 and 2 are castles built by English kings, the first at Richmond, begun in 1089, and the second at Harlech, built between 1283 and 1290. Source 3 is a map of all the castles built in England by William the Conqueror during his reign from 1066 to 1087. As you examine these sources, try to imagine yourself a vassal or subject confronted by castles like these in all the places you see on the map. What message would you get about the power of the king? You can see the strategic value of placing a castle on a hill, because this position allows a clear view of the surrounding countryside. How would such a site also increase the castle's value as a symbol of authority? What other features of the castles shown here increase either their strategic value as fortresses or their symbolic value? The map indicates that the castles built by William were not evenly distributed over the English countryside. Given the information your text provides about the Norman conquest and the problems William faced, why might he have built his castles where he did? Does this pattern of castle building surprise you? (Keep in mind the fact that castles serve both as symbols of power and as a concrete means of enforcing that power, and that all castles may not have been built for the same reason.)

The next three pieces of evidence are all depictions of medieval rulers. Source 4 is a manuscript illumination portrait of the German emperor Otto III (who ruled from 983 to 1002) seated on his throne. Source 5 is a section of the Bayeux Tapestry that shows the nobleman Harold being offered the crown of England in 1066 (left panel), Harold seated on the throne (center panel), and the people acclaiming him as king (right panel). Source 6 is a tomb sculpture from Brunswick Cathedral in Germany of Duke Henry the Lion of Saxony and his wife Matilda, dating from about 1240, shortly after their deaths. The model church Henry holds in his right hand is Brunswick Cathedral, which he completed. What tokens in these pictures depict the sources of royal authority? How do these objects communicate the ruler's secular and religious authority? What types of people are shown with the ruler? What does this choice indicate about the relationships between lord and vassal and between church and state? Think about the impression you have gained so far about the power of medieval kings, both symbolically and in the real world.

Now turn to the written sources, all of which describe various ceremonies of feudal life. Selections 7 and 8, dating from the early twelfth century, are ceremonies of homage in which lords and vassals renewed their feudal ties. Source 7 describes a ceremony involving the vassals of the Count of Flanders; Source 8 lists a number of castles, villages, and manors in southern France that the Viscount of Carcassonne held as fiefs from the abbot of the monastery of St. Mary of Grasse. Selections 9 and 10 record the coronation ceremonies of Emperor Frederick Barbarossa of Germany in 1152 and King Richard the Lionhearted of England in 1189. The last selection is a description of the building and consecration ceremony of the Church of St. Denis near Paris written by Abbot Suger, the official responsible for this project. Building the church took more than ten years, and the consecration was held in 1144.

As you read these descriptions, look first for the marks of power relationships. What titles were given to the participants? What physical objects were used in the ceremonies? Who stood in attendance at the ceremony of homage, coronation, or consecration, and what role did each person play? What types of actions were required of the various participants, either during the ceremony or as part of their later duties?

Once you have identified the symbolic actions and objects in the sources, you must analyze them to answer the central question of this chapter: How did these symbols shape power relationships in the central Middle Ages? Far from being passive reflections of existing power relationships, symbols can be actively manipulated to build up or decrease power. Especially in the ceremonies, what evidence do you see of symbol manipulation by the lords or other participants? Some of the vassalage relationships affirmed in rituals such as the homage ceremony required not only symbolic actions but the actual transfer of goods and services. Do you find mention of property transfer in any of these ceremonies? How might this economic factor have affected the future of such a relationship? What do structures such as castles and large tombs indicate about the economic power of their builders? Another way that symbolic ceremonies worked to change power relationships was by the inclusion of stipulations about what would happen if the agreement were broken by either party. Do you find provisions made here for this possibility?

THE EVIDENCE

Source 1 from the British Tourist Authority.

1. Richmond Castle, Begun 1089

Source 2 from the British Tourist Authority (view); Cadw: Welsh Historic Monuments. Crown copyright (ground plan).

2. View and Ground Plan of Harlech Castle, Built by Edward I Between 1283 and 1290

HARLECH CASTLE GROUND PLAN

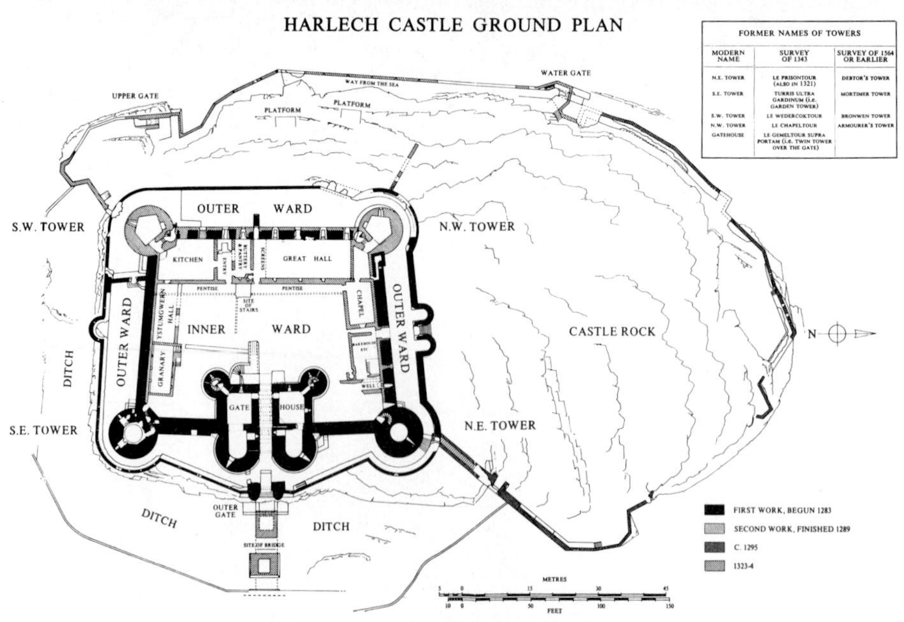

FORMER NAMES OF TOWERS

MODERN NAME	SURVEY OF 1343	SURVEY OF 1564 OR EARLIER
N.E. TOWER	LE PRISONTOUR (ALSO IN 1321)	DEBTOR'S TOWER
S.E. TOWER	TURRIS ULTRA GARDINUM (i.e. GARDEN TOWER)	MORTIMER TOWER
S.W. TOWER	LE WEDERCOKTOUR	BRONWEN TOWER
N.W. TOWER	LE CHAPELTOUR	ARMOURER'S TOWER
GATEHOUSE	LE GEMELTOUR SUPRA PORTAM (i.e. TWIN TOWER OVER THE GATE)	

Source 3 adapted from map in H. C. Darby, Domesday England *(Cambridge: Cambridge University Press, 1977), p. 316.*

3. Major Royal Castles Built During the Reign of William the Conqueror, 1066–1087

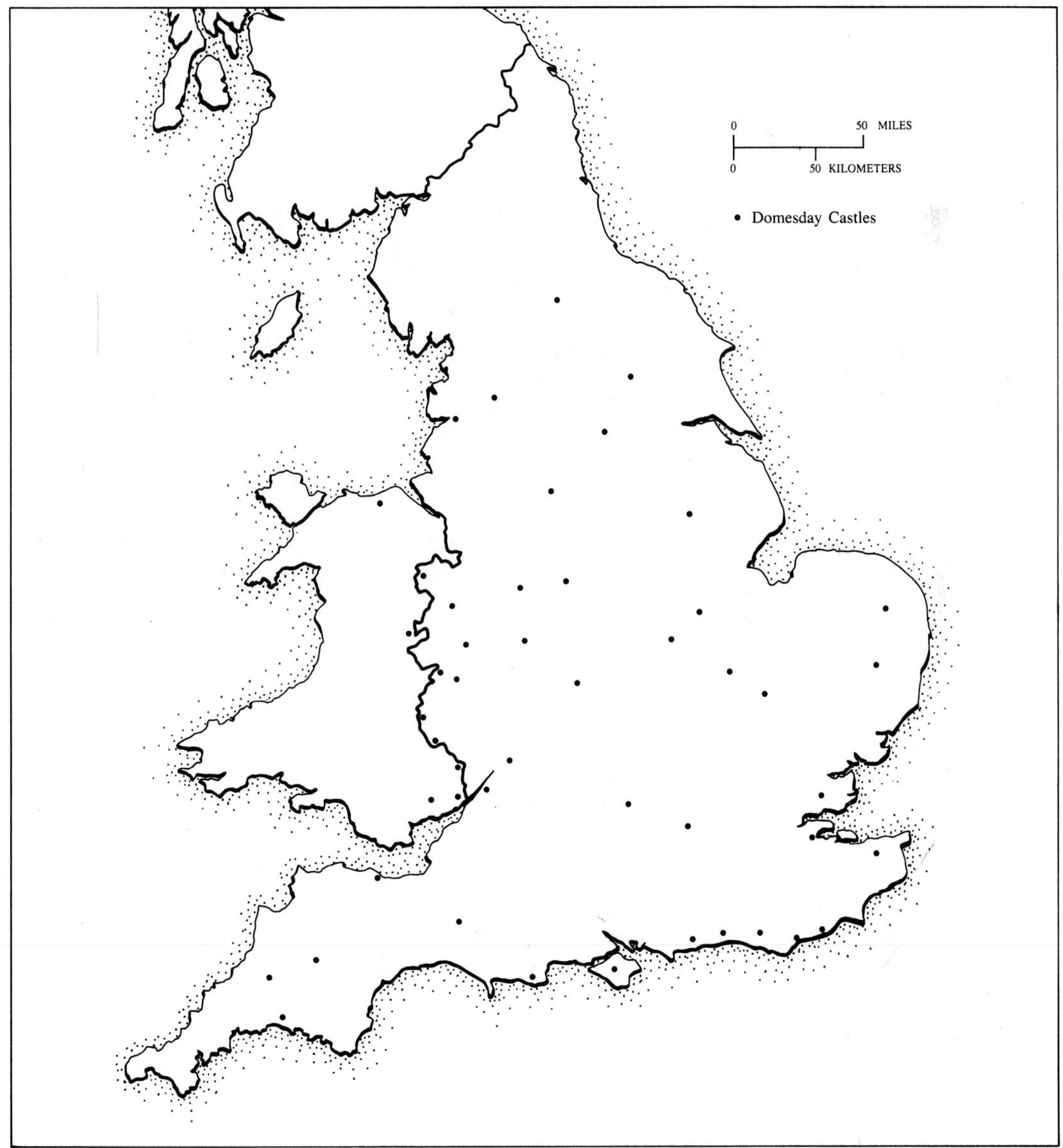

Source 4 from Munich, Staatsbibliothek (Marburg/Art Resource).

4. Portrait of Emperor Otto III (reign 983–1002)

Source 5 from Bayeux, France (Giraudon/Art Resource).

5. From the Bayeux Tapestry, late 11th century

Source 6 from Brunswick Cathedral, Germany (Marburg/Art Resource).

6. Tomb Sculpture of Duke Henry the Lion of Saxony (reign 1142–1195) and His Wife Matilda

Sources 7 and 8 from Edward Cheney, editor and translator, Translations and Reprints from the Original Sources of European History, *vol. 4, no. 3 (Philadelphia: University of Pennsylvania Press, no date), pp. 18–20.*

7. Ceremony of Homage to the Count of Flanders, 1127

Through the whole remaining part of the day those who had been previously enfeoffed[2] by the most pious count Charles did homage to the count, taking up now again their fiefs and offices and whatever they had before rightfully and legitimately obtained. On Thursday the seventh of April, homages were again made to the count being completed in the following order of faith and security.

First they did their homage thus. The count asked if he was willing to become completely his man, and the other replied, "I am willing"; and with clasped hands, surrounded by the hands of the count, they were bound together by a kiss. Secondly, he who had done homage gave his fealty to the representative of the count in these words, "I promise on my faith that I will in future be faithful to count William, and will observe my homage to him completely against all persons in good faith and without deceit," and thirdly, he took his oath to this upon the relics of the saints. Afterward, with a little rod which the count held in his hand, he gave investitures[3] to all who by this agreement had given their security and homage and accompanying oath.

8. Ceremony of Homage to Abbot Leo, 1110

In the name of the Lord, I, Bernard Atton, Viscount of Carcassonne, in the presence of my sons, Roger and Trencavel, and of Peter Roger of Barbazan, and William Hugo, and Raymond Mantellini, and Peter de Vietry, nobles, and of many other honorable men, who have come to the monastery of St. Mary of Grasse, to the honor of the festival of the august St. Mary; since lord Leo, abbot of the said monastery, has asked me, in the presence of all those above mentioned, to acknowledge to him the fealty and homage for the castles, manors, and places which the patrons, my ancestors, held from him and his predecessors and from the said monastery as a fief, and which I ought to hold as they held, I have made to the lord abbot Leo acknowledgment and homage as I ought to do.

2. **enfeoff:** to grant a fief.

3. **investiture:** fief.

Therefore, let all present and to come know that I the said Bernard Atton, lord and viscount of Carcassonne, acknowledge verily to thee my lord Leo, by the grace of God abbot of St. Mary of Grasse, and to thy successors that I hold and ought to hold as a fief in Carcassonne the following: that is to say, the castles of Confoles, of Leocque, of Capendes (which is otherwise known as St. Martin of Sussagues); and the manors of Mairac, of Albars and of Musso; also, in the valley of Aquitaine, Rieux, Traverina, Hérault, Archas, Servians, Villatritoes, Tansiraus, Presler, Cornelles. Moreover, I acknowledge that I hold from thee and from the said monastery as a fief the castle of Termes in Narbonne; and in Minerve the castle of Ventaion, and the manors of Cassanolles, and of Ferral and Aiohars; and in Le Rogès, the little village of Longville; for each and all of which I make homage and fealty with hands and with mouth to thee my said lord abbot Leo and to thy successors, and I swear upon these four gospels of God that I will always be a faithful vassal to thee and to thy successors and to St. Mary of Grasse in all things in which a vassal is required to be faithful to his lord, and I will defend thee, my lord, and all thy successors, and the said monastery and the monks present and to come and the castles and manors and all your men and their possessions against all malefactors and invaders, at my request and that of my successors at my own cost; and I will give to thee power over all the castles and manors above described, in peace and in war, whenever they shall be claimed by thee or by thy successors.

Moreover I acknowledge that, as a recognition of the above fiefs, I and my successors ought to come to the said monastery, at our own expense, as often as a new abbot shall have been made, and there do homage and return to him the power over all the fiefs described above. And when the abbot shall mount his horse I and my heirs, viscounts of Carcassonne, and our successors ought to hold the stirrup for the honor of the dominion of St. Mary of Grasse; and to him and all who come with him, to as many as two hundred beasts, we should make the abbot's purveyance[4] in the borough of St. Michael of Carcassonne, the first time he enters Carcassonne, with the best fish and meat and with eggs and cheese, honorably according to his will, and pay the expense of the shoeing of the horses, and for straw and fodder as the season shall require.

And if I or my sons or their successors do not observe to thee or to thy successors each and all the things declared above, and should come against these things, we wish that all the aforesaid fiefs should by that very fact be handed over to thee and to the said monastery of St. Mary of Grasse and to thy successors.

I, therefore, the aforesaid lord Leo, by the grace of God abbot of St. Mary of Grasse, receive the homage and fealty for all the fiefs of castles and manors

4. **purveyance:** food provisions.

and places which are described above; in the way and with the agreements and understandings written above; and likewise I concede to thee and thy heirs and their successors, the viscounts of Carcassonne, all the castles and manors and places aforesaid, as a fief, along with this present charter, divided through the alphabet. And I promise to thee and thy heirs and successors, viscounts of Carcassonne, under the religion of my order, that I will be good and faithful lord concerning all those things described above.

Source 9 from James Bruce Ross and Mary Martin McLaughlin, editors, The Portable Medieval Reader *(New York: Viking, 1949), pp. 262–264. Selection translated by James Bruce Ross.*

9. Coronation of Emperor Frederick Barbarossa, 1152

In the year . . . 1152, after the most pious King Conrad had died in the spring . . . in the city of Bamberg . . . there assembled in the city of Frankfurt from the vast expanse of the transalpine kingdom [Germany], marvellous to tell, the whole strength of the princes, not without certain of the barons from Italy, in one body, so to speak. Here, when the primates were taking counsel about the prince to be elected—for the highest honour of the Roman Empire claims this point of law for itself, as if by special prerogative, namely, that the kings do not succeed by heredity but are created by the election of the princes—finally Frederick, duke of Swabia, son of Duke Frederick, was desired by all, and with the approval of all, was raised up as king. . . .

When the king had bound all the princes who had assembled there in fealty and homage, he, together with a few whom he had chosen as suitable, having dismissed the others in peace, took ship with great joy on the fifth day and, going by the Main and Rhine, he landed at the royal palace of Sinzig. There, taking horse, he came to Aachen on the next Saturday; on the following day, Sunday [March 9th] . . . led by the bishops from the palace to the church of the blessed Virgin Mary, and with the applause of all present, crowned by Arnold, archbishop of Cologne, assisted by the other bishops, he was set on the throne of the Franks, which was placed in the same church by Charles the Great. Many were amazed that in such a short space of time not only so many of the princes and nobles of the kingdom had assembled but also that not a few had come even from western Gaul, where, it was thought, the rumour of this event could not yet have penetrated. . . .

Nor should I pass over in silence that on the same day in the same church the bishop-elect of Münster, also called Frederick, was consecrated as bishop by the same bishops who had consecrated the king; so that in truth the highest king and the priest believed this to be a sort of prognostication[5] in the present joyfulness that, in one church, one day saw the unction[6] of two persons, who alone are anointed sacramentally with the institution of the old and new dispensations and are rightly called the anointed of Christ.

Source 10 from J. A. Giles, editor and translator, Roger of Wendover's Flowers of History, *vol. 2 (London: H. G. Bohn, 1849), pp. 79–81.*

10. Coronation of Richard the Lionhearted, 1189

Duke Richard, when all the preparations for his coronation were complete, came to London, where were assembled the archbishops of Canterbury, Rouen, and Treves, by whom he had been absolved for having carried arms against his father after he had taken the cross. The archbishop of Dublin was also there, with all the bishops, earls, barons, and nobles of the kingdom. When all were assembled, he received the crown of the kingdom in the order following: First came the archbishops, bishops, abbots, and clerks, wearing their caps, preceded by the cross, the holy water, and the censers, as far as the door of the inner chamber, where they received the duke, and conducted him to the church of Westminster, as far as the high altar, in a solemn procession. In the midst of the bishops and clerks went four barons carrying candlesticks with wax candles, after whom came two earls, the first of whom carried the royal sceptre, having on its top a golden cross; the other carried the royal sceptre, having a dove on its top. Next to these came two earls with a third between them, carrying three swords with golden sheaths, taken out of the king's treasury. Behind these came six earls and barons carrying a chequer,[7] over which were placed the royal arms and robes, whilst another earl followed them carrying aloft a golden crown. Last of all came Duke Richard, having a bishop on the right hand, and a bishop on the left, and over them was held a silk awning. Proceeding to the altar, as we have said, the holy Gospels were placed before him together with the relics of some of the saints, and he swore, in presence of the clergy and people, that he would observe peace, honour, and reverence, all his life, towards God, the holy Church and its ordinances: he swore also that he would exercise true justice towards the people committed to his charge, and abrogating all bad laws and unjust customs, if any such might be found in his dominions, would steadily observe those which were good. After this they stripped him of all his clothes except his breeches and shirt, which had been ripped apart over

5. **prognostication:** prophecy.
6. **unction:** anointing.
7. **chequer:** a small table.

his shoulders to receive the unction. He was then shod with sandals interwoven with gold thread, and Baldwin archbishop of Canterbury anointed him king in three places, namely, on his head, his shoulders, and his right arm, using prayers composed for the occasion: then a consecrated linen cloth was placed on his head, over which was put a hat, and when they had again clothed him in his royal robes with the tunic and gown, the archbishop gave into his hand a sword wherewith to crush all the enemies of the Church; this done, two earls placed his shoes upon his feet, and when he had received the mantle, he was adjured by the archbishop, in the name of God, not to presume to accept these honours unless his mind was steadily purposed to observe the oaths which he had made: and he answered that, with God's assistance, he would faithfully observe everything which he had promised. Then the king taking the crown from the altar gave it to the archbishop, who placed it upon the king's head, with the sceptre in his right hand and the royal wand in his left; and so, with his crown on, he was led away by the bishops and barons, preceded by the candles, the cross and the three swords aforesaid. When they came to the offertory of the mass, the two bishops aforesaid led him forwards and again led him back. At length, when the mass was chanted, and everything finished in the proper manner, the two bishops aforesaid led him away with his crown on, and bearing in his right hand the sceptre, in his left the royal wand, and so they returned in procession into the choir, where the king put off his royal robes, and taking others of less weight, and a lighter crown also, he proceeded to the dinner-table, at which the archbishops, bishops, earls, and barons, with the clergy and people, were placed, each according to his rank and dignity, and feasted splendidly, so that the wine flowed along the pavement and walls of the palace.

Source 11 from Roland H. Bainton, The Medieval Church *(Princeton: D. VanNostrand, 1962), pp. 86–92, 104, 112, 116–118, 120. Selection translated by Roland H. Bainton.*

11. Abbot Suger's Description of the Building and Consecration of St. Denis, 12th century

Our former church was constructed with royal munificence by the glorious and famous king of the Franks, Dagobert, who, in response to a vision of the saints, erected in their honor a basilica of marble adorned with jewels of incomparable splendor. In time this edifice became too small to accommodate the throngs who came to kiss the holy relics of the Lord, the nail and the crown of thorns. Such was the press that men were as immobile as statues, women took on the pallor of death and cried out as in travail and others, lifted by the men, crawled over them as on a pavement.

I knew not where to find marble for the new church and thought of bringing columns from the baths of Diocletian at Rome through the Mediterranean under convoy even of the Saracens, then by the English Sea and the tortuous Seine, when the Almighty revealed to us a quarry nearby at Pontoise. The columns were hauled by common folk and noble who alike harnassed themselves as beasts of burden. Similarly I knew not where to find adequate timber and supposed that it would be necessary to go to remote Auxerre. I resolved, however, to search the forest of Iveline, though told that it had already been stripped of larger timbers for fortifications. I penetrated the thickets and found twelve trees which the Lord Jesus had protected from the plunderers and reserved for Himself and the Holy Martyrs.

The plan was to build a new church and to integrate the old with the new, except for the gracious and laudable extension of a cluster of chapels by which the entire sanctuary should be suffused with a marvelous and perpetual light from the most holy windows, adding lustre to the beauty within.

Summer and winter for three years we labored and when the church was done we resolved to build a new reliquiary[8] for the remains of our patron saints and in front of this to construct an altar, to which peers, princes and bishops sent precious stones and the illustrious king himself presented exquisite emeralds. The consecration was set for the second Sunday in June and was attended by our Lord King Louis, Queen Eleanor, the Queen Mother and divers peers, archbishops and bishops from France and the Archbishop of Canterbury. When the king and the nobility beheld the chorus of such pontiffs in white vestments with mitres, bejewelled orphreys and croziers,[9] processing to celebrate the nuptials of the Eternal Spouse, to them it appeared that this was rather a heavenly than an earthly chorus, a ceremony less human than divine.

When the reliquiary executed under King Dagobert was opened and the bodies of the saints exposed, the king and all the nobles chanted and wept with joy unspeakable. The most Christian king received the silver chasse[10] of our special patron and led the procession of those bearing candles and crosses. After the consecration of the main altar and of twenty others, a solemn mass was celebrated whose melody, ravishing in consonance and congruent harmony, seemed rather a heavenly than an earthly symphony, and all with one heart and voice acclaimed, "Blessing, honor and glory be unto Thy name, Lord Jesus Christ, (Rev. 5:13) whom God the Father hath anointed High Priest with the oil of gladness above Thy fellows. (Heb. 1:9, Ps. 45) By this most holy chrism[11] and through reception of the most holy

8. **reliquiary:** container for relics.

9. **orphreys:** bands on the front of ecclesiastical robes; **crozier:** staff carried by bishops and other church officials.

10. **chasse:** case for the relics of a saint.

11. **chrism:** consecrated oil.

Eucharist Thou dost conjoin the corporeal with the spiritual, the human with the divine and through visible benedictions dost invisibly restore and wondrously transform this present into the celestial kingdom, through power and mercy making us and the angelic creature, both heaven and earth into one commonwealth, Thou who livest and reignest, God forever and ever, Amen."

QUESTIONS TO CONSIDER

So far we have focused our discussion on symbols of power and their function, but another approach would be to focus on the human participants. The power relationships we have investigated involve three main groups in medieval European society: the nobles, the Church, and the rulers. To examine these groups, you will need to extract information from each of the sources and then compare your findings.

Take the nobles first. How would you compare the role of the nobles in the ceremonies of homage and coronation? What do documents 8, 9, and 11 indicate about the relationship of the nobles with Church officials? How is their relationship to the ruler expressed in the pictures of Otto III and Harold? What differences do you see in the status of the noble class in Germany and in England, as expressed in the coronation ceremonies?

Turning to the Church, what types of religious objects appear in the ceremonies and the depictions of rulers? Does their presence express the power of the Church as an institution or the power of another party? What do these objects tell you about medieval religious beliefs and practices? What evidence do you find of the Church's economic power? How would you compare the roles played by Church officials and the ruler in the coronation and consecration ceremonies? What does document 8 tell you about the relationship between the Church and the nobles? (Remember that a vassalage relationship could also work the other way; that is, a churchman could be a vassal of a noble and pay homage to him in a similar ceremony.) What do the portrait of Otto III and the tapestry likeness of Harold indicate about the relationship between the ruler and Church officials?

The most prominent group in the sources are secular rulers. How would you compare the three visual depictions of these rulers? Might any of the differences you see be explained by differences in the function of these pieces of art—in the fact, for example, that the last is a tomb sculpture? Why might these rulers have wished to express certain features of their rule while they were still alive and ensure other features were stressed for posterity after they were dead? The two coronation ceremonies, Sources 9 and 10, date from the period when the institution of feudal monarchy was being established. What evidence do you see in these ceremonies of both the old and new notions of the king: as the greatest of the nobles and as God's ordained?

How might Abbot Suger's position as Church official have affected his description of the building and dedication of the St. Denis church? Remember that most literate people in the Middle Ages were clerics; thus all the documents included here were probably written by priests or monks. How might this fact have affected their account of the events? Given what you have read and examined here, how would you weigh the importance of symbols and ceremonies against other instruments of power that medieval kings possessed, such as armies and law codes?

EPILOGUE

The expansion of royal power at the expense of the noble class and the Church was only begun during the second feudal age. Monarchs in the later Middle Ages, the Renaissance, and the early modern period continued to build up their authority, devising new methods of taxation to raise revenue, creating a centralized legal system under firm royal control, reducing the role of or doing away with feudal assemblies of nobles, hiring middle-class lawyers and bureaucrats as their advisors and officials, and forbidding the nobles to maintain their own armies while building up royal armies led by generals whom they chose for loyalty.

This expansion of royal power was made easier in many countries by the Protestant Reformation in the sixteenth century. Rulers such as Henry VIII of England who resented the independent power of the Church gladly embraced Protestant theology, which denounced the papacy as evil and declared the secular ruler the proper source of religious authority. Some rulers became Protestant out of sincere religious conviction; for others, the chance to take over Church property and appoint Church officials was the strongest motivation to abandon Roman Catholicism.

The growth of royal power was accompanied, as you would expect after working through this chapter, by changes in the theory underlying kingship and in the symbols used to portray the king. In the late sixteenth and seventeenth centuries, political theorists developed the idea of the divine right of kings, whereby kings derived their power directly and virtually only from God, making them not answerable to their subjects for their behavior. You can detect the seeds of this idea in the documents you have just read and will see it developed to its furthest extent in the last chapter in this book, when we will examine *absolutism*, as this concept of total royal power is called. To gain some idea of the symbols of absolutism, turn to the illustrations in Chapter 14. How would you compare the emblems of power used by monarchs from these two historical periods?

Centralized monarchy did not develop in all parts of Europe, however.

Germany and Italy remained divided and in fact did not become unified nations until the late nineteenth century, just a little over a hundred years ago. From the description of Frederick Barbarossa's coronation, you can determine one reason for this: the fact that the emperorship was elected rather than hereditary. The lack of strong central governments in Germany and Italy was one reason for their decreasing political importance in the early modern period. Because the rulers of western Europe had far greater financial resources than their less unified neighbors, they could maintain large armies and encourage economic development. After the voyages of the Portuguese and Spanish opened up new lands and new trade routes to the East, these rulers also encouraged and subsidized exploration and colonization, which further increased royal and national power. All nations in Europe grew out of the same feudal structure, but the rulers of France, England, and Spain were most successful at manipulating political power and the symbols of that power to build up their own authority and end the fragmented localized network of feudalism.

CHAPTER SEVEN

LIFE AT A MEDIEVAL UNIVERSITY

THE PROBLEM

Centers of learning grew up in several European cities—particularly Paris and Bologna, Italy—during the twelfth and thirteenth centuries. In Paris scholars, drawn by excellent teachers such as Peter Abelard, gathered at the bishop's cathedral school. Because only an official of the bishop, called the *scholasticus* or chancellor, had the responsibility of issuing licenses to teach, students and teachers clustered around the cathedral of Notre Dame, located on an island in the Seine. This educational community soon grew so large that it required additional housing on the left bank of the river, which came to be known as the "Latin Quarter" after the official academic language. Special residence halls for students, called *colleges*, were opened, though the teachers themselves had no classrooms and simply rented rooms on their own for lecturing.

As the number of students in Paris increased, the teachers joined together into a "universal society of teachers," or *university* for short. Believing that the chancellor often either granted the right to teach to unqualified parties or simply sold licenses outright, they began to require that prospective teachers pass an examination set by the university besides getting the chancellor's approval. This certificate to teach was the earliest form of academic degree, granting the holder one of the titles, *master* or *doctor*, that we still use today. (Bachelor's degrees were to come later.) Most of the students studied theology, and Paris became the model for later universities such as Oxford and Cambridge in England and Heidelberg in Germany.

Colleges at many universities changed their character over the centuries. Originally no more than residence halls, the colleges gradually began to sponsor lectures and arrange for courses; the university became simply the institution that granted degrees. This process was especially noticeable at the English universities of Oxford and Cambridge. When colleges were first established in the United States, they generally modeled themselves on the colleges of Oxford and Cambridge; because they were not part of larger universities, the colleges also granted degrees themselves. Thus modern U.S. colleges may be either completely independent institutions or part of a university, such as the College of Engineering or the College of Letters and Science found at many universities. In most cases, colleges that are part of modern universities have completely lost their original function as residences.

The University of Bologna had somewhat different roots and a different emphasis. Professional schools for the training of notaries and lawyers had grown up in Bologna in the twelfth century because the city, located at the crossing of the main trade routes in northern Italy, was a center of commerce. The university developed from these professional schools, and consequently the students were older and more sophisticated than those at Paris. Here, the students themselves banded into a university; they determined the fees teachers would be paid, the hours of classes, and the content of lectures. The most important course of study at Bologna was law. Bologna became the model for European universities such as Orleans or Padua, where students have retained their traditional power through modern times.

Because all those associated with the universities were literate, a great many records survive detailing every aspect of university life both inside and outside the classroom. We can observe the process by which universities were established, read the rules students were required to live by, and learn what they were supposed to be studying (as well as what they actually spent time doing!). Much of medieval university life will seem familiar to us, for modern colleges and universities have inherited a great deal from their medieval predecessors. Indeed, most of the universities that had their beginning in the Middle Ages are still thriving today, making universities one of the few medieval institutions we can evaluate to some extent as insiders, rather than the outsiders we are when looking at such vanished social forms as serfdom or feudalism.

Because of the many parallels between medieval and modern universities, your task in this chapter will be twofold. First, you will be asked to use a variety of records to answer this question: What was life like for students at a medieval university? You can then use this description as well as your own experiences as a student to answer the second question: How would you compare medieval with modern student life, and what factors might account for the differences?

SOURCES AND METHOD

You will be using three types of sources in this chapter. The first type (Sources 1 through 4) consists of rules for university or college life issued by the founders. These are prescriptive documents, setting forth standards of functioning and behavior. The second type (Sources 5 through 8), written by teachers at medieval universities, describes their methods of teaching or presents the area on which they concentrated. These sources provide us with information about how and what students studied or were supposed to study and so have both prescriptive and descriptive qualities. Selections of the third type (Sources 9 through 12) describe actual student life or were written by students themselves. These sources are thus fully descriptive, recounting real events or the problems and desires of real students.

As you read each selection, keep in mind the identity of its author and his position in the university. (No women were allowed to attend medieval universities in any capacity, so we can be sure all authors, even anonymous students, were male.) Then as now, the perspective of administrators, those who established and ran the universities, was very different from that of students and faculty. It is also important to identify the source as prescriptive or descriptive. Prescriptive rules were often written in response to real problems, but the standards they laid down should never be mistaken for reality.

Begin your analysis of medieval university life with a careful reading of Sources 1 through 4. Source 1 describes privileges granted to the students at the University of Paris by the king of France in 1200. Though the University of Paris was originally started by the teachers themselves, the king took the scholars under his special protection and guaranteed them certain extraordinary rights. What privileges are they granted in this document?

Source 2 consists of the statutes issued for the University of Paris by Cardinal Robert Courçon in 1215. Courçon, a representative of Pope Innocent III, took a special interest in the university and approved rules governing academic life. Innocent had been a student at Paris himself and wanted to ensure the university's tradition of theological orthodoxy and high levels of scholarship and behavior. As you read the selection, note the restrictions placed on those allowed to teach the arts. What restrictions are placed on teachers of theology? Why would Innocent be stricter about theology? What other areas did he believe important to regulate? What matters were the masters and students allowed to decide for themselves?

Source 3 contains further statutes issued for the University of Paris by Pope Gregory XI in 1231. What rules did he set for the chancellor's granting of teaching licenses? What issues was the university permitted to decide for itself? What special legal protections did students and teachers have? As pope, Gregory was particularly concerned with the manner in which theology was taught. What special restrictions did he lay down for students and teachers of theology? How would you compare these rules with the earlier ones established by Innocent III?

Source 4 is a series of rules governing life in one of the residential colleges, not the university as a whole. They were issued by Robert de Sorbonne, the man who established the college in the thirteenth century. This college was originally a residence hall for students of theology. By the sixteenth century, however, the word *Sorbonne* was used to describe the faculty of theology; since the nineteenth century the entire University of Paris has been called the Sorbonne.

As you can see from Source 4, Sorbonne's establishment was simply a residence hall with none of the broader functions that colleges later assumed. What aspects of student life did he regulate? What qualities did he attempt to encourage in the students living at his college?

By reading these four prescriptive sources, you have gained some information about the structure of one university (Paris), the hierarchy of authority, special student privileges, daily life in a residential college, and the handling of rule infractions. You have also learned something about the ideals held by authorities and patrons, for the popes and Sorbonne established these rules because they held certain beliefs about how students should behave. What qualities would their ideal student exhibit? What did they see as the ultimate aim of the university? You can also use these sources to assess how Church and secular leaders reacted to scholars, students, and the university in general. How would you describe their attitude—patronizing, respectful, hostile? How might their opinions about members of the university community have influenced other citizens of these university towns?

Besides informing us of standards, rules can also expose real-life problems because those who set the regulations were often responding to events in their environment. Which rules were specifically aimed at halting acts that were already taking place? Which rules seem most likely to have been a response to actual behavior? What kinds of acts did the authorities appear most upset about? Why do you think they believed these acts were important? Judging by the information in these sources, how would you describe relations between university students and the other residents of Paris? Before you go on to the next selections, write a brief description of medieval university life as you now see it. What types of sources would help you test whether your assumptions at this point are correct?

You have probably realized that so far you do not know very much about what or how students actually studied, other than those writings the popes recommended or forbade. The next four selections provide specific academic information. Sources 5 and 6 were written by teachers of theology and philosophy at Paris; Sources 7 and 8, by teachers of law at Bologna. Source 5 is the introduction to Peter Abelard's *Sic et Non*, a philosophical treatise introducing students and other readers to the *scholastic method* of inquiry, which applied logic to Christian theology. Source 6 is a demonstration of the scholastic method by one philosopher, Anselm of Canterbury, to prove the existence of God. If you are not familiar with philosophical works, you will need to read these excerpts very carefully, with special attention to the author's main points and the way in which logic is used to advance arguments. Because scholastic philosophers regarded logic as the most important aid to human understanding, it is fair for you to be critical if you see any flaws in their own logic. In making this analysis, you will be engaging in an activity that students in medieval universities both did themselves and were encouraged to do.

Begin with Abelard's introduction. How did he suggest to students that they read the works of the Church fathers? How were they to handle seeming contradictions? Was all literature to be treated in this way? What, for Abelard, was the most important quality a student could possess? How was education supposed to strengthen this quality? Proceed to Anselm's proof, which you may need to read a number of times. Do you see any flaws in the logic? If you were a student disputing his proof, where would you begin?

Source 7 is an announcement of lectures in law by Odofredus, a teacher at the University of Bologna, written about 1250. Because teachers were paid directly by their students, Odofredus did not simply announce his course but advertised it in a way to make it attractive. What did he see as the positive qualities of his teaching method? How did he propose to handle a text? What specific skills was he trying to teach his students?

Source 8 is the introduction to the *Digest*, the main part of the collection of laws and commentaries made by the Emperor Justinian in the sixth century and one of the basic legal texts taught by Odofredus and his colleagues at Bologna. Like many textbooks, it opens with definitions of what would be taught. What distinctions among types of law does it present? What is the ultimate aim of legal education to be? Return to the description of university life you wrote after reading the first group of sources. What can you now add about the way teachers approached their subjects or the way in which material was taught? What do you now know about the content of courses in medieval universities?

Students did not spend all their time studying, nor did they always behave in the ways popes or patrons hoped they would. The final group of sources come from students themselves or describe what might be termed their extracurricular activities. Source 9 is an anonymous account of a riot in Oxford in 1298; Source 10 a description of student life at Paris written by Jacques de Vitry, a high-minded scholar and historian who had studied at Paris himself. Source 11 consists of two letters, one from a student at Oxford to his father and another from a father to his son, a student at Orleans; Source 12 contains three anonymous short poems written originally in Latin by twelfth-century students.

The account of the riot is relatively straightforward and objective, like a story you might read in a newspaper today. What does this incident indicate about the relations between university scholars and townspeople? Who did the two sets of disputants ask to decide the matter?

The other selections are more subjective than this account, so you must keep the point of view and the intent of the authors in mind as you read them. What kind of language does Vitry use to describe students? With what authority did he criticize their actions? How would you describe his general opinion of university life? What tactics did the student use to convince his father to send money? How would you compare the father's attitude with Vitry's?

Most medieval student poetry was written by young scholars who wandered from university to university and took much longer at their studies than normal, if they ever finished at all. It is important when reading from this genre to remember that the authors were not describing the daily grind but celebrating their wild escapades, in the same way you might talk about an academic year in terms of homecoming parties, weekend bashes, and early morning cramming for exams. This does not mean we should reject their poetry as a valid historical source; rather, we must simply be aware of its intent and limitations. Keeping this in mind, how do the poets describe themselves and their problems? How does this description of student life reinforce or change what you have learned so far?

Return to your original description of university life. What would you add now?

THE EVIDENCE

Sources 1 through 3 from Dana Carleton Munro, editor and translator, Translations and Reprints from the Original Sources of European History, *vol. 2, no. 3 (Philadelphia: University of Pennsylvania Press, no date), pp. 4–5; pp. 12–15; pp. 7–11.*

1. Royal Privileges Granted to the University of Paris by the King of France, 1200

In the Name of the sacred and indivisible Trinity, amen. Philip, by the grace of God, King of the French. . . .

Concerning the safety of the students at Paris in the future, by the advice of our subjects we have ordained as follows: we will cause all the citizens of Paris to swear that if any one sees an injury done to any student by any layman, he will testify truthfully to this, nor will any one withdraw in order not to see [the act]. And if it shall happen that any one strikes a student, except in self-defense, especially if he strikes the student with a weapon, a club or a stone, all laymen who see [the act] shall in good faith seize the malefactor or malefactors and deliver them to our judge; nor shall they withdraw in order not to see the act, or seize the malefactor, or testify to the truth. Also, whether the malefactor is seized in open crime or not, we will make a legal and full examination through clerks or laymen or certain lawful persons; and our count and our judges shall do the same. And if by a full examination we or our judges are able to learn that he who is accused, is guilty of the crime, then we or our judges shall immediately inflict a penalty, according to the quality and nature of the crime; notwithstanding the fact that the criminal may deny the deed and say that he is ready to defend himself in single combat, or to purge himself by the ordeal by water.

Also, neither our provost nor our judges shall lay hands on a student for any offence whatever; nor shall they place him in our prison, unless such a crime has been committed by the student, that he ought to be arrested. And in that case, our judge shall arrest him on the spot, without striking him at all, unless he resists, and shall hand him over to the ecclesiastical judge, who ought to guard him in order to satisfy us and the one suffering the injury. And if a serious crime has been committed, our judge shall go or shall send to see what is done with the student.

2. Statutes for the University of Paris Issued by Robert Courçon, 1215

R., servant of the cross of Christ, by the divine mercy cardinal priest of the title of St. Stephen in Monte Celio and legate of the apostolic seat, to all the masters and scholars at Paris—eternal safety in the Lord.

Let all know, that having been especially commanded by the lord pope to devote our energy effectively to the betterment of the condition of the students at Paris, and wishing by the advice of good men to provide for the tranquillity of the students in the future, we have ordered and prescribed the following rules:

No one is to lecture at Paris in arts before he is twenty-one years old. He is to listen in arts at least six years, before he begins to lecture. He is to promise that he will lecture for at least two years, unless he is prevented by some good reason, which he ought to prove either in public or before the examiners. He must not be smirched by any infamy. When he is ready to lecture, each one is to be examined according to the form contained in the letter of lord P. bishop of Paris (in which is contained the peace established between the chancellor and the students by the judges appointed by the lord pope, approved and confirmed namely by the bishop and deacon of Troyes and by P., the bishop, and J., the chancellor of Paris).

The treatises of Aristotle on logic, both the old and the new, are to be read in the schools in the regular and not in the extraordinary courses. The two Priscians,[1] or at least the second, are also to be read in the schools in the regular courses. On the feast-days nothing is to be read except philosophy, rhetoric, *quadrivialia*, the Barbarism, the Ethics, if they like, and the fourth book of the Topics. The books of Aristotle on Metaphysics or Natural Philosophy, or the abridgements of these works, are not to be read, nor the writings of Master David of Dinant, the heretic Amauri, or the Spaniard Mauricius.[2]

In the promotions and meetings of the masters and in the confutations or arguments of the boys or youths there are to be no festivities. But they may call in some friends or associates, but only a few. We also advise that donations of garments and other things be made, as is customary or even to a greater extent, and especially to the poor. No master lecturing in arts is to wear anything except a cope,[3] round and black and reaching to the heels—at least, when it is new. But he may well wear a pallium.[4] He is not to wear under the round cope embroidered shoes and never any with long bands.

If anyone of the students in arts or theology dies, half of the masters of arts are to go to the funeral one time, and the other half to the next funeral. They are not to withdraw until the burial is completed, unless they have some good reason. If any master of arts or theology dies, all the masters are to be present at the vigils, each one is to read the psalter or have it read. Each one is to remain in the church, where the vigils are celebrated, until midnight or later, unless prevented by some good reason. On the day when the master is buried, no one is to lecture or dispute.

We fully confirm to them the meadow of St. Germain in the condition in which it was adjudged to them.

Each master is to have jurisdiction over his scholars. No one is to receive either schools or a house without the consent of the occupant, if he is able to obtain it. No one is to receive a license from the chancellor or any one else through a gift of money, or furnishing a pledge or making an agreement. Also, the masters and students can make among themselves or with others

1. **Priscian:** a Roman grammarian whose two works presented models of correct letters and legal documents.

2. Aristotle's treatises on metaphysics and natural philosophy were forbidden by the pope because they stated that the world was eternal (rather than created by God) and that the human soul was not immortal. The last three authors the Church regarded as heretics.

3. **cope:** a long cloak or cape.

4. **pallium:** a white stole usually worn by popes and archbishops as a symbol of their authority. In this case, a master teacher was allowed to wear one as an indication of his level of academic achievement and its corresponding institutional authority; the cope thus served a function similar to the master's or doctoral hood.

agreements and regulations, confirmed by a pledge, penalty or oath, about the following matters: namely, if a student is killed, mutilated or receives some outrageous injury—if justice is not done; for fixing the prices of lodgings; concerning the dress, burial, lectures and disputations; in such a manner, however, that the university is not scattered or destroyed on this account.

We decide concerning the theologians, that no one shall lecture at Paris before he is thirty-five years old, and not unless he has studied at least eight years, and has heard the books faithfully and in the schools. He is to listen in theology for five years, before he reads his own lectures in public. No one of them is to lecture before the third hour on the days when the masters lecture. No one is to be received at Paris for the important lectures or sermons unless he is of approved character and learning. There is to be no student at Paris who does not have a regular master.

3. Statutes for the University of Paris Issued by Pope Gregory XI, 1231

Gregory, the bishop, servant of the servants of God, to his beloved sons, all the masters and students of Paris—greeting and apostolic benediction. . . .

Concerning the condition of the students and schools, we have decided that the following should be observed: each chancellor, appointed hereafter at Paris, at the time of his installation, in the presence of the bishop, or at the command of the latter in the chapter at Paris—two masters of the students having been summoned for this purpose and present in behalf of the university—shall swear that, in good faith, according to his conscience, he will not receive as professors of theology and canon law any but suitable men, at a suitable place and time, according to the condition of the city and the honor and glory of those branches of learning; and he will reject all who are unworthy without respect to persons or nations. Before licensing anyone, during three months, dating from the time when the license is requested, the chancellor shall make diligent inquiries of all the masters of theology present in the city, and of all other honest and learned men through whom the truth can be ascertained, concerning the life, knowledge, capacity, purpose, prospects and other qualities needful in such persons; and after the inquiries, in good faith and according to his conscience, he shall grant or deny the license to the candidate, as shall seem fitting and expedient. The masters of theology and canon law, when they begin to lecture, shall take a public oath that they will give true testimony on the above points. The chancellor shall also swear, that, he will in no way reveal the advice of the masters, to their injury; the liberty and privileges being maintained in their full vigor for the canons at Paris, as they were in the beginning. Moreover, the chancellor shall promise to examine in good faith the masters in medicine and arts and in the other branches, to admit only the worthy and to reject the unworthy.

In other matters, because confusion easily creeps in where there is no order, we grant to you the right of making constitutions and ordinances regulating the manner and time of lectures and disputations, the costume to be worn, the burial of the dead; and also concerning the bachelors,[5] who are to lecture and at what hours, and on what they are to lecture; and concerning the prices of the lodgings or the interdiction of the same; and concerning a fit punishment for those who violate your constitutions or ordinances, by exclusion from your society. And if, perchance, the assessment of the lodgings is taken from you, or anything else is lacking, or an injury or outrageous damage, such as death or the mutilation of a limb, is inflicted on one of you; unless through a suitable admonition satisfaction is rendered within fifteen days, you may suspend your lectures until you have received full satisfaction. And if it happens that any one of you is unlawfully imprisoned, unless the injury ceases on a remonstrance from you, you may, if you judge it expedient, suspend your lectures immediately.

We command, moreover, that the bishop of Paris shall so chastise the excesses of the guilty, that the honor of the students shall be preserved and evil deeds shall not remain unpunished. But in no way shall the innocent be seized on account of the guilty; nay rather, if a probable suspicion arises against anyone, he shall be detained honorably and on giving suitable bail he shall be freed, without any exactions from the jailors. But if, perchance, such a crime has been committed that imprisonment is necessary, the bishop shall detain the criminal in his prison. The chancellor is forbidden to keep him in his prison. We also forbid holding a student for a debt contracted by another, since this is interdicted by canonical and legitimate sanctions. Neither the bishop, nor his official, nor the chancellor shall exact a pecuniary penalty for removing an excommunication or any other censure of any kind. Nor shall the chancellor demand from the masters who are licensed an oath, or obedience, or any pledge; nor shall he receive any emolument[6] or promise for granting a license, but be content with the above-mentioned oath.

Also, the vacation in summer is not to exceed one month, and the bachelors, if they wish, can continue their lectures in vacation time. Moreover, we prohibit more expressly the students from carrying weapons in the city, and the university from protecting those who disturb the peace and study. And those who call themselves students but do not frequent the schools, or acknowledge any master, are in no way to enjoy the liberties of the students.

Moreover, we order that the masters in arts shall always read one lecture on Priscian, and one book after the other in the regular courses. Those books

5. **bachelor:** a student who had his first degree and could teach beginning-level subjects.

6. **emolument:** fee.

on natural philosophy which for a certain reason were prohibited in a provincial council, are not to be used at Paris until they have been examined and purged of all suspicion of error. The masters and students in theology shall strive to exercise themselves laudably in the branch which they profess; they shall not show themselves philosophers, but they shall strive to become God's learned. And they shall not speak in the language of the people, confounding the sacred language with the profane. In the schools they shall dispute only on such questions as can be determined by theological books and the writings of the holy fathers.

It is not lawful for any man whatever to infringe this deed of our provision, constitution, concession, prohibition and inhibition or to act contrary to it, from rash presumption. If anyone, however, should dare to attempt this, let him know that he incurs the wrath of almighty God and of the blessed Peter and Paul, his apostles.

Given at the Lateran, on the Ides of April [April 13], in the fifth year of our pontificate.

Source 4 from Lynn Thorndike, editor and translator, University Records and Life in the Middle Ages *(New York: Columbia University Press, 1944), pp. 88–98.*

4. Robert de Sorbonne's Regulations for His College (before 1274)

I wish that the custom which was instituted from the beginning in this house by the counsel of good men may be kept, and if anyone ever has transgressed it, that henceforth he shall not presume to do so.

No one therefore shall eat meat in the house on Advent, nor on Monday or Tuesday of Lent, nor from Ascension Day to Pentecost.

Also, I will that the community be not charged for meals taken in rooms. If there cannot be equality, it is better that the fellow eating in his room be charged than the entire community.

Also, no one shall eat in his room except for cause. If anyone has a guest, he shall eat in hall. If, moreover, it shall not seem expedient to the fellow to bring that guest to hall, let him eat in his room and he shall have the usual portion for himself, not for the guest. If, moreover, he wants more for himself or his guest, he should pay for it himself. . . .

Also, the fellows should be warned by the bearer of the roll that those eating in private rooms conduct themselves quietly and abstain from too much noise, lest those passing through the court and street be scandalized and lest the fellows in rooms adjoining be hindered in their studies. . . .

Also, the rule does not apply to the sick. If anyone eats in a private room because of sickness, he may have a fellow with him, if he wishes, to entertain and wait on him, who also shall have his due portion. What shall be the portion of a fellow shall be left to the discretion of the dispenser. If a fellow shall come late to lunch, if he comes from classes or a sermon or business of the community, he shall have his full portion, but if from his own affairs, he shall have bread only. . . .

Also, all shall wear closed outer garments, nor shall they have trimmings of vair or grise[7] or of red or green silk on the outer garment or hood.

Also, no one shall have loud shoes or clothing by which scandal might be generated in any way.

Also, no one shall be received in the house unless he shall be willing to leave off such and to observe the aforesaid rules.

Also, no one shall be received in the house unless he pledges faith that, if he happens to receive books from the common store, he will treat them carefully as if his own and on no condition remove or lend them out of the house, and return them in good condition whenever required or whenever he leaves town.

Also, let every fellow have his own mark on his clothes and one only and different from the others. And let all the marks be written on a schedule and over each mark the name of whose it is. And let that schedule be given to the servant so that he may learn to recognize the mark of each one. And the servant shall not receive clothes from any fellow unless he sees the mark. And then the servant can return his clothes to each fellow. . . .

Also, for peace and utility we propound that no secular person living in town—scribe, corrector, or anyone else—unless for great cause eat, sleep in a room, or remain with the fellows when they eat, or have frequent conversation in the gardens or hall or other parts of the house, lest the secrets of the house and the remarks of the fellows be spread abroad.

Also, no outsider shall come to accountings or the special meetings of the fellows, and he whose guest he is shall see to this.

Also, no fellow shall bring in outsiders frequently to drink at commons, and if he does, he shall pay according to the estimate of the dispenser.

Also, no fellow shall have a key to the kitchen.

Also, no fellow shall presume to sleep outside the house in town, and if he did so for reason, he shall take pains to submit his excuse to the bearer of the roll. . . .

Also, no women of any sort shall eat in the private rooms. If anyone violates this rule, he shall pay the assessed penalty, namely, sixpence.[8] . . .

Also, no one shall form the habit of talking too loudly at table. Whoever after he has been warned about this by the prior shall have offended by

7. **vair:** squirrel fur. **grise:** any type of gray fur.

8. This was a substantial amount for most students to pay.

speaking too loudly, provided this is established afterwards by testimony of several fellows to the prior, shall be held to the usual house penalty, namely two quarts of wine.

The penalty for transgression of statutes which do not fall under an oath is twopence, if the offenders are not reported by someone, or if they were, the penalty becomes sixpence in the case of fines. I understand "not reported" to mean that, if before the matter has come to the attention of the prior, the offender accuses himself to the prior or has told the clerk to write down twopence against him for such an offence, for it is not enough to say to the fellows, "I accuse myself."

Source 5 from James Harvey Robinson, editor and translator, Readings in European History, *vol. 1 (Boston: Ginn, 1904), pp. 450–452.*

5. Introduction to Peter Abelard's *Sic et Non*, ca 1122

There are many seeming contradictions and even obscurities in the innumerable writings of the church fathers. Our respect for their authority should not stand in the way of an effort on our part to come at the truth. The obscurity and contradictions in ancient writings may be explained upon many grounds, and may be discussed without impugning the good faith and insight of the fathers. A writer may use different terms to mean the same thing, in order to avoid a monotonous repetition of the same word. Common, vague words may be employed in order that the common people may understand; and sometimes a writer sacrifices perfect accuracy in the interest of a clear general statement. Poetical, figurative language is often obscure and vague.

Not infrequently apocryphal works are attributed to the saints. Then, even the best authors often introduce the erroneous views of others and leave the reader to distinguish between the true and the false. Sometime, as Augustine confesses in his own case, the fathers ventured to rely upon the opinions of others.

Doubtless the fathers might err; even Peter, the prince of the apostles, fell into error; what wonder that the saints do not always show themselves inspired? The fathers did not themselves believe that they, or their companions, were always right. Augustine found himself mistaken in some cases and did not hesitate to retract his errors. He warns his admirers not to look upon his letters as they would upon the Scriptures, but to accept only those things which, upon examination, they find to be true.

All writings belonging to this class are to be read with full freedom to criticise, and with no obligation to accept unquestioningly; otherwise the way would be blocked to all discussion, and posterity be deprived of the excellent intellectual exercise of debating difficult questions of language and presentation. But an explicit exception must be made in the case of the Old and New Testaments. In the Scriptures, when anything strikes us as absurd, we may not say that the writer erred, but that the scribe made a blunder in copying the manuscripts, or that there is an error in interpretation, or that the passage is not understood. The fathers make a very careful distinction between the Scriptures and later works. They advocate a discriminating, not to say suspicious, use of the writings of their own contemporaries.

In view of these considerations, I have ventured to bring together various dicta of the holy fathers, as they came to mind, and to formulate certain questions which were suggested by the seeming contradictions in the statements. These questions ought to serve to excite tender readers to a zealous inquiry into truth and so sharpen their wits. The master key of knowledge is, indeed, a persistent and frequent questioning. Aristotle, the most clear-sighted of all the philosophers, was desirous above all things else to arouse this questioning spirit, for in his *Categories* he exhorts a student as follows: "It may well be difficult to reach a positive conclusion in these matters unless they be frequently discussed. It is by no means fruitless to be doubtful on particular points." By doubting we come to examine, and by examining we reach the truth.

[*Abelard provides arguments for and against 158 different philosophical or theological propositions. The following are a few of the questions he discusses.*]

Should human faith be based upon reason, or no?
Is God one, or no?
Is God a substance, or no?
Does the first Psalm refer to Christ, or no?
Is sin pleasing to God, or no?
Is God the author of evil, or no?
Is God all-powerful, or no?
Can God be resisted, or no?
Has God free will, or no?
Was the first man persuaded to sin by the devil, or no?
Was Adam saved, or no?
Did all the apostles have wives except John, or no?
Are the flesh and blood of Christ in very truth and essence present in the sacrament of the altar, or no?
Do we sometimes sin unwillingly, or no?
Does God punish the same sin both here and in the future, or no?
Is it worse to sin openly than secretly, or no?

Source 6 from Roland H. Bainton, The Medieval Church *(Princeton: D. VanNostrand, 1962), pp. 128–129.*

6. St. Anselm's Proof of the Existence of God, from his *Monologium*, ca 1070

I sought if I might find a single argument which would alone suffice to demonstrate that God exists. This I did in the spirit of faith seeking understanding. . . . Come now, O Lord my God, teach my heart where and how it may seek Thee. O Lord, if Thou art not here where shall I seek Thee absent, and if Thou art everywhere why do I not see Thee present? Surely Thou dwellest in light inaccessible. When wilt Thou enlighten our eyes? I do not presume to penetrate Thy profundity but only in some measure to understand Thy truth, which my heart believes and loves, for I seek not to understand that I may believe, but I believe in order that I may understand.

Now the fool will admit that there can be in the mind something than which nothing greater can be conceived. This, being understood, is in the mind, but it cannot be only in the mind, because it is possible to think of something which exists also in reality and that would be greater. If, therefore, that than which nothing greater can be conceived is only in the mind, that than which a greater cannot be conceived is that than which a greater can be conceived and this certainly cannot be. Consequently, without doubt, that than which nothing greater can be conceived exists both in the mind and in reality. This, then, is so sure that one cannot think of its not being so. For it is possible to think of something which one cannot conceive not to exist which is greater than that which can be thought not to exist. Consequently, if that a greater than which cannot be conceived can be thought not to exist, it is not that a greater than which cannot be conceived. But this does not make sense. Therefore, it is true that something than which a greater cannot be conceived is not able to be conceived as not existing. This art Thou, O Lord, my God.

Source 7 from Lynn Thorndike, editor and translator, University Records and Life in the Middle Ages *(New York: Columbia University Press, 1944), pp. 66–67.*

7. Odofredus Announces His Law Lectures at Bologna, ca 1255

If you please, I will begin the *Old Digest*[9] on the eighth day or thereabouts after the feast of St. Michael[10] and I will finish it entire with all ordinary and extraordinary, Providence permitting, in the middle of August or thereabouts. The *Code*[11] I will always begin within about a fortnight of the feast of St. Michael and I will finish it with all ordinary and extraordinary, Providence permitting, on the first of August or thereabouts. The extraordinary lectures used not to be given by the doctors. And so all scholars including the unskilled and novices will be able to make good progress with me, for they will hear their text as a whole, nor will anything be left out, as was once done in this region, indeed was the usual practice. For I shall teach the unskilled and novices but also the advanced students. For the unskilled will be able to make satisfactory progress in the position of the case and exposition of the letter; the advanced students can become more erudite in the subtleties of questions and contrarieties. I shall also read all the glosses, which was not done before my time. . . .

For it is my purpose to teach you faithfully and in a kindly manner, in which instruction the following order has customarily been observed by the ancient and modern doctors and particularly by my master, which method I shall retain. First, I shall give you the summaries of each title before I come to the text. Second, I shall put forth well and distinctly and in the best terms I can the purport of each law. Third, I shall read the text in order to correct it. Fourth, I shall briefly restate the meaning. Fifth, I shall solve conflicts, adding general matters (which are commonly called *brocardica*) and subtle and useful distinctions and questions with the solutions, so far as divine Providence shall assist me. And if any law is deserving of a review by reason of its fame or difficulty, I shall reserve it for an afternoon review.

9. **Old Digest:** the first part of the *Digest*, the emperor Justinian's collation of laws, commentaries, and interpretations of laws by Roman jurists.

10. **feast of St. Michael:** September 29.

11. **Code:** another part of Justinian's collation of laws reflecting the additions to Roman law that came about after Christianity became the official religion of the empire.

Source 8 from Anders Piltz, The World of Medieval Learning, *translated by David Jones (Totowa, New Jersey: Barnes & Noble, 1981), p. 97.*

8. Introduction to *Digest* of Emperor Justinian, 6th century

Public law is the legislation which refers to the Roman state, *Private law* on the other hand is of value to the individual. Common law contains statutes about sacrifices, the priesthood and civil servants. Private law can be divided into three parts: it comprises regulations based on natural law and regulations governing the intercourse of nations and of individuals. *Natural law* is what is taught to all living creatures by nature itself, laws which apply not only to mankind but to every living creature on the earth, in the heavens or in the seas. It is this that sanctions the union of man and woman, which is called marriage, and likewise the bearing and upbringing of children: we can see that other living creatures also possess understanding of this law. *International law* is the [commonly recognized set of] laws applied by every nation of the world. As can be seen it differs from natural law in that the latter is the same for all living creatures whereas the former only concerns human intercourse. . . . *Civil law* does not deviate completely from natural law but neither is it subordinate to it. . . . It is either written or unwritten. . . . Its sources are laws, popular decisions, decisions of the senate, the decrees of princes and the opinions of jurists. . . . *Justice* is the earnest and steadfast desire to give every man the rights he is entitled to. The injunctions of the law are these: live honestly, do no man injury, give to every man what he is entitled to.

Jurisprudence is knowledge of divine and human things, the study of right and wrong.

Source 9 from Cecil Headlam, The Story of Oxford *(London: Dent, 1907), pp. 234–235.*

9. Anonymous Account of a Student Riot at Oxford, 13th century

They [the townsmen] seized and imprisoned all scholars on whom they could lay hands, invaded their inns, made havoc of their goods and trampled their books under foot. In the face of such provocation the Proctors[12] sent their

12. **proctor:** university official who maintained order and supervised examinations.

bedels[13] about the town, forbidding the students to leave their inns. But all commands and exhortations were in vain. By nine o'clock next morning, bands of scholars were parading the streets in martial array. If the Proctors failed to restrain them, the mayor was equally powerless to restrain his townsmen. The great bell of S. Martin's rang out an alarm; oxhorns were sounded in the streets; messengers were sent into the country to collect rustic allies. The clerks,[14] who numbered three thousand in all, began their attack simultaneously in various quarters. They broke open warehouses in the Spicery, the Cutlery and elsewhere. Armed with bows and arrows, swords and bucklers, slings and stones, they fell upon their opponents. Three they slew, and wounded fifty or more. One band, led by Fulk de Neyrmit, Rector of Piglesthorne, and his brother, took up a position in High Street between the Churches of S. Mary and All Saints', and attacked the house of a certain Edward Hales. This Hales was a longstanding enemy of the clerks. There were no half measures with him. He seized his crossbow, and from an upper chamber sent an unerring shaft into the eye of the pugnacious rector. The death of their valiant leader caused the clerks to lose heart. They fled, closely pursued by the townsmen and country-folk. Some were struck down in the streets, and other who had taken refuge in the churches were dragged out and driven mercilessly to prison, lashed with thongs and goaded with iron spikes.

Complaints of murder, violence and robbery were lodged straight-way with the King by both parties. The townsmen claimed three thousand pounds' damage. The commissioners, however, appointed to decide the matter, condemned them to pay two hundred marks, removed the bailiffs, and banished twelve of the most turbulent citizens from Oxford. Then the terms of peace were formally ratified.

Source 10 from Dana Carleton Munro, editor and translator, Translations and Reprints from the Original Sources of European History, *vol. 2, no. 3 (Philadelphia: University of Pennsylvania Press, no date), pp. 19–21.*

10. Jacques de Vitry's Description of Student Life at Paris, ca 1225

Almost all the students at Paris, foreigners and natives, did absolutely nothing except learn or hear something new. Some studied merely to acquire knowledge, which is curiosity; others to acquire fame, which is vanity; others

13. **bedel:** assistant to the proctor.

14. **clerks:** here, students and teachers.

still for the sake of gain, which is cupidity and the vice of simony. Very few studied for their own edification, or that of others. They wrangled and disputed not merely about the various sects or about some discussions; but the differences between the countries also caused dissensions, hatreds and virulent animosities among them, and they impudently uttered all kinds of affronts and insults against one another.

They affirmed that the English were drunkards and had tails; the sons of France proud, effeminate and carefully adorned like women. They said that the Germans were furious and obscene at their feasts; the Normans, vain and boastful; the Poitevins, traitors and always adventurers. The Burgundians they considered vulgar and stupid. The Bretons were reputed to be fickle and changeable and were often reproached for the death of Arthur. The Lombards were called avaricious, vicious and cowardly; the Romans, seditious, turbulent and slanderous; the Sicilians, tyrannical and cruel; the inhabitants of Brabant, men of blood, incendiaries, brigands and ravishers; those of Flanders, fickle, prodigal, gluttonous, yielding as butter, and slothful. After such insults, from words they often came to blows.

I will not speak of those logicians, before whose eyes flitted constantly "the lice of Egypt," that is to say, all the sophistical subtleties, so that no one could comprehend their eloquent discourses in which, as says Isaiah, "there is no wisdom." As to the doctors of theology, "seated in Moses' seat," they were swollen with learning, but their charity was not edifying. Teaching and not practicing, they have "become as sounding brass or a tinkling cymbal," or like a canal of stone, always dry, which ought to carry water to "the bed of spices." They not only hated one another, but by their flatteries they enticed away the students of others; each one seeking his own glory, but caring not a whit about the welfare of souls.

Having listened intently to these words of the Apostle, "If a man desire the office of a bishop, he desireth a good work," they kept multiplying the prebends,[15] and seeking after the offices; and yet they sought the work decidedly less than the preëminence, and they desired above all to have "the uppermost rooms at feasts and the chief seats in the synagogue, and greetings in the market." Although the Apostle James said, "My brethren, be not many masters," they on the contrary were in such haste to become masters, that most of them were not able to have any students, except by entreaties and payments. Now it is safer to listen than to teach, and a humble listener is better than an ignorant and presumptuous doctor. In short, the Lord had reserved for Himself among them all, only a few honorable and timorous men, who had not stood "in the way of sinners," nor sat down with the others in the envenomed seat.

15. **prebends:** that part of church revenues paid as a clergyman's salary.

Sources 11 and 12 from Charles Homer Haskins, The Rise of Universities *(Ithaca, New York: Cornell University Press, 1957), pp. 77–80; pp. 85–87.*

11. Two Letters, 13th century

B. to his venerable master A., greeting. This is to inform you that I am studying at Oxford with the greatest diligence, but the matter of money stands greatly in the way of my promotion,[16] as it is now two months since I spent the last of what you sent me. The city is expensive and makes many demands; I have to rent lodgings, buy necessaries, and provide for many other things which I cannot now specify. Wherefore I respectfully beg your paternity that by the promptings of divine pity you may assist me, so that I may be able to complete what I have well begun. For you must know that without Ceres and Bacchus Apollo[17] grows cold.

To his son G. residing at Orleans P. of Besançon sends greetings with paternal zeal. It is written, "He also that is slothful in his work is brother to him that is a great waster." I have recently discovered that you live dissolutely and slothfully, preferring license to restraint and play to work and strumming a guitar while the others are at their studies, whence it happens that you have read but one volume of law while your more industrious companions have read several. Wherefore I have decided to exhort you herewith to repent utterly of your dissolute and careless ways, that you may no longer be called a waster and your shame may be turned to good repute.

12. Three Anonymous Student Poems, 12th century

I, a wandering scholar lad,
  Born for toil and sadness,
Oftentimes am driven by
  Poverty to madness.

Literature and knowledge I
  Fain would still be earning,
Were it not that want of pelf[18]
  Makes me cease from learning.

These torn clothes that cover me
  Are too thin and rotten;
Oft I have to suffer cold,
  By the warmth forgotten.

Scarce I can attend at church,
  Sing God's praises duly;
Mass and vespers both I miss,
  Though I love them truly.

16. **promotion:** that is, attaining his degree.
17. **Ceres:** Roman god of grain. **Bacchus:** god of wine. **Apollo:** god of wisdom.
18. **pelf:** a contemptuous term for money.

Oh, thou pride of N——,
  By thy worth I pray thee
Give the suppliant help in need,
  Heaven will sure repay thee.

Take a mind unto thee now
  Like unto St. Martin;
Clothe the pilgrim's nakedness,
  Wish him well at parting.

So may God translate your soul
  Into peace eternal,
And the bliss of saints be yours
  In His realm supernal.

We in our wandering,
Blithesome and squandering,
  Tara, tantara, teino!

Eat to satiety,
Drink with propriety;
  Tara, tantara, teino!

Laugh till our sides we split,
Rags on our hides we fit;
  Tara, tantara, teino!

Jesting eternally,
Quaffing infernally:
  Tara, tantara, teino!
    etc.

Some are gaming, some are drinking,
Some are living without thinking;
And of those who make the racket,
Some are stripped of coat and jacket;
Some get clothes of finer feather,
Some are cleaned out altogether;
No one there dreads death's invasion,
But all drink in emulation.

QUESTIONS TO CONSIDER

You have now examined medieval universities and colleges from three points of view—of the authorities who established them, the teachers who taught in them, and the students who attended them. In refining your description of university life, think first about points on which a number of sources agree. What role did religious and secular authorities play in the universities, both in their founding and in day-to-day operations? What privileges were extended to teachers and students, and how did these benefits affect their relationship with townspeople? Given these privileges along with student attitudes and actions, what opinion would you expect townspeople to have of students? Which of Sorbonne's rules would you expect to have been frequently broken? What qualities did authorities and teachers alike see as vital to effective teaching? What qualities did both try to encourage in students? Would students have agreed about any of these? What problems did the authorities, teachers, and students all agree were most pressing for students?

Now turn to points on which you have contradictory information. How would you compare Jacques de Vitry's and Peter Abelard's beliefs about the role of logic in education? How might de Vitry have viewed Anselm's attempt to prove the existence of God through reason? How would Abelard have regarded the pope's attempts to forbid the reading of certain books and authors? Would he have believed the rules for students set out in Sources 1 through 4 helped or hindered the learning process? What suggestions for educational improvements might a philosopher like Abelard have made? Would Anselm and Odofredus have agreed about the proper methods and aims of education? How would you compare the relationship between authorities and teachers as described by the teachers and by the students?

Some of these contradictions are inherent in the highly different points of view of the three groups and are irreconcilable. You must, however, make some effort to resolve those contradictions that involve conflicting points of *fact* rather than simply conflicting *opinions*. Historians resolve contradictions in their sources by a variety of methods: by assessing the authors' intent and possible biases, giving weight to evidence that is likely to be most objective; by judging each source as partially valid, speculating on how each author's point of view might have affected his or her description; by trying to find additional information confirming one side or the other. At this point you can use the first two methods in your own thinking: Which observers do you judge as most objective? Why did the students, teachers, and officials have different viewpoints in the first place? (You can also think about the third method historians use to resolve contradictions in their evidence: What other types of sources would you examine to confirm what you have discovered here?) Once you have made these judgments, you can complete your description of medieval university life.

Now move on to the second part of your task in this chapter, which is to compare medieval and modern university life. Some of the more striking contrasts have probably already occurred to you, but the best way to proceed is to think first about your evidence. What types of sources would give you the information for modern universities that you have unearthed for medieval ones? What are the modern equivalents of the medieval rules and ordinances? Of descriptions of student actions? Of student poetry? Of course announcements? Of philosophical treatises? Besides such parallel sources, where else can you find information about modern universities? What types of sources generated from modern universities, or from their students and teachers, have no medieval equivalent?

After considering these points of similarity and difference in sources, we are ready to make a specific comparison of university life in medieval and modern times. Because higher education in the United States is so diverse—some colleges and universities are public and some private, some religious and some nonsectarian, some residential and some commuter—it would be best if you compared your own institution with the more generalized description of medieval universities you have developed. Do you see any modern equivalents to the privileges granted students by popes and kings? To the frequent clashes between universities and their surrounding communities? How would you compare the relationship between religious and political authorities in medieval universities and in your own institution? The concern of authorities for the methods and content of higher education? How would you compare student residential life? Student problems? The students themselves? Relations between students and their parents? How would you compare the subjects taught? The method of teaching? The status of the faculty? Relations between students and teachers? Teachers' and students' views of the ultimate aims of education?

Once you have drawn up your comparison, you will need to perform what is often the most difficult task of any historical inquiry, which is to suggest reasons for what you have discovered. In doing this, you need to speculate not only about why some things have changed, but also about why others have remained the same. In your view, what is the most important difference between medieval and modern universities, and why?

EPILOGUE

The pattern set by Paris and Bologna was a popular one; by 1500, more than eighty universities were in existence throughout Europe. Often a dispute at one university, particularly among the faculty of theology, would lead a group of teachers and students to move elsewhere to form their own university. Sometimes they left one city because they felt the townspeople were overcharging them for food and lodging. Students often traveled from university to university in search of the best teachers or most amenable surroundings; because there were no admission forms or credits required for graduation, transferring from school to school was much easier in the Middle Ages than it is today.

As you have deduced from the sources, medieval students and teachers were criticized for all the seven deadly sins: greed, sloth, pride, lust, gluttony, envy, and anger. Toward the end of the Middle Ages, the university system itself came under attack for being too remote from worldly concerns, for providing students only with useless philosophical information that would never help them in the real world of politics and business. Especially in Italy, independent teachers of speech and writing began to offer young men who wanted an education an alternative to universities, setting up academies to teach practical rhetorical and literary skills for those who planned to engage in commerce, banking, or politics. This new program of study, called *humanism*, emphasized language and literature rather than theology and philosophy.

Though the universities initially opposed the humanist curriculum, by the sixteenth century a considerable number, especially the newer ones, began to change their offerings. They established endowed chairs for teachers of Latin, Greek, and Hebrew, particularly because students who had trained at humanist secondary schools demanded further language training. Some of the oldest universities, such as Paris, were the slowest to change, but eventually they modified their program to keep students from going elsewhere.

The gradual introduction of humanism set a pattern that universities were to follow when any new body of knowledge or subject matter emerged. Innovative subjects and courses were first generally taught outside the universities in separate academies or institutes, then were slowly integrated into the university curriculum. In the seventeenth and eighteenth centuries, natural science was added in this way; in the nineteenth century, the social sciences and modern languages; and, in the twentieth, a whole range of subjects such as agriculture, engineering, and the fine arts. (The University of Paris continued to be the slowest to change well into the twentieth century; for example, it did not add sociology as a discipline until the 1960s. Modernization of curriculum was one of the demands of the 1968 student revolt in Paris.) Thus, even though the university has survived since the Middle Ages, Peter Abelard or Robert de Sorbonne might have difficulty recognizing the institution in its present-day form.

CHAPTER EIGHT

THE "COMMERCIAL REVOLUTION"

THE PROBLEM

Western Europe during the early Middle Ages was a largely rural society. The cities of the Roman Empire had shrunk into small villages and the roads the Romans had built were allowed to fall into disrepair. Manors and villages were relatively self-sufficient in basic commodities such as grain and cloth, and even in times of famine could not import the food they needed because the cost of transportation was too high. When standardized Roman coinage was no longer available, villages, towns, monasteries, and individual nobles all minted their own coins, which were often accepted as legitimate tender only in very limited areas. Much local trade was carried out by barter; many people rarely used or even saw coins. Such long-distance trade as existed was handled by Jews, Greeks, and Syrians, who imported luxury goods like spices, silks, and perfumes from the Near East. These extremely expensive commodities were purchased only by nobles and high-ranking churchmen. The pervasive lack of trade is reflected in the almost complete absence of sources about trade before the tenth century. Commercial documents are extremely rare, and both public and private records testify to the agrarian nature of early medieval society.

This situation began to change in the tenth century, when Vikings in the north and Italians in the south revived European commerce. The Vikings initially raided and plundered along the coasts of northern Europe but soon turned to trading with the very people whose lands they had threatened. Their swift boats carried northern products like furs, timber, wax, and amber to all the towns of the North Sea and the north Atlantic; Swedish Vikings went eastward, trading down the Russian rivers as far as Constantinople and the Muslim world. Because these traders for the most part were illiterate, few written accounts of their far-flung enterprises survive. Those we have often come from their eastern trading partners in the Byzantine and Muslim empires, who were much more likely to be able to read and write.

The Italians, on the other hand, have left voluminous records of their business activities. Most Italian merchants were literate, and Italian artisans learned from the Muslims how to make paper, which provided a writing surface much cheaper than parchment or vellum, products made from the skin of calves and goats. At the same time that the Vikings were trading in northern Europe, merchants from the cities of Genoa, Pisa, and Venice were taking over former Muslim trade routes in the western Mediterranean. After the Crusades in the twelfth century, merchants from these cities also became involved in the lucrative trade of the eastern Mediterranean, importing such Oriental luxuries as spices and silks and exporting slaves, timber, and iron. When European cities began to produce manufactured products, including fancy wool cloth, armaments, and leather goods, Italian merchants traded these items both within Europe and to the East. They began to keep increasingly elaborate records of their transactions and devised new methods of bookkeeping to keep track of their ventures. They wrote manuals of advice for other merchants on these new business techniques, on practical arithmetic and geography, and on the customs and practices of the foreign lands they visited.

Though the profits of such trading ventures could be enormous, the risks were equally great. Travel was difficult and dangerous, for few inns were available for travelers and highway robbers and pirates posed a threat by land and sea. Shipwrecks were common, and in many places local residents claimed the right to anything that could be salvaged from a wreck. Italian merchants began to devise ways to share the risks, pooling their capital and talents and sharing the profits if the venture was a success. They formalized these agreements with various forms of contracts, ranging from temporary partnerships called *commenda* or *societas* that would be dissolved once the venture was over to more permanent partnerships called *compagnie* (literally, "bread together"; i.e., sharing bread, the root of the word *company*). Many of these *compagnie* began as agreements between brothers or other relatives and in-laws but quickly grew to include nonfamily members. In addition, these partnerships began to include individuals who invested only their money, leaving the actual running of the business to the active partners. Along with long-distance trade, the *compagnie* became involved in purely banking activities, taking deposits, making loans, and investing in enterprises other than long-distance trade, primarily mining. Some partnerships also began to provide insurance for others, thus transferring the risk entirely.

This explosion of trade encountered two serious difficulties in medieval Europe. One was the problem of money. The amount of gold and silver available for coins was simply not adequate for the increased flow of commerce. How did merchants get around this obstacle? Records reveal a range of inventive ways employed to solve the need for money, the most important of which was the development of paper letters of exchange and deposit statements that could be used in place of metal coinage. This innovation freed up coinage for other business and also relieved merchants of the burden of always having to carry a cashbox with several guards to protect it.

The second problem was a moral and theological one. The Christian church in the West forbade *usury*, that is, the charging of interest on a loan. The Church had developed this doctrine in the early Middle Ages, when loans were intended mainly for consumption—tiding someone over, for instance, until the next harvest. Theologians reasoned that it was wrong for a Christian to take advantage of the bad luck or need of another Christian, so loans should be made *pro amore* (out of love), not with an eye for profit. This restriction on Christians is the reason that Jews were the primary moneylenders in early medieval society, for as a group outside the Christian community they were not subject to the same restrictions. Moneylending was also one of the few occupations at which Jews could make a living, for in many areas they were forbidden to own land or to engage in most trades. At the same time that Christians imposed these restrictions on Jews, they also harbored a deep grudge against the Jews for their moneylending activities. This economic resentment is one of the roots of Christian anti-Semitism, which was very strong in the Middle Ages and flared up in intermittent campaigns of persecution or mass murder.

The Church's prohibition on usury meant that merchants often felt compelled to hide their interest, which they did by adding the interest into the principal in a loan agreement without stating this practice explicitly or by repaying the loan in a different currency without noting that the amount repaid was more than the original sum. Gradually the Church relaxed its sanction against charging interest, declaring that some interest was legitimate as a payment for the risk the investor was taking and that only interest above a certain level would be considered usury. The Church itself then became a moneylender, opening pawnshops whose stated purpose was to help the poor by charging a lower rate of interest than secular moneylenders did.

The stigma attached to moneylending carried over in many ways to all the activities of a medieval merchant. Trade was not like agriculture or manufacturing, for a merchant merely handled goods produced by someone else. To the medieval sensibility, making a profit from manipulating money was a dubious undertaking; the investment of labor, skill, and time warranted a profit, but did the investment of mere money? Merchants themselves, sharing these attitudes to some degree, gave generous donations to the Church and to charities and agreed, at least in principle, that profit should be limited to what was judged to be fair and just. They also took pains not to flaunt their wealth but to dress and furnish their homes in a way that would convey financial stability rather than flashy extravagance. By the end of the Middle Ages, society had somewhat come to accept the role of the merchant: Preachers in Italian cities compared merchants to Christ, who had "redeemed" the human race from the devil just as merchants redeemed loans and merchandise.

Historians often call this expansion and transformation of the European economy the *Commercial Revolution* and mark it as the beginning of our modern capitalist economy. Though you may be most familiar with the word *revolution* as a way to describe a violent political rebellion like the American Revolution or the French Revolution, the term is also used more broadly to describe economic and intellectual changes such as the Industrial Revolution or the Scientific Revolution. These social transformations do not necessarily involve violence and may occur over a much longer period of time than political revolutions. What makes them true revolutions is the extent of their effects on society. In calling this broad-based economic change the Commercial Revolution, historians point not only to the growth of new forms of business but also to the development of a "capitalist spirit"—of the idea that making a profit is good in itself, regardless of the uses to which that profit is put. Your task in this chapter will be to examine some of the documentary evidence for this historical judgment. What kinds of records did medieval merchants leave that have caused historians to speak of a Commercial Revolution? How did medieval merchants regard their own activities and social role?

SOURCES AND METHOD

In analyzing the development of medieval commerce and trade, historians have a wide variety of documents at their disposal. The most basic evidence, and the basis of business both then and now, consists of the contracts drawn up between individuals and firms. These were generally written by a notary and were witnessed by men who had a reputation for honesty. Copies of these notarial contracts were often preserved by towns that recognized the importance of business, such as Genoa or Florence, where they can be found today in city and private archives. Then as now, the language is matter of fact and often somewhat formalized and legalistic, quite similar to that found in contemporary legal documents. Because these contracts were written for other people in business and lawyers, they often assume a knowledge of the relevant laws and coinage systems, but they are still fairly straightforward because both parties in the contract wanted to make sure the terms were clear and easily understood.

The first six documents are notarial contracts made by Italian merchants, arranged in chronological order. The first point to determine is the central purpose of each contract. Is it a loan? A business partnership? An insurance agreement? A deposit statement? Are the responsibilities of each party clearly laid out—that is, if you had been one of the parties, would you have known from this contract what was expected of you and what you could expect from the other parties? Did the contract end at a specific time, or was it ongoing? What were the penalties for failure to fulfill the contract? If merchandise was involved, what was it and where was it going?

Along with notarial contracts, historians also use personal letters and account books to document the expansion of commerce. Source 7 is a letter from an Italian merchant conducting business in southern France. Notice the dates of the letter and the payment ordered. What kind of transaction is discussed here? What rate of interest is the investor to receive? Why does the merchant choose to call this an "exchange" rather than a "loan"? Sources 8 and 9 are extracts from two merchants' account books, the first from the early part and the second from the very end of the fourteenth century. Do you find any difference in the way the two merchants kept their accounts? Why did the second merchant divide his book into two columns? Which account do you find easier to use?

Though Source 7 and several of the notarial contracts openly mention interest, other records left by merchants provide evidence that this was not a unanimously accepted practice. Document 10 is a letter in the form of a contract written by a notary on behalf of a merchant and sent to a Church official. What does it reveal about the merchant? What does he promise to do? Why might he act in such a way at this point in his life? (The phrase "from this illness" provides a clue here.)

Think about the material you have read so far, which is only a small sample of the thousands of such contracts, letters, and personal accounts preserved in the archives of Italian cities. (And those surviving are themselves a small portion of all the commercial documents drawn up during this period, for many were thrown away once the contract was no longer valid and many more were destroyed over time by flood, fire, mice, and rot.) How are these contracts and accounts similar to their modern counterparts? How are they different? Can we see in them the beginnings of our modern capitalist system?

Historians can tell a great deal about commercial practices from contracts, letters, and accounts, but such sources do not reveal much about what medieval merchants thought about themselves and their activities. For this we need to look at more reflective and introspective sources, the best of which are the manuals of advice written by merchants for their sons or other merchants. These manuals are all *prescriptive*—that is, they tell people how they should behave. Before using prescriptive sources, historians must first ask several questions: Who is writing? For who is he or she writing? Why is he or she writing? Only after these questions have been answered is it possible to evaluate the actual content.

Because it is primarily based on theories about human nature, much prescriptive literature has a limited foundation in reality or personal experience. In Chapter 2 you read some prescriptive sources in which Athenian writers described the ways husbands and wives should behave based on notions about the male and female character. You will find further examples in Chapter 11, in which middle-class Renaissance men instruct women and rulers alike in rules of behavior, basing their advice on theories about women's nature and political structures. Such literature gives us very little information about how men, women, or rulers of this era actually conducted themselves, but the merchants' manuals we are examining here are somewhat different. All were written by older merchants, document 11 by an unknown thirteenth-century Norwegian merchant and the last three by fourteenth-century Florentines. Thus they tell us not only how these men thought merchants should behave but also reflect their own experiences in trade. The problems and situations they describe were thus quite familiar to them and not simply drawn from abstract theories.

As you read this evidence, keep in mind that even though the manuals are intended to instruct and guide, they also reflect real experience. What suggestions does each of the authors make for merchants? How do they feel merchants should behave? What should merchants avoid doing? What assumptions do the authors make about human nature? What judgment might these authors make about the contracts and accounts you have just read?

THE EVIDENCE

Sources 1 through 10 from Robert S. Lopez and Irving W. Raymond, editors and translators, Medieval Trade in the Mediterranean World *(New York: Columbia University Press, 1955), p. 145, no. 61; pp. 169–170, no. 78; p. 179, no. 84; p. 164, no. 73; p. 214, no. 103; pp. 260–261, no. 136; p. 231, no. 115; pp. 362–363, no. 179; p. 373, no. 182; pp. 159–160, no. 68.*

1. Notarial Contract

[Genoa], January 14, 1156

I, Rinaldo Gauxone, promise you, Lamberto Grillo, or your accredited messenger, £6½ in pepper or in coin [to be delivered any time] up to next Easter; otherwise [I will pay] the penalty of the double, under pledge of my orchard in Sozziglia. And you may enter into [possession] of it for the principal and the penalty on your own authority and without order by the consuls. Done in the chapter house, 1156, on the fourteenth day from the beginning of January, third indiction. Witnesses: Sismondo Muscula, B. Papa Canticula Macobrio, notary, Baldo Rubeo, watchman.

2. Notarial Contract

Constantinople, December, 1158

In the name of the Lord God and our Savior, Jesus Christ. In the year of the Lord 1158, in the month of December, seventh indiction, in Constantinople. I, Pietro Cornaro of the section of Sant' Apollinare, together with my heirs, openly declare to you, Sebastiano Ziani of the section of Santa Giustina, and to your heirs that I have received from Stefano Ziani, your brother, 100 gold hyperpers of the old weight[1] belonging to you. And with these I am to go and to do business wherever it seems good to me. And I am to carry with me the aforesaid goods (*habere*) by the convoy of ships which will come to Venice from Constantinople or from Alexandria in this first coming September, or [I am] to send the same goods from the aforesaid territories to Venice by a reliable man in the witness of good men. And then, within thirty days after that convoy of ships from the aforesaid territories enters [the waters of] Venice, I am to give and to deliver, personally or through my messenger, to you or your messenger in Venice, 125 gold hyperpers of the old weight. The aforesaid goods, however, are to remain at your risk from sea[2] and [hostile] people, provided [the risk] is proved. If I do not observe all these [conditions] for you as written above, then I, together with my heirs, am to restore to you and to your heirs all the aforesaid hyperpers in the double out of my lands and houses and of all that I am known to own in this world. And let the same capital and [the penalty of] the double bear interest of six per five every year from that time forward.

I, Pietro Cornaro, signed by my own hand.
I, Pietro Lambardo, witness, signed.
I, Marco Signorello, witness, signed.
I, Marco Bembo, witness, signed.
I, Giovanni da Noale, subdeacon and notary, completed and certified [this instrument].

3. Notarial Contract

[Genoa,] September 29, 1163

Witnesses: Simone Bucuccio, Ogerio Peloso, Ribaldo di Sauro, and Genoardo Tasca. Stabile and Ansaldo Garraton have formed a *societas* in which, as they mutually declared, Stabile contributed £88 [Genoese][3] and Ansaldo

1. **hyperpers of the old weight**: a type of Byzantine gold coin.

2. Here Cornaro indicates that he is not assuming the risk for the merchandise.

3. Each city in Italy issued its own silver coinage, often called a pound (£) though it did not weigh a pound. Each city's pound contained a different amount of silver, so contracts generally specify which city's pound is involved.

£44. Ansaldo carries this *societas*, in order to put it to work, to Tunis or to wherever goes the ship in which he shall go—namely, [the ship] of Baldizzone Grasso and Girardo. On his return [he will place the proceeds] in the power of Stabile or of his messenger for [the purpose of] division. After deducting the capital, they shall divide the profits in half. Done in the chapter house, September 29, 1163, eleventh indiction.

In addition, Stabile gave his permission to send that money to Genoa by whatever ship seems most convenient to him [to Ansaldo].

4. Notarial Contract

Genoa [February 12, 1190]

Witnesses: Giovanni Patrio, Quilego, and Ugo Caniverga. We, Guglielmo Riccuomo and Egidio de Uxel, have received from you, Rufo, banker, and Bernardo, banker, an amount of exchange for which we promise to pay to you or to your accredited messenger £69 Pavese[3] by mid-Lent. Otherwise we promise you the penalty of the double, [both of us liable] for the whole amount, etc. Done in Genoa, in the bank of Rufo, in the shop of Ogerio Vento, on the same day.

5. Notarial Contract

[Genoa,] November 7, 1200

I, Oberto, banker, of Pollanexi, acknowledge that I have received from you, Maria, wife of Rolando Generificio, £50 Genoese[3] in *accomendacio*,[4] which belong to your husband, the aforesaid Rolando. I am to keep them in the bank and to employ [them] in trade in Genoa as long as it shall be your pleasure; and I promise to give you the profit according to what seems to me ought to come to you. Moreover, I promise to return and to restore the aforesaid £50 or just as much instead of them, myself or through my messenger, to you or to your husband or to your accredited messenger, within eight days after you tell me and make the request, and similarly [to give you] the profit; otherwise the penalty of the double and the seizure of my goods as security. Done in the house of the late Baldovino de Arato. Witnesses: Rufo de Arato and Aimerico, cooper. In the year of the Nativity of the Lord 1200, third indiction, the seventh day of November.

4. **accomendacio**: a *commenda* contract.

6. Notarial Contract

[Palermo, March 24, 1350]

On the twenty-fourth of the same month. Luchino de Mari and Leonardo Cattaneo, of Genoa, of their own free will, each of them for one half, insured (*assecuraverunt*) Filippo Cavegra of Voltri, captain of that *panfilo*[5] called "Saint Ampelius," which today departed from the port of Palermo, for 200 gold florins[6] on said *panfilo* and its equipment and the right to the freight charges of the present voyage of the said *panfilo* against every risk, peril, and fortune of God, the sea, and [hostile] people which may happen to come to the aforesaid *panfilo* and its tackle and equipment from the port of Palermo and from that moment at which said *panfilo* departs from there [to the time of its arrival] at the shore of Sciacca, and from that shore as far as the port of Tunis, and from the port of Tunis as far as the port of Mazara or of Trapani—viz., as far as the one of the aforesaid ports to which said *panfilo* shall go in order to make port, going, loading, unloading, returning, [each insurer] pro rata, provided the voyage is not altered without a legitimate impediment of God, the sea, and [hostile] people. [The aforesaid is to be done] in such a way that if perchance total disaster happens to overtake the aforesaid *panfilo* and its equipment and the right to the aforesaid freight charges, said Luchino and Leonardo are to be bound to give and to pay said 200 gold florins to the same Filippo in Palermo within one month after receiving positive news; and if a partial [disaster] occurs, [they are bound to give and to pay] by that proportion and part according to which [loss] has occurred. In consideration of this insurance thus made as above the said Luchino and Leonardo, in the presence and on request of the said Filippo, solemnly acknowledged that they have had and have received from the same Filippo 28 gold florins, waiving, etc.

Witnesses: Pellegrino Coccorello, Martino Leccavela, and Giovanni Salvago.

7. Letter from an Italian Merchant

Avignon, October 5, 1339

In the name of God, amen. To Bartolo and partners [*compagni*], Barna of Lucca and partners [send] greetings from Avignon.

You shall pay by this letter on November 20, [1]339, to Landuccio Busdraghi and partners, of Lucca, gold florins three hundred twelve and three fourths

5. **panfilo**: a type of ship.

6. **florin**: a large gold coin issued by the city of Florence.

for the exchange [*per cambio*] of gold florins three hundred, because I have received such money today from Tancredi Bonagiunta and partners at the rate [*raxione*] of $4\frac{1}{4}$ per 100 to their advantage. And charge [it] to our account. •Done on October 5, [1]339.

Francesco Falconetti has ordered us to pay in your behalf 230 gold *scudi*[7] to the Acciajuoli [*compagnia*].

[*Address on the outside;*]

To Bartolo Casini and partners, in Pisa.

[*Mark of Barna of Lucca*]

8. Merchant's Account Book

Carcassonne, 1340

Senher Ber. of St. Esteve, nobleman, lord of Lastours, owes s.4[8] which we lent him. To be paid . . . on October 3.

Mosenher the major judge of Carcassonne owes s.18 for 3 palms of medley French [cloth], which was for the lining of the cape which Maestro Crestiá Rocafort took. Paid s.18. . . .

Riquart, wife of the late En Adam of Rovenay, of the city of Carcassonne, owes s.10 for 2 palms of vermilion and for $1\frac{1}{2}$ palms of white [cloth], which was for hose with edging for her, which she took on Wednesday, October 4. Also, she owes d.1. Also, she owes d.1. Also, she owes d.1. Also, she owes d.1. Remains [to be paid] s.10 d.4. Also, she owes d.1. Paid s.3 d.11 medal. Paid s.6 d.5 medal.

Senher Uc Garie, £11 for 4 *canas* of *cameli*.[9] Paid £11.

Senher Peyre Fabre of Pomas owes s.4 which we lent to Jacme Rog of Villefranche de Conflent. Also, he owes 15 gold *dobles*[10] because of what we lent him on Sunday, October 8. Paid in full.

7. **scudi**: a gold coin issued by various Italian cities.

8. Most money systems in medieval Europe were based on the following equivalents: 1 pound (£) = 20 shillings (s) = 240 pence (d). A medal was worth $\frac{1}{2}$ pence.

9. **cameli**: a type of cloth.

10. **doble:** a gold coin issued in Spain.

9. Merchant's Account Book

[Milan], 1396

Andreolo of Concorezzo must give—Credited to the account of Giovannino of Dugnano on folio 8 on March 17 £16 s.-d.-

Item—[credited] to Marco Serrainerio on folio 6 on March 31—[for money] which he [Marco] paid to him £4 s.16 d.-

Item—[credited] to said Marco on folio 6 on April 28—[for money] deposited in [the bank of] Manno, [son] of Ser Jacopo £10 s.-d.-

Item—[credited] to said Marco, on folio 6 on May 6—[for money] deposited in [the bank of] Paolino of Osnago £6 s.8 d.-

Item—[credited] to said Marco on folio 6 on May 16—[for money] deposited in [the bank of] Paolino of Osnago for the remainder £12 s.-d.-

Item—for the balance posted to the common credit, profit, and loss [of the partnership] on folio 20 on aforesaid day £ -s.7 d.6

Total £49 s.11 d.6

He [*Andreolo*] *must have*—Debited to the account of Merceries on folio 18 on March 6—for 12 thousand needles for sacks, marked Antonio £10 s.16 d.-

Item, posted as above on aforesaid day, for 12 thousand long needles, marked Masso, at s.13 [per thousand] £7 s.16 d.-

Item, posted as above; for 24 thousand long needles, marked Stefano, at s.12 d.9 [per thousand] £15 s.6 d.-

Item, posted as above, for 12 thousand old woman's needles . . . marked with a ship, at s.8 [per thousand] £4 s.16 d.-

Item, posted as above, for 12 thousand old woman's needles, large, marked with a ship, at s.12 d.9 [per thousand] £7 s.14 d.-

Item, posted as above, for 3 thousand needles for fine shoes, at s.21 d.6 [per thousand] £3 s.4 d.6

Total £49 s.11 d.6

10. Letter from a Merchant to a Church Official

[Siena, September 27, 1221]

On the same day. I, Aringhiero d'Altavilla, promise you, Magister Pietro, rector of the church of S. Pietro delle Scale, and I swear on the holy Gospels of God that if I escape from this illness I shall be and remain [obedient] to the order of the lord bishop of Siena in regard to the usuries which I have collected up to this day, satisfying whoever proves to me his legal [claims] in regard to them and making restitution of these [usuries] as he [the bishop] shall charge me. And in regard to the excommunication laid upon me in the case of the money of Boncompagno, late of the monastery, I shall likewise be [obedient] to his order, so far as it concerns my part.

And I, Mezzolombardo d'Altavilla, in his behalf promise you and swear that if said Aringhiero dies from this illness, I shall remain [obedient] to and shall observe, in regard to the aforesaid, the order of the lord bishop, according to the form and content mentioned above. In the presence of Tornampuglia, [son] of Salsidone, Rustichino, [son] of Sinibaldo, Bartolo of Leonessa, and many others invited.

Source 11 from L. M. Larson, editor and translator, The King's Mirror *(New York: American Scandinavian Foundation, 1917), pp. 79–81, 84–85.*

11. Letter from a Norwegian Merchant, 13th century

The man who is to be a trader will have to brave many perils, sometimes at sea and sometimes in heathen lands, but nearly always among alien peoples; and it must be his constant purpose to act discreetly wherever he happens to be. On the sea he must be alert and fearless.

When you are in a market town, or wherever you are, be polite and agreeable; then you will secure the friendship of all good men. Make it a habit to rise early in the morning, and go first and immediately to church. . . .

When the services are over, go out to look after your business affairs. If you are unacquainted with the traffic of the town, observe carefully how those who are reputed the best and most prominent merchants conduct their business. You must also be careful to examine the wares that you buy before the purchase is finally made to make sure that they are sound and flawless. And whenever you make a purchase, call in a few trusty men to serve as witnesses as to how the bargain was made.

You should keep occupied with your business till breakfast or, if necessity demands it, till midday; after that you should eat your meal. Keep your table well provided and set with a white cloth, clean victuals, and good drinks. Serve enjoyable meals, if you can afford it.

Finally, remember this, that whenever you have an hour to spare you should give thought to your studies, especially to the law books; for it is clear that those who gain knowledge from books have keener wits than others, since those who are the most learned have the best proofs for their knowledge. Make a study of all the laws. . . . If you are acquainted with the law, you will not be annoyed by quibbles when you have suits to bring against men of your own class, but will be able to plead according to law in every case.

But although I have most to say about laws, I regard no man perfect in knowledge unless he has thoroughly learned and mastered the customs of the place where he is sojourning. And if you wish to become perfect in knowledge, you must learn all the languages, first of all Latin and French, for these idioms are most widely used; and yet, do not neglect your native tongue or speech.

And further, there are certain things which you must beware of and shun like the devil himself: these are drinking, chess, harlots, quarreling, and throwing dice for stakes. For upon such foundations the greatest calamities are built; and unless they strive to avoid these things, few only are able to live long without blame or sin.

Observe carefully how the sky is lighted, the course of the heavenly bodies, the grouping of the hours, and the points of the horizon. Learn also how to mark the movements of the ocean and to discern how its turmoil ebbs and swells; for that is knowledge which all must possess who wish to trade abroad. Learn arithmetic thoroughly, for merchants have great need of that.

If you come to a place where the king or some other chief who is in authority has his officials, seek to win their friendship; and if they demand any necessary fees on the ruler's behalf, be prompt to render all such payments, lest by holding too tightly to little things you lose the greater. . . . If you can dispose of your wares at suitable prices, do not hold them long; for it is the wont of merchants to buy constantly and to sell rapidly. . . .

If you attend carefully to all these things, with God's mercy you may hope for success. This, too, you must keep constantly in mind, if you wish to be counted a wise man, that you ought never to let a day pass without learning something that will profit you. Be not like those who think it beneath their dignity to hear or learn from others such things even as might avail them much if they knew them. For a man must regard it as great an honor to learn as to teach, if he wishes to be considered thoroughly informed. . . .

Keep your temper calm though not to the point of suffering abuse or bringing upon yourself the reproach of cowardice. Though necessity may force you into strife, be not in a hurry to take revenge; first make sure that your effort will succeed and strike where it ought. Never display a heated temper when you see that you are likely to fail, but be sure to maintain your honor at some later time, unless your opponent should offer a satisfactory atonement.

If your wealth takes on rapid growth, divide it and invest it in a partnership trade in fields where you do not yourself travel; but be cautious in selecting partners. Always let Almighty God, the holy Virgin Mary, and the saint whom you have most frequently called upon to intercede for you be counted among your partners. Watch with care over the property which the saints are to share with you and always bring it faithfully to the place to which it was originally promised.

Sources 12 through 14 from Robert S. Lopez and Irving W. Raymond, editors and translators, Medieval Trade in the Mediterranean World *(New York: Columbia University Press, 1955), p. 422, no. 204; pp. 423–424, no. 205; pp. 425–426, no. 208.*

12. An Italian Merchant's Advice

[Florence, 1393]

If you engage in the wool or French-cloth business, do [it] on your own and do not try to grow rich in two days. Manage on your own money and never borrow for profit's sake. Transact your business with trustworthy persons who enjoy good reputation and credit and who have something to show for their name. And if you ever get cheated by them, do not again fall into their clutches. Do not sell your merchandise to persons who may be willing to overpay for it; never be ensnared by greed for [high] prices; always demand flawless records; better go slowly, [but] do go safely.

If you exercise the wool craft (*Arte di Lana*), manage on your own money. Be not eager to send your merchandise abroad unless you have someone to whom it matters as much as to you. If you can do without a partner (*compagno*) do so. If you cannot, get a partner wisely—a good and rich man, and not one higher than you, especially in [social] status or in [connection with] families with overbearing manners.

Do not exercise any trade or business in which you have no experience. Do what you are able to do and beware of everything else, for [otherwise] you would be cheated. And if you want to become experienced in anything, practise it as a child, be in shops (*fondachi*) and in banks with others, go abroad, frequent merchants and merchandise, see with [your own] eyes the places and countries where you have in mind to do business. Try a friend—or rather the man whom you believe to be a friend—a hundred times before you rely upon him a single time, and never rely upon anyone so deeply that he may ruin you. Go cautiously in [placing] your confidence, and do not be gullible, and the more one shows himself loyal to you and wise in words, the less trust him. And do not trust at all one who makes overtures to you in anything. Enjoy listening to tall talkers, braggers, and men lavish of compliments, and give words [in return] for words; but do not give any credit that may bring harm to you, and do not rely upon them at all. As for Pharisees and hypocrites smiting themselves and covering themselves with the cloak of religion, rely not upon them but sooner [rely] upon a soldier. Have nothing to do with one who has often changed his business, partners, and masters. And with one who gambles, lives in luxury, overdresses, feasts himself, or is a scatterbrain—do not get involved by entrusting your goods or committing your business to him.

If you do business abroad, go often yourself—at least once a year—to see and to settle the accounts. Watch what [kind of] life the man who is abroad in your behalf leads—whether he spends too much. [Make sure] that he extends sound credits, that he does not rush to [start] things or lies down too low[?], that he acts cautiously and never oversteps instructions. Should he cheat you in anything, fire him.

And always behave with wisdom and do not get involved. And never show off your wealth but keep it hidden, and always by words and acts make people believe that you possess one half as much as you have. By following this course you cannot be too badly cheated, neither you nor those who will be left after you.

13. Giovanni Frescobaldi, *A Bit of Advice for Those Who Cross to England*

[Florence, early fourteenth century]

Wear modest colors, be humble, be dull in appearance but in fact be subtle: if the Englishman [tries to] floor you, woe to him!

Flee cares as well as any one who fights you; spend bravely, and do not show yourself mean.[11]

Pay on the day [when payment is due and be] courteous in collecting, showing that need is driving you to the grave. Make no more demands than you are entitled to.

Buy in [good] time if you have good prospects—and do not get involved with people at court. Obey the orders of those who are in authority.

It behooves you to club together with your nation, and see to it that your doors are well bolted early.

14. Dino Compagni, *Song on Worthy Conduct*

[Florence, beginning of the fourteenth century]

A merchant wishing that his worth be great
Must always act according as is right;
And let him be a man of long foresight,
And never fail his promises to keep.
Let him be pleasant, if he can, of looks,
As fits the honor'd calling that he chose;
Open when selling, but when buying close;
Genial in greeting and without complaints.
He will be worthier if he goes to church,
Gives for the love of God, clinches his deals
Without a haggle, and wholly repeals
Usury taking. Further, he must write
Accounts well-kept and free from oversight.

11. **mean**: cheap.

QUESTIONS TO CONSIDER

This period of European history has been dubbed the Commercial Revolution for three reasons: an increase in the sheer volume of trade in Europe, increasing sophistication and complexity of business procedures, and a new attitude toward business and making money. The evidence you have examined does not give you information about the first reason, but it can help you assess the latter two.

To evaluate the change in business procedures, we need to return to the first ten documents, paying particular attention to their dates and to the smaller details that indicate change. Economic revolutions do not occur within a few years the way political revolutions do, but we should be able to notice economic change over time. Look again at these documents, one by one. What problem of the medieval economy does the first document reveal? Do any of the later documents refer to this method of payment? What did the borrower pledge as security for his loan? What does that pledge reveal about the flow of capital? Do any of the other documents hint at the source of the investors' money? What risks are described in the second document? Do any of the later documents discuss these same risks? Do they suggest any ways of avoiding the risks?

What does the third document reveal about family relationships? Do any of the other contracts give you further information about families? Why did the partners in document 3 get an equal return on their investments when their original investments were not the same? You have probably noticed that the original amount in document 4 was not specified. Why might this be? Document 5 is a male banker's contract with a woman. Who determined how much profit she is to receive? How does this arrangement differ from the practices in other contracts you have read? What might account for the differences?

Document 9 is an account book with debits and credits listed separately, a procedure known as *double-entry bookkeeping*. Why has this been called the most important change in the history of accounting? Did you also notice any differences in the types of currencies described in the two accounts? Why might the use of these currencies be significant?

Though the Church disapproved of charging interest on a loan, most of the contracts openly discuss interest. Why do you think they do this? Does your explanation fit with what you have learned from document 10? Do you think this merchant would have agreed with the advice given in the final four documents?

The new "capitalist spirit" toward making money is much harder to document than changes in business procedure. Why so? As you read the selections from the advice manuals, what attitude toward profit and money did you detect? Do you find evidence of older attitudes as well? How would you compare the advice given by these merchants with that you might expect to receive from a professor at the Harvard Business School? Are you surprised by the similarities or the differences?

EPILOGUE

The Commercial Revolution was a slow and gradual process like every major economic change. The new business procedures developed by the Italians spread only very slowly to the rest of Europe; not until the fifteenth or sixteenth century, for example, did northern European merchants take up double-entry bookkeeping. As more small investors combined their resources to fund trading ventures, the concept of *limited liability* developed so that, in case of a shipwreck or failed venture, investors lost only their original investments, and not all their property, as stipulated in the contracts you have just read.

The European banking and monetary system remained chaotic for several more centuries. The banks that developed out of the *compagnie* partnerships often made enormous loans to rulers and then collapsed when the rulers defaulted on their loans; when a bank collapsed, the investments of all depositors were lost. (This state of affairs remained unchanged until the bank collapses of the Great Depression of the 1930s, when governments began to see the need for insuring bank deposits.) Merchants continued to handle many different currencies, although gradually certain currencies, such as the Venetian ducat and the English pound, became more favored and automatically acceptable throughout Europe. All paper tender was still issued by private banks; not until the seventeenth century did any nation begin issuing paper currency.

Attitudes toward merchants also changed gradually. Though the Church relaxed its absolute position on usury and conceded that merchants might be allowed entrance to heaven, widespread resentment was still directed against merchants and bankers, especially when some merchant families began to accumulate wealth that was almost unimaginable by that era's standards. Less discreet about their wealth than the advice manuals recommended, merchants irritated and offended the often less wealthy noble class. As Italian bankers began to replace the Jews as Europe's prime moneylenders, they were insulted and occasionally physically attacked, though not to the degree that Jews were abused. (Shakespeare's plays, for example, refer to "greedy Lombards," or Italians.)

Despite the slow speed of these economic and attitudinal changes, Italian business practices gradually spread to the rest of Europe. Northern European merchants, especially the Dutch and the English, took the lead in the seventeenth century and developed such economic institutions as the stock market. They also turned medieval attitudes toward business upside down by formulating the idea that success in business was a sign of God's favor and poverty a sign of moral and spiritual degeneracy. When the Europeans established colonies, they took capitalism with them. By the nineteenth century, most of the world had experienced a Commercial Revolution.

CHAPTER NINE

CRAFT GUILDS: ECONOMIC CHANGE AND SOCIAL CONFLICT

THE PROBLEM

The Commercial Revolution of the eleventh and twelfth centuries, with its reinvigoration of trade and development of a strong merchant class, came with, and was one of the causes for, a rebirth of town life. Especially in Italy and the Low Countries, but in many other parts of Europe as well, towns began to spring up around cathedrals, monasteries, and castles, or at locations favorable for trade such as ports or major crossroads. Some were totally new cities, but many developed on the sites of former Roman towns or Roman border camps.

As a town grew, its merchants and traders often joined together to form a guild that prohibited nonmembers from trading in the town. These same merchants often made up the earliest town government, serving as mayors and members of the city council, so that a town's economic policies were determined by its merchants' self-interests. Acting through the city council, the merchants' guilds determined the hours that markets would be open, decided which coins would be accepted as currency, and set prices on imported and local goods. Foreign affairs were also guided by the merchants, who chose as their allies either good trading partners or those who could prove useful against a competitor city. In many cities and towns, the merchants' guild was to all intents the city government, despite the official distinction between the two institutions.

Though the initial impetus to establish a town often came from trade and commerce, towns quickly became centers of production as well. A growing population attracted food and clothing producers; the wealth of the merchants drew producers of luxury goods. Merchants often imported raw materials such as wool or metals and supported the development of industries that manufactured products such as cloth and weaponry from these materials, then exported the finished products to other areas. Certain cities became known for their fine woolens or silks, their rugged arms and armor, or their elegant gold and silver work.

Like merchants, producers recognized the benefits of organization. The twelfth century witnessed the birth of craft guilds that regulated most aspects of production. Each guild set standards of quality for its products and regulated the size of workshops, the training period required to become a member, and the conduct of members. In most cities individual guilds, such as those of the shoemakers or blacksmiths, achieved a monopoly in the production and sales of one product, forbidding nonmembers to work at their trade. In some towns each craft formed its own guild; by the thirteenth and fourteenth centuries more than one hundred separate craft guilds had been formed in many cities throughout Europe. In other towns related crafts were combined within larger guilds.

Each guild set the pattern by which its members were trained. To become a shoemaker, for instance, it was necessary to spend about seven years as an apprentice and then at least that long as a journeyman working in the shop of a master shoemaker. At this time the journeyman was entitled to make his *masterpiece*. If the masterpiece was approved by the other master shoemakers and if they thought the market for shoes large enough in their town to accommodate another shoemaker, the journeyman became a master and opened his own shop. Though the time required to be an apprentice and journeyman varied slightly from guild to guild, all guilds followed this same three-stage process. Apprentices and journeymen usually lived with the master and his family and were often forbidden to marry. Conversely, most guilds required that masters be married, as they believed a wife was absolutely essential to the running of the shop and household and, moreover, that married men were likely to be more stable and dependable.

The master's wife assisted in running the shop, often selling the goods her husband had produced. Their children, both male and female, worked alongside the apprentices and journeymen; sons were sometimes formally apprenticed but daughters were not, because most guilds limited formal membership to males. Most guilds did allow a master's widow to continue operating a shop for a set period of time after her husband's death, for they recognized she had the necessary skills and experience. Such widows paid all the required guild dues but did not vote or hold office in the guilds because they were not considered full members. The fact that women were not formally guild members did not mean that they did not work in guild shops, however; along with the master's wife and daughters, female domestic servants often performed the tasks requiring less skill. In addition, a few all-female guilds were formed in several European cities, particularly Cologne and Paris, in which girls were formally apprenticed in the same way boys were in regular craft guilds.

Practitioners of a craft or trade required the permission of the city council to form a guild. Once this permission was granted, the guild could write its own ordinances and regulations. At first these ordinances were usually very brief, but over the centuries they were expanded as new problems arose or the guild tried to clear up ambiguities. The guild often set up a court to hear disputes between members, though a town's municipal court established by the city council remained the final arbiter; this municipal court also handled disputes between two guilds or between a guild and a nonmember. Guilds were jealous of their rights and privileges and quick to complain when they felt someone was infringing on their monopoly. They were also careful to maintain the quality of their products by appointing several members to be inspectors; these inspectors visited workshops frequently, confiscating or destroying any product not up to standard. Guilds discouraged competition between masters by limiting the amount of raw materials each master could own and the size of the workshops, thus assuring each master that his household-workshop would be able to support itself.

Guilds were not simply economic organizations but also systems of social support. Though hostile to outsiders, they were protective and supportive of their own. They supported elderly masters who could no longer work as well as widows and orphans. Guilds maintained an altar at a city church and paid for the funerals of members and the baptisms of their children. Guild members marched together in city parades, reinforcing their feelings of solidarity by special ceremonies and distinctive dress.

As craft guilds grew in economic power, they began to demand a share of the political power in their city and thus came into conflict with the city councils, which were dominated by merchants. After its first emergence in the fourteenth century, this conflict was to continue for centuries in many cities. In some cities, particularly in the Low Countries, the guilds triumphed, taking over control of the city's political as well as economic life. In others, the merchants triumphed and excluded all craftsmen from political power. In still others, a compromise was reached whereby the guilds were allowed some members on the council and the council some power over the guilds.

During periods of high growth in their towns and times of economic prosperity, the guilds welcomed new members and the establishment of more and larger workshops. These workshops provided an important means of education and socialization for young people, placing them together with others their age learning the same skills. Apprentices and journeymen identified both with their peer group of young people at the same level of training and with the masters in their craft, whom they sought to emulate. Guilds also facilitated the mobility of labor, for a journeyman carrying a letter of apprenticeship could travel from town to town in search of the best opportunity for opening up a shop; theoretically, at least, he was entitled to be taken on by any master. (This period of travel is the origin of the term *journeyman.*)

During periods of economic depression the guilds were not so successful. At these times they generally tried to limit membership so that supply of their product would not exceed demand. Only sons who inherited a shop from their fathers, or men who married masters' widows or daughters, were allowed to become masters. This meant that journeymen might remain journeymen their entire lives and never become masters. Journeymen who had been deprived of full guild membership in this way lost their sense of solidarity with the masters in their craft. In some cities they formed separate journeymen's guilds to defend their interests against those of the masters, demanding changes in their conditions of employment, including the right to marry and live in their own households as well as the right to determine who would work in the shop. To ensure workplaces for themselves, the journeymen tried to exclude anyone who was not an apprentice or journeyman. In some cases they even tried to prevent the master's wife and children from working, though in this effort they were rarely successful. These conflicts within guilds were accompanied by increasing conflicts between guilds and the city council, for councils felt the guilds' restrictive policies did not work to the economic advantage of the town as a whole.

Though in every town some production—especially of simple items such as soap, candles, and wooden dishes—remained free of guild control, the craft guilds were the most important institutions shaping patterns of employment and daily life in medieval towns. Often the majority of a town's population worked in guild shops and lived in households headed by master craftsmen. Guild records consequently provide information not only about guilds themselves but also about many other economic and social issues. In particular, they highlight the varying responses of different groups of people to conflicts and problems in late medieval urban life. Your task in this chapter will be to use guild records to explore economic and social change in late medieval cities. What sorts of changes did the guilds view as problems, and how did they respond? What do their reactions tell us about the attitudes of this group of what we might term "middle-class" people?

SOURCES AND METHOD

We can find information about medieval craft guilds in a huge variety of sources, because record keeping was an important facet of guild activity. In general these sources can be divided into two basic types, a division that holds equally for sources from many other historical periods, as we have seen in Chapter 8. The first type is prescriptive—laws, regulations, and ordinances describing how the guild was supposed to operate and how the masters who wrote the ordinances hoped things would be. These documents do not simply describe an ideal, however, but were generally written in response to events already taking place, and so can tell us about real problems and the attitudes of the guild masters toward these problems. What they cannot tell us is if any of the proposed solutions worked, or what problems the solutions themselves caused. For this we have to turn to the second type of primary evidence, descriptive documents such as court records, city council minutes, and petitions and supplications submitted by individuals. Through these records we can observe how the guilds attempted to enforce their regulations and how these regulations were circumvented or ignored. As you read the guild records, then, the first question you must ask yourself is whether a given document is prescriptive or descriptive, for confusing the two types of evidence can give a very skewed view of what life in a medieval city was like. (This kind of discrimination must be applied to any historical source, of course, and is not always an easy task. Sometimes even prominent historians have built a whole pyramid of erroneous theories about the past by assuming that prescriptive sources accurately described reality. We investigated only one example of this in Chapter 2 on classical Athens.)

The first eight selections are all taken from guild ordinances: Sources 1 and 2 from fourteenth-century England, Source 3 from thirteenth-century Paris, Sources 4 through 8 from sixteenth-century Germany. Read each carefully, both for the problems discussed explicitly and for the underlying concerns and attitudes of the masters writing these ordinances. At this point you may want to begin a three-column list or chart, one column for explicitly stated problems, a second for the solutions proposed in the documents, and a third for your speculations about the reasons that certain events were seen as problems or that a given solution was suggested. The regulations also provide a great deal of general information on conditions of apprenticeship, maximum size of the workshop, length of the workday, and noneconomic functions of the guild such as religious activities and support of impoverished members.

Though all these selections are guild ordinances, some differences exist among them that may shape your conclusions. Source 3 concerns a women's guild, the silk spinners of Paris; all the others pertain to the more common men's guilds. Do you see any gender-related features in the regulations of the all-female guild? How would you describe the work of women in the other guilds? Sources 4 through 8 all come from the sixteenth century, a time when many guilds felt threatened and grew increasingly restrictive. What specific measures did the guilds take to reduce competition? Were these steps completely new, or did they follow a pattern that had been set by earlier ordinances as represented by the first and second documents?

Documents 9 through 11 are supplications or petitions. Source 9 is addressed to the English Parliament by the silk women of London; and

Sources 10 and 11 to the city council of Frankfurt, Germany by two widows. What problems were they seeking redress for? What solutions did they propose? Documents 10 and 11 discuss actions already taken by a guild. How do these actions reflect the guild's aims? What sorts of regulations were the guild trying to enforce?

The sources you have read so far have given you some impression not only of the guild masters and their aims and attitudes, but also of the relationship between the guilds and the city council. Before proceeding to the last group of sources, look at your list, or reread the previous documents, to assess the role of the town's political authorities. When did they become involved in the enforcement of guild regulations? How do the regulations and supplications refer to these authorities? When did individuals go to the city council or other authorities for assistance?

Now read the last four sources, which describe decisions or actions by a city council that relate to guild matters. Sources 12 and 13 come from fourteenth-century Flanders; Sources 14 and 15 from sixteenth-century Germany. These documents also bring up problems, propose solutions, and reflect attitudes, and so can be added to your list, though of course they reflect the opinions of the city council, not of the guild masters. Compare the information on your list from these sources with that from the earlier selections. Which problems did both groups consider important? How did the solutions proposed by the city council differ from those proposed by the guilds? What does this divergence tell you about the underlying attitudes of the two groups and about possible sources of conflict within the city?

THE EVIDENCE

Source 1 from James Harvey Robinson, editor and translator, Readings in European History, *vol. 1 (Boston: Ginn, 1904), pp. 409–411.*

1. Ordinance of the Spurriers' [Spurmakers'] Guild of London, 1345

Be it remembered, that on Tuesday, the morrow of St. Peter's bonds, in the nineteenth year of the reign of King Edward III, the articles underwritten were read before John Hammond, mayor, Roger de Depham, recorder, and the other aldermen; and seeing that the same were deemed befitting, they were accepted and enrolled in these words.

In the first place, that no one of the trade of spurriers shall work longer than from the beginning of the day until curfew rings out at the church of

St. Sepulcher, without Newgate;[1] by reason that no man can work so neatly by night as by day. And many persons of the said trade, who compass[2] how to practice deception in their work, desire to work by night rather than by day; and then they introduce false iron, and iron that has been cracked, for tin, and also they put gilt on false copper, and cracked.

And further, many of the said trade are wandering about all day, without working at all at their trade; and then, when they have become drunk and frantic, they take to their work, to the annoyance of the sick and all their neighborhood as well, by reason of the broils[3] that arise between them and the strange folk who are dwelling among them. And then they blow up their fires so vigorously, that their forges begin all at once to blaze, to the great peril of themselves and of all the neighborhood around. And then, too, all the neighbors are much in dread of the sparks, which so vigorously issue forth in all directions from the mouths of the chimneys in their forges.

By reason thereof it seems unto them that working by night should be put an end to, in order to avoid such false work and such perils; and therefore the mayor and the aldermen do will, by the assent of the good folk of the said trade and for the common profit, that from henceforth such time for working, and such false work made in the trade, shall be forbidden. And if any person shall be found in the said trade to do the contrary hereof, let him be amerced,[4] the first time in forty pence,[5] one half to go to the use of the Chamber of the Guildhall of London, and the other half to the use of the said trade; the second time, in half a mark;[5] and the third time, in ten shillings,[5] to the use of the same Chamber and trade; and the fourth time, let him forswear the trade forever.

Also, that no one of the said trade shall hang his spurs out on Sundays, or on any other days that are double feasts; but only a sign indicating his business; and such spurs as they shall so sell, they are to show and sell within their shops, without exposing them without or opening the doors or windows of their shops, on the pain aforesaid.

Also, that no one of the said trade shall keep a house or shop to carry on his business, unless he is free of the city;[6] and that no one shall cause to be sold, or exposed for sale, any manner of old spurs for new ones, or shall garnish them or change them for new ones.

Also, that no one of the said trade shall take an apprentice for a less term than seven years, and such apprentice shall be enrolled according to the usages of the said city.

1. **without Newgate:** just outside the gate to the city called Newgate.
2. **compass:** know.
3. **broil:** fight.
4. **amerced:** fined.
5. **pence:** small silver coins; 12 pence = 1 shilling; 160 pence = 1 mark.
6. **free of the city:** a citizen.

Also, that if any one of the said trade, who is not a freeman, shall take an apprentice for a term of years, he shall be amerced as aforesaid.

Also, that no one of the said trade shall receive the apprentice, serving man, or journeyman of another in the same trade, during the term agreed upon between his master and him, on the pain aforesaid.

Also, that no alien of another country, or foreigner of this country, shall follow or use the said trade, unless he is enfranchised before the mayor, aldermen, and chamberlain; and that, by witness and surety[7] of the good folk of the said trade, who will go surety for him, as to his loyalty and his good behavior.

Also, that no one of the said trade shall work on Saturdays, after *nones*[8] has been rung out in the city; and not from that hour until the Monday morning following.

Source 2 from Edward P. Cheney, editor and translator, Translations and Reprints from the Original Sources of European History, *vol. 2, no. 1 (Philadelphia, University of Pennsylvania Press, no date), pp. 23–25.*

2. Ordinance of the White-Tawyers'[9] Guild of London, 1346

In honor of God, of Our Lady, and of All Saints, and for the nurture of tranquillity and peace among the good folks the megucers, called white-tawyers, the folks of the same trade have, by assent of Richard Lacer, mayor, and of the aldermen, ordained the points under-written.

In the first place, they have ordained that they will find a wax candle, to burn before our Lady in the church of Allhallows, near London wall.

Also, that each person of the said trade shall put in the box such sum as he shall think fit, in aid of maintaining the said candle.

Also, if by chance any one of the said trade shall fall into poverty, whether through old age or because he cannot labor or work, and have nothing with which to keep himself, he shall have every week from the said box 7d. for his support, if he be a man of good repute. And after his decease, if he have a wife, a woman of good repute, she shall have weekly for her support 7d. from the said box, so long as she shall behave herself well and keep single.

And that no stranger shall work in the said trade, or keep house for the same in the city, if he be not an apprentice, or a man admitted to the franchise of the said city.

7. **surety:** guarantee.
8. **nones:** about 3 p.m.
9. **white-tawyer:** a person who dressed leather with salt, alum and other substances, giving it a white surface.

And that no one shall take the serving-man of another to work with him, during his term, unless it be with the permission of his master.

And if any one of the said trade shall have work in his house that he cannot complete, or if for want of assistance such work shall be in danger of being lost, those of the said trade shall aid him, that so the said work be not lost.

And if any one of the said trade shall depart this life, and have not wherewithal to be buried, he shall be buried at the expense of their common box. And when any one of the said trade shall die, all those of the said trade shall go to the vigil, and make offering on the morrow.

And if any serving-man shall conduct himself in any other manner than properly towards his master, and act rebelliously toward him, no one of the said trade shall set him to work, until he shall have made amends before the mayor and aldermen; and before them such misprision[10] shall be redressed.

Also,— that the good folks of the same trade shall once in the year be assembled in a certain place, convenient thereto, there to choose two men of the most loyal and benefitting of the same trade, to be overseers of work and all other things touching the trade for that year; which persons shall be presented to the mayor and aldermen for the time being, and sworn before them diligently to inquire and make search, and loyally to present to the said mayor and aldermen such defaults as they shall find touching the said trade without sparing anyone for friendship or for hatred, or in any other manner. And if any one of the said trade shall be found rebellious against the said overseers, so as not to let them properly make their search and assay, as they ought to do; or if he shall absent himself from the meeting aforesaid, without reasonable cause, after due warning by the said overseers, he shall pay to the Chamber, upon the first default, 40d.; and on the second like default, half a mark; and on the third one mark; and on the fourth, 20s., and shall forswear the trade forever.

Also, that if the overseers shall be found lax and negligent about their duty, or partial to any person for gift or for friendship, maintaining him or voluntarily permitting him to continue in his default, and shall not present him to the mayor and aldermen, as before stated, they are to incur the penalty foresaid.

Also, that each year, at such assemblies of the good folks of the said trade, there shall be chosen overseers, as before stated. And if it be found that through laxity or negligence of the said governors such assemblies are not held, each of the said overseers is to incur the said penalty.

Also, that all skins falsely and deceitfully wrought in their trade which the said overseers shall find on sale in the hands of any person, citizen or foreigner, within the franchise shall be forfeited to the said chamber, and the worker thereof amerced in manner aforesaid.

10. **misprision:** misconduct.

Also, that no one who has not been an apprentice, and has not finished his term of apprenticeship in the said trade, shall be made free of the same trade; unless it be attested by the overseers for the time being, or by four persons of the said trade, that such person is able and sufficiently skilled to be made free of the same.

Source 3 from Julia O'Faolain and Lauro Martines, editors, Not in God's Image: Women in History from the Greeks to the Victorians *(New York: Harper & Row, 1973),* pp. 137–139.

3. Ordinance of the Silk Spinsters in Paris, 1254–1271

Any woman who wishes to be a silk spinster on large spindles in the city of Paris—i.e., reeling, spinning, doubling and retwisting—may freely do so, provided she observe the following customs and usages of the craft:

No spinster on large spindles may have more than three apprentices, unless they be her own or her husband's children born in true wedlock; nor may she contract with them for an apprenticeship of less than seven years or for a fee of less than 20 Parisian sols[11] to be paid to her, their mistress. The apprenticeship shall be for eight years if there is no fee, but she may accept more years and money if she can get them. . . .

No woman of the said craft may hire an apprentice or workgirl who has not completed her years of service with the mistress to whom she was apprenticed. If a spinster has assumed an apprentice, she may not take on another before the first has completed her seven years unless the apprentice die or forswear the craft forever.[12] If an apprentice spinster buy her freedom before serving the said seven years, she may not herself take on an apprentice until she has practiced the craft for seven years. If any spinster sell her apprentice, she shall owe six deniers to the guardians appointed in the King's name to guard the [standards of the] craft. The buyer shall also owe six deniers. . . .

If a working woman comes from outside Paris and wishes to practice the said craft in the city, she must swear before two guardians of the craft that she will practice it well and loyally and conform to its customs and usages.

If anyone give a woman of the said craft silk to be spun and the woman pawn it and the owner complain, the fine shall be 5 sols.

11. **sol, denier:** silver coins minted in France. In general, 12 deniers = 1 sol.

12. This appears to conflict with the first sentence in the second paragraph, but can be explained if we understand that **apprentice** in this paragraph is shorthand for **apprentice-spinster**, or what in other guilds would be called **journeyman** (there is no female equivalent in French for journeyman). Thus a girl would be an apprentice for seven or eight years (as stated in the second paragraph), an apprentice-spinster for another seven years, and finally a spinster.

No workwoman shall farm out another's silk to be worked upon outside her own house.

The said craft has as guardians two men of integrity sworn in the King's name but appointed and changed at the will of the provost of Paris. Taking an oath in the provost's presence, they shall swear to guard the craft truly, loyally, and to their utmost, and to inform him or his agents of all malpractices discovered therein.

Any spinster who shall infringe any of the above rules shall pay the King a fine of 5 sols for each offense . . . [from which the craft guardians deduct their own expenses].

Source 4 from Merry E. Wiesner, translator, unpublished ordinance in Memmingen Stadtarchiv, Zünfte, 471-1.

4. Tailors' Ordinance from Memmingen (Germany), 1543

Concerning seamstresses: All seamstresses who are not citizens here are to be sent away and forbidden to do any work as seamstresses in this city.

For those who are citizens, it is ordered that no one shall serve an apprenticeship of less than one year, and after this a period as a journeyman for at least one year, before she is allowed to become a master. She is also never to do anything which is limited to members of the tailors' or furriers' guild, and is to pay the guild five shillings [when she is taken on as a master]. She is to obey all regulations and ordinances. A woman who wants to become master is to appear before the sworn overseers,[13] who will test her on what she knows and explain the ordinances, which she will be expected to follow from that point on.

Those who do not follow the above regulations on one or more points are to be appropriately corrected and punished by the sworn overseers.

13. **overseer:** official in charge of the guild, who swore an oath to enforce its rules.

Sources 5 through 8 from Merry E. Wiesner, translator, unpublished ordinances in Nuremberg Stadtarchiv, Quellen zur Nürnbergische Geschichte, Rep. F5, no. 68/II, fol. 663; no. 68/I, fol. 441; no 68/I, fol. 29; no. 68/I, fol. 115.

5. Ringmakers' Guild Ordinance, Nuremberg (Germany), 16th century

No one is to make use of any domestic servant to do any work in this craft from now on. This includes any and all work or assistance, with a fine of four pounds for each infraction.

Some journeymen are now marrying before they become masters, and using their wives to assist them in the craft, which has led to disputes. Therefore this ordinance is expanded: Because it is forbidden for female domestic servants to do anything associated with the craft, those women whose husbands are not yet masters are also forbidden to work. Masters' daughters who are not yet married are allowed to work for their fathers as long as they live in their fathers' household, but those who have hired themselves out to another master as a maid can only do the work of a domestic servant, and nothing in the craft.

6. Needlemakers' Guild Ordinance, Nuremberg, 16th century

No master in this craft [needlemakers] is to teach or make use of a female domestic servant in place of a journeyman or apprentice for any type of work, under penalty of one pound per day. They can still teach their own children, however.

7. Ordinance for All Guilds in Nuremberg, 1543

To prevent further errors in regard to apprentices, it is ordered that from now on no widow in any craft is to take on a new apprentice, on the grounds that he will not be able to get a letter of apprenticeship from her as there was never a master in the shop. If, when the master dies, there is already an apprentice in the shop, he can complete his training with the widow.

8. Goldsmiths' Guild Ordinance, Nuremberg, 1535

If, when a goldsmith dies, there is no son who wants to inherit the shop or continue on in the craft, or none who is skilled or old enough to make the masterpiece at that time, his widow will be allowed to continue the shop (if she wants) three years after the death of her husband and no longer, unless she marries someone who is a master goldsmith or who makes his masterpiece during this time. Every widow who is continuing a shop will have to obey all the guild ordinances and bring her work to be inspected, and be liable to the same fines as a master if she breaks any regulations.

Source 9 from Julia O'Faolain and Lauro Martines, editors, Not in God's Image: Women in History from the Greeks to the Victorians *(New York: Harper & Row, 1973), pp. 159–160.*

9. Petition from the Silk Women of London to Parliament, 1455

[Petition from] the silk women and throwsters[14] of the crafts and occupation of silk work within the city of London . . . [hitherto, thanks to the silk industry] many a woman lived full honorably, and therewith many households kept, and many gentlewomen and others in great number like as there now be more than a thousand, have been drawn under them in learning the same crafts and occupation. . . . [But] lately divers Lombards [Italians] and other alien strangers imagining to destroy the same crafts and all such virtuous occupations for women within this land, to the intent to enrich themselves and put such occupations to other lands, bring now daily into this land wrought silk, thrown ribbons, and laces falsely and deceivably wrought, and no silk unwrought, to the great hurt of all such as shall wear or occupy the same and the utter destruction of all the same crafts and occupations: The sufferance whereof hath caused and is like to cause great idleness amongst gentlewomen and other women of worship. . . . In reformation whereof [they ask Parliament to get the King to ban all finished silk from coming into] this land from beyond the sea.

14. **throwster:** a woman who twists silk fibers into silk thread.

Sources 10 and 11 from Merry E. Wiesner, translator, unpublished supplications in Frankfurt Stadtarchiv, Zünfte, Ugb. C-50, Ss, no. 4; Ugb. C-32, R, no. 1.

10. Widow's Supplication to the Frankfurt City Council, late 16th century

Distinguished and honorable sirs, I, a poor and distressed widow, wish to respectfully report in what manner earlier this year I spun some pounds of yarn, 57 to be exact, for the use of my own household. I wanted to take the yarn to be woven into cloth, but didn't know whom I should give it to so that I could get it worked into cloth the quickest and earliest.

Therefore I was talking to some farm women from Bornheim, who were selling their produce in front of the shoemakers' guild house, and they told me about a weaver that they had in Bornheim who made good cloth and could also make it quickly. I let him know—through the farmers' wives—that I wanted him to make my cloth. I got the yarn together and sent my children to carry it to him; as they were on their way, the weavers here grabbed the yarn forcefully from my children, and took it to their guild house. They said they had ordinances which forbade taking yarn to foreigners to weave, and told me they would not return it unless I paid a fine.

I then went to the lord mayors, asking them about this ordinance that would let people confiscate things without warning from the public streets. They said they didn't know about any such ordinance, and that my yarn should have long been returned to me. I then went to the overseer of the guild, master Adlaff Zimmermann who lives by the Eschenheimer tower, who answered me with rough, harsh words that they would in no way return my yarn to me, and that the guild did have such an ordinance.

Therefore I respectfully request, if they do have such an ordinance, I didn't know anything about it, and so ask you humbly and in God's name to tell the weavers to return my yarn. If, according to this ordinance, I am supposed to pay a fine, they should take it from the yarn, and give the rest back. I ask this of your honorable sirs, as the protectors of widows and orphans, and pray that you will help me.

Your humble servant, Agatha, the widow of the late Conrad Gaingen.

11. Widow's Supplication to the Frankfurt City Council, late 16th century

Most honorable and merciful gentlemen, you certainly know what a heavy and hard cross God has laid on me, and in what a miserable situation I find myself, after the much too early death of my late husband, with my young children, all of them still minors and some still nursing. This unfortunate situation is well known everywhere.

Although in consideration of my misfortune most Christian hearts would have gladly let me continue in my craft and occupation, and allowed me to earn a little piece of bread, instead the overseers of the woolweavers' guild came to me as soon as my husband had died, in my sorrow and even in my own house. Against all Christian charity, they began to order changes in my workshop with very harsh and menacing words. They specifically ordered that my apprentice, whom I had raised and trained at great cost and who had just come to be of use to me in the craft, leave me and go to them, which would be to their great advantage but my greater disadvantage. They ordered this on the pretense that there was no longer a master here so he could not finish his training.

Honorable sirs, I then humbly put myself under the protection of the lord mayors here, and asked that the two journeymen and the apprentice be allowed to continue on in their work as they had before unimpeded until a final judgment was reached in the matter. Despite this, one of the weavers began to shout at my journeymen whenever he saw them, especially if there were other people on the street. In his unhindered and unwarranted boldness, he yelled that my workshop was not honorable, and all journeymen who worked there were thieves and rascals. After doing this for several days, he and several others came into my workshop on a Saturday, and, bitter and jealous, pushed my journeymen out. They began to write to all places where this craft is practiced to tell other masters not to accept anyone who had worked in my workshop.

I now humbly beg you, my honorable and gracious sirs, protect me and my hungry children from such abuse, shame, and insult. Help my journeymen, who were so undeservedly insulted, to regain their honor. I beg you, as the protector of humble widows, to let my apprentice stay with me, as apprentices are allowed to stay in the workshops of widows throughout the entire Holy Roman Empire, as long as there are journeymen, whether or not there is a master present. Protect me from any further insults of the woolweavers' guild, which does nothing to increase the honor of our city, which you, honorable sirs, are charged to uphold. I plead with you to grant me my request, and allow me to continue my workshop.

Sources 12 and 13 from Carolly Erickson, The Records of Medieval Europe *(Garden City, New York: Anchor, 1971), p. 238. Translated by Carolly Erickson.*

12. Judgment Against a Draper[15] in Flanders, mid-14th century

When Jacquemars des Mares, a draper, brought one of his cloths to the great cloth hall of Arras and sold it, the aforesaid cloth was examined by the *espincheurs*[16] as is customary, and at the time they had it weighed, it was half a pound over the legal weight. Then, because of certain suspicions which arose, they had the cloth dried, and when it was dry, it weighed a half pound less than the legal weight. The *espincheur* brought the misdeed to the attention of the Twenty;[17] Jacquemars was fined 100 shillings.

13. Dispute Between Master Fullers[18] and Their Apprentices in Flanders, 1345

A point of discussion was mooted between the apprentice fullers on the one hand, and the master fullers on the other. The apprentices held that, as they laid out in a letter, no one could have work done in his house without taking apprentices. . . . For they complained of fulling masters who had their children work in their houses, without standing [for jobs] in the public square like the other apprentices, and they begged that their letter be answered. The fulling masters stated certain arguments to the contrary. The aldermen sent for both parties and for the Twenty also and asked the masters if indeed they kept their children as apprentices; each master said he did. It was declared by the aldermen that every apprentice must remain in the public square, as reason demanded.

Done in the year of 1344 [1345], in the month of February, and through a full sitting of the aldermen.

15. **draper:** a person who made woolen cloth.
16. **espincheur:** cloth inspector.
17. **Twenty:** court of twenty men, made up of members of the city council.
18. **fuller:** a person who beat finished cloth with sticks in order to clean and thicken it.

Sources 14 and 15 from Merry E. Wiesner, translator, unpublished decisions in Nuremberg Stadtarchiv, Quellen zur Nürnbergische Geschichte, Rep. F5, no. 68/I, fol. 58 (1577); fol. 99 (1581).

14. Decision by the Nuremberg City Council, 1577

The honorable city council has decided to deny the request of Barbara Hansmesser that she be allowed to dye wool because the blanketweavers' guild has so adamantly opposed it. Because her husband is not a citizen, they are both ordered to get out of the city and find work in some other place, with the warning that if they are found in the vicinity of this city, and are doing any work here, work will be taken from them and the yarn cut to pieces. They can count on this.

15. Decision by the Nuremberg City Council, 1581

Anna Pentzin, a widow and citizen, is to be allowed to make tin boxes as she has requested, despite the objections of the tinsmiths' guild, until she has remarried or has begun to earn her living in another way. Regarding her children: she is not to have her son help her in any way, but her daughter can help her occasionally. Once her mother marries, or they move apart from each other, the daughter is not to have anything more to do with the craft of tinsmithing.

QUESTIONS TO CONSIDER

The records you have read have shed some light on a wide variety of issues in the medieval city. Along with learning about the guilds themselves, you have also found out about economic development, political conflicts, urban social structure, and family relationships. To draw some general conclusions and answer the questions for this chapter, you will need to divide the information from your sources according to these topical categories. This is exactly what historians who use such records do, especially if they are interested in more general questions such as economic or social change and are using guild records as only one of their sources. Investigating specific historical issues involves not only uncovering sources that deal with your problem directly but also extracting small bits of information from sources that cover a great many other areas. This is especially the case in the matter of social change, for the effects of such changes can often be detected in many different facets of everyday life.

The easiest way to approach broad historical questions is by starting with the narrowest and most specific category of information, in this case with material about the guilds themselves. Looking at your list, which problems were solely internal guild affairs? How did the guilds enforce their solutions to these problems? What impact did their solutions have on people who were not members of the guild? How did the guild regulate relations between master, journeymen, apprentices? What noneconomic functions of the guild were regarded as important and worthy of regulating?

Now move to more general economic issues. What changes did the guilds regard as threatening? What actions did they take to answer these threats? Do their actions and fears seem justified in all cases? Political conflicts were very often combined with these economic concerns, as we would expect in societies like these, in which the two areas are so closely linked. How would you describe the relations between the guilds and the city councils? How did individuals use the town's political conflicts to their own advantage? (The best examples here are the supplications: To whom did individuals turn for help, and why? What sort of language do they use to persuade authorities to help them?) The guild records provide information about not only internal city politics but external affairs as well. What was the general attitude toward foreigners, who people in the Middle Ages regarded as anyone who did not live in their own town?

Next, turn to issues of social change and social structure. How would you describe the relations between masters and servants after reading these sources? How would you characterize the atmosphere in most shops—collegial and friendly or divided and somewhat hostile? What about relations between men and women in the shops? How were these relations affected by whether the man was a master or a journeyman, and the woman a widow or a domestic servant? What was the attitude of the political authorities toward women working within the guild structure? What was the attitude of the guilds toward elderly or suffering workers? Do you see changes over time?

As you have no doubt noticed, guilds did not regulate simply individual workers but their families as well. What special privileges were given to members of the master's family? Who objected to these privileges, and why? What measures did the guilds take in regard to the wives and children of other workers? How did the guilds treat widows of their members? Would you regard the guilds as generally helpful to families or only to certain types of families?

You are now ready to suggest some answers to the questions posed by this chapter: What economic and social changes did medieval guilds consider to be problems? What solutions did they propose? How did their attitudes toward men and women of different social classes shape their solutions? How did guild actions both reflect and affect the political structure of medieval cities?

EPILOGUE

Despite frequent conflicts with city councils and other political authorities, the craft guilds of most European cities were able to maintain their monopoly on production throughout the sixteenth century. Though in the short run this was beneficial to the guild masters, in the long run the restrictions imposed by the guilds contributed to economic and social problems that eventually worked to the detriment of both the guilds and the cities.

Limitations on workshop size and hours of production as well as strict regulations on product quality prevented individuals from experimenting with new and faster processes that required more workers or that produced lower-quality and therefore cheaper goods. Prohibitions against the use of machinery saved skilled jobs but also kept guild shops from expanding their output or making their products cheaper. Restrictions on the number of workshops not only led to conflicts between masters and journeymen, but also increased the number of people in the cities who had no opportunity to enter the guild system at all and who therefore had no sympathy with the aims of the guild masters. City councils recognized that these people needed employment and that their employment would have to come from outside the guild system.

To escape guild restrictions, people who wanted to make products on a larger scale than guilds would allow set up workshops in the country or in small villages, often hiring many households with each household performing only one step of the process. This production process is called *cottage industry* or the *putting-out system*, and by the fifteenth and sixteenth centuries it was in open competition with urban guild production in some areas, especially the manufacture of cloth. These new industries could produce goods much more inexpensively than the guilds, and those who set them up were able to persuade cities to allow their cheaper products to be sold, a practice that undercut local guild production. Some city councils also recognized that these new industries could provide jobs for the increasingly large portion of the urban population that could not be absorbed into the guild system. They took away guild monopolies on production and allowed new industries to be established within cities themselves, so that part of the late medieval urban economy also came to be organized as a putting-out system.

Though most guilds fought this trend, more enterprising or wealthier masters recognized the benefits of the putting-out system and began to hire other households to work for them, promoting a greater division within the guild between wealthier masters and the poorer masters and journeymen they hired. Some masters became so wealthy that they no longer had to work in a shop themselves, nor did their wives and family members.

The individuals who established these new industries invested their money in the same way the merchants and traders we examined in the last chapter did, so these cottage industries are also regarded as capitalist. Economic historians see capitalism in the West as developing through several stages. In the first stage, *mercantile capitalism,* capital was primarily invested in trade and commerce. In the second stage, investors put their money into production as well as trade; this period, beginning with the putting-out system, is often termed *proto-industrial capitalism.* Whereas the master craftsman in guild shops both worked with and owned the tools and raw materials, the investor in capitalist production did not perform any of the actual labor himself but simply provided the raw materials—and, in some cases, the tools—and paid households for their work. This division between labor and investment is seen, particularly by labor historians, as the hallmark of proto-industrial capitalism. During the eighteenth century capitalism entered a third stage, known as *industrial capitalism,* in which workers were gathered in factories instead of working in their own homes and were paid as individuals rather than as families. By this time work and family were increasingly separated in a way they had not been in proto-industrial capitalism.

The rise of capitalist production did not bring an immediate end to the guilds, however. Guilds were still to be found in some industries and in some parts of Europe as late as the nineteenth century, though their power was much less than it had been in the Middle Ages. The political function of guilds was largely assumed by the new centralized states, which also regulated the economy. Their social functions, such as educating young people and caring for the elderly, were taken over by the schools and the relief agencies set up by the national governments. The guilds' decline in power paralleled that of the cities, which largely enjoyed independence in many parts of Europe during the Middle Ages but by the seventeenth century were controlled by larger regional governments or by dynastic states.

CHAPTER TEN

LAY PIETY AND HERESY IN THE LATE MIDDLE AGES

THE PROBLEM

During the late Middle Ages, the Christian church went through a period of turmoil and disunity, with corruption and abuse evident at all levels of its hierarchy. Though the Church was officially an independent institution, many of its officials, such as bishops and archbishops, were actually chosen by secular nobles and rulers, who picked their own relatives or others who would do as they were told. Officials who were elected or appointed from within the Church itself were often selected for their administrative and legal skills, not for their piety, high moral standards, or religious devotion. These problems extended all the way to the papacy, which for much of the fourteenth century was located not in Rome but in Avignon in southern France, where it was dominated by the French monarchy. During this time the papacy lost its stature as an international power and had difficulty raising revenue from many parts of Europe, especially from the English, who rightly suspected that money sent to the pope might end up in the coffers of the French king, with whom they were at war. The Avignon popes had ever-increasing needs for revenue because they had to hire mercenaries to keep the Papal States in Italy under control, build palaces and churches in Avignon that reflected the power and prestige of the papacy, and pay the salaries of a growing corps of lawyers and bureaucrats who administered the papal empire.

The papacy devised a number of ways to meet its increasing need for money. Though the outright selling of Church offices, termed *simony,* was strictly forbidden, the popes required all candidates to pay for the privilege of taking over a vacant office, then hand over a large share of their first year's revenues directly to the papacy. Official prohibitions, such as those against priests having concubines or giving Church land to family members, could be ignored if the cleric paid the pope for a special dispensation. The papacy also collected money directly from laypeople, charging fees for clerical services such as marriage or baptism and for dispensations that legitimized children born out of wedlock.

The most lucrative source of income for the papacy proved to be the granting of *indulgences.* Indulgences were based on three doctrines developed by the medieval Church—the sacrament of penance, the concept of Purgatory, and the Treasury of Merit. To partake of the sacrament of penance, a believer was to confess all sins to a priest and be truly sorry, or contrite, for them, after which the priest absolved the believer, often requiring him or her to carry out certain acts as penance for these sins such as saying prayers or going on pilgrimages. According to Church doctrine, this punishment did not end with death but might be extended into Purgatory, where Christians spent time atoning for the sins for which they had not done earthly penance. Only after a set time in Purgatory could most Christians be admitted to heaven. (Those who were going to hell, on the other hand, went directly there.)

Along with the doctrines of penance and Purgatory, the Church also developed the idea of the Treasury of Merit. This Treasury was seen as a collection of all the superlative good deeds and meritorious acts that the apostles, saints, and other good people had done during their lives, which the pope as head of the Church could dispense as he wished through the granting of indulgences. The recipient of an indulgence received a share in the Treasury of Merit that took the place of having to do individual penance. Originally granted to people who performed special services for the Church, such as participating in crusades, indulgences gradually came to be exchanged for cash contributions. Though official theology taught that priestly absolution and true contrition were still necessary, unscrupulous indulgence peddlers often sold them outright as easy substitutes for penance. Indulgences also began to be granted to relieve people of time in Purgatory and even to allow believers to shorten deceased relatives' time in Purgatory. To many people it seemed the Church was teaching that one could buy one's way into heaven, though this was not actually so.

Because Church officials at all levels were often chosen for their family connections or legal and financial skills, they also bent official doctrines and saw their posts primarily in terms of income rather than spiritual duties. Bishops spent much of their time at the papal court trying to win the pope's favor and squeezed all possible revenues out of their dioceses in order to pay for their offices. These absentee officials, who left the affairs of the diocese in the hands of substitutes, often had very little idea about the needs or problems of their territory. Those who were successful in gaining papal backing might be appointed to many different offices simultaneously; they collected the income from all their posts, appointed badly paid proxies to carry out their duties, and might actually never even visit the diocese over which they were bishop.

With so little supervision, parish priests and monks were sometimes lax in their standards of morality and spiritual observance. Frequently parish priests were poor and badly educated, for most of the Church's wealth stayed in the hands of higher officials, who provided no opportunity for priests to gain an education; some priests did not even know Latin but simply recited the Mass by rote without understanding what they were saying. During the week they farmed just as their parishioners did, for the income from tithes was not sufficient to support them. Some of the monasteries and convents maintained high standards, but others, caught in the squeeze for revenue, admitted any applicant who would pay the entrance fee without determining if this person was fit for the monastic life.

With the Church embroiled in these problems, we might expect that people would turn away from religion to concentrate on other aspects of life, but this was not the case. Religion continued to dominate the lives of people in the late Middle Ages, which was in fact perhaps the most religious period in all of European history. What did change, however, is how people expressed and experienced their Christian faith. Not surprisingly, they turned away somewhat from the institutional Church and sought more direct paths to God through individual actions.

Much of this lay piety was supported by the Church hierarchy because it did not question basic theological doctrines such as life after death; the importance of the sacraments of baptism, communion, and penance; the honor owed to saints and their relics; and the right of the pope to grant indulgences, collect taxes, and determine correct doctrine. Pious laypeople also made frequent donations, which swelled the Church's revenue. Some individuals and groups went beyond personal piety, however, to question the Church's wealth and many of its central doctrines. The Church declared such people heretics and set up inquisitorial courts to investigate, try, and condemn them.

Your task in this chapter will be to examine late medieval lay piety and religious practices, both those approved by the institutional Church and those condemned as heresy. How did common people in the Middle Ages experience and express their religious faith? How did the Church as an institution respond to laypeople's ideas and actions?

SOURCES AND METHOD

Medieval Christianity, multifaceted in nature, may be explored from a number of angles. In Chapter 4 we looked at the Church's development as a political and economic institution and at the close relations that grew up between Church leaders and rulers. Christianity was not only an institution, however, but also a faith shared by most people living in Europe, whether they were highly educated or uneducated, wealthy or poor. We can find information about how educated men understood and interpreted Christianity fairly easily by reading theological treatises and official Church decisions, but these may not accurately reflect the religious views of the majority. For this perspective we must turn to a much smaller group of sources that throw light on the religious beliefs of the common people.

Learning about and reconstructing the ideas of common people in the premodern period is extremely difficult, for such people were by and large illiterate. The surviving written records of their thoughts and actions thus all come through the filter of literate observers whose perspective and understanding of events might differ radically from the participants'. This is especially a problem when we are examining religious ideas, for most people who could read and write in the Middle Ages were clerics and thus part of the institutional Church. It was often hard for such observers to be objective about criticism directed against the Church, or even to comprehend how uneducated people interpreted and understood theological concepts.

Because of these problems, we must ask several questions before turning to any written source about popular religious belief. Who actually wrote the document? Was the writer recording the words of an illiterate person or simply describing actions he or she had observed? Why was this piece written? If the writer is recording the words of someone else, did he or she clearly understand the language being spoken or might there be some problems because of dialect? Is the writer translating a vernacular language such as English or French into Latin, and so possibly mistranslating religious ideas? Why were this person's thoughts recorded—did that person wish it or did the authorities, as was the case with trial records?

Artistic evidence might seem more direct, for people who could not read or write sculpted, painted, and made stained-glass windows. They did not always choose their own subject matter or sign their works, however, so medieval art does not directly express the individual personality and concerns of the artist in the way that modern art does. What it does reveal, however, is how common people learned about religion from windows and statues depicting Biblical and other Christian scenes. We can also use frequently recurring images as a rough guide to popular religious sentiments, for individuals and groups commissioned art that reflected their own concerns. The dominance of certain images shifted throughout the Middle Ages as people's attitudes toward the Church and the right way to approach God changed.

Using artistic evidence as a source of information about popular belief requires a different set of initial questions than written evidence. Where and when was the piece probably made? Can we learn anything about the artist or patron, such as his or her identity? Where was the piece originally displayed? Are the materials simple enough that the piece could be ordered or purchased by someone who was not wealthy? Is the image common or unusual?

Keeping in mind the limitations we have noted, turn now to the written sources. The first three are *sermon stories*, tales of miracles that learned preachers used in their public sermons; later they were collected by many different preachers and used widely in sermons all over Europe. These stories are consequently not written *by* laypeople but *for* them and reflect official Church doctrines. They do not present sophisticated theology, however, but show us how common people learned about Christianity. As you read, note the kinds of people who appear as main characters. Why would preachers use characters like these?

In the first sermon, to whom does the woman turn for assistance? When her prayers are not answered immediately, what does she do? Why would the preacher condone such a dramatic action? (To answer this question, think about the impact this story would have on the female members of the audience; Mary may not have responded instantly to prayer, but, like most mothers, did so immediately once her child was taken from her.) What qualities of Mary does this story emphasize?

The second sermon discusses an important element in lay piety, the belief in saints and relics. Does the author support or condemn these beliefs? Are the relics themselves important or faith in them? Why would the author, himself a priest, describe the priest in the story as "wily" and "wicked"? (Again, keep in mind the audience. Given the problems most people recognized in the Church, how would a lay audience respond to a story in which the hero is also a layperson?)

The third sermon also involves devotion to the Virgin. How does the main character express his faith? Why does he feel his actions are unworthy? How does the author show that the tumbler's actions are deemed worthy? Taking these three sermons together, what types of actions do you think preachers were trying to encourage in people? What traits of lay piety did they praise?

The remaining written sources directly record the thoughts and actions of laypeople, some of whom the Church supported and some of whom it condemned. None could read or write Latin and so qualify as unlearned by medieval standards, though some could read their own vernacular language. Source 4 is taken from the *Revelations* of Bridget of Sweden, a noblewoman who lived from 1303 to 1373. After her husband's death, Bridget traveled to Rome, where she began to see visions and give advice based on these visions to both laypeople and Church officials. Because she could not speak Latin, she wrote or dictated her visions in Swedish; these were later translated by her confessors and eventually were published in Latin. At the end of her life, Bridget made a pilgrimage to Jerusalem, where she had the visions reprinted here. How would you describe these visions? How did the fact that she was a woman shape her religious experience?

Source 5 is drawn from the first autobiography ever written in English, that of Margery Kempe, who was probably born in 1373, the same year Bridget died. Kempe, a middle-class woman from the town of King's Lynn, was illiterate in English as well as Latin. Although she was married and had fourteen children, she began to see visions in which Christ demanded that she set herself apart from most women. At the end of her most unusual life, she dictated her autobiography to several male scribes, who wrote it down in English. As you read, note how Kempe describes her actions and behavior. What made her most open to criticism? How does she defend her actions? She refers to herself, always in the third person, as "this creature." What does this practice indicate about her self-consciousness? Do her actions reflect this self-image? What aspects of Christianity most inspire or disturb her? How was the official reaction to her influenced by the fact that she was a woman?

The last two written sources come from trial records. Source 6 contains three testimonies from the Inquisition carried out between 1318 and 1325 by Jacques Fournier, Bishop of Pamiers in southern France. All three accused were illiterate peasants who spoke Occitan, a regional dialect; their words were translated by scribes into Latin. Fournier launched the Inquisition because he suspected large numbers of people in his district to be *Albigensians* (also called Cathars), followers of a heretic movement that rejected many basic Church doctrines. Albigensians regarded the material world as evil and not made by God and did not believe in the possibility of eternal life. They denied the power of many Church ceremonies and rituals and urged that any Church leader, including the pope, should not be obeyed if he did not live up to rigorous moral standards.

As you read the testimonies, note which specific Christian beliefs were being challenged. Given their statements, would you call the peasants who were being questioned Christians? How might problems of translation have affected the records? How might the fact that this was a trial have affected what the individuals said?

Source 7 comes from a heresy trial of sixty people suspected of Lollard beliefs, conducted in the diocese of Norwich, England between 1428 and 1431. Lollards followed the ideas of John Wyclif, an English scholar who lived in the fourteenth century; the selection itself presents all of the basic Lollard beliefs. Most of the trial record is in Latin because it was conducted by ecclesiastical authorities and recorded by clerics, but a few of the confessions were written down in English. The selection here is one of those, with the spelling modernized. What does the accused admit to having believed? The list of unacceptable beliefs in many heresy trials reflects not only the ideas of the person confessing but also those the inquisitors thought were especially dangerous and in need of suppression. What did the inquisitors in this case appear particularly concerned about? How would this emphasis have shaped the confession? How was the accused to prove he had given up his heresy? Given his beliefs, would you call the person under questioning a Christian?

Now examine the two visual sources. Both are wooden statues carved in the fourteenth or fifteenth century by unknown artists and originally placed in churches in southern Germany. They are examples of the two most common religious images of the late Middle Ages. What aspects of popular belief that you have identified from the written sources do they reflect? Mary is shown wearing a crown and holding an orb, a sphere with a cross on top representing the world that normally was carried by monarchs. What qualities are emphasized through this depiction? Christ is shown in a dramatic pose of suffering. What does this attitude emphasize about his nature? Given what you now know about how common people understood Christianity, why would these two subjects be the most popular? Why do you think there is no depiction of God the Father?

THE EVIDENCE

Source 1 from C. C. S. Bland, editor and translator, Miracles of the Blessed Virgin Mary *(London: Routledge, 1928), p. 118.*

1. A Sermon Story About the Virgin Mary, 13th century

A certain woman of simple and upright life used to worship the Holy Mary, Mother of God, often strewing flowers and herbs before her image.

Now it chanced that the woman's only son was taken prisoner. And the mother weeping for him would not be comforted, and prayed with all her heart to the Blessed Virgin Mary for her son's deliverance. But seeing it was all in vain, she entered the church and thus addressed the image of the Blessed Virgin, "O Blessed Virgin Mary, often have I asked thee for the deliverance of my son and thou hast not heard me. Therefore, as my son was taken from me, so will I take away thine and will put him in durance as hostage for mine."

And taking the image of the Child from the bosom of Mary, she went home, wrapped him up in a clean cloth, and shut him up carefully in a chest. And, behold, the following night the Blessed Mary appeared to the captive youth bidding him to go forth and said to him: "Tell your mother to give me my Son." And he coming to his mother, described how he had been set free. But she with great rejoicing carried back the image of Jesus to Mary and gave her thanks.

Source 2 from Dana Carleton Munro, editor and translator, Translations and Reprints from the Original Sources of European History, *vol. 2, no. 4 (Philadelphia: University of Pennsylvania Press, no date), p. 14.*

2. A Sermon Story About Relics, 13th century

A certain knight loved most ardently the above-mentioned martyr, St. Thomas of Canterbury,[1] and sought everywhere to obtain some relic of him. When a certain wily priest, in whose house he was staying, heard of this he said to him, "I have by me a bridle which St. Thomas used for a long time, and I have often experienced its virtues." When the knight heard this, and believed it, he joyfully paid the priest the money which the latter demanded and received the bridle with great devotion.

God truly, to whom nothing is impossible, wishing to reward the faith of the knight and for the honor of his martyr, deigned to work many miracles through the same bridle. The knight seeing this founded a church in honor of the martyr and in it he placed as a relic the bridle of that most wicked priest.

Source 3 from Eugene Mason, translator, Aucassin and Nicolette and Other Mediaeval Romances and Legends *(New York: Dutton, 1910), pp. 53–62.*

3. "Our Lady's Tumbler," a Sermon Story, 13th century

Amongst the lives of the ancient fathers, wherein may be found much profitable matter, this story is told for a true ensample.[2] I do not say that you may not often have heard a fairer story, but at least this is not to be despised, and is well worth the telling. Now therefore will I say and narrate what chanced to this minstrel.

He erred up and down, to and fro, so often and in so many places, that he took the whole world in despite, and sought rest in a certain holy order.

1. **Thomas Becket:** the Archbishop of Canterbury who was murdered on the steps of the cathedral on the orders of Henry II for opposing the king's wishes. He was quickly made a saint and Canterbury became the most popular pilgrimage site in England.
2. **ensample:** example.

Horses and raiment and money, yea, all that he had, he straightway put from him, and seeking shelter from the world, was firmly set never to put foot within it more. For this cause he took refuge in this holy order, amongst the monks of Clairvaux. Now, though this dancer was comely of face and shapely of person, yet when he had once entered the monastery he found that he was master of no craft practiced therein. In the world he had gained his bread by tumbling and dancing and feats of address.[3] To leap, to spring, such matters he knew well, but of greater things he knew nothing, for he had never spelled from book—nor Paternoster,[4] nor canticle,[5] nor creed, nor Hail Mary, nor aught concerning his soul's salvation. . . .

The tumbler moved amongst his fellows like a man ashamed, for he had neither part nor lot in all the business of the monastery, and for this he was right sad and sorrowful. He saw the monks and the penitents about him, each serving God, in this place and that, according to his office and degree. He marked the priests at their ritual before the altars; the deacons at the gospels; the subdeacons at the epistles; and the ministers about the vigils. . . . Then he said. . . "Ah, St. Mary, alas, what words are these I say! These men are calling on the mercy of God, but I—what do I here! Here there is none so mean or vile but who serves God in his office and degree, save only me, for I work not, neither can I preach. Caitiff[6] and shamed was I when I thrust myself herein, seeing that I can do nothing well, either in labor or in prayer. I see my brothers upon their errands, one behind the other; but I do naught but fill my belly with the meat that they provide. If they perceive this thing, certainly shall I be in an evil case, for they will cast me out amongst the dogs, and none will take pity on the glutton and the idle man. Truly am I a caitiff, set in a high place for a sign." Then he wept for very woe, and would that he was quiet in the grave. "Mary, Mother," quoth he, "pray now your heavenly Father that he keep me in his pleasure, and give me such good counsel that I may truly serve both him and you; yea, and may deserve that meat which now is bitter in my mouth."

Driven mad with thoughts such as these, he wandered about the abbey until he found himself within the crypt, and took sanctuary by the altar, crouching close as he was able. Above the altar was carved the statue of Madame St. Mary. Truly his steps had not erred when he sought that refuge; nay, but rather, God who knows his own had led him thither by the hand. When he heard the bells ring for mass he sprang to his feet all dismayed. "Ha!" said he; "now am I betrayed. Each adds his mite to the great offering, save only me. Like a tethered ox, naught I do but chew the cud, and waste good victuals on a useless man. Shall I speak my thought? Shall I work my

3. **feats of address:** gymnastics.
4. **Paternoster:** rosary beads, used as an aid to prayer.
5. **canticle:** hymn.
6. **caitiff:** evil, mean, cowardly.

will? By the Mother of God, thus am I set to do. None is here to blame. I will do that which I can, and honor with my craft the Mother of God in her monastery. Since others honor her with chant, then I will serve with tumbling."

He takes off his cowl, and removes his garments, placing them near the altar, but so that his body be not naked he dons a tunic, very thin and fine, of scarce more substance than a shirt. So, light and comely of body, with gown girt closely about his loins, he comes before the Image right humbly. Then raising his eyes, "Lady," said he, "to your fair charge I give my body and my soul. Sweet Queen, sweet Lady, scorn not the thing I know, for with the help of God I will essay to serve you in good faith, even as I may. I cannot read your Hours nor chant your praise, but at the least I can set before you what art I have. Now will I be as the lamb that plays and skips before his mother. Oh, Lady, who art nowise bitter to those who serve you with a good intent, that which thy servant is, that he is for you."

Then commenced he his merry play, leaping low and small, tall and high, over and under. Then once more he knelt upon his knees before the statue, and meekly bowed his head. "Ha!" said he, "most gracious Queen, of your pity and your charity scorn not this my service." Again he leaped and played, and for holiday and festival, made the somersault of Metz. Again he bowed before the Image, did reverence, and paid it all the honor that he might. Afterwards he did the French vault, then the vault of Champagne, then the Spanish vault, then the vaults they love in Brittany, then the vault of Lorraine, and all these feats he did as best he was able. Afterwards he did the Roman vault, and then, with hands before his brow, danced daintily before the altar, gazing with a humble heart at the statue of God's Mother. "Lady," said he, "I set before you a fair play. This travail I do for you alone; so help me God, for you, Lady, and your Son. Think not I tumble for my own delight; but I serve you, and look for no other guerdon on my carpet. My brothers serve you, yea, and so do I. Lady, scorn not your villein, for he toils for your good pleasure; and, Lady, you are my delight and the sweetness of the world." Then he walked on his two hands, with his feet in the air, and his head near the ground. He twirled with his feet, and wept with his eyes. "Lady," said he, "I worship you with heart, with body, feet and hands, for this I can neither add to nor take away. Now am I your very minstrel. Others may chant your praises in the church, but here in the crypt will I tumble for your delight. Lady, lead me truly in your way, and for the love of God hold me not in utter despite." Then he smote upon his breast, he sighed and wept most tenderly, since he knew no better prayer than tears. Then he turned him about, and leaped once again. "Lady," said he, "as God is my Savior, never have I turned this somersault before. Never has a tumbler done such a feat, and, certes, it is not bad. Lady, what delight is his who may harbor with you in your glorious manor. For God's love, Lady, grant me such fair hostelry, since I am yours, and am nothing of my own." Once again he did the vault of Metz; again he danced and tumbled. Then when the chants rose louder from the choir, he, too, forced the note, and put forward all his skill. So long as the priest was about that mass, so long his flesh endured to dance, and leap and spring, till at the last, nigh fainting, he could stand no longer upon his feet, but fell for weariness on the ground. From head to heel sweat stood upon him, drop by drop, as blood falls from meat turning upon the hearth. "Lady," said he, "I can no more, but truly will I seek you again." Fire consumed him utterly. He took his habit once more, and when he was wrapped close therein, he rose to his feet, and bending low before the statue, went his way. "Farewell," said he, "gentlest Friend. For God's love take it not to heart, for so I may I will soon return. Not one Hour shall pass but that I will serve you with right goodwill, so I may come, and so my service is pleasing in your sight." Thus he went from the crypt, yet gazing on his Lady. "Lady," said he, "my heart is sore that I cannot read your Hours. How would I love them for love of you, most gentle Lady! Into your care I commend my soul and my body."

In this fashion passed many days, for at every Hour he sought the crypt to do service, and pay homage before the Image. His service was so much to his mind that never once was he too weary to set out his most cunning feats to distract the Mother of God, nor did he ever wish for other play than this. Now, doubtless, the monks knew well enough that day by day he sought the crypt, but not a man on earth—save God alone—was aware of aught that passed there; neither would he, for all the wealth of the world, have let his goings in be seen, save by the Lord his God alone. For truly he believed that were his secret once espied he would be hunted from the cloister, and flung once more into the foul, sinful world, and for his part he was more fain to fall on death than to suffer any taint of sin. But God considering his simplicity, his sorrow for all he had wrought amiss, and the love which moved him to this deed, would that this toil should be known; and the Lord willed that the work of his friend should be made plain to men, for the glory of the Mother whom he worshipped, and so that all men should know and hear, and receive that God refuses none who seeks his face in love, however low his degree, save only he love God and strive to do his will.

Now think you that the Lord would have accepted this service, had it not been done for love of him? Verily and truly, no, however much this juggler tumbled; but God called him friend, because he loved him much. Toil and labor, keep fast and vigil, sigh and weep, watch and pray, ply the sharp scourge, be diligent at Matins[7] and at mass, owe no man anything, give alms of all you have—and yet, if you love not God with all your heart, all these good deeds are so much loss—mark well my words—and profit you naught for the saving of your soul. Without charity and love, works avail a man

7. **Matins:** an evening or midnight prayer service.

nothing. God asks not gold, neither for silver, but only for love unfeigned in his people's hearts, and since the tumbler loved him beyond measure, for this reason God was willing to accept his service. . . .

[*The abbot heard about the tumbler's activities and went to investigate.*]

Whilst the abbot looked, forthwith there came down from the vault a Dame so glorious, that certainly no man had seen one so precious, nor so richly crowned. She was more beautiful than the daughters of men, and her vesture was heavy with gold and gleaming stones. In her train came the hosts of heaven, angel and archangel also; and these pressed close about the minstrel, and solaced and refreshed him. When their shining ranks drew near, peace fell upon his heart; for they contended to do him service, and were the servants of the servitor of that Dame who is the rarest Jewel of God. Then the sweet and courteous Queen herself took a white napkin in her hand, and with it gently fanned her minstrel before the altar. Courteous and debonair, the Lady refreshed his neck, his body and his brow. Meekly she served him as a handmaid in his need. But these things were hidden from the good man, for he neither saw nor knew that about him stood so fair a company.

The holy angels honor him greatly, but they can no longer stay, for their Lady turns to go. She blesses her minstrel with the sign of God, and the holy angels throng about her, still gazing back with delight upon their companion, for they await the hour when God shall release him from the burden of the world and they possess his soul.

Source 4 from Katharina M. Wilson, editor, Medieval Women Writers *(Athens: University of Georgia Press, 1984), p. 245. Selection translated by Barbara Obrist.*

4. Two Visions of Bridget of Sweden, 1370s

After this the Virgin Mary appeared again to me, in the same place, and said: it has been a long time since in Rome I promised you that I would show you here in Bethlehem how my offspring had been born. And although in Naples I showed you something of it, that is to say the way I was standing when I gave birth to my son, you still should know for sure that I stood and gave birth such as you have seen it now—my knees were bent and I was alone in the stable, praying; I gave birth to him with such exultation and joy of my soul that I had no difficulties when he got out of my body or any pain. Then I wrapped him in swaddling clothes that I had prepared long ago. When Joseph saw this he was astonished and full of joy and happiness, because I had given birth without any help.

At the same place where the Virgin Mary and Joseph were adoring the boy in the cradle, I also saw the shepherds, who had been watching their flocks, coming so that they could look at the child and adore it. When they saw the child, they first wanted to find out whether it was a male or a female, for angels had announced to them that the savior of the world had been born, and they had not said that it was a savioress. Then the Virgin Mary showed to them the nature and the male sex of the child. At once they adored him with great awe and joy. Afterward they returned, praising and glorifying God for all they had heard and seen.

Source 5 from W. Butler-Bowdon, editor, The Book of Margery Kempe *(London: Oxford University Press, 1936), pp. 41–42, 86–88, 161–165, 167–168.*

5. From the Autobiography of Margery Kempe, ca 1430

This creature, when Our Lord had forgiven her her sin, as has been written before, had a desire to see those places where He was born, and where He suffered His Passion,[8] and where He died, with other holy places where He was in His life, and also after His resurrection.

As she was in these desires, Our Lord bade her, in her mind, two years ere she went, that she should go to Rome, to Jerusalem and to Saint James,[9] and she would fain have gone but she had no money.

And then she said to Our Lord:—"Where shall I get money to go with to these Holy Places?"

Our Lord answered to her:—"I shall send thee friends enough in divers countries of England to help thee. And, daughter, I shall go with thee in every country and provide for thee, I shall lead thee thither, and bring thee back again in safety. And no Englishman shall die in the ship that thou art in. I shall keep thee from all wicked men's power. And, daughter, I say to thee that I will that thou wearest clothes of white and no other colour, for thou shalt be arrayed after My will."

"Ah! Dear Lord, if I go arrayed in other manner than other chaste women do, I dread the people will slander me. They will say I am a hypocrite and wonder at me."

8. **Passion:** the crucifixion.

9. **St. James of Compostella:** a cathedral in northwestern Spain.

"Yea, daughter, the more ridicule that thou hast for My love, the more thou pleasest Me."

Then this creature durst not otherwise do than she was commanded in her soul. . . .

So they went forth into the Holy Land till they could see Jerusalem. And when this creature saw Jerusalem, riding on an ass, she thanked God with all her heart, praying Him for His mercy that, as He had brought her to see His earthly city of Jerusalem, He would grant her grace to see the blissful city of Jerusalem above, the city of Heaven. Our Lord Jesus Christ, answering her thought, granted her to have her desire.

Then for the joy she had, and the sweetness she felt in the dalliance with Our Lord, she was on the point of falling off her ass, for she could not bear the sweetness and grace that God wrought in her soul. Then two pilgrims, Duchemen, went to her, and kept her from falling; one of whom was a priest, and he put spices in her mouth to comfort her, thinking she had been sick. And so they helped her on to Jerusalem, and when she came there, she said:—

"Sirs, I pray you be not displeased though I weep sore in this holy place where Our Lord Jesus Christ was quick and dead."

Then went they to the temple in Jerusalem and they were let in on the same day at evensong time, and abode there till the next day at evensong time. Then the friars lifted up a cross and led the pilgrims about from one place to another where Our Lord suffered His[10] . . . and His Passion, every man and woman bearing a wax candle in one hand. And the friars always, as they went about, told them what Our Lord suffered in every place. The aforesaid creature wept and sobbed as plenteously as though she had seen Our Lord with her bodily eye, suffering His Passion at that time. Before her in her soul she saw Him verily by contemplation, and that caused her to have compassion. And when they came up on to the Mount of Calvary,[11] she fell down because she could not stand or kneel, and rolled and wrested with her body, spreading her arms abroad, and cried with a loud voice as though her heart would have burst asunder; for, in the city of her soul, she saw verily and clearly how Our Lord was crucified. Before her face, she heard and saw, in her ghostly sight, the mourning of Our Lady, of Saint John, and Mary Magdalene and of many others that loved Our Lord.

And she had such great compassion and such great pain, at seeing Our Lord's pain that she could not keep herself from crying and roaring though she should have died for it. And this was the first cry[12] that ever she cried in any contemplation. And this manner of crying endured many years after

10. Word missing in ms.

11. **Calvary:** where Jesus is believed to have been crucified.

12. **cry:** outcry, scream.

this time, for aught any man might do, and therefore, suffered she much despite and much reproof. The crying was so loud and so wonderful that it made the people astounded unless they had heard it before, or unless they knew the cause of the crying. And she had them so often that they made her right weak in her bodily might, and especially if she heard of Our Lord's Passion. . . .

[She returned to England, where her crying upset many people and she was called to appear before the Archbishop of York.]

On the next day she was brought into the Archbishop's Chapel, and there came many of the Archbishop's retinue, despising her, calling her "Lollard" and "heretic" and swearing many a horrible oath that she should be burnt.

And she, through the strength of Jesus, spoke back to them:—

"Sirs, I dread ye shall be burnt in Hell without end, unless ye amend in your swearing of oaths, for ye keep not the Commandments of God. I would not swear as ye do for all the money in this world."

Then they went away, as if they had been shamed. She then, making her prayer in her mind, asked grace so to be demeaned that day as was most pleasure to God, and profit to her own soul, and good example to her fellow Christians.

Our Lord, answering her, said it should be right well. At the last, the said Archbishop came into the chapel with his clerks, and sharply he said to her:—

"Why goest thou in white? Art thou a maiden?"

She kneeling on her knees before him, said:—

"Nay, sir, I am no maiden. I am a wife."

He commanded his retinue to fetch a pair of fetters and said she should be fettered, for she was a false heretic.

Then she said:—"I am no heretic, nor shall ye prove me one."

The Archbishop went away and left her standing alone. Then she made her prayers to Our Lord God Almighty to help her and succour her against all her enemies, ghostly and bodily, a long while, and her flesh trembled and quaked wonderfully, so that she was fain to put her hands under her clothes, so that it should not be espied.

Afterwards the Archbishop came again into the Chapel with many clerks, amongst whom was the same doctor who had examined her before, and the monk that had preached against her a little time before in York. Some of the people asked whether she were a Christian woman or a Jew; some said she was a good woman; some said "Nay."

Then the Archbishop took his seat and his clerks also, each of them in his degree, many people being present.

And during the time while the people were gathering together and the Archbishop taking his seat, the said creature stood all behind, making her prayers for help and succour against her enemies with high devotion, so long that she melted all into tears.

And at the last she cried aloud therewith, so that the Archbishop and his clerks and many people had great wonder of her, for they had not heard such crying before. When her crying was passed, she came before the Archbishop and fell down on her knees, the Archbishop saying full boisterously unto her:—

"Why, weepest thou, woman?"

She, answering, said:—"Sir, ye shall wish some day that ye had wept as sore as I."

Then anon, the Archbishop put to her the Articles of our Faith,[13] to which God gave her grace to answer well and truly and readily without any great study, so that he might not blame her. Then he said to the clerks:—

"She knoweth her Faith well enough. What shall I do with her?"

The clerks said:—"We know well that she can say the Articles of the Faith, but we will not suffer her to dwell amongst us, for the people hath great faith in her dalliance, and, peradventure, she might pervert some of them." . . .

Then said the Archbishop to her:—"Thou shalt swear that thou wilt neither teach nor challenge the people in my diocese."

"Nay, sir, I shall not swear," she said, "for I shall speak of God, and rebuke those that swear great oaths wheresoever I go, unto the time that the Pope and Holy Church hath ordained that no man shall be so bold as to speak of God, for God Almighty forbiddeth not, sir, that we shall speak of Him. And also the Gospel maketh mention that, when the woman had heard Our Lord preach, she came before Him with a loud voice and said:—"Blessed be the womb that bore Thee, and the teats that gave Thee suck." Then Our Lord again said to her, "Forsooth, so are they blessed that hear the word of God and keep it." And therefore, sir, methinketh that the Gospel giveth me leave to speak of God."

"Ah! Sir," said the clerks, "here wot we well that she hath a devil within her, for she speaketh of the Gospel."

As quickly as possible, a great clerk brought forth a book and laid Saint Paul, for his part, against her, that no woman should preach.

She answering thereto said:—"I preach not, sir; I come into no pulpit, I use but communication and good words, and that I will do while I live." . . .

She, kneeling down on her knees, asked his blessing. He, praying her to pray for him, blessed her and let her go.

13. **Articles of Faith:** a standard series of questions, in which a person suspected of heresy was asked if they believed in the central doctrines of Christianity—the Trinity, the Virgin Birth, the efficacy of the sacraments, heaven and hell, the power of the Pope.

Then she, going again to York, was received by many people and full worthy clerks, who rejoiced in Our Lord, Who had given her, unlettered, wit and wisdom to answer so many learned men without disgrace or blame, thanks be to God.

Source 6 from Edward Peters, editor, Heresy and Authority in Medieval Europe: Documents in Translation *(Philadelphia: University of Pennsylvania Press, 1980), pp. 259–261. Selection translated by Steven Sargent.*

6. Testimony from the Inquisition Led by Jacques Fournier, Bishop of Pamiers, 1318–1325

Testimony of Arnaud de Savinhan

"He said that as long as he could remember, which might be about thirty years since he was then about forty-five years old, he had believed completely that God had not made the world, namely heaven, earth, and the elements, but that it had always been existing in and of itself, and was not made by God nor by anyone else. Nevertheless he always had believed that Adam was the first man and that God had made him, and thereafter there had been human generation. But before God had made Adam, the world had lasted infinitely into the past; and he [the witness] did not believe that the world had had a beginning.

"He also said that he had believed for all that time up to the beginning of May in the present year that the world had never had a beginning, and thus that it would never end, and that the world would go on in the same way in the future as it did now; and that just as men were generated now and as they had been generated from Adam onward, there would always be in the future the generation of men, and of vines, and of the other plants, and of all animals; nor would that generation ever end. He believed that there was no other world except the present one."

Testimony of Raimond de l'Aire, of Tignac

An older man told him that a mule has a soul as good as a man's; "and from this belief he had by himself deduced that his own soul and those of other men are nothing but blood, because when a person's blood is taken away, he dies. He also believed that a dead person's soul and body both die, and that after death nothing human remains, because he didn't see anything leave the mouth of a person when he dies. From this he believed that the human soul after death has neither good nor evil, and that there is no hell or paradise in another world where human souls are rewarded or punished."

Testimony of Guillemette Benet

"Asked if, since she believed that human souls died with the bodies, she also believed that men would be resurrected and would live again after death, she answered that she did not believe that the resurrecting of the human body would happen, since she believed that as the dead body was buried, the soul was buried with the body; and since she saw that the body putrefied, she believed that it would never be resurrected. . . .

"Asked if she believed that the soul of Jesus Christ, who died on the cross, had died with his body, she answered yes, because although God is not able to die, nevertheless Jesus Christ died and therefore, even though she believed that God always existed, nevertheless she did not believe that Christ's soul lived and existed. . . .

"Asked if she believed that Christ was resurrected, she said yes and that God had done this."

Testimony of Arnaud Gelis, of Pamiers

Arnaud's beliefs	*Roman Catholic orthodoxy*
1. The souls of dead people do not do any other penance except to wander from church to church, some faster, some slower according to their sinfulness.	1. All souls of dead people go to purgatory, where they do the penance they had not completed on earth. And when this is done they go to the heavenly paradise where Christ, Mary, the angels, and the saints reside.
2. After they are finished going around to churches through the streets, the souls go to the place of rest, which is on this earth. They stay there until the judgment day.	2. When their penance is done, the souls of the dead go to the joy of the celestial paradise, which is no place of rest on earth, but rather in heaven.
3. No soul of any man except the most saintly goes directly to heaven or the heavenly kingdom. Souls do this on the day of judgment.	3. All souls of the dead, when their penance is done in purgatory (if they had need of it), enter the heavenly kingdom.
4. Souls of children who died before baptism go to an obscure place until the judgment day. There they feel neither pain nor pleasure. After the judgment day they enter paradise.	4. The souls of unbaptized children will never be saved or enter the kingdom of heaven.

5. No soul of a dead person, no matter how evil, has entered or will enter hell.

5. The souls of all evil persons—i.e., those who perpetrate great crimes that they do not confess or do penance for—go immediately after death to hell, where they stay and are punished for their sins.

6. At the last judgment God will have mercy on all who held the Christian faith and no one will be damned, no matter how evil he was.

6. All souls that held the Christian faith and accepted its sacraments and obeyed its commandments will be saved; but those who, even though holding the faith and accepting the sacraments, did not live according to the commandments will be damned.

7. Christ will have mercy on the souls of all heretics, Jews, and pagans; therefore none of them will be damned.

7. All souls of heretics, pagans, and Jews, who did not want to believe in Christ, will be damned. They will be punished eternally in hell.

8. Human souls, both before the body's death and after, have their own bodily form just like their external body. And the souls have distinct members like hands, eyes, feet, and the rest.

8. Human souls, both while in the body and after its death, because they are spirits, are not corporeal, nor do they have corporeal members, nor do they eat or drink, nor do they suffer such corporeal necessities.

9. Hell is a place only for demons.

9. Hell is a place for demons and for wicked people, where each is punished eternally as he deserves.

Disbelief in Indulgences: Testimony of Guillelme Cornelhano

"He also said that about two years before around the feast of Pentecost . . . a seller of indulgences passed by [him and Guillelma Vilara, wife of Arnald Cuculli] who had with him many indulgences. And after he had left them, Guillelma said, "Do you believe that any man is able to indulge or absolve anyone of his sins? Don't believe it, because no one can absolve anyone except God." And when he himself said that the pope and all priests could absolve man from sins, Guillelma answered that it was not so, only God could [do that]."

Testimony of Peter Sabatier

"When questioned, Peter said and confessed willingly that about three years ago on a certain day in the village of Varillis . . . when he returned from the church [to his house], he said that whatever things the priests and clerics were chanting and singing in the church were lies and tricks; but he never doubted, rather always believed, that the sacraments of the church and its articles of faith were true."

He persisted in this belief "for about a year, and believed out of silliness that priests and clerics, in singing and chanting those things in the church while performing the divine offices, sang and chanted in order to have the contributions, and that there was no good effect wrought by those divine offices."

Source 7 from Norman P. Tanner, editor, Heresy Trials in the Diocese of Norwich, 1428–1431, *Camden Fourth Series, vol. 20 (London: Royal Historical Society, 1977), pp. 111–113. Selection translated by Merry E. Wiesner.*

7. From a Norwich Heresy Trial, 1428–1431

In the name of God, before you, the worshipful father in Christ, William, by the grace of God bishop of Norwich, I, John Reve, a glover from Beccles in your diocese, your subject, feeling and understanding that I have held, believed, and affirmed errors and heresies which be counted in this confession, that is to say:

That I have held, believed, and affirmed that the sacrament of baptism done in water in the form customary to the church is of no avail and not to be demanded if the father and mother of the child are christened and of Christian beliefs.

Also that the sacrament of confirmation done by a bishop is not profitable or necessary to man's salvation.

Also that confession ought not to be made to any priest, but only to God, for no priest has the power to forgive a man of sin.

Also that I have held, believed and affirmed that no priest has the power to make God's body in the sacrament of the altar, and that after the sacramental words said by a priest at mass nothing remains except a loaf of material bread.

Also that only consent of love in Jesus Christ between a man and woman of Christian beliefs is sufficient for the sacrament of matrimony, without any contract of words or solemnizing in church.

Also that I have held, believed and affirmed that only God has power to make the sacraments, and no other creature.

Also that I have held, believed and affirmed that no creature of Christian belief is required to fast in Lent, on the Umber Days, Fridays, vigils of saints nor any other times which the Church commands should be fasted, but it is lawful for people of Christian beliefs to eat meat at all such times and days. And in affirming this opinion I have eaten meat on Fridays and the other aforementioned days.

Also I have held, believed and affirmed that it is lawful for all Christ's people to do all bodily work on Sundays and all other days which the Church has commanded to be held holy, if people keep themselves from other sins at such days and times.

Also I have held, believed, and affirmed that every man may lawfully and without sin withhold and withdraw his tithes and offerings from churches and curates, if it is done prudently.

Also I have held, believed and affirmed that it is lawful for God's people to act contrary to the precepts of the Church.

Also that censures of the Church and sentences of cursing whether from bishops, prelates, or other ordinaries are not to be taken into account or dreaded, for as soon as such bishops or ordinaries curse any man, Christ himself assails him.

Also that I have believed, held, and affirmed that no manner of worship ought to be done to any images of the crucifix, of Our Lady or of any other saints.

Also that no manner of pilgrimages ought to be done to any places of saints, but only to poor people.

Also that I have held and believed that it is not lawful to swear in any case.

Also that I have held, believed, and affirmed that the pope of Rome is the Antichrist and has no power in the Holy Church as St. Peter had unless he follows in the steps of Peter in his manner of living.

Also that all bishops, prelates and priests of the Church are the Antichrist's disciples.

Also that I have held, believed and affirmed that it is as meritorious and as profitable to all Christ's people to be buried in meadows or in wild fields as it is to be buried in churches or churchyards.

Because of which and many other errors and heresies which I have held, believed, and affirmed within your diocese, I am called before you, worshipful father, who has the cure of my soul. And you are fully informed that the said my holding, believing, and affirming are judged errors and heresies and contrary to the Church of Rome, wherefore I willingly follow the doctrine of holy Church and depart from all manner of heresy and error and turn with good heart and will to the unity of the Church. Considering that holy Church will not spare her bosom to him that will return nor God will the death of a sinner but rather that he be returned and live, with a pure heart I confess, detest and despise my said errors and heresies, and the said opinions I confess as heretical and erroneous and repugnant to the faith of the Church at Rome and all universal holy Church. And for as much as I showed myself corrupt and unfaithful through the said things that I so held, believed, and affirmed, from henceforth I will show myself uncorrupt and faithful, and I promise to keep the faith and doctrine of the holy Church truly. And I abjure and forswear all manner of error and heresy, doctrine and opinion against the holy Church and the determination of the Church of Rome—namely the opinions listed before—and swear by these holy gospels which I am bodily touching that from henceforth I shall never hold error nor heresy nor false doctrine against the faith of holy Church and the determination of the Church of Rome. No such things shall I obstinately defend. I shall defend no person holding or teaching such things openly or privately. I shall never after this time be an assistor, counselor, or defender of heretics or of any person suspected of heresy. I shall never ally myself with them. I shall not wittingly show fellowship to them, nor give them counsel, gifts, succor, favor, or comfort. If I know any heretics or any persons suspected of heresy, or people who counsel, assist or defend them, or any persons holding private conventicles or meetings, or holding any singular opinions different from the common doctrine of the Church, I shall let you, worshipful father, or your vicar general in your absence or the diocesans of such persons know soon and immediately. So help me God at holy doom and these holy gospels.

In witness of which things I subscribe here with my own hand a cross—X. And to this part intended to remain in your register I set my sign. And that other part I receive with your seal to keep with me until my life's end. Given at Norwich in the chapel of your palace, xviii day of the month of April in the year of our Lord one thousand four hundred and thirty.

Source 8 from Bayerisches Nationalmuseum, Munich.

8. Madonna, Germany, ca 1430

Source 9 from Cathedral of St. Vitus, Prague (Marburg/Art Resource).

9. Crucifix, Germany, 14th century

QUESTIONS TO CONSIDER

The written sources and the religious statues have provided you with evidence for the two central questions of this chapter. Looking again at those questions, you can see that the first concerns the religious beliefs and practices of laypeople, and the second the official Church reaction to those beliefs and practices. You now need to sort through the sources to separate the information you have gained about each question.

Look first at lay piety itself. Which Christian beliefs were numbers of people attracted to? Why were these beliefs especially appealing? Why might it have been difficult for most people to respond to more esoteric points of theology such as the Trinity? Many of the sources have described or depicted the extremely important role of the Virgin Mary in lay piety. Why do you think people turned to her, rather than to God the Father, in their prayers and devotions? In official Christian theology, Mary is not a goddess but completely human, and believers were urged to honor but not to worship her. From the sources, do you think most laypeople understood this distinction? Looking at the first and third sermon stories, which relate beliefs and practices approved of by the Church, was this distinction always made clear to laypeople?

You have seen that religion was not simply a matter of belief for most people but also of real-world practices and acts. What practices were most popular? How did people see these as contributing to their spiritual lives? Two of the sermon stories and the works of Bridget and Margery Kempe refer matter-of-factly to visions and miracles. What does this imply about the divisions between the natural and supernatural in most people's minds?

The two heresy trials record beliefs that deviated from those officially accepted. Do you find evidence of similar beliefs, though perhaps not carried so far, in any of the other sources? For example, what religious beliefs and practices of Margery Kempe opened her to the accusation of heresy? How would you compare the two heresies from the sources reprinted here? Does either appear to deviate further from official Church teachings than the other? Which teachings do both dispute? Can you make any generalizations about late medieval heresy from these examples, or are the differences between them more striking than the similarities?

Now turn to the second question. Official Church reaction to lay piety was both positive and negative. Positive reactions included attempts by preachers and priests to shape popular belief and to encourage certain actions that they felt strengthened the Church. Judging by the sermon stories, what beliefs and practices were preachers trying to encourage in their listeners? Did the religious statuary encourage similar ideas? How did the archbishop try to influence Margery Kempe? Negative reactions included the Church's attempts to eradicate unacceptable beliefs and behavior, with sanctions ranging from mild scoldings to execution for heresy. Judging from the heresy trials and Margery Kempe's autobiography, what kinds of beliefs were Church officials especially worried about? Did they appear to be more concerned with beliefs or with behavior?

Many of those charged with heresy or with suspect beliefs in the late Middle Ages were women, and the Church hierarchy was of course totally male. Thinking particularly of the experience of Margery Kempe, do you find evidence of gender differences in official attitudes toward lay piety? Even women whose ideas were initially accepted could later be judged heretical. For example, Bridget of Sweden was made a saint less than twenty years after her death, but only forty years later the authenticity of her visions was questioned and she was dismissed by some Church officials as a chatterbox deluded by the devil. Do you find anything in the visions printed here that might have been disturbing to the all-male clerical establishment?

Both lay piety and official reaction to it were shaped by political and economic factors as well as by theology and doctrine. From your sources, which beliefs and practices encouraged or condemned by the Church would have had economic repercussions? Especially in the Norwich heresy trial, which ideas did the Church view as a political threat? Why would the ideas expressed in that trial have been seen as more dangerous than those of Margery Kempe? Reread the discussion in your text of the political and economic changes that late medieval Europe experienced. How was the Church involved in these changes? Do your sources provide evidence for any of the developments described in your text?

You are now ready to answer the two central questions of this chapter: How did common people in the Middle Ages experience and express their religious faith? How did the Church as an institution respond to laypeople's beliefs and practices? Are your answers more complex or less complex than you expected?

EPILOGUE

Most of the strong lay piety in the late Middle Ages remained inside the boundaries judged acceptable by the Church. Groups branded as heretics were usually small, and they were quite successfully wiped out by intensive inquisitions and campaigns of persecution such as those carried out against the Albigensians and Lollards.

Persecution did not put an end to dissatisfaction with the institutional Church, however, nor were preachers and priests ever able to exert total control over the beliefs or activities of common people. Indeed, the more historians study the beliefs of "unlearned" people, the more they discover that people do not passively absorb what they are told but add to it their own ideas. Illiteracy does not preclude imagination or intelligence, and influence between the learned elite and the common people runs in both directions.

Though lay dissatisfaction persisted, it did not cause the institutional Church to change or initiate reforms during the late Middle Ages. In 1377, the papacy returned to Rome, and when the pope died the following year the Roman people forced the college of cardinals, the body of church officials who chose the popes, to elect an Italian pope. This pope, Urban VI, tried to reform some of the Church's problems but did so in such a belligerent way that he set most of the college of cardinals against him. They responded by declaring that the pope's election was invalid because they had been put under duress and, calling for his resignation, elected another pope. Urban did not step down, however, and a forty-year power split began in which two and later three popes simultaneously excommunicated the others, collected taxes, made appointments, and granted indulgences. The Great Schism, as this period is called, was probably the low point in the history of organized Christianity in the West, but the eventual reunification of the Church in 1417 did not resolve all problems. For the next century, the popes concentrated their energies on artistic patronage and expansion of their political power in Italy; despite several major attempts at reform and increasing recognition of internal problems by many Church officials and scholars throughout Europe, low standards of discipline and morality, and high levels of corruption, persisted.

Martin Luther's break with the Catholic church in the early sixteenth century began as yet another attempt at reform but quickly grew into a revolution that split Western Christianity from that time on. The swift and widespread acceptance of Luther's ideas gave vivid testimony to the depth of popular dissatisfaction with the Church. At the very beginning, at least, common people in many parts of Germany saw the Protestant Reformation as the change they had been looking for, a movement that emphasized personal piety and played down the priest's role in the individual's salvation. Supporting Luther initially, they quickly realized that he was not the leader they had hoped for and that he attacked many of the practices, such as pilgrimages or the veneration of Mary, that were dearest to them. Thus the strong lay piety movement of the late Middle Ages is an important factor in understanding not just medieval Christianity in all its complexity but the roots of the Reformation as well.

CHAPTER ELEVEN

THE RENAISSANCE

MAN AND WOMAN

THE PROBLEM

The age we know as the Renaissance had its beginnings in the fourteenth century as a literary movement among educated, mostly upper-class men in northern Italian cities, notably Florence. Such writers as Petrarch attempted to emulate as closely as possible the literary figures of ancient Rome, believing that these men, especially Cicero, had attained a level of style and a command of the Latin language that had never since been duplicated. Petrarch's fascination with antiquity did not stop with language, however, but also included an interest in classical architecture and art; he spent long hours wandering around the large numbers of Roman ruins remaining in Italy. His obsession with the classical past also led him to reject the thousand-year period between his own time and that of Rome, viewing this as a "dark," "gothic," or at best "middle" age—a deep trough between two peaks of civilization. Though Petrarch himself did not call his own period the *Renaissance*—a word that means "rebirth"—he clearly believed he was witnessing the dawning of a new age.

Writers and artists intending to recapture the glory that was Rome would have to study Roman models, and Petrarch proposed an appropriate course of study or curriculum termed the *studia humanitates*, or simply "liberal studies" or the "liberal arts." Like all curricula, it contained an implicit philosophy, a philosophy that came to be known as *humanism*. Humanism was not a rigorous philosophical system like Aristotelianism, nor an all-encompassing belief system like Christianity, but what we might better call an attitude toward learning and toward life.

This new attitude had a slow diffusion out of Italy, with the result that the Renaissance "happened" at very different times in different parts of Europe. Because it was not a single historical event in the same sense as the French Revolution or the Peloponnesian War, the Renaissance is difficult to date. Roughly, we can say it began in Italy in the fourteenth century; spread to France, Germany, and Spain by the end of the fifteenth century; to England by the early part of the sixteenth century; and not until the seventeenth century to Scandinavia. Thus the Renaissance preceded the Reformation—which *was* an event—in most of Europe, took place at the same time as the Reformation in England, and came after the Reformation in Scandinavia. Shakespeare, for example, is considered a "Renaissance" writer even though he lived 250 years after Petrarch.

Though the chronology may be somewhat confusing, there are certain recurring features of humanism through the centuries. One of these is a veneration of the classical past. Petrarch concentrated primarily on Latin and ancient Rome, but during the mid-fifteenth century humanists also began to emphasize Greek language, art, architecture, philosophy, and literature. Though they disagreed about the relative merits of the classical philosophers and writers, all agreed that classical philosophy and literature were of paramount importance to their own culture.

Another feature of humanism is its emphasis on individualism. Medieval society was corporate—that is, oriented toward, and organized around, people acting in groups. Medieval political philosophy dictated that the smallest component of society was not the individual but the family. An individual ruler stood at the top of medieval society, but this ruler was regarded as tightly bound to the other nobles by feudal alliances and, in some ways, as simply the greatest of the nobles. Workers banded together in guilds; pious people formed religious confraternities; citizens swore an oath of allegiance to their own city. Even art was thought to be a group effort, with the individual artist feeling no more need to sign a work than a baker did to sign each loaf of bread. (We know the names of some medieval artists from sources such as contracts, bills of sale, and financial records, but rarely from the paintings or sculpture themselves.)

Christianity encouraged this sense of community as well. Though Christians were baptized and participated in most other sacraments as individuals, the priest represented the whole community when he alone drank wine at communion, and Christ was believed to have embodied all of Christianity when he died. Christians were encouraged to think of themselves as part of one great "Christendom" and to follow the example of Christ by showing humility and meekness rather than the self-assurance that draws attention to the individual.

These attitudes began to shift during the Renaissance. The family, the guild, and other corporate groups remained important social forces, but some individuals increasingly viewed the group as simply a springboard to far greater individual achievement that could be obtained through talent or hard work. Rather than defining themselves primarily within the context of the group, some prized their own sense of uniqueness and individuality, hiring artists to paint or sculpt their portraits and writers to produce verbal likenesses. Caught up in this new individualism, artists and writers themselves began to paint their own self-portraits and write autobiographies. Visual artists, believing that their skill at painting or sculpture was not simply a result of good training but of individual genius, began to sign their works. Rather than the vices they were to medieval Christians, self-confidence and individualism became virtues for many people. Humanists wrote not only biographies of prominent individuals but also treatises that described the attributes of the ideal person. In their opinion, that person should be well rounded and should also exhibit the quality of *virtu*—a word that does not mean virtue but rather the ability to make an impact in one's chosen field of endeavor.

The notion of individualism includes a belief that the people and objects of this world are important, at least important enough to warrant a picture or a verbal description. This belief, usually called *secularism*, is also a part of humanism. Secularism is a highly charged word in modern American political jargon—even more so when expanded to *secular humanism*—and may be too strong a term to apply to Renaissance thinkers. No one in the Renaissance denied the existence of God or the central importance of religion in human life. What they did reject was the idea that it was necessary to forsake the material world and retire to a life of contemplation in order to worship God. God had created this world full of beauty, including the human body, to be appreciated. The talents of each person should be developed to their fullest through education and then displayed to the world because those talents came from God. Studying pre-Christian philosophers such as Plato or Aristotle could enhance an understanding of Christianity because God could certainly have endowed these thinkers with great wisdom even though they were not Christian.

The basis for all these features of humanism—classicism, individualism, secularism—was learning, and humanists all agreed on the importance of education, not just for the individual but also for society as a whole. During the mid-fifteenth century many humanists, such as Leonardo Bruni, began to stress that a proper liberal education was based on training for service to society as well as on classical models. Medieval education had been primarily an organ of the Church, oriented to its needs. Church and cathedral schools trained students to read and write so that they could copy manuscripts, serve as church lawyers, and write correspondence. Monks, priests, and nuns also used their education to honor the glory of God by reciting prayers, studying the Bible and other religious works, composing and singing hymns, or simply speculating on the nature of God. In the Middle Ages the ultimate aim of human life was to *know*, and particularly to know God, so medieval education was often both inwardly directed and otherwordly, helping individuals to come to a better understanding of God. The Renaissance humanists, on the other hand, believed the ultimate aim of human life was to *act*, so humanist education was resoundingly outwardly directed and this-worldly, emphasizing practical skills such as public speaking and writing that would benefit any politician, diplomat, military leader, or businessman. This education was not to be used in a monastery where only God could see it, but in the newly expanding cities and towns of northern Italy, cities that were growing steadily richer thanks to the development of trade we examined in Chapter 8. The primarily classical humanism of the fourteenth century was gradually transformed into civic humanism as humanists took employment as city secretaries and historians and as merchants and bankers sent their sons to humanist schools.

Humanism underwent a further transformation in the sixteenth century, when the governing of the cities of northern Italy was taken over by powerful noblemen. These rulers hired humanists as secretaries, tutors, diplomats, and advisors, and they established humanist academies in their capital cities. Unlike medieval rulers, who saw themselves primarily as military leaders, Renaissance rulers saw themselves as the leaders of all facets of life in their territories. Thus they supported poets and musicians as well as generals, learned several languages, and established their court as the cultural as well as political center of the territory.

Reflecting this new courtly milieu, humanists began to write biographies of rulers and to reflect on the qualities that were important in the ideal ruler and courtier. The trait of *virtu*, so vital in an individual, was even more critical in a ruler. For a ruler, *virtu* meant the ability to shape society as a whole and leave an indelible mark on history. Humanists held up as models worthy of emulation such classical rulers as Alexander the Great and Julius Caesar.

In many ways, then, Renaissance thinkers broke with the immediate medieval past in developing new ideals for human behavior. For one group, however, this break was not so complete. When humanists described the ideal woman, she turned out to be much more like her medieval counterpart than the "Renaissance man" was. The problem of female education was particularly perplexing for humanists. Medieval women, like medieval men, had been educated to serve and know God. Renaissance men were educated to serve the city or the state, which no humanist felt was a proper role for women. If women were not to engage in the type of public activities felt to be the proper arena for displaying talent and education, why should they be educated at all? Should the new virtues of self-confidence and individualism be extended to include women? Or should women be the link with the older Christian virtues of modesty and humility? In their consideration of the proper "Renaissance woman," humanists often exhibited both the tension between, and their attempts to fuse, the pagan classical and medieval Christian traditions.

In this chapter you will examine the writings of several humanists describing the ideal educational program for boys and girls, the ideal male and female courtier, and the ideal ruler. In addition, you will read one short section from the autobiography of a humanist and another from the biography of a ruler written by a humanist; you will also look at several portraits. How do these authors describe the ideal man, woman, and ruler? How were these ideals expressed in written descriptions and visual portraits of actual Renaissance people?

SOURCES AND METHOD

The written sources in this chapter are primarily prescriptive; in other words, they present ideals their humanist authors hoped people would emulate. In chapter 2 we used prescriptive literature to compare ideals and reality in classical Athens, but here we will explore only the ideals themselves. Our questions and methodology are those of intellectual historians, who are interested in the development of ideas as well as in how those ideas relate to other types of changes. Intellectual history is an especially important dimension of the Renaissance, which was primarily an intellectual rather than political or social movement. The questions you need to keep most in mind, then, relate to the ideas set forth here: What qualities were the ideal man, woman, or ruler supposed to possess? How were these qualities to be inculcated in young people? On the basis of these qualities, what did humanists think was most important in human existence? How did authors and artists portraying real people—in biographies, autobiographies, or portraits—express similar ideals?

Whenever we use prescriptive literature as our historical source, we must first inquire into the author's motives. Why did he believe people had to be instructed in matters of behavior? Were they behaving badly or confronting new situations in which they would not know how to act? The intentions of these humanist authors were fairly straightforward because they believed themselves to be living in a new age, a rebirth of classical culture. In their minds, people needed to be informed about the values of this new age and instructed in the means for putting these values into practice. The humanist authors were thus attempting to mold new types of people to fit a new world, not simply correcting attitudes and behavior they felt were wrong or misguided. Consequently, humanist prescriptive literature concentrates on the positive, telling people what to do rather than what not to do (unlike much other prescriptive literature, such as the Ten Commandments).

Before you read the written selections, look at the three portraits. The first is a self-portrait by the German artist Albrecht Dürer; the second a portrait of an Italian woman known simply as Simonetta, by the Italian artist Sandro Botticelli or a member of his workshop; the third a sculpture of the Venetian general Bartolommeo Colleoni by Andrea del Verrocchio. How would you describe the expressions of the subjects in each of these portraits? Do any of them exhibit the qualities prized by the humanists—individualism, *virtu*, self-confidence? What other traits did the artist choose to emphasize? What differences do you see in the portrait of the woman compared with those of the two men? Now proceed to the written evidence.

Sources 4 and 5 are letters from humanists to members of the nobility. The first, discussing the proper education for men, is from Peter Paul Vergerius to Ubertinus, the son of the ruler of Padua, Italy; the second, discussing the proper education for women, is from Leonardo Bruni to Lady Baptista Malatesta, the daughter of the Duke of Urbino. As you read them, note both the similarities and differences in the two courses of study. What factors might account for this? What is the ultimate purpose of the two educational programs?

Sources 6 and 7 are taken from one of the most popular advice manuals ever written, Baldassare Castiglione's *The Courtier*. Castiglione was himself a courtier in Urbino, Mantua, and Milan, and he wrote this discussion of the perfect courtier and court lady in the form of a dialogue between noblemen. As you did for Sources 4 and 5, compare the qualities prescribed for men and women, respectively. How do these relate to the educational program discussed in Sources 4 and 5?

Source 8 comes from one of the most widely read pieces of political advice ever written, Machiavelli's *The Prince*. Like Castiglione, Niccolo Machiavelli had served various governments and had watched rulers and states rise and fall in late-fifteenth- and early-sixteenth-century Italy. What does he believe is the most critical factor or factors in the training of a prince? What qualities should a ruler possess to be effective and display *virtu*?

The first five documents are all straightforward prescriptive literature, as the authors' frequent use of such words as "ought" and "should" indicates. This was not the only way humanists communicated their ideals, however; biographies of real people also expressed these ideals. To use biographies as a source of ideas we must take a slightly more subtle approach, identifying those personal characteristics the author chose to emphasize, those that might have been omitted, and the way in which each biographer manipulated the true personality of his subject to fit the humanist ideal. These are points to consider as you read the next two documents. Source 9 is from the autobiography of Leon Battista Alberti, which you will note is written in the third person. How does Alberti describe himself? How did his life reflect the new humanist ideals? Why might he have chosen to write in the third person instead of saying "I"? Source 10 is Polydore Vergil's description of Henry VII of England, who ruled from 1485 to 1509. What does it tell us about Renaissance monarchs and also about the author?

Once you have read the written selections, return to the portraits. Do you find anything there you did not see before?

THE EVIDENCE

Source 1 from Alte Pinakothek, Munich.

1. Albrecht Dürer, *Self-Portrait in a Fur Coat*, 1500

Source 2 from Staatliche Museen PK, Kupferstichkabinett, Berlin.

2. Workshop of Botticelli (ca 1444–1510), so-called *Simonetta*

Source 3 from Venice (Alinari/Art Resource/Anderson).

3. Andrea del Verrocchio (ca 1435–1488), Sculpture of General Bartolommeo Colleoni

Sources 4 and 5 from W. H. Woodward, editor and translator, Vittorino da Feltre and Other Humanist Educators *(London: Cambridge University Press, 1897), pp. 102, 106–107, 109, 110; pp. 126–129, 132, 133.*

4. From Peter Paul Vergerius, Letter to Ubertinus of Padua, 1392

3. We call those studies *liberal* which are worthy of a free man; those studies by which we attain and practice virtue and wisdom; that education which calls forth, trains, and develops those highest gifts of body and of mind which ennoble men, and which are rightly judged to rank next in dignity to virtue only. For to a vulgar temper gain and pleasure are the one aim of existence, to a lofty nature, moral worth and fame. It is, then, of the highest importance that even from infancy this aim, this effort, should constantly be kept alive in growing minds. . . .

We come now to the consideration of the various subjects which may rightly be included under the name of "Liberal Studies." Amongst these I accord the first place to History, on grounds both of its attractiveness and of its utility, qualities which appeal equally to the scholar and to the statesman. Next in importance ranks Moral Philosophy, which indeed is, in a peculiar sense, a "Liberal Art," in that its purpose is to teach men the secret of true freedom. History, then, gives us the concrete examples of the precepts inculcated by Philosophy. The one shows what men should do, the other what men have said and done in the past, and what practical lessons we may draw therefrom for the present day. I would indicate as the third main branch of study, Eloquence, which indeed holds a place of distinction amongst the refined arts. By philosophy we learn the essential truth of things, which by eloquence we so exhibit in orderly adornment as to bring conviction to differing minds. And history provides the light of experience—a cumulative wisdom fit to supplement the force of reason and the persuasion of eloquence. For we allow that soundness of judgment, wisdom of speech, integrity of conduct are the marks of a truly liberal temper. . . .

4. The principal "Disciplines" have now been reviewed. It must not be supposed that a liberal education requires acquaintance with them all: for a thorough mastery of even one of them might fairly be the achievement of a lifetime. Most of us, too, must learn to be content with modest capacity as with modest fortune. Perhaps we do wisely to pursue that study which we find most suited to our intelligence and our tastes, though it is true that we cannot rightly understand one subject unless we can perceive its relation to the rest. The choice of studies will depend to some extent upon the character of individual minds. . . .

Respecting the general place of liberal studies, we remember that Aristotle would not have them absorb the entire interests of life: for he kept steadily in view the nature of man as a citizen, an active member of the State. For the man who has surrendered himself absolutely to the attractions of Letters or of speculative thought follows, perhaps, a self-regarding end and is useless as a citizen or as prince.

5. From Leonardo Bruni, Letter to Lady Baptista Malatesta, ca 1405

There are certain subjects in which, whilst a modest proficiency is on all accounts to be desired, a minute knowledge and excessive devotion seem to be a vain display. For instance, subtleties of Arithmetic and Geometry are not worthy to absorb a cultivated mind, and the same must be said of Astrology. You will be surprised to find me suggesting (though with much more hesitation) that the great and complex art of Rhetoric should be placed in the same category. My chief reason is the obvious one, that I have in view the cultivation most fitting to a woman. To her neither the intricacies of debate nor the oratorical artifices of action and delivery are of the least practical use, if indeed they are not positively unbecoming. Rhetoric in all its forms—public discussion, forensic argument, logical fence, and the like—lies absolutely outside the province of woman.

What Disciplines then are properly open to her? In the first place she has before her, as a subject peculiarly her own, the whole field of religion and morals. The literature of the Church will thus claim her earnest study. Such a writer, for instance, as St. Augustine affords her the fullest scope for reverent yet learned inquiry. Her devotional instinct may lead her to value the help and consolation of holy men now living; but in this case let her not for an instant yield to the impulse to look into their writings, which, compared with those of Augustine, are utterly destitute of sound and melodious style, and seem to me to have no attraction whatever.

Moreover, the cultivated Christian lady has no need in the study of this weighty subject to confine herself to ecclesiastical writers. Morals, indeed, have been treated of by the noblest intellects of Greece and Rome. What they have left to us upon Continence, Temperance, Modesty, Justice, Courage, Greatness of Soul, demands your sincere respect. . . .

But we must not forget that true distinction is to be gained by a wide and varied range of such studies as conduce to the profitable enjoyment of life, in which, however, we must observe due proportion in the attention and time we devote to them.

First amongst such studies I place History: a subject which must not on any account be neglected by one who aspires to true cultivation. For it is our duty to understand the origins of our own history and its development; and the achievements of Peoples and of Kings.

For the careful study of the past enlarges our foresight in contemporary affairs and affords to citizens and to monarchs lessons of incitement or warning in the ordering of public policy. From History, also, we draw our store of examples of moral precepts. . . .

The great Orators of antiquity must by all means be included. Nowhere do we find the virtues more warmly extolled, the vices so fiercely decried. From them we may learn, also, how to express consolation, encouragement, dissuasion or advice. . . .

I come now to Poetry and the Poets—a subject with which every educated lady must shew herself thoroughly familiar. For we cannot point to any great mind of the past for whom the Poets had not a powerful attraction. . . . Hence my view that familiarity with the great poets of antiquity is essential to any claim to true education. For in their writings we find deep speculations upon Nature, and upon the Causes and Origins of things, which must carry weight with us both from their antiquity and from their authorship. Besides these, many important truths upon matters of daily life are suggested or illustrated. All this is expressed with such grace and dignity as demands our admiration.

But I am ready to admit that there are two types of poet: the aristocracy, so to call them, of their craft, and the vulgar, and that the latter may be put aside in ordering a woman's reading. A comic dramatist may season his wit too highly: a satirist describe too bluntly the moral corruption which he scourges: let her pass them by. . . .

But my last word must be this. . . . All sources of profitable learning will in due proportion claim your study. None have more urgent claim than the subjects and authors which treat of Religion and of our duties in the world; and it is because they assist and illustrate these supreme studies that I press upon your attention the works of the most approved poets, historians and orators of the past.

Sources 6 and 7 from Baldassare Castiglione, The Book of the Courtier, *translated by Charles S. Singleton (Garden City, New York: Doubleday, 1959), pp. 32, 34, 70–71; pp. 206–208, 211–212.*

6. From Baldassare Castiglione, *The Courtier*, 1508–1516

"I hold that the principal and true profession of the Courtier must be that of arms which I wish him to exercise with vigor; and let him be known among the others as bold, energetic, and faithful to whomever he serves. And the repute of these good qualities will be earned by exercising them in every time and place, inasmuch as one may not ever fail therein without great blame. And, just as among women the name of purity, once stained, is never restored, so the reputation of a gentleman whose profession is arms, if ever in the least way he sullies himself through cowardice or other disgrace, always remains defiled before the world and covered with ignominy. Therefore, the more our Courtier excels in this art, the more will he merit praise." . . .

Then signor Gasparo replied: "As for me, I have known few men excellent in anything whatsoever who did not praise themselves; and it seems to me that this can well be permitted them, because he who feels himself to be of some worth, and sees that his works are ignored, is indignant that his own worth should lie buried; and he must make it known to someone, in order not to be cheated of the honor that is the true reward of all virtuous toil. Thus, among the ancients, seldom does anyone of any worth refrain from praising himself. To be sure, those persons who are of no merit, and yet praise themselves, are insufferable; but we do not assume that our Courtier will be of that sort."

Then the Count said: "If you took notice, I blamed impudent and indiscriminate praise of one's self: and truly, as you say, one must not conceive a bad opinion of a worthy man who praises himself modestly; nay, one must take that as surer evidence than if it came from another's mouth. I do say that whoever does not fall into error in praising himself and does not cause annoyance or envy in the person who listens to him is indeed a discreet man and, besides the praises he gives himself, deserves praises from others; for that is a very difficult thing." . . .

"I would have him more than passably learned in letters, at least in those studies which we call the humanities. Let him be conversant not only with the Latin language, but with Greek as well, because of the abundance and variety of things that are so divinely written therein. Let him be versed in the poets, as well as in the orators and historians, and let him be practiced also in writing verse and prose, especially in our own vernacular; for, beside the personal satisfaction he will take in this, in this way he will never want for pleasant entertainment with the ladies, who are usually fond of such things. And if, because of other occupations or lack of study, he does not attain to such a perfection that his writings should merit great praise, let him take care to keep them under cover so that others will not laugh at him, and let him show them only to a friend who can be trusted; because at least they will be of profit to him in that, through such exercise, he will be capable of judging the writing of others. For it very rarely happens that a man who is unpracticed in writing, however learned he may be, can ever wholly understand the toils and industry of writers, or taste the sweetness and excellence of styles, and those intrinsic niceties that are often found in the ancients.

These studies, moreover, will make him fluent, and (as Aristippus said to the tyrant) bold and self-confident in speaking with everyone. However, I would have our Courtier keep one precept firmly in mind, namely, in this as in everything else, to be cautious and reserved rather than forward, and take care not to get the mistaken notion that he knows something he does not know."

7. From Baldassare Castiglione, *The Courtier*, 1508–1516

I think that in her ways, manners, words, gestures, and bearing, a woman ought to be very unlike a man; for just as he must show a certain solid and sturdy manliness, so it is seemly for a woman to have a soft and delicate tenderness, with an air of womanly sweetness in her every movement. . . .

[Again] . . . many virtues of the mind are as necessary to a woman as to a man; also, gentle birth; to avoid affectation, to be naturally graceful in all her actions, to be mannerly, clever, prudent, not arrogant, not envious, not slanderous, not vain, not contentious, not inept, to know how to gain and hold the favor of her mistress [queen or presiding lady at court] and of all others, to perform well and gracefully the exercises that are suitable for women. And I do think that beauty is more necessary to her than to the Courtier, for truly that woman lacks much who lacks beauty. . . . I say that, in my opinion, in a Lady who lives at court a certain pleasing affability is becoming above all else, whereby she will be able to entertain graciously every kind of man with agreeable and comely conversation suited to the time and place and to the station of the person with whom she speaks, joining to serene and modest manners, and to that comeliness that ought to inform all her actions, a quick vivacity of spirit whereby she will show herself a stranger to all boorishness; but with such a kind manner as to cause her to be thought no less chaste, prudent, and gentle than she is agreeable, witty, and discreet: thus, she must observe a certain mean (difficult to achieve and, as it were, composed of contraries) and must strictly observe certain limits and not exceed them.

Now, in her wish to be thought good and pure, this Lady must not be so coy, or appear so to abhor gay company or any talk that is a little loose, as to withdraw as soon as she finds herself involved, for it might easily be thought that she was pretending to be so austere in order to hide something about herself which she feared others might discover; for manners so unbending are always odious. Yet, on the other hand, for the sake of appearing free and amiable she must not utter unseemly words or enter into any immodest and unbridled familiarity or into ways such as might cause others to believe about her what is perhaps not true; but when she finds herself present at such talk, she ought to listen with a light blush of shame. . . .

And to repeat briefly a part of what has already been said. I wish this Lady to have knowledge of letters, of music, of painting, and know how to dance and how to be festive, adding a discreet modesty and the giving of a good impression of herself to those other things that have been required of the Courtier. And so, in her talk, her laughter, her play, her jesting, in short in everything, she will be most graceful and will converse appropriately with every person in whose company she may happen to be, using witticisms and pleasantries that are becoming to her.

Source 8 from Niccolo Machiavelli, The Prince and the Discourses, *translated by Luigi Ricci, revised by E. R. P. Vincent (New York: Random House, 1950), pp. 4, 53, 55, 56, 61–62.*

8. From Niccolo Machiavelli, *The Prince*, 1513

I desire no honour for my work but such as the novelty and gravity of its subject may justly deserve. Nor will it, I trust, be deemed presumptuous on the part of a man of humble and obscure condition to attempt to discuss and direct the government of princes; for in the same way that landscape painters station themselves in the valleys in order to draw mountains or high ground, and ascend an eminence in order to get a good view of the plains, so it is necessary to be a prince to know thoroughly the nature of the people, and one of the populace to know the nature of princes. . . .

A prince should therefore have no other aim or thought, nor take up any other thing for his study, but war and its organisation and discipline, for that is the only art that is necessary to one who commands, and it is of such virtue that it not only maintains those who are born princes, but often enables men of private fortune to attain to that rank. And one sees, on the other hand, that when princes think more of luxury than of arms, they lose their state. The chief cause of the loss of states, is the contempt of this art, and the way to acquire them is to be well versed in the same. . . .

But as to exercise for the mind, the prince ought to read history and study the actions of eminent men, see how they acted in warfare, examine the causes of their victories and defeats in order to imitate the former and avoid the latter, and above all, do as some men have done in the past, who have imitated some one, who has been much praised and glorified, and have always kept his deeds and actions before them. . . .

It now remains to be seen what are the methods and rules for a prince as regards his subjects and friends. . . .

From this arises the question whether it is better to be loved more than feared, or feared more than loved. The reply is, that one ought to be both feared and loved, but as it is difficult for the two to go together, it is much safer to be feared than loved, if one of the two has to be wanting. For it may be said of men in general that they are ungrateful, voluble, dissemblers, anxious to avoid danger, and covetous of gain; as long as you benefit them, they are entirely yours; they offer you their blood, their goods, their life, and their children, as I have before said, when the necessity is remote; but when it approaches, they revolt. And the prince who has relied solely on their words, without making other preparations, is ruined; for the friendship which is gained by purchase and not through grandeur and nobility of spirit is bought but not secured, and at a pinch is not to be expended in your service. And men have less scruple in offending one who makes himself loved than one who makes himself feared; for love is held by a chain of obligation which, men being selfish, is broken whenever it serves their purpose; but fear is maintained by a dread of punishment which never fails.

Still, a prince should make himself feared in such a way that if he does not gain love, he at any rate avoids hatred; for fear and the absence of hatred may well go together, and will be always attained by one who abstains from interfering with the property of his citizens and subjects or with their women. And when he is obliged to take the life of any one, let him do so when there is a proper justification and manifest reason for it; but above all he must abstain from taking the property of others, for men forget more easily the death of their father than the loss of their patrimony. Then also pretexts for seizing property are never wanting, and one who begins to live by rapine will always find some reason for taking the goods of others, whereas causes for taking life are rarer and more fleeting.

But when the prince is with his army and has a large number of soldiers under his control, then it is extremely necessary that he should not mind being thought cruel; for without this reputation he could not keep an army united or disposed to any duty.

Source 9 from James Bruce Ross and Mary Martin McLaughlin, editors, The Portable Renaissance Reader *(New York: Viking, 1953), pp. 480–485, 490–492. Selection translated by James Bruce Ross.*

9. From Leon Battista Alberti, *Autobiography,* after 1460(?)

In everything suitable to one born free and educated liberally, he was so trained from boyhood that among the leading young men of his age he was considered by no means the last. For, assiduous in the science and skill of dealing with arms and horses and musical instruments, as well as in the pursuit of letters[1] and the fine arts, he was devoted to the knowledge of the most strange and difficult things. And finally he embraced with zeal and forethought everything which pertained to fame. To omit the rest, he strove

1. **letters:** Alberti means the humanist program of study, primarily the study of languages and literature.

so hard to attain a name in modelling and painting that he wished to neglect nothing by which he might gain the approbation of good men. His genius was so versatile that you might almost judge all the fine arts to be his. Neither ease nor sloth held him back, nor was he ever seized by satiety in carrying out what was to be done.

He often said that not even in letters had he noticed what is called the satiety of all things among mortals; for to him letters, in which he delighted so greatly, seemed sometimes like flowering and richly fragrant buds, so that hunger or sleep could scarcely distract him from his books. At other times, however, those very letters swarmed together like scorpions before his eyes, so that he could see nothing at all but books. Therefore, when letters began to be displeasing to him, he turned to music and painting and exercise.

He played ball, hurled the javelin, ran, leaped, wrestled, and above all delighted in the steep ascent of mountains; he applied himself to all these things for the sake of health rather than sport or pleasure. . . .

At length, on the orders of his doctors, he desisted from those studies which were most fatiguing to the memory, just when they were about to flourish. But in truth, because he could not live without letters, at the age of twenty-four he turned to physics and the mathematical arts. He did not despair of being able to cultivate them sufficiently, because he perceived that in them talent rather than memory must be employed. At this time he wrote for his brother *On the Advantages and Disadvantages of Letters*, in which booklet, taught by experience, he discussed whatever could be thought about letters. And he wrote at this time for the sake of his soul several little works: *Ephebia, On Religion, Deiphira*, and more of this sort in prose; then in verse, *Elegies* and *Eclogues*, and *Discourses*, and works on love of such a kind as to inculcate good habits in those who studied them and to foster the quiet of the soul. . . .

Although he was affable, gentle, and harmful to no one, nevertheless he felt the animosity of many evil men, and hidden enmities, both annoying and very burdensome; in particular the harsh injuries and intolerable insults from his own relatives. He lived among the envious and malevolent with such modesty and equanimity that none of his detractors or rivals, although very hostile towards him, dared to utter a word about him in the presence of good and worthy men unless it was full of praise and admiration. Even by these envious ones he was received with honour face to face. But, in truth, when he was absent, those who had pretended to love him most slandered him with every sort of calumny, wherever the ears of the fickle and their like lay open. For they took it ill to be exceeded in ability and fame by him who, far inferior to them in fortune, had striven with such zeal and industry. There were even some among his kinsmen (not to mention others) who, having experienced his humanity, beneficence, and liberality, conspired against him most ungratefully and cruelly in an evil domestic plot, and those barbarians aroused the boldness of servants to strike him with a knife, blameless as he was.

He bore injuries of this kind from his kinsmen with equanimity, more in silence than by indignantly resorting to vengeance or permitting the shame and ignominy of his relatives to be made public. . . .

He could endure pain and cold and heat. When, not yet fifteen, he received a serious wound in the foot, and the physician, according to his custom and skill, drew together the broken parts of the foot and sewed them through the skin with a needle, he scarcely uttered a sound of pain. With his own hands, though in such great pain, he even aided the ministering doctor and treated his own wound though he was burning with fever. And when on account of a pain in his side he was continually in an icy sweat, he called in musicians, and for about two hours he strove by singing to overcome the force of the malady and the agony of the pain. His head was by nature unable to endure either cold or wind; but by persistence he learned to bear them, gradually getting used to riding bareheaded in summer, then in winter, and even in raging wind. By some defect in his nature he loathed garlic and also honey, and the mere sight of them, if by chance they were offered to him, brought on vomiting. But he conquered himself by force of looking at and handling the disagreeable objects, so that they came to offend him less, thus showing by example that men can do anything with themselves if they will. . . .

When his favourite dog died he wrote a funeral oration for him.

Source 10 from Denys Hay, editor and translator, The Anglia Historia of Polydore Vergil, AD 1485–1537, *book 74 (London: Camden Society, 1950), p. 147.*

10. From Polydore Vergil, *Anglia Historia*, ca 1540

Henry reigned twenty-three years and seven months. He lived for fifty-two years. By his wife Elizabeth he was the father of eight children, four boys and as many girls. He left three surviving children, an only son Henry prince of Wales, and two daughters, Margaret married to James king of Scotland, and Mary betrothed to Charles prince of Castile. His body was slender but well built and strong; his height above the average. His appearance was remarkably attractive and his face was cheerful, especially when speaking; his eyes were small and blue, his teeth few, poor and blackish; his hair was thin and white; his complexion sallow. His spirit was distinguished, wise and prudent; his mind was brave and resolute and never, even at moments of the greatest danger, deserted him. He had a most pertinacious memory. Withal he was not devoid of scholarship. In government he was shrewd and prudent, so that no one dared to get the better of him through deceit or guile. He was gracious and kind and was as attentive to his visitors as he was easy of access. His hospitality was splendidly generous; he was fond of having foreigners at his court and he freely conferred favours on them. But those of his subjects who were indebted to him and who did not pay him due honour or who were generous only with promises, he treated with harsh severity. He well knew how to maintain his royal majesty and all which appertains to kingship at every time and in every place. He was most fortunate in war, although he was constitutionally more inclined to peace than to war. He cherished justice above all things; as a result he vigorously punished violence, manslaughter and every other kind of wickedness whatsoever. Consequently he was greatly regretted[2] on that account by all his subjects, who had been able to conduct their lives peaceably, far removed from the assaults and evil doing of scoundrels. He was the most ardent supporter of our faith, and daily participated with great piety in religious services. To those whom he considered to be worthy priests, he often secretly gave alms so that they should pray for his salvation. He was particularly fond of those Franciscan friars whom they call Observants, for whom he founded many convents, so that with his help their rule should continually flourish in his kingdom. But all these virtues were obscured latterly only by avarice, from which (as we showed above) he suffered. This avarice is surely a bad enough vice in a private individual, whom it forever torments; in a monarch indeed it may be considered the worst vice, since it is harmful to everyone, and distorts those qualities of trustfulness, justice and integrity by which the state must be governed.

QUESTIONS TO CONSIDER

The first step in exploring the history of ideas is to focus on and define the ideas themselves. Once you have done that by reading the selections and thinking about the questions proposed in Sources and Method, you need to take the next step, which is to compare the ideas of various thinkers. In this way you can trace the development of ideas, how they originate and mature and change in the mind of one thinker after another. First, ask specific questions, such as: What would Bruni think of Castiglione's court lady? How would Leon Battista Alberti be judged by Castiglione's standards? Did Polydore Vergil and Machiavelli have the same ideas about the personal qualities of a ruler? Would a man educated according to the ideas of Vergerius have fitted into Castiglione's ideal court? Would a ruler have wanted him? Would Bruni's learned lady have made a good member of Castiglione's court? Would Botticelli's Simonetta? Does Machiavelli's prince display the qualities Vergerius envisioned in a liberally educated man? How do the main qualities of Machiavelli's prince compare with those of Castiglione's courtier? Why might they be quite different? From the por-

2. **regretted:** missed after he died.

trait, how might Dürer have been judged by each of the writers? Could we think of Verrocchio's sculpture of Colleoni as a portrait of a Machiavellian ruler? How did the artists' ideals for men, women, and rulers differ from the writers'?

Once you have made these specific comparisons, you can move on to broader comparisons of the basic assumptions of the authors and artists: What was the underlying view of human nature for these writers? Was this the same for men and women? You have probably noticed that all the writers and artists presented here are male. Given what you have now learned about ideals for men and women, would you have expected most Renaissance writers to be male?

Many intellectual historians are interested not only in the history of ideas themselves but also in their social and political origins. These historians want to know what people thought and why they thought the way they did. This type of intellectual history is called the *sociology of knowledge* because it explores the societal context of ideas in the same way that sociology examines past and present social groups. The sociology of knowledge is a more speculative field than the history of ideas alone because it attempts to discover the underlying reasons that cause people to develop different ways of thinking in different historical periods—a process that can be quite difficult to discern. Nevertheless, from the information your text provides about the social and political changes occurring during the Renaissance, you can also consider some sociology of knowledge questions: Why did humanism first arise in northern Italy and not elsewhere in Italy? Why was religion regarded as especially important for women? How did Castiglione's career affect his view of politics? How did Machiavelli's? What transformation of the status of artists during the Renaissance allowed both Alberti and Dürer to depict themselves in the way they did? Given that the documents range from 1392 to 1540, what political changes might have accounted for the varying ideals proposed for the individual? How did the ideals proposed for rulers reflect the actual growth of centralized political power? How might the growth of that power have shaped the ideals set forth by Machiavelli and Polydore Vergil? Questions such as these take us somewhat beyond the scope of our original enquiry, but they are important to ask in looking at any ideological change, particularly a sensibility as far reaching as the Renaissance. Humanism did not spring up in a vacuum but at a very specific time and place.

We must also be careful, however, not to overemphasize social and political background in tracing the development of ideas. Intellectual historians prefer to speak of "necessary conditions" or "background factors" rather than "causes." A movement as diffuse and long lasting as humanism necessarily stemmed from a wide variety of factors, so do not feel concerned if you find yourself qualifying your answers to the questions in the last paragraph with such words as "might," "perhaps," and "possibly."

EPILOGUE

Scholars and writers throughout Western history have attempted to revive the classical past, but none of these efforts before or after were to produce the long-lasting effects of the Italian Renaissance. In many ways Petrarch was right: It was the dawn of a new age. As the ideas and ideals of humanism spread, writers all over Europe felt they had definitely broken with the centuries-long tradition that directly preceded them. It was at this point that historians began the three-part division of Western history that we still use today: antiquity, the Middle Ages or medieval period, and the modern period. (If you pause to reflect on what "middle" implies, you will see that no one living in the tenth century would have described him- or herself as living in the "Middle Ages.")

The effects of the Renaissance were eventually felt far beyond the realms of literature and art. Humanist schools and academies opened throughout Europe, and eventually the older universities changed their curricula to add courses in Latin, Greek, and Hebrew language and literature. In northern Europe, humanists became interested in reforming the Church, bringing it back to the standards of piety and morality they believed had been present in the early Church, in the same way that Petrarch had tried to return the Latin language to its ancient standards. This movement, termed *Christian humanism,* would be one of the background factors behind the Protestant Reformation, as learned people began to realize from their studies that the Church was now far removed from the ideas and standards of the early Christians. The intense Renaissance interest in the physical world, combined with monetary greed and missionary impulses, led to the exploration and eventual colonization of much of the non-European world. This secular spirit was also important in setting the stage for the Scientific Revolution of the seventeenth century.

Humanist ideas about the perfect man, woman, and ruler were originally directed at the upper classes but would eventually find a much larger audience. Castiglione's *The Courtier* was translated into every European language, and the personal characteristics he outlined for the ideal courtier became those expected of the middle-class gentleman. Echoes of the Renaissance ideal for women are still with us; a glance at women's magazines or at contemporary advice manuals for girls will show you that physical beauty, morality, femininity, and religion are often still seen to be the most important personal qualities a woman can possess. Machiavelli's *The Prince* has more dramatic echoes, as many modern dictators clearly would agree that it is more important to be feared than loved.

We should not overemphasize the connections between the Renaissance and the modern world, however, for the Renaissance also kept many close ties with the Middle Ages. Despite the emergence of individualism, family background remained the most important determinant of a person's social and economic standing. Despite an emphasis on the material, secular world, religion remained central to the lives of most Europeans. Though some artists were recognized as geniuses, they were still expected to be dependable, tax-paying members of society—that is, members of the community like everybody else. The fact that so many humanists felt it necessary to set standards and describe ideal behavior gives us a clue that not everyone understood or accepted that they were living in a new age: people have no need to be convinced of what they already believe is true.

CHAPTER TWELVE

THE SPREAD OF THE REFORMATION

THE PROBLEM

In 1517, an Augustinian monk in the German province of Saxony named Martin Luther (1483–1546) began preaching and writing against papal *indulgences*, those letters from the pope that substituted for earthly penance or time in Purgatory for Christians who earned or purchased them. Luther called for an end to the sale of indulgences because this practice encouraged people to believe that sins did not have to be taken seriously but could be atoned for simply by buying a piece of paper. In taking this position he was repeating the ideas expressed more than one hundred years earlier by John Hus (1369?–1415), a Czech theologian and preacher. Many of Luther's other ideas had also been previously expressed by Hus, and even earlier by John Wyclif (1328–1384), an English philosopher and theologian. All three objected to the wealth of the Church and to the pope's claims to earthly power; called for an end to pilgrimages and the veneration of saints; said that priests were no better than other people, and that in fact all believers were priests; and believed that the Bible should be available for all people to read for themselves in their own language.

Though Luther's beliefs were quite similar to those of Wyclif and Hus, their impact was not. Wyclif had gained a large following and died peacefully in his bed; less than twenty years after his death, however, English rulers ordered anyone espousing his beliefs to be burnt at the stake as a heretic and so the movement he started was more or less wiped out. Hus himself was burnt at the stake in 1415 at the Council of Constance, which ordered the bones of Wyclif to be dug up and burnt as well. Hus's followers were not as easily steered back to the fold or stamped out as Wyclif's had been, but his ideas never spread beyond Bohemia (modern-day western Czechoslovakia). Martin Luther's actions, on the other hand, led to a permanent split in western Christianity, dividing an institution that had existed as a unified body for almost

1,500 years. Within only a few years, Luther gained a huge number of followers in Germany and other countries, inspiring other religious reformers to break with the Catholic church in developing their own ideas. This movement has come to be known collectively as the "Protestant Reformation," though perhaps *Revolution* might be a more accurate term.

To understand why Luther's impact was so much greater than that of his predecessors, we need to examine a number of factors besides his basic set of beliefs. As with any revolution, social and economic grievances also played a role. Many different groups in early-sixteenth-century German society were disturbed by the changes they saw around them. Peasants, wanting the right to hunt and fish as they had in earlier times, objected to new taxes their landlords imposed on them. Bitter at the wealth of the Church, they believed the clergy were more interested in collecting money from them than in providing spiritual leadership. Landlords, watching the price of manufactured goods rise even faster than they could raise taxes or rents, blamed urban merchants and bankers, calling them greedy and avaricious. Those with only small landholdings were especially caught in an inflationary squeeze and often had to sell off their lands. This was particularly the case for the free imperial knights, a group of about 3,000 individuals in Germany who owed allegiance directly to the emperor but whose landholdings were often less than one square mile. The knights were also losing their reason for existence because military campaigns increasingly relied on infantry and artillery forces rather than mounted cavalry. All these groups were becoming nationalistic and objected to their church taxes and tithes going to the pope, whom they regarded as primarily an Italian prince rather than an international religious leader.

Political factors were also important in the Protestant Revolution. Germany was not a centralized monarchy like France, Spain, and England, but a collection of hundreds of semi-independent territories loosely combined into a political unit called the Holy Roman Empire, under the leadership of an elected emperor. Some of these territories were ruled by nobles such as princes, dukes, or counts; some were independent cities; some were ecclesiastical principalities ruled by archbishops or bishops; and some were ruled by free imperial knights. Each territory was jealous of the power of its neighbors and was equally unwilling to allow the emperor any strong centralized authority. This effect usually worked to the benefit of the individual territories, but it could also work to their detriment. For example, the emperor's weakness prevented him from enforcing such laws against alleged heretics as the one the English king had used against Wyclif's followers, with the result that each territory was relatively independent in matters of religion. On the other hand, he was unable to place limits on papal legal authority or tax collection in the way the stronger kings of western Europe could, with the result that Germany supported many more indulgence peddlers than England or Spain.

The decentralization of the Holy Roman Empire also left each territory more vulnerable than before to external military threats, the most significant of which in the early sixteenth century was the Ottoman Turks. Originating in central Asia, the Turks had adopted the Muslim religion and begun a campaign of conquest westward. In 1453 they took Constantinople and by 1500 were nearing Vienna, arousing fear in many German rulers. The Turkish threat combined with social and economic grievances among many sectors of society to make western Europeans feel the end of the world was near or to look for a charismatic leader who would solve their problems.

Technological factors also played a role in the Protestant Revolution. The printing press was developed in Germany around 1450, and by Luther's time there were printers in most of the major cities in Europe. The spread of printing was accompanied by a rise in literacy, so that many more people were able to read than in the time of Wyclif or Hus. They were also more able to buy books and pamphlets, for the rag paper used by printers was much cheaper than the parchment or vellum used by copyists in earlier centuries. Owning a Bible or part of a Bible to read in one's own language was now a realistic possibility.

In many ways, then, the early sixteenth century was the right time for a major religious change in western Europe. Your task in this chapter will be to assess how and why that change occurred. How were the ideas of Luther disseminated so widely and so quickly? Why were various groups within German society eager to accept these ideas?

SOURCES AND METHOD

Before you look at the evidence in this chapter, think about how ideas are spread in modern American society. What would be the best ways to reach the greatest number of people if you wanted to discuss a new issue or present a new concept? You might want to use health issues as an example, for these often involve totally new ideas and information on one hand and are regarded as vitally important on the other. Think, for example, about the means by which the dangers of cigarette smoking or information about the spread of AIDS are communicated. To answer the first question, we will need to examine the sixteenth-century equivalents of these forms of communication. Health is an appropriate parallel because the most important such issue for many people in the sixteenth century was the health of their souls, a problem directly addressed by Luther and the other reformers.

The spread of the Reformation was perhaps the first example of a successful multimedia campaign; in consequence, as you might imagine, we will be using a wide variety of sources. As you read the written sources and look at the visual evidence, keep in mind that people were seeing, hearing, and reading all these materials at once. As in any successful advertising or propaganda campaign, certain ideas were reinforced over and over again to make sure the message was thoroughly communicated. You will need to pay particular attention, then, to those points that come up in more than one type of source.

Reinforcement of ideas works best if people are receptive to these ideas in the first place. The second question in this chapter has to do with just this receptivity. As you read and examine the sources, keep in mind the religious, social, and economic grievances of different parts of society in sixteenth-century Germany. What ideas either responded directly to these grievances or might be interpreted as responses to these grievances? What were the authors' or artists' main critiques of the Catholic church? How might the messages have been shaped by what the artists or authors knew their audiences wanted to hear or see? In answering the second question, it is again important to note frequently repeated ideas, for these represent not only what the religious reformers wanted to stress but also what they found to be the most effective images or most widely accepted concepts. Thus as you look at the visual sources and read the written ones, jot down a list of the ideas expressed, both those criticizing existing situations and those making suggestions for improvement. Every time an idea appears, note it; in this way you will begin to see which ideas are central and popular.

Source 1 is a sermon delivered in 1521 by Martin Luther in Erfurt on his way to the Diet of Worms, a meeting of the leaders of the territories in the Holy Roman Empire. It is not based on Luther's own notes but was written down by a person in the audience who then gave the transcript to a local printer. This sermon is thus a record of both how the Reformation message was spread orally—so many people wanted to hear him that the Church where Luther preached could not hold them all—and how it was spread in written form, for seven editions of the sermon appeared in 1521 alone. What teachings of the Catholic church did Luther criticize, and what ideas of his own did he emphasize? In assessing how ideas are spread, we have to pay attention not only to the content of the message but also to the form. In what sorts of words and images did Luther convey his ideas to his large audience?

The next sources—three hymns—also serve as both oral and written evidence. Martin Luther believed congregational hymn singing was an important part of a church service and an effective way to teach people about theology. In this tactic he anticipated modern advertisers, who recognize the power of a song or jingle in influencing people's choices. The first two hymns were written by Luther and the third by Paul Speratus, an early follower. As you read them, pay attention both to their content and their images. What ideas from Luther's sermon are reinforced in the hymns? What sorts of mental pictures do the words produce?

(Keep in mind that you are reading these simply as poetry, whereas sixteenth-century people sang them. You may know the tune of "A Mighty Fortress," which is still sung in many Protestant congregations today, and can use your knowledge of its musical setting to help your assessment of the impact of the hymn and its message.)

The Lutheran message would certainly not have spread as widely as it did if church services were its only forum. The remaining sources are those people might have encountered anywhere. The woodcuts all come from Protestant pamphlets—small, inexpensive paper-bound booklets written in German that were readily available in any city with a printer—or *broadsheets*—single-sheet posters that were often sold alone or as a series. These documents are extremely complex visually and need to be examined with great care. Most of the images used would have been familiar to any sixteenth-century person, but they may not be to you. Here, then, are some clues to help guide your analysis.

In Source 5, the person on the right wearing the triple crown with money on the table in front of him is the pope. The devils in front of the table are wearing the flat hats worn by cardinals; the pieces of paper with seals attached that they are handing out are indulgences. At the bottom are the flames of hell; at the top, heaven with a preacher and people participating in the two Church sacraments that the Protestants retained, baptism and communion.

Source 6, another heaven and hell image, shows Christ at the top deciding who will stay in heaven and a two-headed devil at the bottom dragging various people to hell. The right head of the devil wears the triple-crowned papal tiara, the left head the rolled turban worn by Turks. Included in the hellbound group on the right are men wearing the flat cardinal's hat, the pointed hat of bishops, and the distinctive haircut of monks.

Source 7 comes from a series of woodcut contrasts. The left pictures show Biblical scenes and the right the contemporary Church. The top left picture shows Christ with his disciples; the top right, the pope. From their hats and haircuts you can recognize some of the people gathered in front of the pope; those kneeling are wearing crowns, which in the sixteenth century were worn only by rulers. The bottom left picture shows Christ and the moneylenders at the temple at Jerusalem; the bottom right, the pope and indulgences.

Source 8 is the cover of a pamphlet called "The Wolf's Song." By now you recognize the hats and haircuts of the wolves at the top and sides; some of the geese wear crowns, and many carry jeweled necklaces. The choice of animals is intentional. Wolves were still a threat to livestock in sixteenth-century Europe, and geese were regarded as foolish, silly creatures willing to follow their leader blindly into dangerous situations.

Source 9 is a woodcut by the well-known German artist Lucas Cranach that Luther commissioned to illustrate his pamphlet "Against the Papacy at Rome, Founded by the Devil" (1545). It shows two men defecating into the papal triple crown.

Taking all of the images into account, what message do the woodcuts convey about the pope and other Catholic clergy? About the Protestant clergy? Which images and ideas are frequently repeated? How do these fit in with what was preached or sung in church?

The last source is a pamphlet by an unknown author printed in 1523. It is written in the form of a dialogue, a very common form for these Reformation printed materials. Read it, as you did the sermon and the hymns, for both content and tone. Why do you think the author chose these two characters to convey his message? What do they criticize about Catholic practices? How do the ideas expressed here compare with those in Luther's sermon? Which of the woodcuts might have served as an illustration for this pamphlet?

THE EVIDENCE

Source 1 from John W. Doberstein, editor, Luther's Works, *vol. 51 (Philadelphia: Fortress, 1959), pp. 61–66.*

1. Sermon Preached by Martin Luther in Erfurt (Germany), 1521

Dear friends, I shall pass over the story of St. Thomas this time and leave it for another occasion, and instead consider the brief words uttered by Christ: "Peace be with you" [John 20:19] and "Behold my hands and my side" [John 20:27], and "as the Father has sent me, even so I send you" [John 20:21]. Now, it is clear and manifest that every person likes to think that he will be saved and attain to eternal salvation. This is what I propose to discuss now.

You also know that all philosophers, doctors and writers have studiously endeavored to teach and write what attitude man should take to piety. They have gone to great trouble, but, as is evident, to little avail. Now genuine and true piety consists of two kinds of works: those done for others, which are the right kind, and those done for ourselves, which are unimportant. In order to find a foundation, one man builds churches; another goes on a pilgrimage to St. James'[1] or St. Peter's;[2] a third fasts or prays, wears a cowl, goes barefoot, or does something else of the kind. Such works are nothing whatever and must be completely destroyed. Mark these words: none of our works have any power whatsoever. For God has chosen a man, the Lord Christ Jesus, to crush death, destroy sin, and shatter hell, since there was

1. St. James of Compostella, a cathedral in northern Spain.
2. A cathedral in Rome.

no one before he came who did not inevitably belong to the devil. The devil therefore thought he would get a hold upon the Lord when he hung between the two thieves and was suffering the most contemptible and disgraceful of deaths, which was cursed both by God and by men [cf. Deut. 21:23; Gal. 3:13]. But the Godhead was so strong that death, sin, and even hell were destroyed.

Therefore you should note well the words which Paul writes to the Romans [Rom. 5:12-21]. Our sins have their source in Adam, and because Adam ate the apple, we have inherited sin from him. But Christ has shattered death for our sake, in order that we might be saved by his works, which are alien to us, and not by our works.

But the papal dominion treats us altogether differently. It makes rules about fasting, praying, and butter-eating, so that whoever keeps the commandments of the pope will be saved and whoever does not keep them belongs to the devil. It thus seduces the people with the delusion that goodness and salvation lies in their own works. But I say that none of the saints, no matter how holy they were, attained salvation by their works. Even the holy mother of God did not become good, was not saved, by her virginity or her motherhood, but rather by the will of faith and the works of God, and not by her purity, or her own works. Therefore, mark me well: this is the reason why salvation does not lie in our own works, no matter what they are; it cannot and will not be effected without faith.

Now, someone may say: Look, my friend, you are saying a lot about faith, and claiming that our salvation depends solely upon it; now, I ask you, how does one come to faith? I will tell you. Our Lord Christ said, "Peace be with you. Behold my hands, etc." [John 20:26-27]. [In other words, he is saying:] Look, man, I am the only one who has taken away your sins and redeemed you, etc.; now be at peace. Just as you inherited sin from Adam—not that you committed it, for I did not eat the apple, any more than you did, and yet this is how we came to be in sin—so we have not suffered [as Christ did], and therefore we were made free from death and sin by God's work, not by our works. Therefore God says: Behold, man, I am your redemption [cf. Isa. 43:3]; just as Paul said to the Corinthians: Christ is our justification and redemption, etc. [I Cor. 1:30]. Christ is our justification and redemption, as Paul says in this passage. And here our [Roman] masters say: Yes, *Redemptor,* Redeemer; this is true, but it is not enough.

Therefore, I say again: Alien works, these make us good! Our Lord Christ says: I am your justification. I have destroyed the sins you have upon you. Therefore only believe in me; believe that I am he who has done this; then you will be justified. For it is written, *Justicia est fides,* righteousness is identical with faith and comes through faith. Therefore, if we want to have faith, we should believe the gospel, Paul, etc., and not the papal breves,[3] or

3. **breve:** letter of authority.

the decretals,[4] but rather guard ourselves against them as against fire. For everything that comes from the pope cries out: Give, give; and if you refuse, you are of the devil. It would be a small matter if they were only exploiting the people. But, unfortunately, it is the greatest evil in the world to lead the people to believe that outward works can save or make a man good.

At this time the world is so full of wickedness that it is overflowing, and is therefore now under a terrible judgment and punishment, which God has inflicted, so that the people are perverting and deceiving themselves in their own minds. For to build churches, and to fast and pray and so on has the appearance of good works, but in our heads we are deluding ourselves. We should not give way to greed, desire for temporal honor, and other vices and rather be helpful to our poor neighbor. Then God will arise in us and we in him, and this means a new birth. What does it matter if we commit a fresh sin? If we do not immediately despair, but rather say within ourselves, "O God, thou livest still! Christ my Lord is the destroyer of sin," then at once the sin is gone. And also the wise man says: *"Septies in die cadit iustus et resurgit."* "A righteous man falls seven times, and rises again" [Prov. 24:16].

The reason why the world is so utterly perverted and in error is that for a long time there have been no genuine preachers. There are perhaps three thousand priests, among whom one cannot find four good ones—God have mercy on us in this crying shame! And when you do get a good preacher, he runs through the gospel superficially and then follows it up with a fable . . . or he mixes in something of the pagan teachers, Aristotle, Plato, Socrates, and others, who are all quite contrary to the gospel, and also contrary to God, for they did not have the knowledge of the light which we possess. Aye, if you come to me and say: The Philosopher says: Do many good works, then you will acquire the habit, and finally you will become godly; then I say to you: Do not perform good works in order to become godly; but if you are already godly, then do good works, though without affectation and with faith. There you see how contrary these two points of view are.

In former times the devil made great attacks upon the people and from these attacks they took refuge in faith and clung to the Head, which is Christ; and so he was unable to accomplish anything. So now he has invented another device; he whispers into the ears of our Junkers[5] that they should make exactions from people and give them laws. This way it looks well on the outside; but inside it is full of poison. So the young children grow up in a delusion; they go to church thinking that salvation consists in praying, fasting, and attending mass. Thus it is the preacher's fault. But still there would be no need, if only we had right preachers.

The Lord said three times to St. Peter: *"Petre, amas me? etc.; pasce oves meas"* [John 21:15-17]. "Peter, feed, feed, feed my sheep." What is the meaning of

4. **decretal:** decree on matters of doctrine.

5. **junker:** member of the landowning nobility.

pascere? It means to feed. How should one feed the sheep? Only by preaching the Word of God, only by preaching faith. Then our Junkers come along and say: *Pascere* means *leges dare,* to enact laws, but with deception. Yes, they are well fed! They feed the sheep as the butchers do on Easter eve. Whereas one should speak the Word of God plainly to guide the poor and weak in faith, they mix in their beloved Aristotle, who is contrary to God, despite the fact that Paul says in Col. [2:8]: Beware of laws and philosophy. What does "philosophy" mean? If we knew Greek, Latin, and German, we would see clearly what the Apostle is saying.

Is not this the truth? I know very well that you don't like to hear this and that I am annoying many of you; nevertheless, I shall say it. I will also advise you, no matter who you are: If you have preaching in mind or are able to help it along, then do not become a priest or a monk, for there is a passage in the thirty-third and thirty-fourth chapters of the prophet Ezekiel, unfortunately a terrifying passage, which reads: If you forsake your neighbor, see him going astray, and do not help him, do not preach to him, I will call you to account for his soul [Ezek. 33:8; 34:10]. This is a passage which is not often read. But I say, you become a priest or a monk in order to pray your seven canonical hours and say mass, and you think you want to be godly. Alas, you're a fine fellow! It [i.e., being a priest or monk] will fail you. You say the Psalter, you pray the rosary, you pray all kinds of other prayers, and say a lot of words; you say mass, you kneel before the altar, you read confession, you go on mumbling and maundering; and all the while you think you are free from sin. And yet in your heart you have such great envy that, if you could choke your neighbor and get away with it creditably, you would do it; and that's the way you say mass. It would be no wonder if a thunderbolt struck you to the ground. But if you have eaten three grains of sugar or some other seasoning, no one could drag you to the altar with red-hot tongs.[6] You have scruples! And that means to go to heaven with the devil. I know very well that you don't like to hear this. Nevertheless, I will tell the truth, I must tell the truth, even though it cost me my neck twenty times over, that the verdict may not be pronounced against me [i.e., at the last judgment].

Yes, you say, there were learned people a hundred or fifty years ago too. That is true; but I am not concerned with the length of time or the number of persons. For even though they knew something of it then, the devil has always been a mixer, who preferred the pagan writers to the holy gospel. I will tell the truth and must tell the truth; that's why I'm standing here, and not taking any money for it either. Therefore, we should not build upon human law or works, but rather have true faith in the One who is the destroyer of sin; then we shall find ourselves growing in Him. Then everything that was bitter before is sweet. Then our hearts will recognize God. And when that happens we shall be despised, and we shall pay no regard

6. Because of the rule that the priest must say mass fasting.

to human law, and then the pope will come and excommunicate us. But then we shall be so united with God that we shall pay no heed whatsoever to any hardship, ban, or law.

Then someone may go on and ask: Should we not keep the man-made laws at all? Or, can we not continue to pray, fast, and so on, as long as the right way is present? My answer is that if there is present a right Christian love and faith, then everything a man does is meritorious; and each may do what he wills [cf. Rom. 14:22], so long as he has no regard for works, since they cannot save him.

In conclusion, then, every single person should reflect and remember that we cannot help ourselves, but only God, and also that our works are utterly worthless. So shall we have the peace of God. And every person should so perform his work that it benefits not only himself alone, but also another, his neighbor. If he is rich, his wealth should benefit the poor. If he is poor, his service should benefit the rich. When persons are servants or maidservants, their work should benefit their master. Thus no one's work should benefit him alone; for when you note that you are serving only your own advantage, then your service is false. I am not troubled; I know very well what man-made laws are. Let the pope issue as many laws as he likes, I will keep them all so far as I please.

Therefore, dear friends, remember that God has risen up for our sakes. Therefore let us also arise to be helpful to the weak in faith, and so direct our work that God may be pleased with it. So shall we receive the peace he has given to us today. May God grant us this every day. Amen.

Source 2 from Ulrich Leupold, editor, Luther's Works, *vol. 53 (Philadelphia: Fortress, 1965), p. 305.*

2. Luther, *Lord, Keep Us Steadfast in Thy Word,* hymn, 1541–1542

1. Lord, keep us steadfast in thy Word,
And curb the pope's and Turk's vile sword,
Who seek to topple from the throne
Jesus Christ, thine only Son.

2. Proof of thy might, Lord Christ, afford,
For thou of all the lords art Lord;
Thine own poor Christendom defend,
That it may praise thee without end.

3. God Holy Ghost, who comfort art,
Give to thy folk on earth one heart;
Stand by us breathing our last breath,
Lead us to life straight out of death.

Sources 3 and 4 from Lutheran Book of Worship *(Minneapolis: Augsburg, 1978), hymn 229; hymn 297.*

3. Luther, *A Mighty Fortress Is Our God*, hymn, 1527–1528

1. A mighty fortress is our God,
A sword and shield victorious;
He breaks the cruel oppressor's rod
And wins salvation glorious.
The old satanic foe
Has sworn to work us woe!
With craft and dreadful might
He arms himself to fight.
On earth he has no equal.

2. No strength of ours can match his might!
We would be lost, rejected.
But now a champion comes to fight,
Whom God himself elected.
You ask who this may be?
The Lord of hosts is he!
Christ Jesus, mighty Lord,
God's only Son, adored.
He holds the field victorious.

3. Though hordes of devils fill the land
All threat'ning to devour us,
We tremble not, unmoved we stand;
They cannot overpow'r us,
Let this world's tyrant rage;
In battle we'll engage!
His might is doomed to fail;
God's judgment must prevail!
One little word subdues him.

4. God's Word forever shall abide,
No thanks to foes, who fear it;
For God himself fights by our side
With weapons of the Spirit.
Were they to take our house,
Goods, honor, child, or spouse,
Though life be wrenched away,
They cannot win the day.
The Kingdom's ours forever!

4. Paul Speratus, *Salvation unto Us Has Come*, hymn, 1524

1. Salvation unto us has come
By God's free grace and favor;
Good works cannot avert our doom,
They help and save us never.
Faith looks to Jesus Christ alone,
Who did for all the world atone;
He is our mediator.

2. Theirs was a false, misleading dream
Who thought God's law was given
That sinners might themselves redeem
And by their works gain heaven.
The Law is but a mirror bright
To bring the inbred sin to light
That lurks within our nature.

3. And yet the Law fulfilled must be,
Or we were lost forever;
Therefore God sent his Son that he
Might us from death deliver.
He all the Law for us fulfilled,
And thus his Father's anger stilled
Which over us impended.

4. Faith clings to Jesus' cross alone
And rests in him unceasing;
And by its fruits true faith is known,
With love and hope unceasing.
For faith alone can justify;
Works serve our neighbor and supply
The proof that faith is living.

5. All blessing, honor, thanks, and praise
To Father, Son, and Spirit,
The God who saved us by his grace;
All glory to his merit.
O triune God in heav'n above,
You have revealed your saving love;
Your blessed name we hallow.

Source 5 from Dahlem Museum Kupferstichkabinett, Berlin.

5. Matthias Gerung, Broadsheet, Lauingen (Germany), 1546

Source 6 from the Mitchell Collection, London.

6. Matthias Gerung, Broadsheet, Lauingen, 1546

Source 7 from The Pierpont Morgan Library, New York. PML 58544.

7. Lucas Cranach, Pamphlet, Wittenberg (Germany), 1521

Source 8 from Herzog August Bibliothek, Wolfenbuttel.

8. Unknown Artist, Pamphlet, Augsburg (Germany), 1522

Source 9 from Brieg Gymnasialbibliothek.

9. Lucas Cranach, Pamphlet, Wittenberg, 1545[7]

Bapst hat dem reich Christi gethon
Wie man hie handelt seine Cron.
Machts jr zweifeltig: spricht der geist
Schenckt getrost ein: Gott ists ders heist.
Mart: Luth: D.

7. The lines below the woodcut read, "The pope has done to the kingdom of Christ/What is here being done to his own crown."

Source 10 from Oskar Schade, Satiren und Pasquille aus der Reformationszeit, *vol. 2, no. 15 (Hannover: 1863). Selection translated by Merry E. Wiesner.*

10. Anonymous German Pamphlet, 1523

A dialogue between two good friends named Hans Tholl and Claus Lamp, talking about the Antichrist[8] and his followers.

They are in a good mood while drinking wine and sit and discuss some ideas from the letters of Paul.

PREFACE

Dear Christians and brothers, if we want to recognize and know the Antichrist, we have to go to the brothers who can read, so that they will read us the second chapter of the second letter of Paul to the Thessalonians. There we will clearly find him, with his gestures and manners, how he acted and still acts, how he is now revealed so that we do not have to wait any longer but can know him despite his masks. How the devil sends his followers to knock us down, and how the old women and bath maids see him. We have long been blind to the lies and deceits of Satan, the devil. Because we have not paid attention to the divine warnings from Daniel, Paul, Christ, Peter, and the apocalypse of John, God has tormented us with ghosts and apparitions who will take us all with them to hell. Why should this cause God to suffer when He has offered you His holy word? If you don't want it, then go to the devil, for he is here now. He sees, finds, and possesses.

It happened that Hans Tholl and Claus Lamp were looking for each other and finally found each other in the evening.

CLAUS: My friend Hans, where have you been all day? I've been looking for you. The innkeeper has a good wine for two cents, and I wanted to drink a glass of wine with you.
HANS: Dear friend, I've been in a place that I wouldn't take six glasses of wine for.
CLAUS: So tell me where you have been.
HANS: I've got exciting news.
CLAUS: Well, what is it then? Tell me!
HANS: I was in a place where a friend read to four of us from the Bible. He read in the second chapter of the second letter of Paul to the Thessalonians about the Antichrist and how one is to recognize him.
CLAUS: Oh I would have given a penny to have been there.
HANS: I want you to believe that I haven't heard anything like this in my whole life; I wouldn't have given three pennies to miss it.

8. **Antichrist:** the devil.

CLAUS: Can't you remember anything, Hans? Can you tell me something about it?
HANS: I think I can tell you about almost the whole chapter, and only leave a little out.
CLAUS: So tell me! But let's get some wine first. I'll pay for yours.
HANS: Here's to your money!
CLAUS: Innkeeper, bring some wine.
HANS: What does he get for it?
CLAUS: He gets two cents. Now, tell me! I really want to hear what you will say about the Antichrist.
HANS: I'll tell you, but it will seem strange to you.
CLAUS: Why?
HANS: It seemed strange and odd to me, too, that people or states are the Antichrist.
CLAUS: Go ahead, then, you're boring me.
HANS: Stop that. All right, here's what the chapter says: "Dear brothers," Paul writes to the Thessalonians, "We ask you in the name of the coming of Christ and our coming together for the same, that you not be moved in your senses (or from your senses), or frightened by the spirit or the word or by letters supposedly coming from us, saying that the day of the Lord has come or will be coming soon. Let no one deceive you in any way, it will come only when there is disagreement and disunity (even though they all say they are preaching and believing nothing but the Gospel and Christianity) and the man of lawlessness will be disclosed, the son of damnation, who is against the gospel. Then he will be raised up (here Claus Lamp began to understand) above everything that is called a god (or is worshipped as a god) until he sits in the temple of God and lets himself be prayed to as if he were God." Claus, what are you thinking about? Do you know this man of lawlessness?
CLAUS: Now all the devils will come for you! He is no other beast than the Pope and his realm. I would never in my whole life have realized that if you hadn't been there [to hear it]. I'll buy you a second glass of wine!
HANS: Be quiet! I want to tell you more.
CLAUS: My dear friend, still more?
HANS: Of course. First I'll tell you the reason why I was talked to for so long.
CLAUS: My friend, for God's sake keep talking!
HANS: So listen! Here is the text: Paul says: "Don't you remember the things that I told you when I was with you? And now you know what is holding him (or what you should pay attention to), and that he will be revealed in his time. I tell you, that now he is doing so many evil and underhanded things, that only those who stop it now will stop it when his time comes fully. And then he will be revealed, the lawless one"—listen here, Claus—"who the lord Jesus Christ will slay with the breath of His mouth and will totally destroy with the light of His coming. But the coming of the Antichrist is through the activity of Satan, the devil, with great power and supposed

signs and wonders, and with misguided celebration of the evil of those who will be destroyed. Because they would not accept the love of truth" (this clearly refers to the Gospel) "and be saved, God sends them the results of their errors, a great delusion, so that they believe the lies and are all condemned who did not believe the truth but agreed to the evil (and took it on themselves)." See that, Claus! Now you have heard why God has allowed error. Even though we have long wanted not to do wrong, we still hardheadedly keep doing it.

CLAUS: That says a lot. I would set my life on it, if it were only half as important. Now I hear and see that God allows very little understanding.

HANS: Yes, and why? People don't want to know very much and don't go to the Bible. God has hardened them and we are so godless. God will make us suffer because we don't ask about the truth. If we only had half as much concern about the health of our souls as we have about material goods, we wouldn't have come so far from the right path. As you have just heard, it isn't God who sent the so-called preachers [to lead us astray]. Here, I'll say it to you straight: Paul goes on to say: "Dear brothers, we should give thanks to God at all times because he chose you from the beginning, and he called you through the Gospel" (and not through other fairy-stories, as people are now saying).

CLAUS: Unfortunately you are right. Right now I hear strange things about the beast of the Antichrist from priests and monks. God help us!

HANS: Yes, we need to pray earnestly to God to send us good preachers, that preach the pure Gospel and leave the fairy-stories at home.

CLAUS: My friend, I am still thinking about the Antichrist, that he has begun so many devilish things and made the whole world to be his fool.

HANS: That astonishes me, too. But you have now heard from Paul, when he says: "God has allowed them to be deluded because they have not accepted the truth." We haven't noticed this, and the priests have hidden it from us.

CLAUS: I believe that the devil has possessed them all so that they haven't preached to us about these things.

HANS: They are afraid that people would recognize that their God, the Pope, is the Antichrist. People are supposed to honor and pray to him, just like Paul says about the Antichrist. So they are afraid.

CLAUS: That's really true. They've thought: If we tell the lay people this, they will notice and think about how they have to kiss the Pope's foot and call him "most holy." And some know-it-alls even say: The Pope can't do any wrong; he can't sin.

HANS: It's amazing that God has allowed this to happen for so long, that it hasn't been made clear that we have been so blind. What really matters is that we have deserted the truth, my dear Claus. Let's ask God for the true faith! I see clearly that everything will soon be over, that the Last Judgment stands right before the door!

CLAUS: My dear brother Hans, I've thought that for a long time. Shall we go home?

HANS: Yes, let's drink up and go.

CLAUS: I don't want to drink any more, because I have been so seized by pity and compassion. I see that things will end soon. My dear Hans, I want to take this thing to its end with you, so I have to ask: what do you think about the fact that there is such a commotion now about Luther and his writings?

HANS: I think it's because he has discovered the Antichrist. He can't stand it, and I believe he will make many martyrs. I've heard that it has already started in some places; in Antwerp three people have been burnt because of his teachings. And I've heard that in some places they are imprisoning people and hunting them down.

CLAUS: If that's true, that's what's supposed to happen. I have always heard that the Antichrist will make martyrs and will pay money so that people will kill those who do not believe in him but instead preach the word of God.

HANS: I've heard that, too. Now to the next thing: when I want to hear more things read, I'll tell you.

CLAUS: My dear friend, I'll let everything be open to you, because I see clearly what will come out of it. I see clearly, if I want to be saved, I have to come back to the true faith, from which without a doubt the Antichrist and his horde have led us. God give you a good night!

HANS: Same to you! See that you don't forget what I've said.

CLAUS: I won't for the rest of my life. God be praised.

QUESTIONS TO CONSIDER

In exploring how the Reformation movement grew and took root throughout Europe, many scholars point to the printing press as the key factor in explaining why Luther's reforms had a much greater impact than those of Wyclif and Hus. After examining the sources, would you agree? What difference did it make that Luther's sermons were not only delivered but also printed? That hymns were not simply taught to choirs of monks or clergymen but to congregations of laypeople, out of hymnals that were printed and might be purchased by any fairly well-to-do member? That small pamphlets such as the one reproduced here were written in German and appeared in paperback?

Several historians have also pointed to the opposite effect, that the Protestant emphasis on individual reading of the Bible dramatically increased the demand for books. Judging by the language, what sort of person might have bought Luther's sermon or the pamphlet? What effects would you expect the Protestant Reformation to have had on literacy? The religious conflict itself was also a spur to book production and book buying, and religious works were the bestsellers of the sixteenth century. What techniques did the pamphlet writer use to make his work more appealing to a buyer? How might including some of the woodcuts have affected sales?

Of course, the great majority of people in the sixteenth century could not read, so it may be wrong to overemphasize written sources of communication. As you noticed in the dialogue, however, people who could not read often turned to their neighbors who could, so that printed pamphlets were often heard by many who could not read them themselves. This dialogue itself was probably read out loud and may even have been acted out, which we know was the case with more elaborate dialogues containing stage directions and a whole cast of characters. Do you think this dialogue would have been effective read aloud rather than silently? The printing press also increased the circulation of visual images; woodcuts such as those reproduced here often became bestsellers. Why did so many people purchase these woodcuts? If a person's only contact with Protestant thinking were images such as these, how would his or her beliefs have differed from those of a person who could read Luther's words as well?

To answer the second question—why people were eager to hear the Protestant message—look at your list of frequently repeated ideas and images. What do the sources say about the role of good works in helping a person achieve salvation? The role of faith? Why did people misunderstand what was important? What was wrong with the Catholic clergy? In contrast, what did "good preachers" do and emphasize?

Though ideas and images were often repeated, not everyone understood them in the same way nor was attracted to them for the same reasons. Groups within German society responded to different parts of the Protestant message and must be examined separately. Begin with the peasants. How are they depicted in the various sources? Why did the pamphlet writer and the artist of Source 9 choose to make their characters peasants? In the heaven and hell woodcuts, where are peasants and poor people? Why would peasants have been particularly attracted to the criticism of indulgences? Why would Luther's ideas about the value of good works have appealed to them? Source 5 shows nobles in fancy feathered hats near hell and Source 8 depicts rulers as geese; how would peasants have responded to these images? In the dialogue, Claus and Hans both agree that the Last Judgment is near. Why might sixteenth-century peasants have accepted this idea of the imminence of the end of the world?

Now consider the nobles and rulers. We have already noted that several of the woodcuts portray them negatively. How did Luther portray them in his sermon? Though hostility to nobles and rulers is evident in the Protestant message, many of the movement's ideas and images appealed to this class. Look, for example, at the upper right picture in Source 7. How does this scene reflect the hostility of rulers to the papacy? The noble class was primarily responsible for military actions in sixteenth-century Germany. How would they have responded to the language of the hymns? What effect might linking the Turks and the pope in the second hymn and the woodcut of Source 6 have had? Luther's sermon, the second and third hymns, Source 6, and the final dialogue all include devils attacking people or dragging them to hell at the Last Judgment. Why might nobles have been attracted to such imagery? What message would they have gotten from imagery linking such devils with the pope? In what ways did the reasons why Luther's ideas appealed to nobles contradict the reasons they appealed to peasants?

Other groups in German society appear only rarely in the sources given here, so you will not be able to discover as much about why they received the Protestant message enthusiastically as you can in the case of peasants and nobles. You may, however, want to review the sources for evidence relating to the middle class, which you can find most easily in the woodcuts. Which of your answers about the reasons certain ideas were appealing to peasants or nobles would also apply to middle-class people?

You are now ready to answer both the "how" and "why" questions posed in this chapter. *How* were the basic concepts of the Reformation communicated to a wide range of the population? *Why* were these concepts attractive to different groups?

EPILOGUE

Though Luther's initial message was one of religious reform, people quickly saw its social, economic, and political implications. The free imperial knights used Luther's attack on the wealth of the Church and his ideas about the spiritual equality of all Christians to justify their rebellion in 1521. Quickly suppressed, this uprising was followed by a more serious rebellion by peasants in 1525. Peasants in south Germany added religious demands, such as a call for "good pastors" and an end to church taxes, to their long-standing economic grievances and took up arms. The Peasants' War spread eastward and northward but was never unified militarily, and it was brutally put down by imperial and noble armies later the same year.

Given some of Luther's remarks about rulers and human laws (as you read in the sermon), the peasants expected him to support them. He did not and urged them instead to obey their rulers, for in his opinion religion was not a valid justification for political revolution or social upheaval. When the peasants did not listen and continued their rebellion, Luther turned against them, calling them "murdering and thieving hordes." He supported the rulers in their slaughter of peasant armies, and his later writings became much more conservative than the sermon you read here.

The nobles and rulers who accepted Luther's message continued to receive his support, however.

Many of the German states abolished the Catholic church and established their own Protestant churches under their individual ruler's control. This expulsion led to a series of religious wars between Protestants and Catholics that were finally ended by the Peace of Augsburg in 1555. The terms of the peace treaty allowed rulers to choose between Catholicism and Lutheran Protestantism; they were further given the right to enforce religious uniformity within their territories. By the middle of the sixteenth century, then, the only people who could respond as they chose to the Protestant message were rulers.

Achieving religious uniformity was not as simple a task as it had been earlier, however. Though rulers attempted to ban materials they did not agree with and prevent their subjects from reading or printing forbidden materials, religious literature was regularly smuggled from city to city. Because printing presses could produce thousands of copies of anything fairly quickly, ideas of all types spread much more quickly than earlier. Once people can read, it is much more difficult to control the information they take in; though rulers could control their subjects' outward religious activities, they could not control their thoughts.

Rulers were not the only ones who could not control thinking and the exchange of ideas during the sixteenth century. As Luther discovered to his dismay, once ideas are printed and widely disseminated, they take on a life of their own; no matter how much one might wish, they cannot be called back nor be made to conform to their original meaning. Not only did German knights and peasants interpret Luther's message in their own way, but other religious reformers, building on what he had written, developed their own interpretations of the Christian message. They used the same variety of methods that had been so successful in spreading Luther's ideas to communicate their own, and the Protestant Reformation became a multifaceted movement with many different leaders and numerous plans for action.

The Catholic church, learning from Protestant successes, began to publish its own illustrated pamphlets with negative images of Luther and other Protestant leaders along with explanations of its theology in easy-to-understand language. In this chapter we have looked exclusively at Lutheran propaganda, but the oral, written, and visual techniques of communication presented here were employed by all sides in the sixteenth-century religious conflict. Later they would be adapted for other political and intellectual debates.

CHAPTER THIRTEEN

THE MOTIVATIONS FOR EXPLORATION

THE PROBLEM

Beginning in the fifteenth century, European nations sent their emissaries on voyages of exploration, which later turned into voyages of colonization, a process culminating during the nineteenth century in European control of much of the world. Portugal, the first nation to send its ships far beyond the familiar Mediterranean and north Atlantic coastlines, was followed quickly by Spain, and somewhat later by England, the Netherlands, and France.

A glance at the map of Europe partly explains why Portugal as a coastal nation was the pioneer, but geography was not the only important factor. Portugal, a poor country agriculturally, for centuries had derived its export products and main sources of wealth from the sea. Its sailors and navigators were accustomed to navigating the wide Atlantic—called the "Ocean Sea" in the fifteenth century—unlike their Italian and Greek counterparts, who stayed in the calmer waters of the Mediterranean.

Voyages of exploration required vast amounts of financial backing, and in this circumstance Portugal was again fortunate. The Portuguese monarchy, gradually building up its authority and taking power away from the feudal nobility, developed a new tax base that brought in steady revenue. Now the kings and princes of Portugal looked for further ways to expand both their wealth and political power. A bit more adventurous than other rulers, they were willing to risk the substantial funds necessary to send out ships.

The most influential of these rulers was Prince Henry, called "the Navigator," a younger son of King John I. In 1419 Henry, equally fascinated by the technological aspects of discovery, began to support shipbuilders, mapmakers, sailors, astronomers, and instrument makers, encouraging captains to sail farther down the African coast. Henry has often been romanticized as a seeker of pure knowledge, motivated by a thoroughly modern exploring spirit, but this portrait misrepresents him. As a man of the late Middle Ages, he was motivated to a great extent by religion.

Henry had heard stories of Prester John, ruler of a totally mythical Christian kingdom supposed to exist somewhere in Central Africa, and hoped by sending ships down the coast to avoid the Muslims in North Africa and make contact with Prester John. Economic motivations were also extremely important, for gold mines were rumored to exist in the African interior. Henry also realized that if Portuguese ships could circumnavigate Africa, they might be able to make direct contact with the spice-growing East. Portugal could then establish an alternative route for Eastern spices and luxury products and end the monopoly of Italian merchants, who made enormous profits when they transported Eastern goods across the Mediterranean.

This mix of economic and religious motives drew the Portuguese farther and farther down the African coast. Their search for Prester John was not successful, but the economic rewards were great. Gold, ivory, and slaves provided more than adequate recompense for royal—and later private—investors.

Despite the lure of financial reward, many captains were reluctant to sail out of sight of land for very long, a custom that, given the wind patterns in the eastern Atlantic, made it difficult to get much farther south than present-day Zimbabwe. The next step was achieved somewhat by accident in 1487, when a Portuguese captain, Bartholemew Dias, was blown off course; by the time the winds had died so he could head east again, his ship had passed the southern tip of Africa, the Cape of Good Hope, the most dangerous part of the sea voyage to India. Though Dias had proved the Cape could be rounded, it would take another twelve years for a Portuguese ship to reach India. In 1499, a Portuguese fleet under Vasco de Gama was finally successful, landing at Calicut on the west coast of the subcontinent.

Meanwhile Portugal's much larger and richer neighbor had decided to send out voyages of exploration as well. During the fifteenth century, the Spanish monarchs had been consolidating their authority, gradually stripping the feudal nobility and even the Church of their traditional powers. Spain was also in the final stages of the *reconquista*, the reconquering of Spain from the Muslims that had begun several centuries earlier. By the last decades of the fifteenth century, the Muslims held only the small territory of Granada in the south; in 1492, under the leadership of King Ferdinand of Aragon and Queen Isabella of Castile, Spanish armies conquered Granada. Where would Spaniards looking for conquest and adventure turn now?

Yet another accident provided the answer. Before Dias sailed around the Cape of Good Hope, a Genoese sailor named Christopher Columbus had come to the Portuguese court hoping to obtain financial backing for an expedition to China. Columbus proposed sailing west, not east, believing that Asia lay less than 4,000 miles from Portugal in that direction. His calculations were based on two sources—the Italian Marco Polo's reports about the distance by land across Asia and estimates of the size of the earth made by Ptolemy, a Greek astronomer of the fourth century. Ptolemy, however, estimated that the earth was one-sixth smaller than it actually is, and Polo greatly exaggerated the distance he had traveled. Totally accepting the calculations of both, Columbus carried their books in his sea chest when he finally embarked. Columbus had no luck at the Portuguese court because the astronomers and geographers there were doubtful about Ptolemy's figures, and he turned next to Spain. At first the Spanish monarchs also showed little interest, but the persistence of Columbus, combined with the great success of their rivals the Portuguese, made them change their minds. Because the level of geographic knowledge at the Spanish court was far lower than at the Portuguese court, Ptolemy's estimates were not questioned, and with three tiny ships Columbus set off westward in 1492. He took with him two Arabic interpreters, hoping to use them at the court of the Chinese emperor, for he knew the Arabs had had previous contact with China and assumed someone at the court could speak Arabic.

As we all know, Columbus did not reach China but rather the islands of the Caribbean, located where his estimates predicted China to be. Columbus believed he was in Asia, of course, and, despite three more voyages, would continue to believe this until he died. Ferdinand and Isabella agreed with him and were ecstatic about the new route to Asia; the Portuguese were alarmed and wanted to make sure part of Asia was reserved for them even though they had not gotten there yet. The monarchs turned to the only higher authority they all recognized, the Pope, who drew a line around the world about 300 miles west of the Azores that granted Spain the right to everything west and Portugal everything east. Spain and Portugal signed the Treaty of Tordesillas confirming the papal division in 1494. The Pope and the Spanish monarchs thought the line went down the middle of the Atlantic, but the Portuguese may have already known that it crossed the large land mass of South America. It is not certain if Portuguese sailors had already discovered Brazil. Whatever the case, by the terms of this treaty Portugal received the rights to the eastern part of South America.

For the Pope to divide up the world in this way may seem a bit odd to us today, but from the perspective of western Europe in 1494 it was not that strange an act. All of western Europe was still under the religious authority of the Pope, and only Spain and Portugal had begun to venture much overseas, at least since the largely unknown voyages of the Vikings in the tenth and eleventh centuries. No other countries in Europe were in a position to register a complaint. This still begs the question that we will address in this chapter: What gave the rulers of Portugal and Spain—and eventually those of other countries in western Europe—the conviction that they had the right to divide up the world in this manner? The rulers knew that the lands their ships reached were inhabited yet still announced they were "discovering" and "claiming" these lands for one or another country. What do these proclamations indicate about European attitudes toward the rest of the world?

Though few objections were raised within Europe to the Pope's action (had it been widely known in the non-European world, the treaty would probably have been greeted with laughter), everything had changed by a century later. Half of Europe was now Protestant and no longer heeded the Pope. Even more important, other nations, especially England and the Netherlands, had built up fleets of ships bigger and better than those of Spain and Portugal, and these countries were not going to be kept out of the race for colonies and overseas trading ports. Elizabeth I of England encouraged English explorers and adventurers to search for new routes and to challenge Spain's hold on Central and South America by raids on Spanish colonies and treasure ships. During the seventeenth century, the English, Dutch, and French established colonies in North America, the English in India and Africa as well; the Dutch in the Far East, South America, and southern Africa; and the French in Africa, India, and the Caribbean. Even less powerful European countries such as Sweden and Denmark felt it important to establish colonies.

All these explorations brought Europeans into contact with lands and peoples totally unlike any they had previously experienced. Columbus's discoveries were particularly startling, showing Europe a "New World" that even the ancient Greeks had known nothing about. Educated Europeans were somewhat disturbed by these findings, as they called into question all standard sources of authority. How were these new lands and peoples to be fit in to a worldview that derived from the Bible and the ancient Greeks? How was this great gap in the knowledge of Aristotle and Plato to be explained? Were these New World people also descended from the sons of Noah? Did Christ die for them as well? We would probably be less surprised today to find intelligent life somewhere else in the universe than sixteenth-century Europeans were at meeting the inhabitants of the New World.

Your task in this chapter will be to analyze the writings of several early explorers and other Europeans interested in exploration in order to answer the following questions: What motivated Europeans to travel such great distances, or to subsidize this travel? What was their reaction to the lands and peoples they encountered?

SOURCES AND METHOD

To understand a person's reasons for taking action, historians of the contemporary period often try to interview that person directly; oral history can provide clues that official records do not. This is not possible, of course, for earlier periods, so we must rely on written records. Certain types of written records, such as letters, diaries, and journals, can function in many ways like an oral interview, however, because they are more likely to reveal human thoughts, desires, and motivations than official records such as chronicles or reports. The Renaissance also saw the beginning of the literary form known as the essay, in which an author reflected on a topic and expressed his or her personal opinions. Along with essays, letters and journals can also be quite reflective and thoughtful, combining descriptions of experiences with the writer's reponses to them.

The sources you will be using in this chapter include letters, journals, and essays. Source 1 is taken from a letter from King Manoel of Portugal to King Ferdinand and Queen Isabella of Spain; Source 2 is a letter and the prologue to a journal of Christopher Columbus, both written on his first voyage. The third selection is taken from a letter written by Amerigo Vespucci, a Florentine agent who sailed on Columbus's first voyage to Venezuela in 1499. All these selections date from the very first decade after the discovery of the New World and reflect much of the initial excitement. Source 4 is an extract from the journal of Sir Walter Raleigh, first published in 1596. Raleigh led an English expedition that discovered the country of Guiana in South America. Selections 5 and 6 are from two essays written by Michel de Montaigne (1533–1592), a French nobleman and philosopher who is often called "the father of modern skepticism." Montaigne did not take part in any voyages himself but wrote these essays after hearing and reading reports of the discoveries as well as observing some New World residents at the French court. The last three sources were all written nearly a century after the first three, when Europeans had had more time to reflect on the differences between the Old World and the New World.

As you read the selections, note first those reasons for exploration the author mentions explicitly. Which reasons does he mention first, and which does he return to? When people write letters, they often open and close with what they believe is most important, or what they believe the recipient of the letter most wants to or expects to hear, so you need to pay special attention to these parts of the letters by King Manoel and Columbus. Motivations also emerge less obviously in the way the discoverers describe what they saw. What were they particularly pleased to find? What does this indicate about their motivations? How do the explorers describe their own actions? Does this description give you further, and perhaps different, information about their aims?

Letters, diaries, and journals from the fifteenth and sixteenth centuries cannot be read in the same way that modern private letters and diaries can. In many cases, even though these documents were ostensibly private, the authors fully expected them to be published later and in some cases, such as the selections printed here from Vespucci and Raleigh, even arranged for their publication. As you read, think about how such foreknowledge would have affected the content of these pieces. In addition, letters of any period are written following certain conventions. We traditionally start letters with "Dear" without implying the normal meaning of "dear" and end with "Sincerely" when we may not be sincere at all; we may even end with "Love" to persons whom we would not otherwise address that way. One of the first things a person studying a foreign language must learn are these conventions, and we must learn them for past cultures as well if we want to interpret the personal correspondence of these cultures correctly. What portions of the letters appear to you to be simply conventional—that is, what the recipient would expect to find in any letter? Think about how you write letters to your parents, friends, prospective employers, or the editor of a newspaper. How might these writers also have been affected in their style by the identity of their correspondent?

The second question focuses on the reactions of the explorers and commentators to the New World. Here you must pay close attention both to the descriptions themselves and to the tone they are written in. What kinds of words do the writers use to describe the lands and the peoples they encountered? Is their overall reaction positive or negative? What do their actions in meeting the native people reveal about their beliefs and goals? The earliest explorers, such as Columbus and Vespucci, realized only gradually that they had found a genuinely new world and not simply the eastern extension of the old one. How did their preconceptions about what they would find influence their reactions? Most later explorers like Raleigh, as well as later commentators including Montaigne, recognized that the Americas were not part of the Old World and had not shared in its history. How did recognition of this distinction shape their reactions? What other differences do you see in the earlier reactions as compared to the later ones? What might have accounted for these differences?

THE EVIDENCE

Source 1 from E. G. Ravenstein, editor and translator, A Journal of the First Voyage of Vasco de Gama *(London: Hakluyt Society, 1898), pp. 77–79.*

1. From a Letter by King Manoel, 1499

Most high and excellent Prince and Princess, most potent Lord and Lady!

Your Highnesses already know that we had ordered Vasco da Gama, a nobleman of our household, and his brother Paulo da Gama, with four vessels to make discoveries by sea, and that two years have now elapsed since their departure. And as the principal motive of this enterprise has been with our predecessors, the service of God our Lord, and our own advantage, it pleased Him in His mercy to speed them on their route. From a message which has now been brought to this city by one of the captains, we learn that they did reach and discover India and other kingdoms and lordships bordering upon it; that they entered and navigated its sea, finding large cities, large edifices and rivers, and great populations among whom is carried on all the trade in spices and precious stones, which are forwarded in ships (which these same explorers saw and met with in good numbers and of great size) to Mecca, and thence to Cairo, whence they are dispersed throughout the world. Of these [spices, etc.] they have brought a quantity including cinnamon, cloves, ginger, nutmeg, and pepper, as well as other kinds, together with the boughs and leaves of the same; also many fine stones of all sorts, such as rubies and others. And they also came to a country in which there are mines of gold, of which [gold], as of the spices and precious stones, they did not bring as much as they could have done, for they took no merchandise with them.

As we are aware that your Highnesses will hear of these things with much pleasure and satisfaction, we thought well to give this information. And your Highnesses may believe, in accordance with what we have learnt concerning the Christian people whom these explorers reached, that it will be possible notwithstanding that they are not as yet strong in the faith or possessed of a thorough knowledge of it, to do much in the service of God and the exaltation of the Holy Faith, once they shall have been converted and fully fortified in it. And when they shall have thus been fortified in the faith, there will be an opportunity for destroying the Moors of those parts. Moreover, we hope, with the help of God, that the great trade which now enriches the Moors of those parts, through whose hands it passes without the intervention of other persons or peoples, shall, in consequence of our regulations, be diverted to the natives and ships of our own kingdom, so that henceforth all Christendom, in this part of Europe, shall be able in a large measure to provide itself with these spices and precious stones.

Source 2 from John Boyd Thacher, Christopher Columbus: His Life, His Work, His Remains *(New York: Kraus Reprints, 1967) vol. 1, pp. 513–515, vol. 2, pp. 21–26. Selection translated by John Boyd Thacher.*

2. Journal Prologue and Letter by Christopher Columbus, 1492

PROLOGUE

Because, most Christian and very exalted and very excellent and very powerful Princes, King and Queen of the Spains and of the Islands of the Sea, our Lords, in this present year of 1492 after your Highnesses had made an end to the war of the Moors, who were reigning in Europe, and having finished the war in the very great city of Granada, where in this present year on the 2nd day of the month of January, I saw the Royal banners of your Highnesses placed by force of arms on the towers of the Alhambra, which is the fortress of the said City: and I saw the Moorish King come out to the gates of the City and kiss the Royal hands of your Highnesses, and the hands of the Prince, my Lord: and then in that present month, because of the information which I had given your Highnesses about the lands of India, and about a Prince who is called Great Khan, which means in our Romance language, King of Kings—how he and his predecessors had many times sent to Rome to beg for men learned in our Holy Faith that they might be instructed therein, and that the Holy Father had never furnished them, and so, many peoples believing in idolatries and receiving among themselves sects of perdition, were lost:—your Highnesses, as Catholic Christians and Princes, loving the Holy Christian faith and the spreading of it, and enemies of the sect of Mahomet and of all idolatries and heresies, decided to send me, Christopher Columbus, to the said regions of India, to see the said Princes and the peoples and lands, and learn of their disposition, and of everything, and the measures which could be taken for their conversion to our Holy Faith: and you ordered that I should not go to the east by land, by which it is customary to go, but by way of the west, whence until to-day we do not know certainly that any one has gone. So that, after having banished all the Jews from all your Kingdoms and realms, in the same month of January,[1] your Highnesses ordered me to go with a sufficient fleet to the said regions of India: and for that purpose granted me great favours and ennobled me, that from then henceforward I might entitle myself *Don* and should be High Admiral of the Ocean-Sea[2] and Viceroy and perpetual Governor of all the islands and continental land which I might discover and acquire, and which from now henceforward might be discovered and acquired in the Ocean-Sea, and that my eldest son should succeed in the same manner, and thus from generation to generation for ever after. . . . Also, Lords and Princes, besides describing each night what takes place during the day, and during the day, the sailings of the night, I propose to make a new chart for navigation, on which I will locate all the sea and the lands of the Ocean-Sea, in their proper places, under their winds; and further, to compose a book and show everything by means of drawing, by the latitude from the equator and by longitude from the west, and above all, it is fitting that I forget sleep, and study the navigation diligently, in order to thus fulfil these duties, which will be a great labour.

1. In their attempts to achieve total religious orthodoxy, Ferdinand and Isabella issued a royal edict expelling all practicing Jews from Spain in 1492.

2. **Ocean-Sea:** the Atlantic.

LETTER

Sir:

As I know that you will have pleasure of the great victory which our Lord hath given me in my voyage, I write you this, by which you shall know that, in twenty days I passed over to the Indies with the fleet which the most illustrious King and Queen, our Lords, gave me: where I found very many islands peopled with inhabitants beyond number. And, of them all, I have taken possession for their Highnesses, with proclamation and the royal standard displayed; and I was not gainsaid. . . . There are wonderful pinegroves, and very large plains of verdure, and there is honey, and many kinds of birds, and many various fruits. In the earth there are many mines of metals; and there is a population of incalculable number. Spañola is a marvel; the mountains and hills, and plains and fields, and land, so beautiful and rich for planting and sowing, for breeding cattle of all sorts, for building of towns and villages. There could be no believing, without seeing, such harbours as are here, as well as the many and great rivers, and excellent waters, most of which contain gold. In the trees and fruits and plants, there are great differences from those of Juana. In this, there are many spiceries, and great mines of gold and other metals. The people of this island, and of all the others that I have found and seen or not seen, all go naked, men and women, just as their mothers bring them forth; although some women cover a single place with the leaf of a plant, or a cotton something which they make for that purpose. They have no iron or steel, nor any weapons; nor are they fit thereunto; not because they be not a well-formed people and of fair stature, but that they are most wondrously timorous. They have no other weapons than the stems of reeds in their seeding state, on the end of which they fix little sharpened stakes. Even these, they dare not use; for many times has it happened that I sent two or three men ashore to some village to parley, and countless numbers of them sallied forth, but as soon as they saw those approach, they fled away in such wise that even a father would not wait for his son. And this was not because any hurt had ever been done to any of them:—on the contrary, at every headland where I have gone and been able to hold speech with them, I gave them of everything which I had, as well cloth as many other things, without accepting aught therefor; but such they are, incurably timid. It is true that since they have become more assured, and are losing that terror, they are artless and generous with what they have, to such a degree as no one would believe but he who had seen it. Of anything they have, if it be asked for, they never say no, but do rather invite the person to accept it, and show as much lovingness as though they would give their hearts. And whether it be a thing of value, or one of little worth, they are straightways content with whatsoever trifle of whatsoever kind may be given them in return for it. I forbade that anything so worthless as fragments of broken platters, and pieces of broken glass, and strapbuckles, should be given them; although when they were able to get such things they seemed to think they had the best jewel in the world, for it was the hap of a sailor to get, in exchange for a strap, gold to the weight of two and a half castellanos, and others much more for other things of far less value; while for new blancas they gave every thing they had, even though it were the worth of two or three gold castellanos, or one or two arrobas of spun cotton. They took even pieces of broken barrel-hoops, and gave whatever they had, like senseless brutes; insomuch that it seemed to me ill. I forbade it, and I gave gratuitously a thousand useful things that I carried, in order that they may conceive affection, and furthermore may be made Christians; for they are inclined to the love and service of their Highnesses and of all the Castilian nation, and they strive to combine in giving us things which they have in abundance, and of which we are in need. And they know no sect, or idolatry; save that they all believe that power and goodness are in the sky, and they believed very firmly that I, with these ships and crew, came from the sky; and in such opinion, they received me at every place where I landed, after they had lost their terror. And this comes not because they are ignorant; on the contrary, they are men of very subtle wit, who navigate all those seas, and who give a marvellously good account of everything—but because they never saw men wearing clothes or the like of our ships. And as soon as I arrived in the Indies, in the first island that I found, I took some of them by force, to the intent that they should learn our speech and give me information of what there was in those parts. And so it was, that very soon they understood us and we them, what by speech or what by signs; and those Indians have been of much service. To this day I carry them with me who are still of the opinion that I come from heaven, as appears from much conversation which they have had with me. And they were the first to proclaim it wherever I arrived; and the others went running from house to house and to the neighbouring villages, with loud cries of "Come! come to see the people from heaven!" Then, as soon as their minds were reassured about us, every one came, men as well as women, so that there remained none behind, big or little; and they all brought something to eat and drink, which they gave with wondrous lovingness. . . . I took possession of a large town which I named the city of Navidad. And I have made fortifications there, and a fort which by this time will have been completely finished and I have left therein men enough for such a purpose, with arms and artillery, and provisions for more than a year, and a boat, and a man who is master of all sea-craft for making others; and great friendship with the King of that land, to such a degree that he prided himself on calling and holding me as his brother. And even though his mind might change towards attacking those men, neither he nor his people know what arms are, and go naked. As I have already said, they are the most timorous creatures there are in the world, so that the men who remain there are alone sufficient to destroy all that land, and the island is without personal danger for them if they know how to behave themselves. It seems to me that in all those islands, the men are all content with a single wife; and to their chief or king they give as many as twenty. The women, it appears to me, do more work than the men. Nor have I been able to learn whether they held personal property, for it seemed to me that whatever one had, they all took shares of, especially of eatable things. . . . And in truth I should have done much more if the ships had served me as well as might reasonably have been expected. This is enough; and thanks to eternal God our Lord who gives to all those who walk His way, victory over things which seem impossible; and this was signally one such, for although men have talked or written of those lands, it was all by conjecture, without confirmation from eyesight, importing just so much that the hearers for the most part listened and judged that there was more fable in it than anything actual, however trifling. Since thus our Redeemer has given to our most illustrious King and Queen, and to their famous kingdoms, this victory in so high a matter, Christendom should take gladness therein and make great festivals, and give solemn thanks to the Holy Trinity for the great exaltation they shall have by the conversion of so many peoples to our Holy faith; and next for the temporal benefit which will bring hither refreshment and profit, not only to Spain, but to all Christians. This briefly, in accordance with the facts. Dated on the caravel, off the Canary Islands, the 15 February of the year 1493.

At your command,
The Admiral

Source 3 from C. R. Markham, editor and translator, The Letters of Amerigo Vespucci *(London: Hakluyt Society, 1894), pp. 27–28.*

3. From a Letter by Amerigo Vespucci, 1499

[We] went to another island. We found that this other island was inhabited by very tall people. We landed to see whether there was any fresh water, and not thinking it was inhabited, as we had not seen anyone, we came upon very large foot-marks in the sand, as we were walking along the beach. We judged that if the other measurements were in proportion to those of their feet, they must be very tall. Going in search, we came into a road which led inland. There were nine of us. Judging that there could not be many inhabitants, as the island was small, we walked over it to see what sort of people they were. When we had gone about a league we saw five huts, which appeared to be uninhabited, in a valley, and we went to them. But we only found five women, two old, and three children of such lofty stature that, for the wonder of the thing, we wanted to keep them. When they saw us they were so frightened that they had not the power to run away. The two old women began to invite us with words, and to set before us many things, and took us into a hut. They were taller than a large man who may well be tall, such as was Francesco degli Albizi, but better proportioned. Our intention was to take the young girls by force, and to bring them to Castille as a wonderful thing. While we were forming this design there entered by the door of the hut as many as thirty-six men, much bigger than the women, and so well made that it was a rare thing to behold them. They, in like manner, put us into such a state of perturbation that we rather wished we were on board, than having dealings with such people. They carried very large bows and arrows, and great clubs with knobs. They talked among themselves in a tone as if they wished to destroy us. Seeing ourselves in such danger, we made various suggestions one to another. Some proposed that we should attack them in the hut, and others said that it would be better to do so outside, while others advised that we should not take any action until we saw what the natives were going to do. We at last agreed to go out of the hut, and walk away in the direction of the ships as if nothing had happened, and this we did. Having taken our route to return to the ships, they also came along behind us at a distance of about a stone's-throw, talking among themselves. I believe they had not less fear of us than we of them; for sometimes we stopped to rest, and they did so also without coming nearer. At last we came to the beach, where the boats were waiting for us. We got in, and, when we were some way from the shore, the natives rushed down and shot many arrows; but we then had little fear of them. We replied with two bombard-shots, more to frighten them than to do them harm. They all fled into the woods, and so we took leave of them, thankful to escape after a dangerous adventure. They all went naked like the others. We called this island *the Island of the Giants*, by reason of their stature.

Source 4 from Walter Raleigh, Discovery of the Empire of Guiana *(London: Hakluyt Society, 1894), pp. 60–61, 82. Spelling modernized.*

4. From the Journal of Sir Walter Raleigh, 1596

This Arwacan pilot, with the rest, feared that we would have eaten them, or otherwise have put them to some cruel death, for the Spaniards to the end that none of the people in the passage towards Guiana or in Guiana itself might come to speech with us persuaded all the nations that we were men-eaters and cannibals: but when the poor men and women had seen us and that we gave them meat and to every one some thing or other which was rare and strange to them, they began to conceive the deceit and purpose of the Spaniards, who indeed (as they confessed) took from them both their wives and daughters daily, and used them for the satisfying of their own lusts, especially such as they took in this manner by strength. But I protest before the majesty of the living God, that I neither know nor believe that any of our company one or other, by violence or otherwise, ever knew any of their women, and yet we saw many hundreds, and had many in our power, and of those very young, and excellently favoured which came among us without deceit, stark naked.

Nothing got us more love among them than this usage, for I suffered not any man to take from any of the nations so much as a pina or a potato root without giving them contentment, nor any man so much as to offer to touch any of their wives or daughters: which course, so contrary to the Spaniards (who tyrannize over them in all things) drew them to admire her Majesty, whose commandment I told them it was, and also wonderfully to honour our nation. But I confess it was a very impatient work to keep the meaner sort from spoil and stealing when we came to their houses, which because in all I could not prevent, I caused my Indian interpreter at every place when we departed to know of the loss or wrong done, and if aught were stolen or taken by violence, either the same was restored and the party punished in their sight, or else it was paid for to their uttermost demand. They also much wondered at us after they heard that we had slain the Spaniards at Trinidado, for they were before resolved that no nation of Christians durst abide their presence, and they wondered more when I had made them know of the great overthrow that her Majesty's army and fleet had given them of late years in their own countries. . . .

I never saw a more beautiful country, nor more lively prospects, hills so raised here and there over the valleys, the river winding into divers branches, the plains adjoining without bush or stubble, all fair green grass, the ground of hard sand easy to march on, either for horse or foot, the deer crossing in every path, the birds towards the evening singing on every tree with a thousand several tunes, cranes and herons of white, crimson, and carnation perching on the river's side, the air fresh with a gentle easterly wind, and every stone that we stooped to take up, promised either gold or silver by his complexion.

Source 5 from Donald M. Frame, translator, The Complete Essays of Montaigne *(Stanford: Stanford University Press, 1948), pp. 153, 155–159.*

5. From Michel de Montaigne, *Of Cannibals*, 1572

These nations, then, seem to me barbarous in this sense, that they have been fashioned very little by the human mind, and are still very close to their original naturalness. The laws of nature still rule them, very little corrupted by ours; and they are in such a state of purity that I am sometimes vexed that they were unknown earlier, in the days when there were men able to judge them better than we. I am sorry that Lycurgus and Plato did not know of them; for it seems to me that what we actually see in these nations surpasses not only all the pictures in which poets have idealized the golden age and all their inventions in imagining a happy state of man, but also the conceptions and the very desire of philosophy. . . .

They have their wars with the nations beyond the mountains, further inland, to which they go quite naked, with no other arms than bows or wooden swords ending in a sharp point, in the manner of the tongues of our boar spears. It is astonishing that firmness they show in their combats, which never end but in slaughter and bloodshed; for as to routs and terror, they know nothing of either.

Each man brings back as his trophy the head of the enemy he has killed, and sets it up at the entrance to his dwelling. After they have treated their prisoners well for a long time with all the hospitality they can think of, each man who has a prisoner calls a great assembly of his acquaintances. He ties a rope to one of the prisoner's arms by the end of which he holds him, a few steps away, for fear of being hurt, and gives his dearest friend the other arm to hold in the same way; and these two, in the presence of the whole assembly, kill him with their swords. This done, they roast him and eat him in common and send some pieces to their absent friends. This is not, as people think, for nourishment, as of old the Scythians used to do; it is to betoken an extreme revenge.

I am not sorry that we notice the barbarous horror of such acts, but I am heartily sorry that, judging their faults rightly, we should be so blind to our own. I think there is more barbarity in eating a man alive than in eating him dead; and in tearing by tortures and the rack a body still full of feeling, in roasting a man bit by bit, in having him bitten and mangled by dogs and swine (as we have not only read but seen within fresh memory, not among ancient enemies, but among neighbors and fellow citizens, and what is worse, on the pretext of piety and religion), than in roasting and eating him after he is dead. . . .

So we may well call these people barbarians, in respect to the rules of reason, but not in respect to ourselves, who surpass them in every kind of barbarity.

Their warfare is wholly noble and generous, and as excusable and beautiful as this human disease can be; its only basis among them is their rivalry in valor. They are not fighting for the conquest of new lands, for they still enjoy that natural abundance that provides them without toil and trouble with all necessary things in such profusion that they have no wish to enlarge their boundaries. They are still in that happy state of desiring only as much as their natural needs demand; anything beyond that is superfluous to them. . . . Truly here are real savages by our standards; for either they must be thoroughly so, or we must be; there is an amazing distance between their character and ours.

Three of these men, ignorant of the price they will pay some day, in loss of repose and happiness, for gaining knowledge of the corruptions of this side of the ocean; ignorant also of the fact that of this intercourse will come their ruin (which I suppose is already well advanced: poor wretches, to let themselves be tricked by the desire for new things, and to have left the serenity of their own sky to come and see ours!)—three of these men were at Rouen, at the time the late King Charles IX was there. The king talked to them for a long time; they were shown our ways, our splendor, the aspect of a fine city. After that, someone asked their opinion and wanted to know what they had found most amazing. They mentioned three things, of which I have forgotten the third, and I am very sorry for it; but I still remember two of them. They said that in the first place they thought it very strange that so many grown men, bearded, strong, and armed, who were around the king (it is likely that they were talking about the Swiss of his guard) should submit to obey a child, and that one of them was not chosen to command instead. Second (they have a way in their language of speaking of men as halves of one another), they had noticed that there were among us men full and gorged with all sorts of good things, and that their other halves were beggars at their doors, emaciated with hunger and poverty; and they thought it strange that these needy halves could endure such an injustice, and did not take the others by the throat, or set fire to their houses. . . .

All this is not too bad—but what's the use? The don't wear breeches.

Source 6 from George B. Ives, translator, The Essays of Montaigne *(New York: Heritage, 1946), pp. 1235–1237.*

6. From Michel de Montaigne, *Of Coaches*, 1588

Our world has lately discovered another (and who can assure us that it is the last of its brethren, since the spirits, the sibyls, and we ourselves have known nothing of this one until now?), no less large, as fully peopled and fruitful as our world, but so new and so infantine that it is still taught its A B C; it is not fifty years since it knew neither letters nor weights nor measures nor garments nor corn nor vines; it was still a naked baby in arms, and lived solely on what it received from its mother-nurse. . . . I much fear that we shall have greatly hastened its decline and ruin by our contagion, and that we shall have sold our beliefs and our arts to it very dear. It was an infant world, yet we have not whipped and subdued it to our teaching by the advantage of our worth and native strength, or won its favour by our justice and kindness, or subjugated it by our magnanimity. The greater part of the answers and of the negotiations entered into with them witness that they are in no wise inferior to us in native clearness of mind and pertinence. The startling magnificence of the cities of Cuzco and of Mexico and, among other like matters, the king's garden in which all the trees and fruits and all the plants, in the same arrangement and size that they have in a garden, were wonderfully fashioned of gold—as, in his cabinet, were all the animals native to his land and his waters—and the beauty of their work in precious stones, in feathers, in cotton, and in painting, shew that in craftsmanship also they are in no wise inferior to us.

But as for piety, observance of the laws, kindliness, liberality, loyalty, frankness, it has served us well to have less than they; they were lost by this advantage over us, and sold and betrayed themselves. As for hardiness and courage, as for staunchness, constancy, resolute endurance of pain and of hunger and of death, I should not fear to oppose examples that I could find among them to the most famous ancient examples that we have in the traditions of our world on this side of the ocean. For, as to those who have subjugated them, take away the strategems and trickery which they made use of to deceive them, and the natural amazement which it brought to the latter nations—to see so unexpectedly the arrival of bearded men different from themselves in language, in religion, in bearing, and in aspect, coming from so distant a part of the world which they had never known to be inhabited at all, mounted on great unfamiliar monsters, opposed to those who had never seen, not only a horse, but any beast whatever trained to carry and support a man or any other burden; furnished with a shining and hard skin and armed with a sharp and glittering weapon, opposed to those who bartered great wealth of gold and pearls for the marvel of the gleam of a mirror or a knife, and who had neither knowledge nor substance by which they could in any length of time pierce our steel; and furthermore to the lightning and thunder of our cannon and harquebuses,[3] capable of dismaying even Cæsar, had he been surprised by them as unprepared as were these, opposed to peoples that were naked except where some weaving of cotton had been invented, without other weapons, for the most part, than bows, stones, clubs, and wooden shields, peoples taken by surprise under colour of friendliness and good faith and by curiosity to see strange and unfamiliar things—take away, I say, from the conquerors this disparity and you take from them the whole occasion of so many victories. When I consider the indomitable ardour with which so many thousands of men, women and children so often come forward and fling themselves upon inevitable dangers in defence of their gods and of their liberty—this generous obstinacy in enduring all extremities and difficulties, and death, rather than submit to the domination of those by whom they have been so shamefully deceived, some

3. **harquebus:** hand-held firearm.

choosing rather, when captured, to pine away from hunger and fasting than to accept food from the hands of their enemies, so basely victorious—I perceive that whosoever should have attacked them on equal terms, of weapons and of experience and of numbers, would have been as much in peril as in any war that we know, and even more so.

QUESTIONS TO CONSIDER

To answer the two questions posed in this chapter, you will need to compare all the selections. Beginning with reasons for exploration, what changes do you find over the hundred years covered here? Which motives remained the same? At the time of Columbus, Vespucci, and King Manoel of Portugal, all of Europe practiced one religion. By the time of Montaigne and Raleigh, however, Europe was divided into two bitterly opposed camps of believers and had seen many decades of religious war. How did this altered state of affairs bear on the religious motivation of the explorers?

The numerous dynastic and national rivalries of sixteenth-century Europe also expanded overseas once the individual nations had established trading bases and colonies. From this time onward, most "European" wars involved some fighting far beyond the boundaries of Europe, fighting that in many cases determined the final outcome of the war. As you read these selections, can you detect premonitions or actual indications of internation rivalry? For example, would you regard King Manoel's comments about the pleasure he knows Ferdinand and Isabella will feel about his success as sincere or ironic? How did Raleigh use the long dispute between England and Spain to his own advantage? How did he draw the native inhabitants into this rivalry? (The victory by the forces of Queen Elizabeth he refers to was the defeat of the Spanish Armada in 1588 seven years before.)

In assessing historical reasons, it is important not to take every statement at face value but to consider the honesty or hypocrisy of the author. We have already seen how letters are shaped by convention as well as by the expectation that they might eventually be published. Given the cultural background of the authors, what motivations would you expect them to have emphasized? How might such official explanations have changed over the sixteenth century as the religious and political situation in Europe underwent drastic alteration? Your text can provide information about the actual course of the Spanish and English conquest of the New World. How did this conquest fit in with the stated aims of Columbus and Raleigh? Which would you judge to be the more valid demonstration of a person's true goals, stated aims or actions?

Historians have commented that educated Europeans invented the New World long before they ever discovered it—that is, they saw what was wrong in their own world and imagined a place where life was better. When they finally did "discover" America, they tried to believe it the place they had imagined and were disappointed when it turned out not to be Paradise. Do any of the authors you have read here provide evidence for this assertion? Montaigne especially draws explicit comparisons between the Old World and the New. How do both worlds stand up, in his judgment? Does his view differ from the attitude of the actual explorers, which you can gauge from their actions on meeting the inhabitants? Why might this have been? Do any of the explorers criticize his own culture in the way Montaigne does? Source 5 ends with an ironic comment by Montaigne. What does this remark indicate about the reactions of other contemporary writers to the New World natives?

Many of the explorers were neither highly educated nor searching for anything so idealistic as paradise on earth. Nonetheless, they brought their prejudices and cultural biases with them and did not view the New World or its inhabitants objectively. You can see this cultural bias in many of their descriptions, particularly when you note the observations common to all the explorers. What startled them the most about the inhabitants of America? How do their reactions to the natural products of the New World—fruits, plants, and metals—compare with their reactions to the culture of its human residents? What might have accounted for this difference in reaction? It is also possible to detect some tension between the leaders of the exploration and their men, particularly in the selections from Columbus and Raleigh. How did the leaders try to handle or prevent problems that arose between the native inhabitants and their men? Do you think their efforts were successful?

European exploration of the New World arose from a complicated mixture of motives, but abstract reasons alone would not have been enough without technological innovation. During the fifteenth and sixteenth centuries, improvements in shipbuilding, navigational instruments, and weaponry allowed Europeans to carry out in reality the voyages they had dreamed of. What new devices do the sources mention explicitly? Did the authors recognize the importance of these devices? How did Columbus and Montaigne differ in their estimations of the role of firearms?

In the century between Columbus and Raleigh, Europeans quickly conquered much of the New World. How would the relative effortlessness of this annexation have affected their views of the role of technology? How were later encounters between Europeans and New World residents shaped by this easy conquest? How would it have influenced European views of their own superiority, which you have no doubt noted in even the earliest explorers, Columbus and Vespucci? Though Montaigne recognized the vital role played by sheer superiority of weaponry in the colonization of America, many European commentators did not, attributing the takeover simply to cultural superiority. Do you find evidence of such ethnocentrism in the sources for this chapter? Why might explorers and commentators have wanted to downplay the importance of technology in their explorations and conquests? How did their technological advantage nonetheless shape their reactions to the residents of the New World?

Though our sources of this period were a varied group, you should now be able to make some generalizations about their reasons for sailing to the New World, their reactions to what they found, and the relationship between the two—that is, how did the reality of America begin to influence their motivation once they saw the New World for themselves?

EPILOGUE

European overseas expansion had tremendous consequences both in Europe and in its conquered territories. Especially after the Spanish discovered gold and silver in Central and South America, wealth poured back into the Old World. We would expect Spain to have benefitted from this windfall, but the Spanish economy was not highly developed; Spanish monarchs had to purchase all the manufactured goods their colonists needed from other parts of Europe. In addition, Spain was often involved in wars on the European continent and borrowed money from German bankers to pay for the soldiers and equipment it needed. Thus, much of the New World wealth flowed straight through Spain and directly into the hands of bankers such as the Fuggers of Augsburg.

Overseas holdings were not an unqualified boon for Portugal, either. A small and relatively poor country, it was to find that defending its empire eventually cost more than the wealth gained through spices and other imports. By the end of the sixteenth century, Portugal had lost many of its colonies to the Netherlands.

The nations that most clearly benefited from the age of exploration were not the pioneers but the second wave, particularly the Netherlands and England. The Dutch came to dominate the spice trade, bringing back more goods in their boats than any other nation. The cities of Antwerp and later Amsterdam became the largest trading centers in Europe, and the world's first stock market opened in Amsterdam in 1609. The seventeenth century saw a cultural, intellectual, and artistic flowering in the Netherlands known as the "Golden Age," supported by the wealth from overseas trade. In the long run, however, England was most successful with its overseas conquests, creating the largest network of colonies and becoming the most powerful nation in the world. By 1700 the center of power and wealth in Europe had shifted from the Mediterranean to the Atlantic, with colonies both the result of, and a crucial factor in, the rise to power of the unified nation states of western Europe.

Exploration and colonization thus brought mixed blessings to the Old World. Its impact on the New World, in contrast, was an unmitigated disaster. It is estimated that as much as 90 percent of the pre-Columbian population of Central America died in the first fifty years of Spanish rule, some by warfare but most by disease and forced labor in Spanish mines. Because much of the agriculture and mining in the New World required huge numbers of workers, the Spanish and Portuguese, and later other European colonists, began to import African slaves. This was the world's first enforced mass relocation of a population from one continent to another. It may be hard for us, as twentieth-century witnesses, to understand how most early modern Europeans could have had so little regard for other human beings that neither the massive deaths of the native population nor the horrors of the slave trade bothered them unduly. Possibly your readings in this chapter have given you some insight into the kind of world-view that would allow such things to happen.

CHAPTER FOURTEEN
STAGING ABSOLUTISM

THE PROBLEM

The "Age of Absolutism" is the label historians often apply to the history of Europe in the seventeenth and eighteenth centuries. In many ways it is an appropriate description; although the seventeenth-century conflict between king and Parliament in England resulted in the Civil War (1642–1648) and Glorious Revolution (1688), which severely limited royal power and created parliamentary government, most European monarchs of this era aspired to absolute authority in their realms.

The royal absolutism that evolved in seventeenth-century Europe represents an important step in governmental development. In constructing absolutist states, monarchs and their ministers both created new organs of administration and built on existing institutions of government to supplant the regional authorities of the medieval state with more centralized state power. In principle, this centralized authority was subject to the absolute authority of the monarch; in practice, royal authority was nowhere as encompassing as that of a modern dictator. Poor communication systems, the persistence of traditional privileges that exempted whole regions or social groups from full royal authority, and other factors all set limits on royal power. Nevertheless, monarchs of the era strove for the ideal of absolute royal power, and France was the model in their work of state building.

French monarchs of the seventeenth and early eighteenth centuries more fully developed the system of absolute monarchy. In these rulers' efforts to overcome impediments to royal authority we can learn much about the creation of absolutism in Europe. Rulers in Prussia, Austria, Russia, and many smaller states sought not only the real power of the French kings but also the elaborate court ceremony and dazzling palaces that symbolized that power.

Absolutism in France was the work of Henry IV (r. 1589–1610), Louis XIII (r. 1610–1643) and his minister Cardinal Richelieu, and Louis XIV (r. 1643–1715). These rulers established a system of centralized royal political authority that destroyed many remnants of the feudal monarchy. The reward for their endeavors was great: with Europe's largest population and immense wealth, France was potentially the mightiest country on the continent in 1600 and its natural leader, if only these national strengths could be unified and directed by a strong government. Creation of such a government around an absolute monarch was the aim of French rulers, but they confronted formidable problems, common to many early modern states, in achieving their goal. Nobles everywhere still held considerable power, in part a legacy of the system of feudal monarchy. In France they possessed military power, which they used in the religious civil wars of the sixteenth century and in their Fronde revolt against growing royal power in the mid-seventeenth century. Nobles also exercised considerable political power through such representative bodies as the Estates General and provincial assemblies, which gave form to their claims for a voice in government. Moreover, nobles served as the judges of the great law courts, the *parlements,* that had to register all royal edicts before they could take effect.

A second obstacle to national unity and royal authority in many states, in an age that equated national unity with religious uniformity, was the presence of a large and influential religious minority. In France the Protestant minority was known as the Huguenots. Not only did they forswear the Catholic religion of the king and the majority of his subjects, but they possessed military power in their rights, under the Edict of Nantes,[1] to fortify their cities.

A third and major impediment to unifying a country under absolute royal authority lay in regional differences. The medieval monarchy of France had been built province by province over several centuries, and the kingdom was not well integrated. Some provinces, like Brittany in the north, retained local estates or assemblies with which the monarch actually had to bargain for taxes. Many provinces had their own cultural heritage that separated them from the king's government centered in Paris. These differences might be as simple as matters of local custom, but also as complex as unique systems of civil law. A particular problem was the persistence of local dialects, which made the French of royal officials a foreign and incomprehensible tongue in large portions of the kingdom.

The only unifying principle that could overcome all these centrifugal forces was royal authority. The task in the seventeenth century was to build a theoretical basis for a truly powerful monarch, to endow the king with tangible power that gave substance to theory, and to place the sovereign in a setting that would never permit the country to forget his new power.

To establish an abstract basis for absolutism, royal authority had to be strengthened and reinforced by a veritable cult of kingship. Seventeenth-century French statesmen

1. **Edict of Nantes:** In this 1598 decree, King Henry IV sought to end the civil warfare between French Catholics and Huguenots. He granted the Protestants basic protection, in the event of renewed fighting, by allowing them to fortify some 200 of their cities. The edict also accorded the Protestants freedom of belief with some restrictions and civil rights equal to those of Catholic Frenchmen.

built on medieval foundations in this task. Medieval kings had possessed limited tangible authority but substantial religious prestige; their vassals had rendered them religious oaths of loyalty. French monarchs since Pepin the Short had been anointed in a biblically inspired coronation ceremony in which they received not only the communion bread the Catholic Church administered to all believers, but also the wine normally reserved for clerics; once crowned, they claimed to possess mystical religious powers to heal with the royal touch. All these trappings served to endow the monarch with almost divine powers, separating him from and raising him above his subjects. Many seventeenth-century thinkers emphasized this traditional divine dimension of royal power. Others, as you will see, found more practical grounds for great royal power.

To achieve greater royal power, Henry IV reestablished peace after the religious civil warfare of the late sixteenth century and Cardinal Richelieu curbed the military power of the nobility. With the creation of loyal provincial administrators, the *intendants*, and a system of political patronage that he directed, the Cardinal also established firmer central control in the name of Louis XIII. Richelieu, moreover, ended Huguenot political power by crushing their revolt in 1628, and he intervened in the Thirty Years' War to establish France as a chief European power.

The reign of Louis XIV completed the process of consolidating royal authority in France. Louis XIV created much of the administrative apparatus necessary to centralize the state. The king brought the nobility under even greater control, building in Europe's largest army a force that could defeat any aristocratic revolt and creating in Versailles a court life that drew nobles near to the king, away from provincial plotting, where their actions could be observed. The king also sought to extend royal authority by expanding France's borders through a series of wars and to eliminate completely the Huguenot minority by revoking their religious freedoms embodied in the Edict of Nantes.

The king supplemented his military and political work of state building with other projects to integrate France more completely as one nation. With royal patronage, authors and scholars flourished and, by the example of their often excellent works, extended the French dialect in the country at the expense of provincial tongues. In the king's name, his finance minister, Jean-Baptiste Colbert (1619–1683) sought to realize a vision of a unified French economy. He designed mercantilist policies to favor French trade and to build French industry, and he improved transportation to bind the country together as one unit. The result of Louis's policies, therefore, was not only a stronger king and a more powerful France but a more unified country as well.

Far more than previous French monarchs, Louis XIV addressed the third task in establishing absolutism. In modern terms it consisted of effective public relations, which required visible evidence of the new royal authority. The stage setting for the royal display of the symbols of absolute authority was Versailles, the site of a new royal palace. Built between 1661 and 1682, the palace itself was massive, with a façade one-quarter mile long pierced by 2,143 windows. It was set in a park of 37,000 acres, of which 6,000 acres were embellished with formal gardens. These gardens contained 1,400 fountains that required massive hydraulic works to supply them with water, an artificial lake one mile long for royal boating parties, and 200 statues. The palace grounds contained various smaller palaces as well, including Marly, where the king could entertain small, select groups, away from the main palace that was the center of a court life embracing almost 20,000 persons (9,000 soldiers billeted in the town; and 5,000 royal servants, 1,000 nobles and their 4,000 servants, plus the royal family, all housed in the main palace). Because the royal ministers and their secretaries also were in residence, Versailles was much more than a palace: it was the capital of France.

Royal architects deliberately designed the palace to impart a message to all who entered. As a guidebook of 1681 by Laurent Morellet noted regarding the palace's art:

> The subjects of painting which complete the decorations of the ceilings are of heroes and illustrious men, taken from history and fable, who have deserved the titles of Magnanimous, of Great, of Fathers of the People, of Liberal, of Just, of August and Victorious, and who have possessed all the Virtues which we have seen appear in the Person of our Great Monarch during the fortunate course of his reign; so that everything remarkable which one sees in the Château and in the garden always has some relationship with the great actions of His Majesty.[2]

The court ritual and etiquette enacted in this setting departed markedly from the simpler court life of Louis XIII and were designed to complement the physical presence of the palace itself in teaching the lesson of a new royal power.

In this chapter we will analyze royal absolutism in France. What was the theoretical basis for absolute royal authority? What was traditional and what was new in the justification of royal power as expressed in late sixteenth- and seventeenth-century France? How did such early modern kings as Louis XIV communicate their absolute power in the various ceremonies and symbols of royal authority presented in the evidence that follows?

SOURCES AND METHOD

This chapter assembles several kinds of sources, each demanding a different kind of historical analysis. Two works of political theory that were

2. Laurent Morellet, *Explication historique de ce qu'il y a de plus remarquable dans la maison royale de Versailles et en celle de Monsieur à Saint-Cloud* (Paris, 1681), quoted in Robert W. Hartle, "Louis XIV and the Mirror of Antiquity" in Steven G. Reinhardt and Vaughn L. Glasgow, eds., *The Sun King: Louis XIV and the New World* (New Orleans: Louisiana State Museum Foundation, 1984), p. 111.

influential in the formation of absolutism open the evidence. To analyze these works effectively, you will need some brief background information on their authors and on the problems these thinkers discussed.

Jean Bodin (1530–1596) was a law professor, an attorney, and a legal official. His interests transcended his legal education, however. He brought a wide reading in Hebrew, Greek, Italian, and German to the central problem addressed in his major work, *The Six Books of the Republic* (1576), that of establishing the well-ordered state. Writing during the religious wars of the sixteenth century when government in France all but broke down, Bodin offered answers to this crisis. Especially novel for the sixteenth century was his call for religious toleration. Although at least formally a Catholic[3] and recognizing unity in religion as a strong unifying factor for a country, Bodin was unwilling to advocate force in eliminating Protestantism from France. He believed that acceptance was by far the better policy.

Bodin's political thought was also significant, and his *Republic* immediately was recognized as an important work. Published in several editions and translated into Latin, Italian, Spanish, and German, the *Republic* influenced a circle of men, the *Politiques,* who advised Henry IV. In seeking to explain how to establish the well-ordered state, Bodin contributed much in the process to Western political theory. Perhaps his most important idea was that there was nothing divine about governing power. Men created governments solely to ensure their physical and material security; to meet those needs, the ruling power had to exercise a sovereignty on which Bodin placed few limits.[4] Indeed, Bodin's concept of the ruler's power is his most important contribution to political thought. In the brief selection from Jean Bodin's complex work, examine his conception of the sovereign power required to establish a well-ordered state in France and contrast this conception with the feudal state still partially existing in his time.

The second work of political theory was written by Jacques Bénigne Bossuet (1627–1704), Bishop of Meaux. A great orator who preached at the court of Louis XIV, Bossuet was entrusted with the education of the king's son and heir, the Dauphin. He wrote three works for that prince's instruction, including the one excerpted in this chapter, *Politics Drawn from the Very Words of the Holy Scripture* (1678).

As tutor to the Dauphin and royal preacher, Bossuet expressed what has been called the *divine right* theory of kingship: that is, the king was

3. Bodin's religious thought evolved in the course of his life. Although he was brought up a Catholic and was briefly a Carmelite friar, his knowledge of Hebrew and early regard for the Old Testament led some to suspect he was a Jew. Writings of his middle years indicate some Calvinist leanings. Later in life, his thought seems to have moved beyond traditional Catholic and Protestant Christianity. He was nevertheless deeply religious.

4. Bodin saw the sovereign power limited by natural law and the need to respect property (which meant that the ruler could not tax without his subjects' consent) and the family.

God's deputy on earth, and to oppose him was to oppose divine law. Here, of course, the bishop was drawing on those medieval beliefs and practices imputing certain divine powers to the king. Because Bossuet was an influential member of the court of Louis XIV, his ideas on royal authority carried considerable weight. Trained as a theologian, he buttressed his political theories with scriptural authority. In this selection, determine the extent of the royal link to God. Why might such a theory be particularly useful to Louis XIV?

Source 3 is a selection from the *Memoirs* of Louis de Rouvroy, Duke of Saint-Simon (1675–1755). Saint-Simon's memoirs of court life are extensive, comprising forty-one volumes in the main French edition. They constitute both a remarkable record of life at Versailles and, because of their style, an important example of French literature. As useful and important as the *Memoirs* are, however, they must be read with care. All of us, consciously or unconsciously, have biases and opinions, and memoirists are no exception. In fact, memoir literature illustrates problems that students of history should be aware of in all they read. The way in which authors present events, even what they choose to include or omit from their accounts, reflects their opinions. Because memoir writers often recount events in which they participated, they may have especially strong views about what they relate. Thus, to use Saint-Simon's work profitably, it is essential to understand his point of view. We must also ask if the memoir writer was in a position to know firsthand what he or she is relating or is simply recounting less reliable rumors.

Saint-Simon came from an old noble family recently risen to prominence when his father became a royal favorite. Ironically, no one was more deeply opposed to the policies of Louis XIV, which aimed at destroying the traditional feudal power of the nobility in the name of royal authority, than this man whose position rested on that very authority. Saint-Simon was, quite simply, a defender of the older style of kingship in which sovereignty was limited by the monarch's need to consult with his vassals. His memoirs reflect this view and are often critical of the king. But even with his critical view of the king and his court, Saint-Simon was an important figure there, an individual privy to state business and court gossip, who gives us a remarkable picture of life at Versailles. Analyze the court etiquette and ritual Saint-Simon describes as a nonverbal message from the king to his most powerful subjects. For example, what message did the royal waking and dressing ceremony convey to the most powerful and privileged persons in France, who crowded the royal bedroom and vied for the privilege of helping the king dress? What message did their very presence convey in turn to Louis XIV? Recall Bossuet's ideas of kingship. Why might public religious ritual such as that attending the royal rising be part of the agenda of a king not particularly noted for his piety during the first half of his life?

Studied closely, the three different kinds of written evidence presented—the work of a sixteenth-century political theorist, the writings of a contemporary supporter, and the memoirs of one of the king's opponents—reveal much about the growing power of the French monarchy. What common themes do you find in these works? What were the sources of the king's political authority? From these written sources we move on to pictorial evidence of the symbols of royal authority. Symbols, as you know, are concrete objects possessing a meaning beyond what is immediately apparent. We are all aware of the power of symbols, particularly in our age of electronic media, and we all, perhaps unconsciously, analyze them to some extent. Take a simple example drawn from modern advertising: the lion appears frequently as an image in advertisements for banks and other financial institutions. The lion's presence is intended to convey to us the strength of the financial institution, to inspire our faith in the latter's ability to protect our funds. Using this kind of analysis, you can determine the total meaning of the symbols associated with Louis XIV.

Consider the painting presented as the fourth piece of evidence, *Louis XIV Taking Up Personal Government in 1661*. Louis XIV had been king in name since the age of five after his father's death in 1643, but only in 1661, as an adult, did he assume full power. Remember that such art was generally commissioned by the king and often had an instructional purpose. What do the following elements symbolize: the portrayal of Louis XIV as a Roman emperor; the positioning of a figure representing France on his left; the crowning of the king with a wreath of flowers; the figure of Time (note the hourglass and scythe) holding a tapestry over the royal head; and the presence of herald angels hovering above?

Now go on to the other pictures and perform the same kind of analysis, always trying to identify the symbolic message the painter or architect wished to convey. For Source 5 study the royal pose and such seemingly superficial elements in the picture as the king's dress and the background details. Ask yourself what ideas these were intended to convey. Source 6 presents the insignia Louis XIV chose as his personal symbol, which decorated much of Versailles. Reflect on Louis's reasons for this choice in reading his explanation:

> The symbol that I have adopted and that you see all around you represents the duties of a Prince and inspires me always to fulfill them. I chose for an emblem the Sun which, according to the rules of this art [heraldry], is the noblest of all, and which, by the brightness that surrounds it, by the light it lends to the other stars that constitute, after a fashion, its court, by the universal good it does, endlessly promoting life, joy, and growth, by its perpetual and regular movement, by its constant and invariable course, is assuredly the most dazzling and most beautiful image of the monarch.[5]

With Sources 8 through 13, we turn to analysis of architecture, which of course also served to symbolize royal power. You must ask

5. Quoted in Reinhardt and Glasgow, *The Sun King*, p. 181.

yourself how great that concept was as you look at the pictures of Versailles. The palace, after all, was not only the royal residence but also the setting for the conduct of government, including the king's reception of foreign ambassadors. At the most basic level, notice the scale of the palace. What impression might its size have been intended to convey? At a second level, examine decorative details of the palace. Why might the balustrade at the palace entry have been decorated with statuary symbolizing Magnificence, Justice, Wisdom, Prudence, Diligence, Peace, Europe, Asia, Renown, Abundance, Force, Generosity, Wealth, Authority, Fame, America, Africa, and Victory?

Observe the views of the palace's interior, considering the functions of the rooms and their details. Source 10 offers a view of the royal chapel at Versailles. Richly decorated in marble and complemented with ceiling paintings such as that depicting the Trinity, the chapel was the site of daily masses as well as of royal marriages and celebrations of victories. Note that the king attended mass in the royal gallery, joining the rest of the court on the main floor only when the mass celebrant was a bishop. Why might such a magnificent setting be part of the palace? More important, what significance do you place on the position the king chose for himself in this grand setting?

Sources 11 and 12 present the sites of the royal rising ceremony described by Saint-Simon. The royal bedroom, Source 11, was richly decorated in gilt, red, and white, and was complemented by paintings of biblical scenes. Notice the rich decoration of the Bull's Eye Window Antechamber, just outside the bedroom, where the courtiers daily awaited the king's arising. Why were the rooms decorated in such a fashion?

Source 13 offers an artist's view of Marly. Again, notice the scale of this palace, reflecting that it was, according to Saint-Simon, a weekend getaway spot for Louis XIV and selected favorites. How might the king have used invitations to this château with the closeness to the royal person they entailed? Examine details of the palace. The central château had twelve apartments, four of which were reserved for the royal family, the others for its guests. The twelve pavilions around the lake in the center of the château's grounds each housed two guest apartments and represented the twelve signs of the zodiac. What symbolic importance might you attach to this?

Finally, return to Source 7, which recreates the pageant known as the Carousel of 1662, one of many such entertainments at court. The scale of such festivals could be huge. In 1662, 12,197 costumed people took part in a celebration that included a parade through the streets of Paris and games. Costumed as ancient Romans, Persians, and others, the participants must have made quite an impression on their audience. What kind of impression do you think it was?

What common message runs through the art and architecture you have analyzed? As you unravel the message woven into this visual evidence, combine it with the evidence you derived from Saint-Simon's portrayal of court life and the political theory of absolutism. Remember, too, the unstated message: that the monarchy of Louis XIV possessed in Europe's largest army the ultimate means for persuading its subjects to accept the divine powers of the king. You should be able to determine from all this material what was new in this conception of royal authority and the ways in which the new authority was expressed.

THE EVIDENCE

Source 1 from Francis William Coker, editor, Readings in Political Philosophy *(New York: Macmillan, 1926), pp. 235–236.*

1. From Jean Bodin, *The Six Books of the Republic*, Book I, 1576

The first and principal function of sovereignty is to give laws to the citizens generally and individually, and, it must be added, not necessarily with the consent of superiors, equals, or inferiors. If the consent of superiors is required, then the prince is clearly a subject; if he must have the consent of equals, then others share his authority; if the consent of inferiors—the people or the senate—is necessary, then he lacks supreme authority. . . .

It may be objected that custom does not get its power from the judgment or command of the prince, and yet has almost the force of law, so that it would seem that the prince is master of law, the people of custom. Custom, insensibly, yet with the full compliance of all, passes gradually into the character of men, and acquires force with the lapse of time. Law, on the other hand, comes forth in one moment at the order of him who has the power to command, and often in opposition to the desire and approval of those whom it governs. Wherefore, Chrysostom[6] likens law to a tyrant and custom to a king. Moreover, the power of law is far greater than that of custom, for customs may be superseded by laws, but laws are not supplanted by customs; it is within the power and function of magistrates to restore the operation of laws which by custom are obsolescent. Custom proposes neither rewards nor penalties; laws carry one or the other, unless it be a permissive law which nullifies the penalty of some other law. In short, a custom has compelling force only as long as the prince, by adding his endorsement and sanction to the custom, makes it a law.

6. **Chrysostom:** Saint John Chrysostom (ca 347–407), an early Father of the Greek Church whose religion led him into conflict with the Eastern Roman emperor.

It is thus clear that laws and customs depend for their force upon the will of those who hold supreme power in the state. This first and chief mark of sovereignty is, therefore, of such sort that it cannot be transferred to subjects, though the prince or people sometimes confer upon one of the citizens the power to frame laws (*legum condendarum*), which then have the same force as if they had been framed by the prince himself. The Lacedæmonians bestowed such power upon Lycurgus, the Athenians upon Solon;[7] each stood as deputy for his state, and the fulfilment of his function depended upon the pleasure not of himself but of the people; his legislation had no force save as the people confirmed it by their assent. The former composed and wrote the laws, the people enacted and commanded them.

Under this supreme power of ordaining and abrogating laws, it is clear that all other functions of sovereignty are included; that it may be truly said that supreme authority in the state is comprised in this one thing—namely, to give laws to all and each of the citizens, and to receive none from them. For to declare war or make peace, though seeming to involve what is alien to the term law, is yet accomplished by law, that is by decree of the supreme power. It is also the prerogative of sovereignty to receive appeals from the highest magistrates, to confer authority upon the greater magistrates and to withdraw it from them, to allow exemption from taxes, to bestow other immunities, to grant dispensations from the laws, to exercise power of life and death, to fix the value, name and form of money, to compel all citizens to observe their oaths: all of these attributes are derived from the supreme power of commanding and forbidding—that is, from the authority to give law to the citizens collectively and individually, and to receive law from no one save immortal God. A duke, therefore, who gives laws to all his subjects, but receives law from the emperor, Pope, or king, or has a co-partner in authority, lacks sovereignty.

Source 2 from Richard H. Powers, editor and translator, Readings in European Civilization Since 1500 *(Boston: Houghton Mifflin, 1961) pp. 129–130.*

2. From Jacques Bénigne Bossuet, *Politics Drawn from the Very Words of the Holy Scriptures*, 1678

TO MONSEIGNEUR LE DAUPHIN

God is the King of kings. It is for Him to instruct and direct kings as His ministers. Heed then, Monseigneur, the lessons which He gives them in His Scriptures, and learn . . . the rules and examples on which they ought to base their conduct. . . .

7. **Lacedæmonians:** the Spartans of ancient Greece. **Lycurgus:** traditional author of the Spartan constitution. **Solon:** sixth century B.C. Athenean lawgiver.

BOOK II: OR AUTHORITY. . .

CONCLUSION: Accordingly we have established by means of Scriptures that monarchical government comes from God. . . . That when government was established among men He chose hereditary monarchy as the most natural and most durable form. That excluding the sex born to obey[8] from the sovereign power was only natural. . . .

BOOK III: THE NATURE OF ROYAL AUTHORITY. . .

FIRST ARTICLE: Its essential characteristics. . . . First, royal authority is sacred; Second, it is paternal; Third, it is absolute; Fourth, it is subject to reason. . . .

SECOND ARTICLE: Royal authority is sacred.

FIRST PROPOSITION: God establishes kings as his ministers and reigns over people through them.—We have already seen that all power comes from God. . . .

Therefore princes act as ministers of God and as His lieutenants on earth. It is through them that he exercises His empire. . . .

Thus we have seen that the royal throne is not the throne of a man, but the throne of God himself. So in Scriptures we find "God has chosen my son Solomon to sit upon the throne of the kingdom of Jehovah over Israel." And further, "Solomon sat on the throne of Jehovah as king."

And in order that we should not think that to have kings established by God is peculiar to the Israelites, here is what Ecclesiastes says: "God gives each people its governor; and Israel is manifestly reserved to Him.". . .

SECOND PROPOSITION: The person of the king is sacred.—It follows from all the above that the person of kings is sacred. . . . God has had them anointed by His prophets with a sacred ointment, as He has had His pontiffs and His altars anointed.

But even before actually being anointed, they are sacred by virtue of their charge, as representatives of His divine majesty, delegated by His providence to execute His design. . . .

The title of *christ* is given to kings, one sees them called *christs* or the Lord's *anointed* everywhere.

Bearing this venerable name, even the prophets revered them, and looked upon them as associated with the sovereign empire of God, whose authority they exercise on earth. . . .

THIRD PROPOSITION: Religion and conscience demand that we obey the prince.—After having said that the prince is the minister of God Saint Paul concluded: "Accordingly it is necessary that you subject yourself to him out of fear of his anger, but also because of the obligation of your conscience. . . ."

8. **Sex born to obey:** women. The Salic Law, mistakenly attributed to the medieval Salian Franks, precluded women from inheriting the crown of France.

And furthermore: "Servants, obey your temporal masters in all things. . . ." Saint Peter said: "Therefore submit yourselves to the order established among men for the love of God; be subjected to the king as to God . . . be subjected to those to whom He gives His authority and who are sent by Him to reward good deeds and to punish evil ones."

Even if kings fail in this duty, their charge and their ministry must be respected. For Scriptures tell us: "Obey your masters, not only those who are mild and good, but also those who are peevish and unjust."

Thus there is something religious in the respect which one renders the prince. Service to God and respect for kings are one thing. . . .

Thus it is in the spirit of Christianity for kings to be paid a kind of religious respect. . . .

BOOK IV: CONTINUATION OF THE CHARACTERISTICS OF ROYALTY

FIRST ARTICLE: Royal authority is absolute.

FIRST PROPOSITION: The prince need render account to no one for what he orders. . . .

SECOND PROPOSITION: When the prince has judged there is no other judgment. . . . Princes are gods.

Source 3 from Bayle St. John, translator, The Memoirs of the Duke of Saint-Simon on the Reign of Louis XIV and the Regency, *8th ed. (London: George Allen, 1913), vol. 2, pp. 363–365, vol. 3, pp. 221–27.*

3. The Duke of Saint-Simon on the Reign of Louis XIV

[*On the creation of Versailles and the nature of its court life*]

He [Louis XIV] early showed a disinclination for Paris. The troubles that had taken place there during the minority made him regard the place as dangerous;[9] he wished, too, to render himself venerable by hiding himself from the eyes of the multitude; all these considerations fixed him at St. Germains[10] soon after the death of the Queen, his mother. It was to that place he began to attract the world by fêtes and gallantries, and by making it felt that he wished to be often seen.

9. During the Fronde revolt of 1648–1653, the royal government lost control of Paris to the crowds and the royal family was forced to flee the city. Because Louis XIV was a minor (only ten years of age) when the revolt erupted, the government was administered by his mother, Anne of Austria, and her chief minister, Cardinal Mazarin.

10. **St. Germain-en-Laye:** site of a royal château, overlooking the Seine and dating from the twelfth century, where Louis XIV was born. The court fled there in 1649 during the Fronde.

His love for Madame de la Vallière,[11] which was at first kept secret, occasioned frequent excursions to Versailles, then a little card castle, which had been built by Louis XIII—annoyed, and his suite still more so, at being frequently obliged to sleep in a wretched inn there, after he had been out hunting in the forest of Saint Leger. That monarch rarely slept at Versailles more than one night, and then from necessity; the King, his son, slept there, so that he might be more in private with his mistress; pleasures unknown to the hero and just man, worthy son of Saint Louis, who built the little château.[12]

These excursions of Louis XIV by degrees gave birth to those immense buildings he erected at Versailles; and their convenience for a numerous court, so different from the apartments at St. Germains, led him to take up his abode there entirely shortly after the death of the Queen.[13] He built an infinite number of apartments, which were asked for by those who wished to pay their court to him; whereas at St. Germains nearly everybody was obliged to lodge in the town, and the few who found accommodation at the château were strangely inconvenienced.

The frequent fêtes, the private promenades at Versailles, the journeys, were means on which the King seized in order to distinguish or mortify the courtiers, and thus render them more assiduous in pleasing him. He felt that of real favours he had not enough to bestow; in order to keep up the spirit of devotion, he therefore unceasingly invented all sorts of ideal ones, little preferences and petty distinctions, which answered his purpose as well.

He was exceedingly jealous of the attention paid him. Not only did he notice the presence of the most distinguished courtiers, but those of inferior degree also. He looked to the right and to the left, not only upon rising but upon going to bed, at his meals, in passing through his apartments, or his gardens of Versailles, where alone the courtiers were allowed to follow him; he saw and noticed everybody; not one escaped him, not even those who hoped to remain unnoticed. He marked well all absentees from the court, found out the reason of their absence, and never lost an opportunity of acting towards them as the occasion might seem to justify. With some of the courtiers (the most distinguished), it was a demerit not to make the court their ordinary abode; with others 'twas a fault to come but rarely; for those who never or scarcely ever came it was certain disgrace.

Louis XIV took great pains to be well informed of all that passed everywhere; in the public places, in the private houses, in society and familiar intercourse. His spies and tell-tales were infinite. He had them of all species;

11. **Madame de la Vallière:** Louise de la Baume le Blanc, Duchesse de la Vallière (1644–1710), the king's first mistress.

12. Saint-Simon greatly admired Louis XIII, whom he had never met, and for over half a century attended annual memorial services for the king at the royal tombs in the basilica of St. Denis.

13. Anne of Austria (1601–1666), the mother of Louis XIV.

many who were ignorant that their information reached him; others who knew it; others who wrote to him direct, sending their letters through channels he indicated; and all these letters were seen by him alone, and always before everything else; others who sometimes spoke to him secretly in his cabinet, entering by the back stairs. These unknown means ruined an infinite number of people of all classes, who never could discover the cause; often ruined them very unjustly; for the King, once prejudiced, never altered his opinion or so rarely, that nothing was more rare.

[*On the royal day and court etiquette*]
[*The royal day begins*]

At eight o'clock the chief valet de chambre on duty, who alone had slept in the royal chamber, and who had dressed himself, awoke the King. The chief physician, the chief surgeon, and the nurse (as long as she lived), entered at the same time. The latter kissed the King; the others rubbed and often changed his shirt, because he was in the habit of sweating a great deal. At the quarter, the grand chamberlain was called (or, in his absence, the first gentleman of the chamber), and those who had, what was called the *grandes entrées*. The chamberlain (or chief gentleman) drew back the curtains which had been closed again, and presented the holy water from the vase, at the head of the bed. These gentlemen stayed but a moment, and that was the time to speak to the King, if any one had anything to ask of him; in which case the rest stood aside. When, contrary to custom, nobody had aught to say, they were there but for a few moments. He who had opened the curtains and presented the holy water, presented also a prayer-book. Then all passed into the cabinet of the council. A very short religious service being over, the King called, they re-entered. The same officer gave him his dressing-gown; immediately after, other privileged courtiers entered, and then everybody, in time to find the King putting on his shoes and stockings, for he did almost everything himself and with address and grace. Every other day we saw him shave himself; and he had a little short wig in which he always appeared, even in bed, and on medicine days. He often spoke of the chase, and sometimes said a word to somebody. No toilette table was near him; he had simply a mirror held before him.

As soon as he was dressed, he prayed to God, at the side of his bed, where all the clergy present knelt, the cardinals without cushions, all the laity remaining standing; and the captain of the guards came to the balustrade during the prayer, after which the King passed into his cabinet.

He found there, or was followed by all who had the entrée, a very numerous company, for it included everybody in any office. He gave orders to each for the day; thus within a half a quarter of an hour it was known what he meant to do; and then all this crowd left directly. The bastards, a few favourites, and the valets alone were left. It was then a good opportunity for talking with the King; for example, about plans of gardens and buildings; and conversation lasted more or less according to the person engaged in it.

All the Court meantime waited for the King in the gallery, the captain of the guard being alone in the chamber seated at the door of the cabinet.

[*The business of government*]

On Sunday, and often on Monday, there was a council of state; on Tuesday a finance council; on Wednesday council of state; on Saturday finance council. Rarely were two held in one day or any on Thursday or Friday. Once or twice a month there was a council of despatches[14] on Monday morning; but the order that the Secretaries of State took every morning between the King's rising and his mass, much abridged this kind of business. All the ministers were seated according to rank, except at the council of despatches, where all stood except the sons of France, the Chancellor, and the Duc de Beauvilliers.[15]

[*The royal luncheon*]

The dinner was always *au petit couvert*, that is, the King ate by himself in his chamber upon a square table in front of the middle window. It was more or less abundant, for he ordered in the morning whether it was to be "a little," or "very little" service. But even at this last, there were always many dishes, and three courses without counting the fruit. The dinner being ready, the principal courtiers entered; then all who were known; and the first gentlemen of the chamber on duty, informed the King.

I have seen, but very rarely, Monseigneur[16] and his sons standing at their dinners, the King not offering them a seat. I have continually seen there the Princes of the blood and the cardinals. I have often seen there also Monsieur,[17] either on arriving from St. Cloud to see the King, or arriving from the council of despatches (the only one he entered), give the King his napkin and remain standing. A little while afterwards, the King, seeing that he did not go away, asked him if he would not sit down; he bowed, and the King ordered a seat to be brought for him. A stool was put behind him. Some moments after the King said, "Nay then, sit down, my brother." Monsieur bowed and seated himself until the end of the dinner, when he presented the napkin.

[*The day ends*]

At ten o'clock his supper was served. The captain of the guard announced this to him. A quarter of an hour after the King came to supper, and from

14. **Council of Despatches:** the royal council in which ministers discussed the letters from the provincial administrators of France, the *intendants*.

15. **Duc de Beauvilliers:** Paul de Beauvilliers, Duc de St. Aignan (1648–1714), friend of Saint-Simon and tutor of Louis XIV's grandsons, the dukes of Burgundy, Anjou, and Berry.

16. **Monseigneur:** Louis, Dauphin de France (1661–1711), son of Louis XIV and heir to the throne.

17. **Monsieur:** Philippe, Duc d'Orléans (1640–1701), Louis XIV's only sibling. His permanent residence was at the Château of St. Cloud near Paris.

the ante-chamber of Madame de Maintenon[18] to the table again, any one spoke to him who wished. This supper was always on a grand scale, the royal household (that is, the sons and daughters of France), at table, and a large number of courtiers and ladies present, sitting or standing, and on the evening before the journey to Marly all those ladies who wished to take part in it. That was called presenting yourself for Marly. Men asked in the morning, simply saying to the King, "Sire, Marly." In later years the King grew tired of this, and a valet wrote up in the gallery the names of those who asked. The ladies continued to present themselves.

After supper the King stood some moments, his back to the balustrade of the foot of his bed, encircled by all his Court; then, with bows to the ladies, passed into his cabinet, where on arriving, he gave his orders. He passed a little less than an hour there, seated in an arm-chair, with his legitimate children and bastards, his grandchildren, legitimate and otherwise, and their husbands or wives. Monsieur in another arm-chair; the princesses upon stools, Monseigneur and all the other princes standing.

The King, wishing to retire, went and fed his dogs; then said good night, passed into his chamber to the *ruelle*[19] of his bed, where he said his prayers, as in the morning, then undressed. He said good night with an inclination of the head, and whilst everybody was leaving the room stood at the corner of the mantelpiece, where he gave the order to the colonel of the guards alone. Then commenced what was called the *petit coucher*, at which only the specially privileged remained. That was short. They did not leave until he got into bed. It was a moment to speak to him. Then all left if they saw any one buckle to the King. For ten or twelve years before he died the *petit coucher* ceased, in consequence of a long attack of gout he had had; so that the Court was finished at the rising from supper.

18. **Madame de Maintenon:** Françoise d'Aubigné, Marquise de Maintenon (1635–1719) married Louis XIV after the death of his first wife, Marie Thérèse of Spain.

19. **ruelle:** the area in the bedchamber in which the bed was located and in which the king received persons of high rank.

Sources 4 and 5 from Château de Versailles/Cliché des Musées Nationaux-Paris.

4. Charles Le Brun, *Louis XIV Taking Up Personal Government*, ca 1680, from the Ceiling of the Hall of Mirrors at Versailles

5. Hyacinthe-François-Honoré-Pierre-André Rigaud, *Louis XIV, King of France and Navarre*, 1701

Source 6 from Musée de la Marine, Photographic Service.

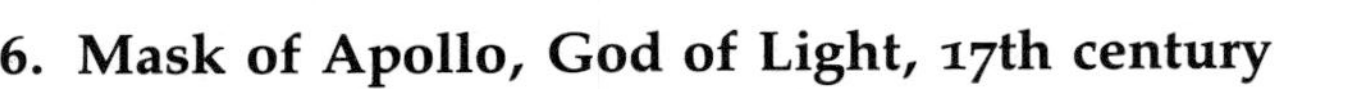

6. Mask of Apollo, God of Light, 17th century

Source 7 from The Boston Athenæum.

7. Rousselet, Louis XIV as "Roman Emperor" in an engraving from the Carousel of 1662

Sources 8 and 9 from French Government Tourist Office.

8. Garden Façade of Versailles

9. Aerial View of Versailles

Sources 10 through 12 from Château de Versailles/Cliché des Musées Nationaux-Paris.

10. The Royal Chapel at Versailles

11. Reconstruction of the King's Chamber at Versailles, after 1701

12. Antechamber of the Bull's Eye Window at Versailles

Source 13 from Château de Versailles/Cliché des Musées Nationaux-Paris.

13. Pierre Denis Martin, *Château of Marly*, 1724

QUESTIONS TO CONSIDER

Louis XIV is reputed to have said, "I am the state." Whether the king actually uttered those words is immaterial for our purpose; they neatly summarize the unifying theme in all this chapter's evidence, which demonstrates how royal power was defined as absolute and how that authority was expressed in deeds, art, and architecture.

Consider first the theories of royal authority, comparing the political ideas of Bodin and Bossuet. What are the origins of sovereignty for Bodin and Bossuet? How do they differ? Why can Bodin be said to have justified absolutism on the basis of expediency, that is, that absolute royal power was the only way to ensure order? Do the two thinkers ultimately arrive at the same conclusions? What is the difference between Bodin's conclusion that the royal power permitted the king to hand down laws to his subjects and receive them from no one and Bossuet's definition of the king as virtually a god on earth?

Royal ceremony and etiquette enforced this view of the king. Consider Saint-Simon's *Memoirs* again. The selection describes only limited aspects of court etiquette, but it conveys to us a vivid image of court life. Who was the center of this court made up of the country's most prominent nobles? Analyze individual elements of court ceremony. How does each contribute to a consistent message? Consider the royal dining ritual. To reinforce the lesson of royal power, who was kept standing during the king's luncheon? Who had the task, for most commoners performed by an ordinary waiter, of handing the king his napkin? A message of royal power is being expressed here in a way that is almost theatrical.

Indeed, the image of theater can be useful in further structuring your analysis. The stage setting for this royal display, the palace of Versailles, shows the work of a skilled director in creating a remarkably uniform message in landscape and architecture alike. Who do you suppose that director was? Examine his statement at Versailles. Look first at the exterior views of both Versailles (Sources 8 and 9) and Marly (Source 13). How do the grounds add to the expression of royal power? What view of nature might they suggest to a visitor? How did the stage set enhance the play described by Saint-Simon? How did it encourage the French to accept the authority of Louis XIV?

Look next at the interior of the palace. It was, of course, a royal residence. But do you find much evidence of its function as a place to live in? Examine the royal bedroom and its outer room (Sources 11 and 12). Modern bedrooms are generally intimate in size and decoration; how does the king's differ? Why? Notice, too, the art and use of symbols in the palace. Why might the king's artists and architects have decorated the palace so richly with Biblical and classical heroes and themes (Sources 8, 9, 10, 11, 12)?

Finally, consider the principal actor, Louis XIV. Notice how his self-presentation is consistent with the trappings of the stage set. We find him consciously acting a role in Source 7, portraying an emperor in the Carousel of 1662. That engraving embodies a great deal of indirect information. What details reinforce the aura of royal power? Why should the king be mounted and in Roman costume? What strikes you about the king's attitude atop the prancing horse? Compare this picture with the Le Brun (Source 4) and Rigaud (Source 5) paintings. What elements do you find these pictures to have in common? How does the royal emblem of the sun (Source 6) contribute to the common message?

With these considerations in mind, return now to the central questions of this chapter. What was the theoretical explanation of royal power expressed in late sixteenth- and seventeenth-century France? How did such early modern kings as Louis XIV communicate their absolute power in the various ceremonies, displays, and symbols of royal authority presented in the evidence?

EPILOGUE

We all know that any successful act produces imitators. In the seventeenth century the monarchy of Louis XIV for a long time looked like the most successful regime in Europe. Royal absolutism had seemingly unified France. Out of that unity came a military power that threatened to overwhelm Europe; an economic strength, based on mercantilism, that increased French wealth; and an intellectual life that gave the culture of seventeenth- and eighteenth-century Europe a distinctly French accent. Imitators of Louis XIV's work were therefore numerous. At the very least, kings sought physically to express the unifying and centralizing monarchical principle of government in palaces recreating Versailles.[20]

But the work of such monarchs as Louis XIV involved far more than the construction of elaborate palaces in which to stage the theater of their court lives. The act of focusing the state on the figure of the monarch began the transition to the centralized modern style of government and marked the beginning of the end of the decentralized medieval state that bound subjects in an almost contractual relationship to their ruler. The king now emerged as theoretically all-powerful and also as a symbol of national unity.

The monarchs of the age did their work of state building so effectively that the unity and centralization they created often survived the monarchy itself. The French monarchy, for example, succumbed to a revolution in 1789 that in large part stemmed from

20. Palaces consciously modeled on Versailles multiplied in the late seventeenth and early eighteenth centuries. They included the Schönbrunn Palace in Vienna (1694), the Royal Palace in Berlin (begun in 1698), Ludwigsburg Palace in Württemberg, Germany (1704–1733), the Würzburg Residenz in Franconia, Germany (1719–1744), and the Stupinigi Palace (1729–1733) near Turin, Italy.

the bankruptcy of the royal government after too many years of overspending on wars and court life in the name of royal glory. But the unified state endured, strong enough to retain its sense of unity despite challenges in war and changes of government that introduced a new politics of mass participation.

The methods employed by Louis XIV and other monarchs also transcended their age. Modern governments understand the importance of ritual, symbolism, and display in creating the sense of national unity that was part of the absolute monarch's goal. Ritual may now be centered on important national observances. The parades on such days as July 4 in the United States, July 14 in France (commemorating one of the earliest victories of the Revolution of 1789), and the anniversary of the October 1917 Revolution in the Soviet Union all differ in form from the rituals of Louis XIV. They are designed for a new political age, one of mass participation in politics, in which the loyalty of the whole people, not just an elite group, must be won. But their purpose remains the same: to win loyalty to the existing political order.

Modern states also use symbolism to build political loyalty. Artwork on public buildings in Washington, D.C. and the capital cities of other republics, for example, often employs classical themes. The purpose of such artwork is to suggest to citizens that their government perpetuates the republican rectitude of Athens and Rome. Display also is part of the political agenda of modern governments, even among governments of new arrivals in the community of nations. This is why newly independent, developing nations of the twentieth century expend large portions of their meager resources on such things as grand new capital cities, the most sophisticated military weaponry, and the latest aircraft for the national airline. These are symbols of their government's successes and thus the basis for these regimes' claims on their peoples' loyalty. These modern rituals, symbols, and displays perform the same function for modern rulers as Versailles did for the Sun King.

Acknowledgments continued from page ii.

125–127: Extract from THE MEDIEVAL CHURCH by Roland H. Bainton © 1962 by Roland H. Bainton. Reprinted by permission of Wadsworth, Inc. Pages 140–142: Extract from Lynn Thorndike, ed. and trans., *University Records and Life in the Middle Ages*. Copyright © 1944 Columbia University Press. Used by permission. Pages 142–143: Extract from James Harvey Robinson, ed. and trans., *Readings in European History*, vol. 1. Published by Silver, Burdett & Ginn, Inc. Page 144: Extract from THE MEDIEVAL CHURCH by Roland H. Bainton © 1962 by Roland H. Bainton. Reprinted by permission of Wadsworth, Inc. Page 145: Extract from Lynn Thorndike, ed. and trans., *University Records and Life in the Middle Ages*. Copyright © 1944 Columbia University Press. Used by permission. Page 146: Extract from Anders Piltz, *The World of Medieval Learning*, trans. David Jones. Permission granted by Basil Blackwell of London and Barnes & Noble Books of Totowa, New Jersey. Pages 146–147: Extract from THE STORY OF OXFORD by Cecil Headlam. Used by permission of J. M. Dent & Sons Ltd. Pages 159–165: Extracts from Robert S. Lopez and Irving W. Raymond, eds. and trans., *Medieval Trade in the Mediterranean World*. Copyright © 1955 Columbia University Press. Used by permission. Pages 165–166: Extract from L. M. Larson, ed. and trans., *The King's Mirror*. Used by permission of American Scandinavian Foundation. Pages 167–168: Extracts from Robert S. Lopez and Irving W. Raymond, eds. and trans., *Medieval Trade in the Mediterranean World*. Copyright © 1955 Columbia University Press. Used by permission. Pages 176–178: Extract from James Harvey Robinson, ed. and trans., *Readings in European History*, vol. 1. Published by Silver, Burdett & Ginn, Inc. Page 186: Extracts from Carolly Erikson, THE RECORDS OF MEDIEVAL EUROPE (Garden City, N.Y.: Doubleday, 1971). Used by permission. Pages 197–198: Extract from C. C. S. Bland, ed. and trans., *Miracles of the Blessed Virgin Mary*. Used by permission of Routledge & Kegan Paul. Pages 198–202: Extract from AUCASSIN AND NICOLETTE AND OTHER MEDIEVAL ROMANCES AND LEGENDS, trans. by Eugene Mason (London: Everyman Library/J. M. Dent & Sons Ltd.). Used by permission. Pages 202–203: Extract from *Medieval Women Writers*, edited by Katharina M. Wilson © 1984. The University of Georgia Press. Pages 203–207: Extract from *The Book of Margery Kempe* edited by W. Butler-Bowdon (1954). Reprinted by permission of Oxford University Press. Pages 207–210: Extract from Edward Peters, ed., *Heresy and Authority in Medieval Europe: Documents in Translation*. Used by permission of University of Pennsylvania Press. Pages 227–229: Extracts from W. H. Woodward, ed. and trans., *Vittorino da Feltre and Other Humanist Educators*. Used by permission of Cambridge University Press. Pages 229–232: Extract from THE BOOK OF THE COURTIER by Baldassare Castiglione, translated by Charles S. Singleton. Copyright © 1959 by Charles S. Singleton and Edgar de N. Mayhew. Reprinted by permission of Doubleday, a division of Bantam, Doubleday, Dell Publishing Group, Inc. Pages 232–233: Extract from THE PRINCE AND THE DISCOURSES by Niccolo Machiavelli, trans. by Luigi Ricci, revised by E. R. P. Vincent (1935). Used by permission of Oxford University Press. Pages 233–235: Extract from THE PORTABLE RENAISSANCE READER, ed. James B. Ross and Mary McLaughlin. Copyright 1953 by The Viking Press, Inc. Copyright renewed © 1981 by Viking Penguin Inc. Pages 235–236: Extract from Denys Hay, ed. and trans., *The Anglia Historia of Polydore Vergil, AD 1485–1537*. Used by permission of the Royal Historical Society. Pages 245–249: Extract from John W. Doberstein, ed., *Luther's Works*, vol. 51. Used by permission of Fortress Press. Page 250: Martin Luther, "A Mighty Fortress Is Our God," reprinted from LUTHERAN BOOK OF WORSHIP, copyright © 1978, by permission of Augsburg Publishing House. Page 251: Paul Speratus, "Salvation unto Us Has Come," copyright © 1941 Concordia Publishing House. Used by permission. Pages 268–269: Extract from E. G. Ravenstein, ed. and trans., *A Journal of the First Voyage of Vasco de Gama*. Used by permission of the Hakluyt Society. Pages 269–273: Extract from John Boyd Thacher, *Christopher Columbus: His Life, His Work, His Remains*. Used by permission of Kraus Reprints. Pages 273–274: Extract from C. R. Markham, ed. and trans., *The Letters of Amerigo Vespucci*. Used by permission of the Hakluyt Society. Pages 275–277: Extract from THE COMPLETE ESSAYS OF MONTAIGNE, translated by Donald M. Frame, with the permission of the publishers, Stanford University Press, © 1958 by the Board of Trustees of the Leland Stanford Junior University. Pages 277–279: Extract from THE ESSAYS OF MONTAIGNE, translated by George B. Ives. Reprinted by permission of the publisher, Harvard University Press. Copyright 1925 by Harvard University Press; © renewed 1953 by Frederick M. Ives. Pages 291–292: Extract from Francis William Coker, ed., *Readings in Political Philosophy*. Used with the approval of Yale University. Pages 294–298: Extract from THE MEMOIRS OF THE DUKE OF SAINT-SIMON ON THE REIGN OF LOUIS XIV, translated by Bayle St. John. Used by permission of the publisher, Unwin Hyman.